Workplace Communication
for the 21st Century

Workplace Communication for the 21st Century

Tools and Strategies That Impact the Bottom Line

Volume 2: External Workplace Communication

Jason S. Wrench, Editor

 PRAEGER

AN IMPRINT OF ABC-CLIO, LLC
Santa Barbara, California • Denver, Colorado • Oxford, England

Library of Congress Cataloging-in-Publication Data

Workplace communication for the 21st century : tools and strategies that
impact the bottom line / Jason S. Wrench, editor.
    v. cm.
  Contents: v. 1. Internal workplace communication — v. 2. External
workplace communication.
  Includes index.
  ISBN 978-0-313-39631-1 (hbk. : alk. paper) — ISBN 978-0-313-39632-8 (ebook)
1. Communication in organizations.   2. Communication in management.
3. Business communication.   4. Interpersonal communication.
I. Wrench, Jason S.
  HD30.3.W667   2013
  658.4'5—dc23   2012011929

ISBN: 978-0-313-39631-1
EISBN: 978-0-313-39632-8

17 16 15 14 13   1 2 3 4 5

This book is also available on the World Wide Web as an eBook.
Visit www.abc-clio.com for details.

Praeger
An Imprint of ABC-CLIO, LLC

ABC-CLIO, LLC
130 Cremona Drive, P.O. Box 1911
Santa Barbara, California 93116-1911

This book is printed on acid-free paper ∞

Manufactured in the United States of America

Contents

Acknowledgments

I want to take a short moment and thank those individuals who have helped me and put up with me as I've worked on this two-volume set.

My departmental family at SUNY New Paltz: Thank you for helping me and supporting me as I've undertaken this endeavor. You wisdom and advice is always appreciated.

Dudley Cahn: Thank you for your wisdom on managing a large editing project. As you already know, you are deeply missed. Now stop writing and enjoy your retirement already!

Chip Hogg: Thank you for your time and patience in the early days of this project. Your enthusiasm was always appreciated as I started and continued through this adventure.

Mary Kahl: Your guidance and friendship during your tenure at SUNY New Paltz truly helped me keep this project on track.

My friends and family: As always, thanks for putting up with the countless number of hours I spend sitting in front of a computer screen. It's great to have such an amazing support network that is always there to listen to me vent and support my various projects.

CHAPTER ONE

How Strategic Workplace Communication Can Save Your Organization

Jason S. Wrench

In today's global economy, business is changing faster than the speed of light. According to Norman W. Edmund (2005), a researcher who investigates the application of the scientific method, by 2020 the amount of knowledge in the world will double every 73 days. To help frame the proliferation of knowledge, Edmund explained that historically the knowledge available to humans has always doubled, but the space between the doubling of knowledge is rapidly decreasing:

1750–1900	150 years
1900–1950	50 years
1950–1960	10 years
1960–1992	5 years

Projection: Knowledge will double every 73 days by the year 2020

While Edmund notes that this projection has yet to occur, "there is little doubt about it—knowledge and knowledge of knowledge are of ever-increasing importance" (13). To apply this phenomenon to the business world is very simple. The bulk of senior managers and executives in the business world today are dealing with phenomena that simply didn't exist when they first entered the workforce. As a result of the technological

revolution of the late 20th century, business as we know it has been forever drastically altered. For example, in a study conducted by Cone, they
found that 93 percent of Americans expect companies to have a presence
in social media (Cone New Media Consumer Study 2009). Furthermore,
85 percent of Americans say companies should interact with consumers
via social media. Last, two-thirds of households making $75,000 or more
feel a stronger connection to brands they interact with online. This kind of
interaction with organizations is a phenomenon of the 21st century, and
organizations are quickly realizing that they must learn to tap into this
phenomenon or be at a competitive disadvantage.

In addition to changing how businesses must interact with their customers, technology has also made a huge impact on how businesses must
interact with their employees as well. According to Gillis (2008), "electronic media—e-mail, intranets, company web sites, blogs, electronic
meetings and e-newsletters, are quickly becoming popular in employee
communication programs" (112). Furthermore, the inclusion of electronic communication was shown to have a direct effect on the productivity of the businesses that utilize them. When asked whether or not the
various technological tools were cost effective for communicating with
their employees, organizations found the tools overwhelmingly cost effective: e-mail (94.4%), electronic mailing lists (90.5%), electronic newslet-
ters (89.5%), and intranets (89.4%).

One of the biggest challenges many organizations face in today's world,
is determining where these new communication challenges should be
handled within the current organizational structure. Historically, these
functions were handled in departments of marketing, human resources,
and/or public relations. However, as the necessity for speed of information
has become essential within the corporate environment, the creation of
single departments with all of these functions has been created. Here is a
sampling of some of the titles these new departments in modern organizations have: office of strategic communications, corporate communications,
office of business communication. No matter what one calls the department, the basic functions of these departments are becoming increasingly
consistent. In a study by Goodman (2006), he found that most corporate communication officers are tasked with specific areas: media relations
(95.7%), public relations (95.7%), crisis communication (93%), executive
communications (speeches—92.5%), employee relations (internal communication—90.3%), and communication policy and strategy (90.3%).

As a result of the changing nature of business/corporate communication
in the modern workplace, the two volumes contained in this set, *Workplace Communication for the 21st Century: Tools and Strategies That Impact
the Bottom Line,* tackle all six of these areas. The first volume in this set

focused on internal communication, which included aspects of both employee relations and communication policy and strategy. The second volume focuses on media relations, public relations, crisis communication, executive communications, and again communication policy and strategy.

The purpose of this chapter is to foreshadow the rest of this volume by first examining the different aspects of modern business communication by differentiating the different subfields that study workplace communication. Next, the chapter will examine the history of workplace communication. Thirdly, the chapter will explore the competency model for workplace communication proposed by the International Association of Business Communicators (IABC). Last, the chapter will propose an extended competency model based on both the IABC competency model and the United States Department of Labor competency models.

Different Names, Different Purposes

When one starts to examine the field of communication in the workplace, you'll find numerous different names that all sound very similar: business and professional communication, managerial communication, organizational communication, and business/corporate communication. In this volume, you'll see instances of all four in play, but I do want to quickly differentiate among the four. While these names have very similar connotations, the names actually refer to very different bodies of academic knowledge and perspectives. Paul Argenti (1996) wrote a seminal essay trying to differentiate between these four distinct areas in hopes of more clearly ascertaining what it is that workplace communication is and does.

Business and Professional Communication

The first term that is commonly seen in academic discourse about communication in the workplace is "business and professional communication." Some times when discussing this idea you'll see it just referred to as business communication or workplace communication, but the more common term is "business and professional communication." Argenti (1996) believes that there are three characteristics that set business and professional communication apart from the other areas of academic study. First, business and professional communication is primarily a course that is aimed at undergraduate students. Often these undergraduate level courses are used as introductory courses within the field of communication studies. In essence, these courses not only discuss the basic principles of human communication, but they also focus on lower level communication skill building.

Second, these courses typically are aimed at helping undergraduates develop specific communication skills sets (e.g., business writing and business public speaking). Other commonly discussed skills within business and professional communication textbooks and courses include team/group functioning, interviewing, leadership, diversity, interpersonal relationships in the workplace, meetings, negotiation/conflict management, and listening (Beebe and Mottet 2010; O'Hair, Friedrich, and Dixon 2011).

Last, business and professional communication courses tend to focus on what Argenti calls microlevel rather than macrolevel aspects of communication. Microlevel aspects of communication focus on how the individual communicator communicates, whereas macrolevel aspects of communication examine how communication functions as a larger picture of the organizational environment.

Of the four subfields being discussed in this section, the study of business and professional communication is by far the oldest. A. E. Phillips (1908) published the first public speaking textbook specifically designed for adults in business, which was quickly followed by other books on the topic (Hoffman 1923; Sandford and Yeager 1929). We should note that Sandford and Yeager's (1929) text *Business and Professional Speaking* was the first text actually written by someone in the speech field. In addition to business speech books, a new trend of public courses for business professionals emerged. Individuals would hold workshops for business professionals on a variety of business topics, which ultimately led to the professionalization of public speaking and workplace learning or training and development. Sanborn (1964) noted that:

> the first popular treatment of communication to come to the attention of the businessman was that of Dale Carnegie, whose writings and courses achieved nationwide popularity in the 1920s and 1930s. Holding out exciting promises of success in business through the development of wondrous powers of speech, memory, "personality," etc., the Carnegie courses have drawn thousands of hopefuls from a generation of businessmen. Conceding the possible usefulness of the Carnegie "therapy" for some people, professionals in the field of communication have tended to regard such approaches as superficial "gimmickery." (5)

While Dale Carnegie's courses and books may have made the idea of business speaking known in the United States, none of his prescriptions were actually based on research. As the research in speech communication became more research focused during the 20th century, so did the teaching of business and professional communication courses.

Managerial Communication

The second academic area of study related to communication in the workplace discussed by Argenti (1996) is managerial communication. Generally speaking, individuals taking courses in managerial communication are students in a Masters of Business Administration (MBA) program. These courses typically focus on how communication functions within the organization in an effort to improve business strategy and the bottom line. For this reason, "management communication focuses on communication strategy; skills, including writing and speaking; process, including teamwork and interpersonal behavior; the global environment, which focuses on cross-cultural communication; and function" (Argenti 1996, 83). In many ways, managerial communication is a hybrid of the other three terms being discussed in this section. However, managerial communication, at its very basic level, is about teaching future businessmen and businesswomen specific communication skills to enhance their personal careers and improve the workplace.

Organizational Communication

The third field noted by Argenti (1996) related to communication in the workplace is organizational communication. As a unique field of study, organizational communication grew out of the body of research originally initiated by scholars in management, organizational behavior, and industrial psychology. Instead of attempting to define the term "organizational communication," Deetz (2001) explains that there are three ways to interpret what is "organizational communication." The first way that scholars commonly think of organizational communication is to see it as a specific area of study within the field of communication studies. As a field, organizational communication draws upon the research from both communication studies and other fields that study organizations (general business, organizational behavior, industrial psychology, organizational sociology, etc.). As such, organizational communication is a hybrid field because it is greatly dependent upon research and insight from a wide array of disciplines. Furthermore, as a separate field of study within communication studies, undergraduate students have the ability to major in organizational communication and even get their doctorates in organizational communication.

The second way that Deetz (2001) explains that people can view organizational communication is "to think of communication as a way to describe and explain organizations. In the same way that psychology, sociology, and economics can be thought of as capable of explaining organizations' processes, communication might also be thought of as a distinct mode of explanation or way of thinking about organizations" (5). In essence, communication scholars have developed ways of analyzing that are uniquely different than psychologists, sociologists, and organizational behaviorists because they come to examining the organization from a theoretically rich tradition in rhetoric and human communication.

Last, Deetz (2001) explains that people can view organizational communication is "as a phenomenon that exists in organizations" (5). Under this conceptualization, organizational communication consists of both microlevel and macrolevel communication issues.

While the field of organizational communication definitely consists of aspects of all three of the other academic areas in workplace communication, the field tends to be more theoretical as a whole and less application-focused. Furthermore, Argenti (1996) notes that "the organizational communication discipline['s development] has been so painfully slow as a result of budget cuts at universities, lack of interest among graduate students looking to enter management education as a career, and the continued interest in the area in other schools outside of the business school environment" (86).

Business/Corporate Communication

The last major academic unit to examine workplace communication is business/corporate communication. According to Goodman (2000), business/corporate communication, "is a vital function in contemporary organizations. It is the total of a corporation's efforts to communicate effectively and profitably. It is a strategic action practiced by professionals within an organization, or on behalf of a client. It is the creation and maintenance of strong internal and external relationships" (69). As discussed earlier, Goodman (2006) found that the top six functions of modern business/corporate communicators are media relations, public relations, crisis communication, executive communication, employee relations, and communication policy and strategy. However, the actual duties that communication executives can have are very broad including "public relations, investor relations, employee relations, community relations, media relations, labor relations, government relations, technical communication, training and employee development, marketing communication, management communication . . . philanthropic activity, crisis and emergency communication, and advertising" (Goodman 2000, 69). Take a look at this list of possible duties that falls into the general heading of "business/corporate communication," and it's not hard to quickly see how complicated the field of business/corporate communication is. On top of all of these functions, often business/corporate communication executives are tasked with working with the information technology departments while creating intranet and Internet communication policies and/or campaigns. Yet other business/corporate communication professionals are asked to write speeches for upper-level management. In essence, business/corporate communication is a giant heading for a great deal of work that is completed in the modern organization (in both for-profit and nonprofit organizations).

Why Workplace Communication Matters

You may be asking yourself by this point, but why should professionals worry about the professional world of workplace communication. In a 2009 study conducted by Corporate Communication International looking at the current trends in business/corporate communication, 95 percent of the respondents had at least a bachelor's degree, but most did not have an advanced degree. In essence, while a master's degree in communication or business administration can definitely help, most of the people who rise to the executive level in business/corporate communication only have a bachelor's degree. However, there are an increasing number of both undergraduate and graduate programs in business/corporate communication; so competition for entry-level positions will continue to increase, and having a strong foundation in the field will be a great way to set yourself apart from others seeking those entry-level positions.

As a side note, some scholars (e.g., Argenti 1996; Goodman 2000) prefer the term "corporate communication" as a standalone term, but the actual field has generally gone by the term "business communication." The two largest professional bodies for business communicators are the IABC and the Association for Business Communication (ABC). Yet others do not differentiate between what is fundamentally called "business communication" or "organizational communication" (Papa, Daniels, and Spiker 2008), which is why we prefer the more general "workplace communication."

The Business Case for Communication

For-profit and nonprofit organizations spend a considerable amount of money today in marketing, creating a web presence, social media, employee intranets, and many other communication vehicles. Unfortunately, people within the workplace communication field have historically not been able to demonstrate why and how their work is beneficial for organizations. For example, Blakeslee (2004) noted that despite the fact that corporations spend over $117 billion in various forms of advertising each year, there is no research that clearly links these advertising dollars to actual increases in sales. As corporations are attempting decrease operating budgets and streamline the business process, demonstrating that what workplace communication professionals do for the bottom line is very important. If workplace communication departments want to keep functioning, they need to build a case for their departments. CEOs want to see how every dollar being spent helps the bottom line. Unfortunately, many workplace communication professionals have a background in an academic subject that does not involve measuring the outcomes of specific business projects. In a study conducted by the IABC in 2005, the researchers found that only 49 percent of communication professionals conduct systematic feedback surveys from key stakeholders, only 34 percent measure whether or not communication projects meet business objectives, and only 30 percent measure whether or not a communication project is actually effective (Rodgers 2006). Clearly, workplace communication professionals need to do a better job of demonstrating the actual value of what they do.

Argenti (2006) notes that there are three major reasons to focus on evaluating the effectiveness of communication projects: (1) workplace communication professionals can more clearly demonstrate how they are meeting the demands of senior executives; (2) workplace communication professionals can justify their budgets; and (3) when senior executives see the benefits of communication projects, they are more willing to cooperate and enable system-wide strategies that lead to stronger business outcomes. While demonstrating how communication programs are beneficial is important, how to go about measuring specific communication projects was discussed in Chapter 15 in volume 1 of this set. Now, I want to explore some of the overarching results found for the benefits of workplace communication.

As discussed in the first volume of this set, one area that has been shown to have a clear impact on market share is the area of employee communication. In a series of studies examining the benefits of effective internal communication on financial outcomes conducted by Watson Wyatt (2004, 2009, 2010), the researchers found that consistently organizations with higher levels of effective internal communication are more profitable. For example, in the 2003–2004 study the researchers found, "Companies with the highest levels of effective communication experienced a 26 percent total return to shareholders from 1998 to 2002, compared to a –15 percent return experienced by firms that communicate least effectively" (1). This finding was again replicated in the 2009–2010 study, "Companies that are highly effective communicators had 47 percent higher total returns to shareholders over the last five years compared with firms that are the least effective communicators" (3). Both of these studies clearly indicate monetarily why businesses today must be interested in the communication function.

History of Workplace Communication

A Brief History of How Humans Have Worked

Humans have gone through numerous very specific cycles of development over many millennia. At first, all societies functioned primarily as hunter-gatherer societies. People would move around on a fairly constant basis to stay with their food supplies. According to Volti (2007), around 10,000 to 12,000 years ago, humans learned that they didn't have to follow the migratory patterns of animals to survive. Instead, humans learned that they could grow plants to eat. With the cultivation of plant life, humans ushered in a new era of human civilization known as the horticultural revolution. By horticulture, we mean the ability to grow plants and use those plants to sustain life. One of the outcomes of this increased dependence on plant cultivation was the increase in community sizes. Volti notes that most hunter-gatherer societies had around 40 people, but horticultural-based societies could have upward of 5,000 members.

Quickly though, people learned that horticultural techniques, which primarily relied on hands and small tools, were not efficient for sustaining large communities. To help support larger communities, humans had to develop new methods and tools for increasing production amounts. Volti calls this new era the agricultural revolution. One of the foundation pieces of the agricultural revolution was the invention of the plow, "A plow turns the soil far more effectively than a hoe or digging stick, and its effectiveness can be augmented by hitching it to a draft anima. Draft animals also have the added benefit of being sources of fertilizer" (8).

One problematic offshoot of the agricultural revolution was the unfortunate cycles that resulted from the earth's environment that led to periods of feast and famine. During periods of feast, peopled would accumulate food supplies and then hopefully live off of those supplies during periods of famine. Unfortunately, during periods of famine, the likelihood of warfare between groups needing food also increased. As conquering and pillaging became part of the normal life cycle of communities, the need for established armies and protection eventually led to the necessity of government. "Initially governing towns or small cities and their outlying environs, a few agrarian states, evolved into vast empires exercising dominion over tens of millions of people, as was the case of ancient Rome and dynastic China" (Volti 2007, 9).

With the increased size and scope of territories, determining how to govern these vast areas became a primary concern. One of the interesting side effects of this problem was the rise in the clerical class, or the class of people who had the ability to read, write, and do basic accounting work.

As empires became increasingly more structured, we also see the invention of the bureaucrat who had to oversee the leader's directives, maintain law and order, and collect taxes.

Also during this period in society, we see the rise of the individual artisan. Artisans were individuals who created materials that could be traded and sold. Volti (2007) estimates that approximately 3 to 5 percent of workers in agricultural societies worked as "potters, smiths, spinners and weavers, brewers, and other specialized artisans" (10). For the most part, these artisans worked independently or in small groups of related artisans. New artisans were created through a process of apprenticeship. In essence, a child would be mentored for a long period of time by a master artisan in a specific skill. Eventually, the apprentice would become a master herself or himself and then train the next generation of workers.

Over a few thousand years, the tools used to create a range of products became faster and larger. Eventually, individual artisans started forming collectives who would work on specific items that could then be marketed. These collectives eventually led to factories where owners would hire artisans to mass produce materials that could be ushered to market. Starting in 1780 the world started to quickly change and a new era called the industrial revolution quickly changed the face of the planet forever. Pioneering economist Joseph Schumpeter created a 50-year model to explain how and why society saw such drastic changes occur (Luthans 2008). Luthans (2008) summarizes Schumpeter's model, "The first wave in modern history (1780s–1840s) brought steam power that drove the Industrial Revolution; next came the railroads (1840s–1890s); followed by electric power (1890s–1930s); and then cheap oil and the automobile (1930s–1980s)" (Luthans 2008, 32).

As the industrial revolution commenced, factories became more rigid and the desire for higher levels of output with fewer resources became the norm (Chandler 1991). With this new model of business in place, learning how to not only increase profits and decrease costs but also to get employees to be productive became the major concern for the new corporate titans. These early years were focused primarily on profit and expansion. Ihator (2004) tells the story of William Henry Vanderbilt of the New York Central Railroad. In 1882 when some of his business partners questioned whether or not the public would go along with a proposal of his, he responded, "The public, why, sir, the public be dammed." This ideology toward the public was very common, and was often the ideology businesses had toward their employees as well.

Volti (2007) argues that one of the primary contributors to the rise of capitalism prior to the industrial revolution was the influence of Protestantism. While early Protestants, such as Martin Luther, were suspicious of the accumulation of wealth, later thinkers such as John Calvin actually celebrated and glorified the accumulation of wealth. Protestants quickly combined the notions of business and religion to create a new perspective where "the Calvinist business man was more than a mere money-grubber; work took on the qualities of a religious 'calling' or vocation. To work hard and prosper was to serve God, while material success provided an indication that death would not be followed by eternal damnation" (Volti 2007, 14). An example of this ideology can be seen in an incident during a 1902 coalmine worker strike. George Baer, a U.S. coalmine operator, decided to stop negotiating with striking coal workers saying, "The rights and interests of the laboring man will be protected and cared for—not by the labor agitators, but by the Christian men to whom God in His infinite wisdom has given the control of the property interests of the country, and upon the successful management of which so much depends" (Brands 1997, 457).

The Rise of the Workplace Communication Professional

During the agricultural revolution, rulers learned that they had to control vast areas in order to maintain the power. Rulers quite often felt the need to illicit help from others to help spread their messages throughout their kingdoms. The oldest known written document in history is the *Precepts of Ke'gemni and Ptah-hotep*, written around 2100 BCE by Ptah-hotep. In Ptah-hotep's *Precepts* he is instructed by the Pharaoh Isesi (of the fifth dynasty in Egypt) to teach the pharaoh's son. Within the 43 paragraphs of Ptah-hotep's *Precepts*, Gray (1946) counted 22 direct or indirect references to some aspect of speech. In essence, this text was not only the first text on public speaking, but also the first text on business communication. Table 1.1 shows a number of the ideas espoused by Ptah-hotep that still are words of advice for modern business communication.

The *Precepts* by Ptah-hotep are hardly the only historic ideas that directly relate to modern business communication, nor was Egypt the only culture to examine communication. Curtin and Gaither (2007) noted that in medieval India, "*sutradhars*, or traveling storytellers, spread rulers' messages, serving a common public relations function" (2). While the idea of having someone communicate the ideas of another is hardly a new phenomenon, the importance of communication quickly became apparent during the late parts of the industrial revolution. Instead of delving into a long narrative of the history of business communication, I have opted to provide you with a general timeline of major historical moments in Table 1.2.

Table 1.1   Precepts of Ptah-hotep

Stanza	Quotation
2	If you meet a debator more capable than yourself, silence will be your best defense.
3	Refute the false arguments of your equal in debate; you will thus appear wiser than he.
8	Avoid stirring up enmities by the perversion of truth; nor should you violate confidence; it is abhorrent to the soul.
13	If you are in the council chamber, follow the procedures as they have been set down for you. Avoid absences or tardiness.
17	If you are in a position of authority, listen graciously to complaints and supplications. Let the supplicant speak freely and without fear, in order that his injury be removed.
24	In council with your superiors, if you would be wise, avoid speaking of that of which you know nothing.
28	If you have occasion to render judgments, speak thou without favouring one side. Let it not be said, "His conduct is that of the nobles, favouring one side in his speech." Turn thine aim toward exact judgments.
40	The fool, on the contrary, mistakes igornace for knowledge, and evil for good. He considers idle chatter to be wisdom, and is shunned because of his misfortunes.

Table 1.2   History of Workplace Communication

1770	The Industrial Revolution starts.
1772	Josiah Wedgwood, an English potter and the inventor of Wedgwood ware, experiments with industrial quality control.
1800s	The Industrial Revolution moves work from the individual, family, or small group to the emerging corporate organization. Training people to work at specific tasks becomes a necessity.
1809	The Masonic Grand Lodge of New York, under De Witt Clinton, establishes vocational-training facilities.
1830	Columbia University establishes a new curriculum for young men "employed in business and mercantile establishments."
1862	The Morrill Act signed by President Abraham Lincoln establishes land-grant agricultural and mechanical colleges. County extension agents begin to train farmers to improve productivity.

(continued)

Table 1.2 *(continued)*

1872	Hoe and Company in New York City establishes the first factory school and curricula was developed based on tasks that were carried out in the factory.
1883	Alexander Kapp, a German adult educator, coins the term "andragogy" referring to adult learning.
1887	William Cooper Procter, grandson of one of the cofounders of Procter and Gamble, introduces a profit-sharing plan.
1892	Francis Galton publishes *Hereditary Genius*, which is the first attempt by nonphysical scientists to measure human behavior (first study in social psychology).
1897	The term "public relations" first appears in *The Year Book of Railway Literature*.
1906	The National Society for the Promotion of Industrial Education is formed.
1908	A. E. Phillips publishes the first public speaking textbook specifically designed for business professionals.
1911	Fredrick W. Taylor publishes *The Principles of Scientific Management*.
1915	Procter and Gamble provides employees with the first disability and death benefits plan.
1916	Henry Fayol declares that the work of managers is to plan, organize, coordinate, and control.
1917	Charles R. Allen uses the "show, tell, do, check" method to train 50,000 shipyard workers. He adapted this framework from the 18th-century German philosopher, psychologist, and educator Johan Friedrich Herbart's five-step framework for pedagogy.
1919	Edward L. Bernays and Doris Fleishman open the first public relations firm.
1920s	Unions set up their first training programs for employees.
	Bell Labs introduces total quality management (TQM) and statistical quality control.
	Edward L. Bernays publishes the first major text on public relations, *Crystallizing Public Opinion*.
1927	The Hawthorne Experiments at the Western Electric Plant in Cicero, IL, reveal the influences of physical and psychological factors on productivity.
1929	The U.S. stock market crashes leading to the Great Depression.
	Edward L. Bernays orchestrates an event on behalf of his tobacco industry client, where he had New York City debutantes marching in the Easter Day Parade light of cigarettes under a campaign called "Torches of Liberty Contingent."

(continued)

Table 1.2   *(continued)*

1931	Professor Erwin H. Schell initiates the MIT executive development program—the first "away-from company" program for executives.
1932	Rensis Likert creates the Likert Scale (e.g., strongly agree, agree, neutral, disagree, strongly disagree) and revolutionizes the measurement of human attitudes, behaviors, and cognitive processes.
1936	Dale Carnegie publishes *How to Win Friends and Influence People*.
1937	Chester Carlson patents xerography—the science behind the photocopier.
1938	Hewlett-Packard creates the "HP Way," a policy that focuses on employee sensitivity (including increased benefits and flex time).
	Franklin Delano Roosevelt signs an executive order stating that the U.S. government, as an employer, should provide training for its employees.
	Chester Barnard publishes *The Functions of the Executive*, and explains, "The first function of the executive is to develop and maintain a system of communication" (226).
1941	Lazarsfeld publishes the first review of the discipline of communication based on his and others' research at the Bureau of Applied Social Research and determines that communication could be broken into four categories: (1) who, (2) said what, (3) to whom, and (4) with what effect.
1942	Peter Drucker publishes *The Future of Industrial Man: A Conservative Approach*.
	The American Society of Training Directors (ASTD) is formed on April 2, 1942, at a meeting of the American Petroleum Institute in New Orleans. Fifteen training directors hold their first meeting on January 12, 1943, in Baton Rouge.
	Alexander R. Heron publishes *Sharing Information with Employees*, which describes the goals, attitudes, and criteria for successful communication with one's employees.
1943	Abraham Maslow publishes "A Theory of Human Motivation" and thus creates his famous hierarchy of needs.
1946	Kurt Lewin first experiments with group dynamics at the Connecticut Interracial Commission.
1947	Public Relations Society of America is created.
	National Training Laboratories conducts its first session in human-relations training—also known as sensitivity training of T-group training.
1948	The Institute of Public Relations in Great Britain is created.
1949	Claude Shannon and Warren Weaver publish *The Mathematical Theory of Communication*, which provides the first major model of human communication (source, message, receiver, noise).

(continued)

Table 1.2 *(continued)*

1950s	Carl Hovland and other researchers at Yale University initiate the first major series of scientific studies examining aspects of persuasion: source credibility, personality traits, argument ordering, explicit versus implicit conclusions, and fear appeals.
1950	The Public Relations Society of America (PRSA) enacts the first "Professional Standards for the Practice of Public Relations."
1953	B. F. Skinner's *Science and Human Behavior* is published, which introduces the idea of behavior modification.
1956	IBM opens the first residential executive-development facility at Sands Point on Long Island, NY.
	International Council of Industrial Editors (ICIE) conducts the first survey of business communicators titled "Operation Tapemeasure."
1957	Osgood, Tannenbaum, and Suci publish *The Measurement of Meaning,* which creates the semantic differential scale used in modern research (e.g., Good 1 2 3 Bad; Right 1 2 3 Wrong; etc.).
1959	Donald L. Kirkpatrick's article establishing the four levels of evaluation for training (reaction, learning, behavior, and results) is published in *Training Directors Journal.*
1960	Douglas M. McGregor's *The Human Side of Enterprise* is published, which introduces theory X and theory Y as opposing viewpoints of people's fundamental perceptions of work.
1961	Lee Thayer publishes *Administrative Communication,* the first book on communication in the workplace written by someone with a background in speech communication.
1964	Robert R. Blake and Jane S. Mouton publish *The Managerial Grid.*
	Charles Redding and George Sanborn publish *Business and Industrial Communication: A Source Book,* which is the first major comprehensive collection of articles on ideals related to communication in the workplace.
1969	ARPANET, a computer networking tool commissioned by the DOD to enable researchers at remote sites to interact, is initiated starting with four remote sites called nodes (University of California–Los Angeles, Stanford Research Institute, University of California–Santa Barbara, and University of Utah).
1970	Members from the American Association of Industrial Editors and the International Council of Industrial Editors create the International Association of Business Communicators (IABC).
1971	Ray Tomlinson invents a program to send messages across the network, which is eventually called electronic mail or e-mail for short.

(continued)

Table 1.2 (*continued*)

1972	In a follow up to the 1956 Operation Tapemeasure, an IABC study found that 59.4% of business communicators were male. Duties included: 95.9% writing and editing, 70.2% internal communication, 44.5% media relations, and 28.9% public relations.
1974	Corporate Communicators Canada joins IABC.
1982	Scott Fahlman suggests that MsgGroup users use ":-)" and ":-(" on September 19th in a Bulletin Board at Carnegie Mellon University.
1987	In response to a congressional request by Senator Al Gore to create a more public presence on the Internet, Gordon Bell and his colleagues write a report for the Office of Science and Technology suggesting the creation of a U.S. research and education network, which would be established four years later by Congress.
1988	Internet Relay Chat (IRC) is developed by Jarkko Oikarinen.
1990	Peter M. Senge publishes *The Fifth Discipline: The Art and Practice of the Learning Organization.*
1991	The World Wide Web (WWW) is released by CERN having been developed by Tim Berners-Lee.
1992	The phrase "surfing the Internet" is coined by Jean Armour Polly.
1993	Bill Clinton creates the Office of Work-Based Learning within the Department of Labor.
	Windows versions of America Online (AOL), CompuServe, and Prodigy enable to the public to easily access the Internet.
1994	Shopping malls arrive on the Internet.
	Arizona law firm Canter & Siegel sends the first "spam" message advertising green card lottery services.
1995	IABC study finds that 70% of the people in business communication are female.
	RealAudio creates an Internet plug-in program to enable Internet users to listen to audio at near real-time rates.
1997	Foster and Jolly release *Corporate Communication Handbook,* the first systematic examination of the field of business communication as a whole.
1999	ASTD begins using the phrase workplace learning and performance (WLP) to describe what was commonly known as training and development.
2001	Peter Senge and George Carstedt predict that the next wave of business will be one powered by information technology.

(*continued*)

Table 1.2   (*continued*)

2002	Blogging, Internet-based diaries/journals available to the public, becomes the new cool thing for people to do on the Internet.
2009	Paul A. Argenti and Courtney M. Barnes publish *Digital Strategies for Powerful Corporate Communications,* which is the first text to specifically address the influx of social media in the modern workplace.

Sources: Gordon (2002), Ihator (2004), Sanborn (1964), Senge and Carstedt 2001; Shaw and Craig (1994), Volti (2007), and Wrench, McCroskey, and Richmond (2008).

An Introduction to the IABC Competency Model

In 1995 several hundred human resource managers and workplace learning professionals gathered in Johannesburg, South Africa, to discuss how to determine the necessary knowledge and skill sets needed for various jobs. In this process, they defined the term "competency" as "a cluster of related knowledge, skills, and attitudes that affects a major part of one's job (a role or responsibility), that correlates with performance on that job, that can be measured against well-accepted standards, and that can be improved via training and development" (Parry 1996, 50). A competency model then "describes the particular combination of knowledge, skills, and characteristics needed to effectively perform a role in an organization and is used as a human resource tool for selection, training and development, appraisal, and succession planning" (Lucia and Lepsinger 1999, 5).

Competency models have been used to determine what it means to be a competent member of a specific sector of business from the viewpoint of workplace learning and performance (Bernthal et al., 2004) to mortgage company sales (Lucia and Lepsinger 1999). Competency modeling has become such an integral part of the modern workplace environment that the United States Department of Labor, Employment and Training Administration (ETA) created a generic competency model for the modern workplace on their website http://www.careeronestop.org/Competency-Model/. Careeronestop.org will even allow you to view a range of competency models for a variety of professions, and build a new one as well.

You may be asking why organizations like competency models. According to the ETA Industry Competency Initiative, the primary reason organizations like competency models is because it allows them to do four basic things: (1) Identify specific employer skill needs; (2) Develop competency-based curricula and training models; (3) Develop industry-defined performance indicators, skill standards, and certifications; (4) Develop resources for career exploration and guidance. In light of these basic reasons for developing competency models, the IABC created a basic competency model for business communicators (Figure 1.1).

Communication Skills	Management Skills	Knowledge Areas
* Writing/Editing * Web content/writing * Writing proposals/RFPS * Research * Presentations *Newsletter Editing/Layout	* Ethics * Communication Planning * Crisis Communication * Publication Management * Database / Distribution Systems * Project Tracking / Measurement * Time Management * Vendor Management * Budgeting *Professional Development	* Marketing Communication * Corporate Reputation / Brand Management *Employee Communications * Media Relations * Issues Management * Crisis Communication Planning * Community Relations * Investory Relations * Govermnet Relations * Labor Relations * Consulting Skills * Problem Solving

Figure 1.1   IABC Competency Model

As you can see, the IABC competency model is built around two major skill sets (communication and management) and a series of knowledge areas important for business communication in the 21st century. When individuals can demonstrate that they are proficient in each of the three areas (both through their body of work and a knowledge examination), they can apply to become accredited business communicators. According to the IABC:

> IABC's accreditation program is the global standard of professional achievement for business communicators. Accredited members practicing around the world apply the same strategic management process in all communication disciplines, across diverse cultures, and in for-profit and nonprofit organizations of all sizes.
>
> This peer-reviewed program challenges candidates to demonstrate their knowledge of strategic communication planning, implementation, measurement and ethics. Candidates who meet all requirements earn the designation Accredited Business Communicator (ABC). (http://www.iabc.com/abc/)

Because the IABC competency model is the standard by which all business communication professionals should be judged, this text is designed around the IABC competency model. However, the IABC competency model is just part of the overall picture. According to ETA's Industry Competency Initiative, industry-specific competencies are toward the top of the competency pyramid. Below the industry-specific competencies, there are a range of other competencies that all employees should have in a thriving economy. These basic competencies are important for all business communicators regardless of their nation of origin. For this reason, Figure 1.2 provides a more detailed competency model for business communication that combines parts of the ETA Competency Initiative and the IABC competency model.

Competency models are quickly becoming very important in the modern workplace, and there is a wealth of literature on the subject of building effective competency models for the modern workplace (e.g., Lucia and Lepsinger 1999; Mansfield 1996; Spicer 2009). As a further extension of the IABC model, I propose the adoption of a more complete model (Figure 1.2, Table 1.3) based on both the IABC model for business communication and fundamental competency modeling parts proposed by the United States Department of Labor's Employment and Training Administration's "building blocks for competency models."

From Competency Model to Book Structure

If one looks at the functions of business communication professionals' levels of the business communicator competency model proposed here, the first volume of this set related to the first building block, internal communication. This volume looks at the last four building blocks: corporate communication, advertising/marketing communication, external communication, and public relations. As a two-volume set devoted to workplace communication as a general construct, the choice to focus one

Figure 1.2   Workplace Communication Competency Model

Table 1.3 Workplace Communication Professional Competency Model

I. Foundations of Workplace Communication[1]

A. Interpersonal Skills

1. *Demonstrating concern for others:* Shows sincere interest in others and their concerns, and demonstrates sensitivity to the needs and feelings of others; helps others resolve sensitive interpersonal problems as appropriate; looks for ways to help people, and pitches in to help others.
2. *Demonstrating insight into behavior:* Recognizes and accurately interprets the verbal and nonverbal behavior of others; shows insight into the actions and motives of others, and recognizes when relationships with others are strained.
3. *Maintaining open communication:* Maintains open lines of communication with others; encourages others to approach him/her with problems and successes; establishes a high degree of trust and credibility with others.
4. *Respecting diversity:* Demonstrates sensitivity and respect for the opinions, perspectives, customs and individual differences of others; values diversity of people and ideas.
5. *Working with diverse people:* Is flexible and open-minded when dealing with a wide range of people; listens to and considers others' viewpoints; works well and develops effective relationships with diverse personalities.
6. *Learning about other cultures:* Takes action to learn about and understand the climate, orientation, needs, and values of other groups, organizations, or cultures.

B. Ethical Understanding

1. *Behaving ethically:* Abides by a strict code of ethics and behavior; chooses an ethical course of action and does the right thing, even in the face of opposition; encourages others to behave accordingly.
2. *Acting fairly:* Treats others with honesty, fairness, and respect; makes decisions that are objective and reflect the just treatment of others.
3. *Taking responsibility:* Takes responsibility for accomplishing work goals within accepted timeframes; accepts responsibility for one's decisions and actions and for those of one's group, team, or department; attempts to learn from mistakes.
4. *Communicating ethically:* Demonstrates respect in one's communication with coworkers, colleagues, and customers; communicates in a manner that is in the best interest for one's company, community, and environment; complies with applicable ethical credos including the National Communication Association's Credo for Ethical Communication and the International Association for Business Communicators' Code of Ethics for Professional Communicators.*

(continued)

Table 1.3 (*continued*)

5. *Business ethics:* Demonstrates respect for coworkers, colleagues, and customers; acts in the best interest of the company, the community, and the environment; complies with applicable laws and rules governing work and reports loss, waste, or theft or company property to appropriate personnel.

C. **Professionalism**
1. *Demonstrating self-control:* Demonstrates self-control by maintaining composure and keeping emotions in check even in very difficult situations; deals calmly and effectively with stressful situations.
2. *Professional appearance:* Maintains a professional demeanor; dresses appropriately for occupation and its requirements; and maintains appropriate personal hygiene.
3. *Substance abuse:* Is free from substance abuse.
4. *Maintains a positive attitude:* Projects a professional image of oneself and the organization; demonstrates a positive attitude toward work; takes pride in one's work and the work of the organization.

D. **Initiative**
1. *Persisting:* Pursues work with energy, drive, and a strong accomplishment orientation; persists and expends extra effort to accomplish tasks even when conditions are difficult or deadlines are tight; persists at a task or problem despite interruptions, obstacles, or setbacks.
2. *Taking initiative:* Goes beyond the routine demands of the job; takes initiative in seeking out new work challenges and increasing the variety and scope of one's job; seeks opportunities to influence events and originate action; assists others who have less experience or have heavy workloads.
3. *Setting challenging goals:* Establishes and maintains personally challenging but realistic work goals; exerts effort toward task mastery; brings issues to closure by pushing forward until a resolution is achieved.
4. *Working independently:* Develops own ways of doing things; is able to perform effectively even with minimal direction, support, or approval and without direct supervision.
5. *Achievement motivation:* Intrinsically driven to succeed and excel; strives to exceed standards and expectations; exhibits confidence in capabilities and an expectation to succeed in future activities.

E. **Dependability and Reliability**
1. *Fulfilling obligations:* Behaves consistently and predictably; is reliable, responsible, and dependable in fulfilling obligations; diligently follows through on commitments and consistently meets deadlines.
2. *Showing up on time:* Demonstrates regular and punctual attendance; rarely is late for meetings or appointments.

(*continued*)

Table 1.3   (*continued*)

3. *Attending to details:* Diligently checks work to ensure that all essential details have been considered; notices errors or inconsistencies that others have missed, and takes prompt, thorough action to correct errors.
4. *Complying with policies:* Follows written and verbal directions; complies with organizational rules, policies, and procedures.

F. **Willingness to Learn**

1. *Demonstrating an interest in learning:* Demonstrates an interest in personal learning and development; seeks feedback from multiple sources about how to improve and develop, and modifies behavior based on feedback or self-analysis of past mistakes.
2. *Participating in training:* Takes steps to develop and maintain knowledge, skills, and expertise necessary to achieve positive results; participates fully in relevant training programs and actively pursues other opportunities to develop knowledge and skills.
3. *Anticipating changes in work:* Anticipates changes in work demands and searches for and participates in assignments or training that address these changing demands; treats unexpected circumstances as opportunities to learn.
4. *Identifying career interests:* Takes charge of personal career development by identifying occupational interests, strengths, options, and opportunities; makes insightful career-planning decisions based on integration and consideration of others' feedback, and seeks out additional training to pursue career goals.

II. **Academic Competencies**

A. **Reading/Comprehension**

1. *Comprehension:* Locates, understands, and interprets written information in prose and in documents such as manuals, reports, memos, letters, forms, graphs, charts, tables, calendars, schedules, signs, notices, applications, and directions; understands the purpose of written materials; attains meaning and comprehends core ideas.
2. *Attention to detail:* Identifies main ideas; notes details and facts; detects inconsistencies; identifies implied meaning and details; identifies missing information; identifies trends.
3. *Integration:* Critically evaluates and analyzes information in written materials; integrates and synthesizes information from multiple written materials.
4. *Application:* Integrates what is learned from written materials with prior knowledge; applies what is learned from written material to follow instructions and complete specific tasks; applies what is learned from written material to future situations.

(*continued*)

Table 1.3 (*continued*)

B. Writing

1. *Organization and development:* Creates documents such as letters, directions, manuals, reports, graphs, and flow charts; communicates thoughts, ideas, information, messages, and other written information, which may contain technical material, in a logical, organized and coherent manner; ideas are well developed with supporting information and examples.
2. *Mechanics:* Uses standard syntax and sentence structure; uses correct spelling, punctuation, and capitalization; uses appropriate grammar (e.g., correct tense, subject-verb agreement, no missing words).
3. *Tone:* Writes in a manner appropriate for business; uses language appropriate for the target audience; uses appropriate tone and word choice (e.g., writing is professional and courteous).

C. Mathematics/Statistics

1. *Quantification:* Reads and writes numbers; counts and places numbers in sequence; recognizes whether one number is larger than another.
2. *Computation:* Adds, subtracts, multiplies, and divides with whole numbers, fractions, decimals, and percents; calculates averages, ratios, proportions and rates; converts decimals to fractions; converts fractions to percents.
3. *Physical measurement and estimation:* Takes measurements of time, temperature, distances, length, width, height, perimeter, area, volume, weight, velocity, and speed; uses and reports measurements correctly; converts from one measurement to another (e.g., from standard to metric).
4. *Psychological/communication measurement and evaluation:* The ability to plan, implement, and evaluate psychometrics related to psychology and communication.*
5. *Application:* Performs basic math computations accurately; translates practical problems into useful mathematical expressions, and uses appropriate mathematical formulas and techniques.

D. Science and Technology

1. *Comprehension:* Understands basic scientific principles and to use commonly available technology; understands the scientific method (i.e., identifies problems, collects information, forms opinions, and draws conclusions); understands overall intent and proper procedures for setup and operation of equipment.
2. *Application:* Applies basic scientific principles and technology to complete tasks.

(*continued*)

Table 1.3 (*continued*)

E. Listening and Speaking

1. *Speaking:* Expresses information to individuals or groups taking into account the audience and the nature of the information (e.g., technical or controversial); speaks clearly and confidently; information is organized in a logical manner; speaks using common English conventions including proper grammar, tone and pace; tracks audience responses and reacts appropriately to those responses; effectively uses eye contact and nonverbal expression.

2. *Listening:* Receives, attends to, interprets, understands, and responds to verbal messages and other cues; picks out important information in verbal messages; understands complex instructions; appreciates feelings and concerns of verbal messages.

3. *Two-way communication:* Practices meaningful two-way communication (i.e., speaks clearly, pays close attention and seeks to understand others, listens attentively, and clarifies information); attends to nonverbal cues and responds appropriately.

4. *Persuasion/influence:* Influences others; persuasively presents thoughts and ideas; gains commitment and ensures support for proposed ideas.

F. Critical and Analytical Thinking

1. *Reasoning:* Possesses sufficient inductive and deductive reasoning ability to perform job successfully; critically reviews, analyzes, synthesizes, compares, and interprets information; draws conclusions from relevant and/or missing information; understands the principles underlying the relationship among facts and applies this understanding when solving problems.

2. *Mental agility:* Identifies connections between issues; quickly understands, orients to, and learns new assignments; shifts gears and changes direction when working on multiple projects or issues.

G. Active Learning

1. *Learning strategies:* Applies a range of learning techniques to acquire new knowledge and skills; processes and retains information; identifies when it is necessary to acquire new knowledge and skills.

2. *Application:* Integrates newly learned knowledge and skills with existing knowledge and skills; uses newly learned knowledge and skills to complete specific tasks; uses newly learned knowledge and skills in new or unfamiliar situations.

H. Computer Skills

1. *Comprehending the basics:* Understands and efficiently uses basic computer hardware (e.g. PCs, printers) and software (e.g. word processing

(*continued*)

Table 1.3   (*continued*)

software, spreadsheet software) to perform tasks; understands common computer terminology (e.g., program, operating system) and is familiar with the fundamental capabilities of computers.

2. *Entering data:* Enters data into computer files quickly, with an acceptable degree of accuracy; double-checks data entry carefully; notices when data are missing or look wrong and takes steps to ensure computer files are complete and accurate.

3. *Preparing documents:* Uses word processing programs to create, edit, and retrieve document files; types materials quickly and accurately; checks work carefully and identifies/corrects typographical errors; uses basic reference materials and tools (e.g., spell check) to ensure accuracy.

III. Workplace Competencies

A. Teamwork

1. *Acknowledging team membership and role:* Accepts membership in the team; shows loyalty to the team; determines when to be a leader and when to be a follower depending on what is needed to achieve the team's goals and objectives; encourages others to express their ideas and opinions; identifies and draws upon team members' strengths and weaknesses to achieve results; learns from other team members.

2. *Establishing productive relationships:* Develops constructive and cooperative working relationships with others; exhibits tact and diplomacy and strives to build consensus; shows sensitivity to the thoughts and opinions of other team members; delivers constructive criticism and voices objections to others' ideas and opinions in a supportive, nonaccusatory manner; responds appropriately to positive and negative feedback.

3. *Identifying with the team and its goals:* Identifies the goals, norms, values, and customs of the team; is a team player and contributes to the group's effort; uses a group approach to identify problems and develop solutions based on group consensus; effectively communicates with all members of the group or team to achieve team goals and objectives.

4. *Resolving conflicts:* Brings others together to reconcile differences; handles conflicts maturely by exercising a give-and-take approach to achieve positive results for all parties; reaches formal or informal agreements that promote mutual goals and interests, and obtains commitment to those agreements from individuals or groups.

B. Adaptability/Flexibility

1. *Employing unique analyses:* Employs unique analyses and generates new, innovative ideas in complex areas; integrates seemingly unrelated information to develop creative solutions; develops innovative methods of obtaining or using resources when insufficient resources are available.

(*continued*)

Table 1.3 *(continued)*

2. *Entertaining new ideas:* Is open to considering new ways of doing things; actively seeks out and carefully considers the merits of new approaches to work; willingly embraces new approaches when appropriate and discards approaches that are no longer working.
3. *Dealing with ambiguity:* Takes effective action when necessary without having to have all the necessary facts in hand; easily changes gears in response to unpredictable or unexpected events, pressures, situations, and job demands; effectively changes plans, goals, actions, or priorities to deal with changing situations.

C. Planning and Organizing

1. *Planning:* Approaches work in a methodical manner; plans and schedules tasks so that work is completed on time; keeps track of details to ensure work is performed accurately and completely.
2. *Prioritizing:* Prioritizes various competing tasks and performs them quickly and efficiently according to their urgency; finds new ways of organizing work area or planning work to accomplish work more efficiently.
3. *Allocating resources:* Estimates resources needed for project completion; allocates time and resources effectively and coordinates efforts with all affected parties; keeps all parties informed of progress and all relevant changes to project timelines.
4. *Anticipating obstacles:* Anticipates obstacles to project completion and develops contingency plans to address them; takes necessary corrective action when projects go off-track.

D. Creative Thinking

1. *Generating innovative solutions:* Uses information, knowledge, and beliefs to generate original, innovative solutions to problems; reframes problems in a different light to find fresh approaches; entertains wide-ranging possibilities others may miss; takes advantage of difficult or unusual situations to develop unique approaches and useful solutions.
2. *Seeing the big picture:* Has broad knowledge and perspective; pieces together seemingly unrelated data to identify patterns and trends and to see a bigger picture; understands the pieces of a system as a whole and appreciates the consequences of actions on other parts of the system; possesses a big-picture view of the situation.

E. Working with Tools and Technology

1. *Selecting tools:* Selects and applies appropriate tools or technological solutions to frequently encountered problems; carefully considers which tools or technological solutions are appropriate for a given job,

(continued)

Table 1.3 (*continued*)

and consistently chooses the best tool or technological solution for the problem at hand.

2. *Keeping current:* Demonstrates an interest in learning about new and emerging tools and technologies; seeks out opportunities to improve knowledge of tools and technologies that may assist in streamlining work and improving productivity.

3. *Troubleshooting:* Learns how to maintain and troubleshoot tools and technologies.

F. **Problem Solving and Decision Making**

1. *Identifying the problem:* Anticipates or recognizes the existence of a problem; identifies the true nature of the problem by analyzing its component parts; uses all available reference systems to locate and obtain information relevant to the problem; recalls previously learned information that is relevant to the problem.

2. *Locating, gathering, and organizing relevant information:* Effectively uses both internal resources (e.g., internal computer networks, company filing systems) and external resources (e.g., Internet search engines) to locate and gather information; examines information obtained for relevance and completeness; recognizes important gaps in existing information and takes steps to eliminate those gaps; organizes/reorganizes information as appropriate to gain a better understanding of the problem.

3. *Generating alternatives:* Integrates previously learned and externally obtained information to generate a variety of high-quality alternative approaches to the problem; skillfully uses logic and analysis to identify the strengths and weaknesses, the costs and benefits, and the short- and long-term consequences of different approaches.

4. *Choosing a solution:* Decisively chooses the best solution after contemplating available approaches to the problem; makes difficult decisions even in highly ambiguous or ill-defined situations; quickly chooses an effective solution without assistance when appropriate.

5. *Implementing the solution:* Commits to a solution in a timely manner, and develops a realistic approach for implementing the chosen solution; observes and evaluates the outcomes of implementing the solution to assess the need for alternative approaches and to identify lessons learned.

G. **Workplace Computer Applications**

1. *Keyboarding and word processing:* Skillfully uses word-processing software; streamlines document processing by employing a variety of common software functions; uses correct style and format, even when confronted by uncommon requirements that deviate from standard guides; consults appropriate manuals when uncertain about the correct style and format.

(*continued*)

Table 1.3   (*continued*)

2. *Internet applications:* Effectively uses the Internet and web-based tools to manage basic workplace tasks (e.g., timekeeping, maintaining employee records, conducting information searches); understands and performs Internet functions requiring the use of log-in and password information; is aware of company guidelines surrounding Internet usage and complies with those guidelines.

3. *E-mailing:* Composes professional e-mails to communicate business-related information to coworkers, colleagues, and customers; understands the company e-mail system and its basic functions (e.g., replying to or forwarding messages, using electronic address books, attaching files); ensures that key stakeholders are kept informed of communications by copying (i.e., CCing) them on important e-mails when appropriate.

4. *Social networking:* The ability to leverage Web 2.0 applications to further one's ability to network with coworkers, professional peers, clients, and other organizational stakeholders.*

5. *Spreadsheets/statistical software:* Uses spreadsheet software to enter, manipulate, edit, and format text and numerical data; effectively creates and saves worksheets, charts, and graphs that are well organized, attractive, and useful.*

6. *Presentation software:* The ability to competently utilize a range of presentation software packages (e.g., PowerPoint, Prezi, Slide Rocket, etc.) in a manner that enhances one's oral presentation of specific informative or persuasive content.*

H. Scheduling and Coordinating

1. *Arranging:* Makes arrangements (e.g. for traveling, meetings) that fulfill all requirements as efficiently and economically as possible; handles all aspects of arrangements thoroughly and completely with little or no supervision.

2. *Informing:* Responds to the schedules of others affected by arrangements; informs others of arrangements, giving them complete, accurate, and timely information; insures that others receive needed materials in time.

3. *Verifying:* Takes steps to verify all arrangements; recognizes problems, generates effective alternatives, and takes corrective action.

4. *Coordinating in distributed environments:* Coordinates schedules of colleagues, coworkers, and clients in regional locations (i.e., across time zones) to ensure that inconvenience is minimized and productivity is enhanced; leverages technology (e.g., Internet, teleconference) to facilitate information sharing in distributed work environments; takes advantage of team member availability throughout business hours in multiple time zones to enhance productivity.

5. *Shiftwork:* Effectively coordinates the transition of employees at the beginning and end of each work shift; disseminates crucial information

(*continued*)

Table 1.3 *(continued)*

in an organized manner to rapidly bring employees up to speed at the start of their shifts; ensures that employees are updated on work completed on past shifts and work that still needs to be completed.

I. **Checking, Examining, and Recording**

1. *Detecting errors:* Detects and corrects errors, even under time pressure; notices errors or inconsistencies; forwards or processes forms in a timely and accurate manner.
2. *Completing forms:* Selects and completes appropriate forms quickly and completely; attends to and follows through on important information in paperwork; expedites forms, orders or advances that require immediate attention.
3. *Obtaining information:* Obtains appropriate information, signatures, and approvals promptly; verifies that all information is present and accurate before forwarding materials.
4. *Maintaining logs:* Keeps logs, records, and files that are up-to-date and readily accessible; updates logs, files, and records, noting important changes in status.

J. **Business Fundamentals**

1. *Situational awareness:* Understands the organization's mission and functions; recognizes one's role in the functioning of the company and understands the potential impact one's own performance can have on the success of the organization; grasps the potential impact of the company's well-being on employees.
2. *Market knowledge:* Understands market trends in the industry and the company's position in the market; knows who the company's primary competitors are, and stays current on organizational strategies to maintain competitiveness.

IV. **Communication Professional Competencies[2]**

A. **Communication Skills**

1. *Writing/editing:* Writing clear, concise materials that are free of spelling, grammar, and punctuation problems for diverse audiences.
2. *Web content/writing:* Understand best practices for web-based content that meets organizational goals and end-user needs.
3. *Editing/layout:* Skills related to planning, editing, and publishing written materials for a range of business goals.
4. *Writing proposals/requests for proposals (RFPs):* Ability to write a business proposal and write a request for a proposal that aligns with strategic business goals.
5. *Secondary research:* Ability to locate, organize, and present relevant literature on topics of importance for organizational needs.

(continued)

Table 1.3   (*continued*)

6. *Primary research:* Ability to conduct and present original research that either (1) helps determine the organization's needs and/or goals, or (2) evaluates communication campaigns after they've been implemented to determine effectiveness.
7. *Presentation preparation:* The ability create effective presentation materials using a range of presentation software and other visual aids for one's self or other organizational members.
8. *Presentation delivery:* The ability to orally and nonverbally communicate a specific informative or persuasive message to further an organization's goals.
9. *Meeting participation:* The ability to prepare for meetings and competently contribute during meetings with a variety organizational stakeholders.
10. *Meeting management:* The ability to put together an agenda, run a meeting effectively and efficiently, and prepare accurate and timely minutes that report the happenings of meetings for a variety of stakeholders.

B. **Knowledge Area Skills**

1. *Marketing communication:* The ability to conduct effective marketing research that leads to marketing plans that can be implemented and then evaluated for effectiveness in improving brand awareness and/or market share.
2. *Brand management:* Understand an organization's brand elements and how to position that brand for a variety of stakeholders.
3. *Employee communications:* Develop, write, edit, and produce materials designed for internal communication.
4. *Media relations:* Effectively interact with media representatives and deliver timely and accurate information that helps further an organization's goals.
5. *Issues management:* Prioritize and proactively address concerns that could negatively affect an organization or its success.
6. *Crisis communication planning:* Create a clear and concrete plan for how communication will occur during a crisis to ensure a consistent message is transmitted to various stakeholders.
7. *Stakeholder relations:* Prioritizing and proactively establishing methods for communicating, interacting, and maintaining a mutually beneficial relationship with various stakeholder groups.
8. *Consulting skills:* Providing advice to various organizational stakeholders outside one's division in an effort to help further the organization's goals.
9. *Problem solving skills:* The ability to think through the specific details of a problem to reach a solution.

(*continued*)

Table 1.3   (*continued*)

10. *Decision making skills:* The ability to examine a specific problem facing an organization, develop possible decision alternatives, evaluate those alternatives using specific criteria, and come to a decision that furthers the organization's goals.

C. **Management Skills**

1. *Ethics:* Know and implement ethical standards for both business and communication ethics.
2. *Communication planning:* Develop and implement strategic communications for a range of organizational goals.
3. *Crisis communication:* The ability to plan and implement an organization's crisis communication plan.
4. *Database management:* Ability to create and maintain a database for a range of organizational purposes.
5. *Knowledge management:* Create and maintain electronic content management systems to enable the gathering and sharing of knowledge throughout an organization.
6. *Project management:* The ability to take a project from its inception through the measurement and analysis of the project post-implementation.
7. *Time management:* The ability to organize one's priorities in an effort to meet organizational/stakeholder deadlines.
8. *Vendor management:* Work with vendors outside the organization to find products and/or services to help an organization achieve its basic goals.
9. *Budgeting:* The ability to set a budget, work with budgeting software, and evaluate project returns-on-investments.
10. *Professional development:* Seeks out additional developmental opportunities to maximize strengths and minimize known personal weaknesses.

V. **Two Functions of Workplace Communication Professionals***

A. **Internal Communication:** Create and distribute informative and persuasive communication targeted specifically at internal organizational stakeholders.
B. **External communication:** Create and distribute informative and persuasive communication target specifically at external organizational stakeholders.

---

[1] All of the definitions come from Career One Stop (2012) unless marked by an asterisk. In the case where an entire section consists of original definitions, the heading is marked instead of individual items. The Communication Professional Competencies is based in part on the IABC Accreditation Council's competency model (IABC, 2008).

[2] All definitions in this section were created for this chapter.

Sources: Career One Stop. Competency model clearing house [U.S. Department of Labor website], 2012. Retrieved from http://www.careeronestop.org/CompetencyModel/; IABC Accreditation Council. Communicator's Competency Model [IABC website], 2008. Retrieved from http://www.iabc.com/abc/pdf/CompetencyModel1.pdf.

volume on internal communication and one volume on external communication made logical sense. While this volume does not attempt to cover all possible aspects of external organizational communication, the volume does provide a general overview of the different major areas within external communication and how they apply in the 21st century.

In chapter 2, Tony Jaques examines the interrelationship between reputation, crisis management, and issue management, and how effective joint implementation can deliver real value to the bottom line. The chapter emphasizes the damage to reputation that can be caused by a crisis, and positions issue management as a proven strategic tool to help prevent crisis from occurring the first place.

In chapter 3, Mary L. Kahl explains various techniques for effective business presentations. Public, oral communication is still one of the primary tools for the transference of information in the corporate world. This chapter discusses five common speech types that executives are often called to deliver: technical briefing, proposal presentation, speeches of introduction, manuscript speeches, and extemporaneous speeches.

In chapter 4, Tina A. Coffelt examines why communicating with customers is an important aspect of business that has positive consequences for profitability. This chapter covers communication norms when working with customers as well as pointers on recovering after a service failure. Considerations for technology, call centers, and culture are mentioned at the end of the chapter.

In chapter 5, Jackson Hataway discusses the importance of communication in sales. He explains that the importance of impression management and relational communication to long-term sales communication strategies are highly intertwined.

In chapter 6, Erin E. Gilles, Shannon M. Brogan, Doreen M. S. Jowi, and Jason S. Wrench focus broadly on the purpose of corporate marketing plans and how to think about marketing communication in the 21st century. The chapter then examines general marketing trends with a focus on international issues and then tackles emerging issues in social media marketing by explaining a new model for understanding marketing and Web 2.0.

In chapter 7, Catherine Karl Wright focuses on how modern organizations can utilize social media and Web 2.0 technologies to further their interaction with customers and other stakeholders.

In chapter 8, Don W. Stacks examines the impact of reputation through personal branding and image on communication in the workplace. The chapter focuses on the influencers of reputation—credibility, confidence, relationship, and trust. The chapter further focuses on message strategies, to enhance or correct reputation through branding yourself.

In chapter 9, Pamela Shockley-Zalabak and Sherwyn Morreale describe a research-based model for organizational trust and the model's five drivers of trust: competence, openness and honesty, concern for employees/stakeholders, reliability, and identification. Strategies for using the model in 21st century organizations are provided throughout this chapter.

In chapter 10, LaKesha N. Anderson and Daniel L. Walsch explore the case of the Northern Illinois University campus shootings and how this event was managed using strategic risk and crisis communication methods. Included in this chapter is a discussion of effective crisis and risk communication strategies, such as the CAUSE model. In addition, strategic communication will be examined as a complement to crisis and risk communication, rather as a separate form of communication.

In chapter 11, Timothy L. Sellnow, Morgan Wickline, and Shari R. Veil summarize a comprehensive list of best practices for effectively managing crisis planning, crisis response, and postcrisis recovery.

In chapter 12, Kristin Roeschenthaler Wolfe looks at the benefits and drawbacks of corporate blogging and helps a company to decide if it should start a blog. The chapter will also examine the different types of blogs; what should and should not be included on a blog; how to handle comments; and how to utilize the corporate blog to benefit the company at all times, and especially during a crisis such as the onset of a rumor regarding the company or one of its products. Finally, the chapter explains the steps in setting up the corporate blog.

In chapter 13, Eric Bergman provides insight into a media training approach that emphasizes win-win outcomes as the best-possible end state during exchanges with journalists. It defines the media and introduces a model for managing polarization. The chapter also examines the fine line between spin and sin, provides insight into strategically targeting interviews, and adds value with four defensive strategies that can be applied when necessary.

In chapter 14, J. David Johnson and Anna Goodman Hoover examine how successful organizations must maintain good relationships with a variety of external stakeholders. In this chapter, the authors focus on key external stakeholders, especially government officials and investors, and the tactics they have available to obtain information they need from organizations. In turn organizations should effectively match their stakeholders' needs in the amount and types of information that they make available through their information architecture.

In chapter 15, Mary M. Meares presents an overview of globalization in organizations and the challenges that accompany working with individuals from different cultural backgrounds. She focuses on how cultural values can be used to better understand the dynamics at play when organizational members have different expectations and frames of reference. She concludes with a number of suggestions for working with those from different countries and cultures in order to move beyond ethnocentrism are provided.

Conclusion

In this volume, the authors discuss a wide range of topics related to how one should communicate with one's external stakeholders. Feel free to read straight through the entire volume or search out those chapters that are the most useful for you right now. We hope this volume doesn't just sit on your shelf but becomes the go-to guide for helping you with a range of external communication problems in your organization.

Key Takeaways

1. Knowledge is increasing in such a rapid fashion that knowing how to shift through and organize information is a paramount business skill.
2. There are many terms commonly associated with workplace communication. The four most common are business and professional communication, managerial communication, organizational communication, and business/corporate communication.
3. The history of understanding how to lead and get others to follow dates back to the Egyptians and the Precepts of Ke'gemni and Ptah-hotep.
4. Competency models are important for the development of knowledge, skills, and attitudes within a workplace relating to specific jobs and job tasks.

Glossary

Business and professional communication: Term related to workplace communication that specifies a body of knowledge taught to undergraduate students that focuses on the development of specific communication skills.

Business/corporate communication: Term related to workplace communication that examines the strategic use of communication in six functional areas: media relations, public relations, crisis communication, executive communication, employee relations, and communication policy and strategy.

Competency: "a cluster of related knowledge, skills, and attitudes that affects a major part of one's job (a role or responsibility), that correlates with performance on that job, that can be measured against well-accepted standards, and that can be improved via training and development" (Parry 1996, 50).

Competency model: A hierarchical model that "describes the particular combination of knowledge, skills, and characteristics needed to effectively perform a role in an organization and is used as a human resource tool for selection, training and development, appraisal, and succession planning" (Lucia and Lepsinger 1999, 5).

Managerial communication: Term related to workplace communication relating to students in an MBA program that focuses on "communication strategy; skills, including writing and speaking; process, including teamwork and interpersonal behavior; the global environment, which focuses on cross-cultural communication; and function" (Argenti 1996, 83).

Organizational communication: Term related to workplace communication that can refer to three distinct areas of interest: (1) an area of studies within the field of communication studies; (2) a way to describe and explain organizations; or (3) a phenomenon that exists within organizations.

References

Argenti, Paul. A. "Communications and Business Value: Measuring the Link." *Journal of Business Strategy* 27 (2006): 29–40.

Argenti, Paul. A. "Corporate Communication as a Discipline." *Management Communication Quarterly* 10 (1996): 73–97.

Beebe, Steven. A., and Timothy P. Mottet. *Business and Professional Communication: Principles and Skills for Leadership.* Boston: Allyn & Bacon, 2010.

Bernthal, Paul R., Karen Colteryahn, Patty Davis, Jennifer Naughton, William J. Rothwell, and Rich Wellins. *ASTD Competency Study: Mapping the Future—New Workplace Learning and Performance Competencies.* Alexandria, VA: ASTD Press, 2004.

Blakeslee, Sandra. "If You have a 'Buy Button' in Your Brain, What Pushes it?" *New York Times,* October 19, 2004, p. 12.

Brands, H. W. *T. R.: The Last Romantic.* New York: Basic Books, 1997.

Chandler, Alfred D., Jr. *Mass Productions and the Beginnings of Scientific Management.* Cambridge, MA: Harvard Business School, 1991.

Cone New Media Consumer Study. http://www.coneinc.com/consumer-new-media-study, 2009.

Curtin, Patricia. A., and T. Kenn Gaither. *International Public Relations: Negotiating Culture, Identity, and Power.* Thousand Oaks, CA: Sage, 2007.

Deetz, Stanley. "Conceptual Foundations." In *The New Handbook of Organizational Communication: Advances in Theory, Research, and Methods,* edited by Fredric M. Jablin and Linda L. Putnam, 3–46. Thousand Oaks, CA: Sage, 2001.

Edmund, Norman W. *End the Biggest Educational and Intellectual Blunder in History.* Ft. Lauderdale, FL: Scientific Method Publishing Co, 2005.

Gillis, Tamara. *The Human Element: Employee Communication in Small to Medium-Sized Businesses.* San Francisco: International Association of Business Communicators, 2008.

Workplace Communication for the 21st Century

Goodman, Michael B. "Corporate Communication: The American Picture." *Corporate Communications: An International Journal* 5 (2000): 69–74.

Goodman, Michael B. "Corporate Communication Practice and Pedagogy at the Dawn of the New Millennium." *Corporate Communications: An International Journal* 11 (2006): 196–213. doi: 10.1108/13563280610680803.

Gordon, Gloria. "A History of IABC Communicators: Forty-Six Years of Shaping the Corporate Word." *Communication World* August–September (2002): 31–33.

Gray, Giles Wilkeson. "The 'Precepts of Kagemni and Ptah-Hotep'." *Quarterly Journal of Speech* 32 (1946): 446–54.

Hoffman, William. G. *Public Speaking for Business Men.* New York: McGraw Hill, 1923.

Ihator, Augustine S. "Corporate Communication: Reflections on Twentieth Century Change." *Corporate Communications: An International Journal* 9 (2004): 243–53.

Lucia, Anntoinette D., and Richard Lepsinger. *The Art and Science of Competency Models: Pinpointing Critical Success Factors in Organizations.* San Francisco: Jossey-Bass/Pfeiffer, 1999.

Luthans, Fred. *Organizational Behavior.* 11th ed. New York McGraw-Hill, 2008.

Mansfield, Richard S. "Building Competency Models: Approaches for HR Professionals." *Human Resource Management* 35, no. 1 (1996): 7–18.

O'Hair, Dan, Gustav W. Friedrich, and Lynda Dee Dixon. *Strategic Communication in Business and the Professions.* 7th ed. Boston: Allyn & Bacon, 2011.

Papa, Michael J., Tom D. Daniels, and Barry K. Spiker. *Organizational Communication: Perspectives and Trends.* Thousand Oaks, CA: Sage, 2008.

Parry, Scott. B. "The Quest for Competencies." *Training* 33 (1996): 48–56.

Phillips, Arthur Edward. *Effective Speaking.* Chicago: The Newton Company, 1908.

Rodgers, Vicci. "The Future of Measurement in Corporate Communication." In *The IABC Handbook of Organizational Communication: A Guide to Internal Communication, Public Relations, Marketing, and Leadership,* edited by Tamara L. Gillis, 453–61. San Francisco: Jossey-Bass, 2006.

Sanborn, George. A. "Communication in Business: An Overview." In *Business and Industrial Communication: A Source Book,* edited by W. Charles Redding and George A. Sanborn, 3–26. New York: Harper & Row, 1964.

Sandford, William Phillips, and Willard Hayes Yeager. *Business and Professional Speaking.* New York: McGraw-Hill, 1929.

Senge, Peter M., and Gordon Carstedt. "Innovating Our Way to the Next Industrial Revolution." *MIT Sloan Management Review* 42 no. 2 (2001): 24–38.

Shaw, H. Walter, and Robert L. Craig. "The Coming of Age of Workplace Learning: A Timeline." *T&D* 48, no. 5 (1994): s5–s12.

Spicer, Carol. "Building a Competency Model: Screening Job Candidates for Desired Competencies Pays Off in Higher Sales and Lower Turnover." *Human Resources* April (2009): 34–36.

Volti, Rudi. *An Introduction to the Sociology of Work and Occupations.* Los Angeles: Sage, 2007.

Wyatt, Watson. "Capitalizing on Effective Communication: How Courage, Innovation and Discipline Drive Business Results in Challenging Times." *2009/2010 Communication ROI Report,* 2010. http://www.watsonwyatt.com.

Wyatt, Watson. "Connecting Organizational Communication to Financial Performance." *2003/2004 Communication ROI Report,* 2004. http://www.watsonwyatt.com.

Wyatt, Watson. "Secrets of Top Performers: How Companies with Highly Effective Employee Communication Differentiate Themselves." *2008/2009 Communication ROI Report,* 2009. http://www.watsonwyatt.com.

Wrench, Jason. S., James C. McCroskey, and Virginia P. Richmond. *Human Communication in Everyday Life: Explanations and Applications.* Boston: Allyn & Bacon, 2008.

CHAPTER TWO

Protecting Reputation and Preventing Crisis: The Strategic Use of Issue Management

Tony Jaques

Getting Segway onto the Pavement

As the Segway company got ready to launch their unique two wheeled, electric People Transporter (PT) in 2002, they realized that most American states and some cites had laws that banned motorized vehicles being driven on pavements. In addition, being classified as a motor vehicle meant that in some cases the PT might be required to have taillights, turn signals and license plates, and the operator might even need a driving license and registration. A ban from use on pavements would have spelled a potential crisis for the product and what followed was a classic strategic issue management (SIM) campaign.

A prioritized lobbying effort focusing on key states worked to eliminate regulatory barriers, while a large-scale public relations effort emphasized the PT's environmental benefits in replacing motorcars for short trips. At the same time the U.S. Postal Service and National Park Service were persuaded to adopt the device, establishing the PT as a serious productivity tool and not just a toy. In addition interest group issues were identified and addressed, including pedestrian safety advocates concerned about the risk of collision, especially for children, senior citizens and the blind; bicycle advocates concerned about protecting exclusive bike trails; and public health advocates concerned about lack of exercise and obesity.

As a result of these efforts, within a year of the product launch, two-thirds of states enacted laws to allow the PT to be used on pavements, and a further seven states followed suit within the next six months. Today all but four American states permit the Segway, as well as most EU countries and many other international markets.

In the same way that public relations is about relationships with both internal and external publics, the deeper, more strategic aspects of communication are often about the relationship between core professional disciplines, which can work together to provide integrated strategies and solutions. One of the most important of these integrated relationships is the nexus between reputation, issue management, and crisis management.

The purpose of this chapter is not to revisit in detail the individual aspects of these three communication disciplines, which are all fully developed, stand-alone activities, each with its unique strengths, language, tools, models, taxonomy, and champions at both the academic and practitioner levels. The purpose here is to explore and emphasize how they interrelate and how effective joint implementation can deliver real value to the bottom line. The structure will be to describe the relationship between reputation and crisis; discuss how potential crises are identified; explore the emerging new style of crisis management that emphasizes a far more strategic approach; describe the development of issue management as a response to the need for organizations to be more proactive; and finally to show how issue management should be the tool of choice for a strategic approach to reputation protection and crisis prevention.

Relationship between Reputation and Crisis

> Branding is what you say about yourself. Reputation is what other people say about you.

Nothing destroys an organization's reputation faster and deeper than a high-profile crisis. Yet for many organizations, crisis management still appears to be regarded as a tactical responsibility with no real link to reputation and strategic planning. As investment guru Warren Buffett once famously noted: "It takes 20 years to build a reputation and five minutes to ruin it. If you think about that you'll do things differently." One of those areas where things are now starting to be done differently is within crisis management, where leading executives are moving from crisis response—getting ready for a crisis when it strikes—toward a greater emphasis on crisis prevention—taking steps to reduce the risk of a crisis before it happens.

The impact of a corporate crisis can be devastating. For example, a study of major Australian crises over a decade showed that about one in four of the organizations impacted by a major crisis went out of business completely (Coleman 2004). Even when the organization survives, no matter how well it responds to a crisis, there is inevitable damage to market value, reputation, and the corporate bottom line, sometimes persisting over years.

Share value is often regarded as a realistic measure of an organization's reputation, and news headlines regularly report a dramatic plunge in stock price after a crisis threat to corporate reputation, such as a major accident, a product recall, or revelation of executive wrongdoing. In fact, some analysts believe that up to 60–70 percent of a company's value can be credited to reputation and other intangible assets, and that a company can lose up to 30 percent of its share value as the result of a well-publicized crisis. Furthermore, organizations that are well prepared for a crisis have been shown to suffer less loss of market value, and to recover more quickly.

This phenomenon was explored in a famous study at Oxford University (Knight and Pretty 1999), which examined organizations struck by a crisis and analyzed the impact on stock price. This groundbreaking research found that for companies with an effective crisis response in place, the immediate impact on share price was a fall of 5 percent, yet after 12 months the price on average had increased by 7 percent from its precrisis level. By contrast, for companies with no effective crisis response in place, the initial stock price loss was 10 percent, and after 12 months the stock price was an average of 15 percent below its precrisis level. In other words, the stock price initially fell twice as far, and after 12 months there was a delta of 22 percent difference in value from companies that had effective crisis response in place.

Turning from academic analysis to the unforgiving world of modern business, 2010 was a year marked by some of the most dramatic high-profile corporate crises for decades. In response to announcing a very damaging vehicle recall, Toyota shares fell $30 billion in four weeks on the Tokyo stock exchange (January 2010); during the disastrous BP oil spill in the Gulf of Mexico, failure to cap the leaking well saw BP shares lose £12 billion in one day (April 20, 2010); and when the U.S. Justice Department accused Goldman Sachs of fraud, the investment banker's shares lost $12.4 billion in one afternoon (April 16, 2010) and $20 billion in a week.

This link between crisis, reputation, and company value was subsequently underlined by *Forbes* magazine under the provocative headline "What's reputation worth? Just ask Toyota, Goldman and BP" (Tannen 2010). The article concluded: "If reputation risk wasn't a top issue for CEOs and boards of directors prior to 2010, the watershed events of the first half of this year should make them reconsider their priorities."

But repeated research continues to reveal failure to turn that priority into action. For example, the U.K.-based Association for Insurance and Risk Managers showed that while 80 percent of managers claimed reputation risk as their top concern, only 43 percent believed they had formal and well-managed plans to tackle it (Baylis 2010). In the same vein, a study of more than 500 major corporate and public sector organizations in Australian and New Zealand ranked damage to brand and image as the single most important risk concern for a fourth year in succession (AON 2011). And an earlier study by the New York–based Conference Board's Reputation Risk Research Working Group showed that 82 percent of the risk management executives surveyed said their companies were making a substantial effort to manage reputation risk and 59 percent said assessing reputation risk was among their highest-ranked challenges (Beal 2009). Meanwhile less than half (49%) said management of reputation risk was highly integrated into their enterprise risk management.

While the link between crisis and reputation is well established and recognized, corporate preparedness for a crisis remains consistently low. In the aftermath of the terrorist attacks on September 11, 2001, the American Management Association surveyed its members and customers and found that only 49 percent had a crisis management plan and only 39 percent had ever carried out a drill or simulation (AMA 2002). The following year the number increased quite sharply to 64 percent, although subsequent AMA surveys showed the number of American companies with a crisis management plan in place soon started to fall again (Ebersole 2005).

> "When things go bad it doesn't matter who's at fault or whether critics are being unfair—management is responsible. Crises are failures of performance." —Peter Firestein

More recently, financial analysts and investor relations officers at companies across Canada and the United States surveyed about operational and corporate crisis preparedness revealed no evidence of any improvement (Canadian Investor Relations Institute 2011). The survey found that while many companies are mindful of the potential damage crises can cause to their sales, reputation, and share value, few have an effective crisis management plan in place to deal with negative scenarios—and if they do it is likely out of date. Of responding analysts, 85 percent said a corporate crisis had the greatest negative impact on a company's value, yet over 50 percent said their company plan prepared them only for an operational crisis, and 50 percent didn't even know if their company conducted crisis simulations.

One of the challenges for organizational communication is that while reputation is commonly seen as a strategic issue that properly deserves the full attention of executive management, crisis management is often assigned to tactical middle managers with little involvement in the development of corporate strategy. What causes this contradiction and what can be done about it?

Traditionally, crisis management has been widely seen as a technical function, which is critical and needs to be carried out professionally and effectively. But this traditional tactical approach is focused primarily on crisis response and on systems tools such as manuals, checklists, simulation exercises, and media training.

By contrast, crisis prevention requires more strategic involvement of senior management. Preventing crises before they happen means implementing effective processes that stretch back before the triggering event, fully aligned with existing activities such as risk assessment, issue management, stakeholder relations, strategic planning, and issue prioritization. It is this strategic approach that positions organizations to identify potential problems early and take preventive action rather than simply responding when the situation goes bad. It also focuses executive attention on problems beyond the obvious.

Identifying Potential Crises

Crises are not just difficult problems. They are the manifestation of risk, and represent a real threat to the organization, more than merely a passing concern. The British crisis expert Denis Smith has observed: "The definition of crisis has generated considerable debate within the academic literature and there is no real collective acceptance about the precise meaning of the term" (2005, 319).

While it is certainly true that there are scores of different definitions (for an overview see Jaques 2009b), one of the most consistently cited is Pearson and Clair, "An organizational crisis is a low-probability, high-impact event that threatens the viability of the organization and is characterized by ambiguity of cause, effect, and means of resolution, as well as by a belief that decisions must be made swiftly" (1998, 60).

This was later adapted by Gregory: "Crises are high consequence, low probability, overlaid with risk and uncertainty, conducted under time-pressure, disruptive of normal business and potentially lethal to organizational reputation" (2005, 313).

Within this definitional construct every industry has obvious sector-specific crisis risks, sometimes called natural risks. These are the familiar risks where organizations are most comfortable. For example, a chemical manufacturer would typically be well prepared to deal with crises arising from spills, leaks, and fires; a transport company would be well prepared to deal with a major road or rail accident; and banks would be well prepared to deal with issues of security and privacy.

In this way, organizations often focus most attention on risks associated with their particular industry, where their sector-specific experience increases the feeling of control. These natural risks are frequently technical problems commonly associated with mechanical or physical failures, which are relatively easy to fix.

Meantime research into the incidence of crises shows that organizations are equally vulnerable to generic risks, which apply to all industries, which can be just as damaging, or even more so. These nonspecific crisis risks could include fraud, employee misconduct, industrial unrest, high-profile litigation, wrongful dismissal, or allegations about sexual harassment or racial discrimination.

Such reputational risks are much harder to deal with, especially as they may implicate individuals, often at a high level in the organization. According to Gaines-Ross (2008), in a survey of 950 business executives worldwide, the leading trigger of reputation crises included financial irregularities (72%), unethical behavior (68%), and executive misconduct (64%). The most recent figures from the Institute for Crisis Management (www.crisisexperts.com) show that two-thirds of business crises reported in the news media are not sudden events but smoldering crises, where action could have—and should have—been taken much earlier.

> According to the Institute for Crisis Management, 51 percent of crises are caused by management, 31 percent by employees, and only 18 percent result from other causes.

To help this identification process, organizations need to have effective mechanisms not just for recognizing problems with the potential to become crises, but mechanisms that also provide for issues to be prioritized and for turning concern into action. There is an obvious close link between systemic causes of failure to recognize potential issues and failure to detect signals. This is shown by postcrisis legal proceedings—such as inquiries, inquests, and class actions—which frequently reveal that information from within the organization was blocked or ignored. Managements need to create an environment that encourages reporting of near misses, which promotes the upward flow of information, especially bad news; and which openly accepts dissenting opinions from both inside and outside the organization.

While identifying issues early and taking planned action is an essential part of crisis prevention, most issues don't exist in a vacuum. They often reflect structural or systemic weakness in the organization, which can only be properly addressed at the executive level.

At the same time an organizational crisis can create a major hurdle to achievement of strategic goals. Crisis prevention then is essential to the organization's bottom line, and integrating issue and crisis management into strategic planning helps optimize the move from tactical crisis response to executive involvement in strategic crisis prevention. This is where the process approach to crisis management proves effective.

The Process Approach to Crisis Management

The traditional or "event" approach to crisis management treats a crisis as "a sudden and unexpected event that threatens to disrupt an organization's operations and poses both a financial and reputational threat" (Coombs 2007, 164). This approach is closely aligned to incident response and has a strong emphasis on getting ready for a crisis before it occurs, and responding quickly and effectively when it strikes. In this context it is regarded as a largely tactical or operational activity that would fall naturally within the responsibility of functions such as security, emergency response, business continuity, and operational recovery with corporate communications in support.

These functions are primarily reactive—dealing with the problem—and as such they are very important. But in general they do nothing to prevent the crisis from occurring in the first place. In other words, their focus is largely on damage control.

Given the terrible potential impact of crises—on life, property, market value, reputation, and even corporate survival—organizations need to move beyond *crisis preparedness*—getting ready for the crisis if it happens—toward *crisis prevention*—taking steps to reduce the chances of its happening at all. As the British crisis expert Denis Smith has said: "To be effective crisis management should, almost by definition, include systematic attempts to prevent crisis from occurring" (Smith 2005, 312).

The process approach to crisis management is more than simply being proactive. It recognizes that crises are part of an ongoing process, which starts long before the triggering event. One early pioneer of the process approach concluded that "crises are not events, but processes extended in time and place" (Shrivastava 1995, 2). Smith later added: "Crises evolve within organizations, they do not simply appear and they are not divorced from the actions of those managers who may ultimately be required to deal with the management of such events" (2004, 350).

A European champion of the concept, Roux-Dufort (2007), has described a crisis as "an accumulation of imperfections" and says that while the event approach sees the triggering event as the crisis, the process approach sees it is only the *amplifier* for a process that started long before.

The essential element of the process approach is to see crisis management as part of a continuum of activity, integrated deep within the responsibilities of the top management of an organization. Typically, this would include core strategic activities such as early problem identification, risk assessment, issue management, and resource allocation requiring the direct involvement or imprimatur of top executives to achieve successful crisis prevention. And all of this work is predicated on the capacity of management to identify and respond to the red flags or warning signs, which prolific crisis scholar Ian Mitroff (2002) has argued, precede most organizational crises.

Contrary to the notion that most crises are sudden, unexpected events, the Institute for Crisis Management's finding that two-thirds of business crisis reported in the news media should have been predicted is strongly reinforced by crisis scholars who warn that while most crisis preceded by clear warning signals, these are frequently ignored.

For example, James and Wooten concluded: "Smouldering crises nearly always leave a trail of red flags and warning signals that something is wrong. These signals often go unheeded by management" (2005, 143). Mitroff went even further, asserting that in every crisis he had ever studied, there were always a few key people on the inside of an organization or on its edge, who saw the early warning signs and tried to warn their superiors. "In every case," he concluded, "the signals were either ignored or blocked from getting to the top or having any effect" (2002, 20).

However, it is acknowledged that recognizing warning signs is not always easy. When the French bank Société Générale lost $US7 billion (€4.9 billion) from the activities of a rogue trader, an independent panel found the company failed to act on 75 red flags or early warnings over a period of 18 months (Clark 2008). Shortly afterward in the United States, in the wake of the $65 billion Madoff investment scandal, SEC Inspector General David Kotz admitted that the agency missed "numerous red flags" from 1992 until the fraudster was arrested in December 2008 and conceded that five separate failed investigations into the affair had been bungled (Stout 2009).

Environmental scanning and signal detection is an essential management skill, which may involve techniques such as strategic forecasting, contingency planning, issue analysis, scenario analysis, community relations, government affairs, stakeholder relations, and many others. But central to this activity is the need to identify problems early and take positive, planned actions within a formal strategic framework—and the discipline that brings these activities together is called issue management.

The Strength of Issue Management

> The proper focus of issue management is not issues. The proper focus of issue management is management.

Issue management did not begin primarily as a tool to assist in crisis prevention. The term "issue management" was coined 35 years ago by the American Howard Chase (1976) in the inaugural issue of his new publication *Corporate Public Issues and Their Management*. Chase was then already over 65 years old and had a long and distinguished career in corporate and government communications. Moreover he was one of six founders of the Public Relations Society of America in 1947 and was its president in 1956.

Chase and his colleagues were concerned by what they believed was increasing influence of NGOs and other groups in the formation of public policy, which had potentially adverse impact on business. In this way, issue management was conceived as a business-based discipline designed specifically to enable corporations to participate in, and not just respond to, public policy issues.

In his typically colorful language Chase said its purpose was to enable the private sector to be "co-equal with the government and citizens in the formation of public policy, rather than being the tail of a policy kite flown by others" (1984a, 10).

On another occasion, when critics questioned whether issue management was really a new concept or was maybe simply a "pretentious" new term for everyday activities (Ehling and Hesse 1983), Chase responded in an opinion piece for the *Wall Street Journal,* which he impishly entitled "No Matter How Well Packaged, Corporate Fads Fail Fast" Chase declared:

> Issue-oriented management process, systematically integrated into line-management decision-making, is the enemy of corporate faddism. Once the high-priority issue is identified, filtered through issue task forces drawn from both line and staff, the designated issue action program produces more lasting results than any quick-fix dreamed up by the most inventive faddists. When all is said and done, the Issue Management process offers the opportunity for alleged rugged individualists to act less like sheep. (1984b, 28)

Behind his rhetoric and outspoken advocacy, Chase and others worked hard to develop formal tools and processes to provide a structured framework for policy participation, which became the foundation of issue management as it is known today. The first formal issue management model, published by Chase and Barrie Jones, was a simple five-step process, which became known as the Chase-Jones process model (Chase and Jones 1977), and is still regarded as "the most influential issue management model" (Coombs and Holladay 2007).

The Chase-Jones Model

The five-step Chase-Jones model presented the process in a cyclical format with linking actions between each step.

- *Issue Identification,* leading through theory and research to
- *Issue Analysis,* followed by judgment and priority setting to reach
- *Issue Change Strategy Options,* leading through policy for change strategy to
- *Issue Action Program,* which leads through support for policy decision to
- *Accomplishment of Issue Action Program Goal/Evaluation of Results,* then looping back to the first step.

Chase himself defined issue management as "the capacity to understand, mobilize, coordinate and direct all strategic and policy planning functions, and all public affairs/public relations skills, toward achievement of one objective: meaningful participation in creation of public policy that affects personal and institutional destiny" (Chase 1982, 1).

And in an early academic study, Wartick and Rude (1986, 124) said: "Issue management attempts to minimize surprises which accompany social and political change by serving as an early warning system for potential environmental threats and attempts to promote more systematic and effective responses to particular issues by serving as a coordinating and integrating force within the corporation." Similarly, Renfro concluded: "The overriding goal of an issues management function is to enhance the current and long-term performance and standing of the corporation by anticipating change, promoting opportunities and avoiding or mitigating threat" (1993, 107).

While the corporate and public policy focus in these definitions was very consistent, two major developments since that time have characterized the evolution of issue management, which in turn have had a great significance for the link between issue management, crisis management, and reputation.

Migration of Issue Management

The first of these evolutionary developments was the migration of issue management beyond the corporate environment and its adoption by government agencies and by activists and other community groups.

Observers may think it is somewhat ironic that issue management techniques would come to be used not to resist or modify public policy as originally conceived by the corporate founders of the discipline, but to promote and implement such policies. For example, Ferguson (1993) has described the use of issue management by Canadian Federal Government agencies, and it is now common to see governments mobilizing issue management tools and processes in relation to controversial issues, such as genetically modified organisms (Henderson 2005) or to respond in the aftermath of crisis situations such as a major public health scare (Gregory 2005).

Issue management techniques have also been widely adopted by NGOs and other community groups, even though they generally avoid the corporate language of the discipline (Jaques 2006). This trend has certainly been accelerated by the development of new technology such as the Internet, which encourages adoption of issue management by such "resource poor" groups, giving them a new facility to frame issues and to compete on a more level playing field (e.g., Demetrious 2001; Walton 2007). As Titley commented, "Resources that were once the preserve of governments and large corporations, such as access to intelligence and an ability to communicate and mobilize (both globally and instantaneously), are now available to anyone for the price of a cup of coffee in a cybercafé" (2003, 86).

Repositioning Issue Management

The second major evolutionary development has been the repositioning of issue management as part of the process of crisis prevention. As early as 1979 the insurance executive Archie Boe said issue management has arisen as a response to "an unprecedented battering of business" and enabled business to move to a precrisis management posture and participate in the public policy process. "The pre-crisis management approach is called issue management and is an important management tool available today's business leaders" (1979, 4).

Despite this viewpoint, there was an understandable reluctance to allow the new discipline to be subsumed into organizational crisis management, which was also developing at the time, and some of the early literature emphasized strongly how issue management and crisis management were different, and why it was important to maintain that distinction.

Even today it remains essential to recognize that issue management and traditional, tactical crisis management are distinct activities, which utilize different tools, processes and personnel, and are typically established in different parts of the organization. And it also needs to be recognized that both are very important separate roles. But the emergence of the more strategic process approach to crisis management, as previously outlined, has begun to blur these boundaries and issue management is now increasingly seen as an integral part of management activity.

One integrated model (Jaques 2007) positions issue management in two distinct areas of the crisis management continuum: in the precrisis phase as one of the activities devoted to crisis prevention (Jaques 2009c) and also in the postcrisis phase, dealing with issues that arise after the crisis event has passed and while the organizations is still in recovery mode (Jaques 2010). For the present discussion the focus is on issue management as an important part of strategic crisis prevention.

Issue Management as a Strategic Discipline

Issue management clearly began as a discipline with a strong focus on the achievement of strategic corporate objectives, especially in the area of public policy. And that strategic focus continues today, for corporations and also other users of issue management.

Unfortunately, the word "strategic" has more recently lost some of its specific meaning and there is a tendency to use strategic as an all-purpose alternative for important, or priority, or urgent. Some commentators even suggest the word has become so devalued that it is sometimes little more than corporate jargon used to impress or to secure executive attention. Nevertheless, understanding the real meaning of strategic is important to proper understanding of issue management, particularly because the alternative term "strategic issue management" (SIM) is widely used as a virtual synonym for issue management (e.g., Ansoff 1980; Camillus and Datta 1991; Heath 1997; Heath and Palenchar 2008; Schwarz 2005).

In spite of this language, the difficulty is that not every important issue is a strategic issue, and not all issue management is carried out at the strategic level within an organization. Or put another way, not all issue management is management of strategic issues, and not all strategic management is to do with issues (see Jaques 2009a for a detailed analysis of the relationship between issue management and strategic planning).

> "While emerging issues may be complicated and difficult to un-
> derstand, the process by which issues are dealt with should not
> be." —Bill Ashley

Issue management has historically been closely linked to the formal practice of strategic planning, and a useful definition can be drawn from this parallel discipline. "The elements of the strategic planning process concern an understanding of the changing environment in which a company finds itself, of the basic mission of the organization or basic company purposes, or long-range planning objectives, and of programs, policies and strategies" (Steiner and Miner 1982, as cited in Buchholz, Evans, and Wagley 1989, 39).

A crucial difference is that while strategic planning is a recognized discipline with formal methodologies that have not migrated substantially outside its business origins, the very fluid and changing nature of issue management makes rigid methodology far less appropriate. In one attempt to capture this difference, the American academic John Mahon suggested: "The emphasis in strategic planning focuses on identifying opportunities and threats to product/market issues. The emphasis in issue management is identifying and addressing social and political issues not usually resolved in the market place" (Mahon 1989 as cited in Greening 1992, 3). And as Ansoff (1980) has pointed out, issue management is not just a process for *planning* the corporate response but for *resolving* the issue.

The important point here is the emphasis on resolving issues. It has been said that problems are *solved* (find the right answer), whereas issues must be *resolved* (an answer must be negotiated). In other words, the focus is not only on identifying, prioritizing, and planning for issues, but achieving resolution that is aligned with the strategic objectives of the organization. Or as Heath (1997) put it, issue management cannot have its full impact if it is not part of the organization's strategic planning process.

Issue management is ideally suited to alignment with organizational strategic planning. The proven process of identifying problems or issues early and putting planned actions in place is fundamental to delivering bottom-line results for business, governments, or NGOs.

> The Issue Management Council of Leesburg, VA, has developed Best
> Practice Indicators to help organizations benchmark their process and
> performance and to help identify steps for implementation. Go to
> www.issuemanagement.org.

The strategic use of issue management is not new. Indeed, issues were being managed using the basic principles long before the discipline had a name. An instructive example was the systematic campaign by Thomas Edison in the 1880s to have direct current (DC) accepted as the electricity supply system rather than alternating current (AC) promoted by his European rival Nikola Tesla (Bissell 2000). Edison ultimately failed and DC is now the international standard. However, the same early issue management techniques were more successful a few years later with the integrated campaign before World War I to persuade American house-wives to use vegetable fat instead of lard and butter (Pendleton 1999). And of course this early health issue campaign has strong parallels with the modern issue strategies used around the world by the contending parties in relation to obesity and fast food (see, e.g., Darmon, Fitzpatrick, and Bronstein 2008; Sheehan 2005).

Many strategic issue campaigns are never revealed in the news media, and their success or failure often remains out of public view. Then again there are many other published examples of how issue management has been used to deliver genuine strategic objectives and bottom-line results. The case of how Segway successfully avoided their two-wheel people mover being classified as a road vehicle is spelled out at the beginning of this chapter (Toohey, Dailida, and Bartholomew 2003). Other examples would include:

- Introduction of "dolphin safe" tuna to respond to animal welfare activists (Fearn-Banks 1996),
- Starbucks working with NGOs to promote Fair Trade coffee (Argenti 2004),
- Unilever's response to genetic-modification concerns in Europe (Heugens 2006),
- A Nobel Prize–winning activist's campaign against landmines (Williams 1999),
- Persuading authorities to permit oil drilling off Norway (Ihlen and Nitz 2008),
- Preventing Disney building a theme park near a Civil War battlefield in Virginia (Wiebner 1995),
- America's high fructose corn syrup industry defending itself against health critics (Mizell 2010), and
- How Whirlpool changed home appliance design to preempt water and energy concerns (Catania 2002).

Most of these campaigns, and many more like them, have helped deliver organizational objectives and have also helped prevent potential crises. The great strength of issue management is its effectiveness in such crisis prevention, and that it provides a formal framework for strategic intervention.

Linking Reputation, Issue Management, and Crisis Prevention

If it is clear that one of the greatest risks to reputation is a crisis and that issue management is an optimal tool for crisis prevention, why do issues continue to be badly managed, and why do preventable crises continue to wreak havoc with organizational and personal reputations? The answer lies to a great extent in the previous conclusion that most crises are preceded by numerous warning signs, and that these signs are regularly missed or ignored. The link between information and action lies at the heart of effective signal detection and, while the literature provides hundreds of instances of failed issue scanning and inadequate response, two examples at opposite ends of the scale serve to illustrate the difficulty.

After Hurricane Katrina struck New Orleans in August 2005, with massive loss of life and damage to property, Homeland Security Secretary Michael Chertoff argued that the event was "particularly unpredictable" and "exceeded the foresight of planners, and maybe anybody's foresight" (Lipton and Shane 2005). Yet in July 2004, a massive simulation had been staged by U.S. Federal and State emergency planners in which the fictional "Hurricane Pam" struck New Orleans in a catastrophic scenario almost identical to what occurred in reality only 12 months later. Critics at the time argued that the simulated event was unrealistic.

The sad facts of the matter were examined in detail by a U.S. House of Representatives Bipartisan Select Committee set up to investigate the preparation and response to Hurricane Katrina. Their 520-page report, aptly titled *A Failure of Initiative*, concluded: "While there was no failure to predict the inevitability and consequences of a monster Hurricane— Katrina in this case—there was a failure of initiative to get beyond design and organizational compromises to improve the level of protection afforded" (Select Bipartisan Committee 2006, 97).

At the other end of the scale in terms of human and environmental impact, is the notoriously tone-deaf response of an airline that failed to provide adequate customer service, failed to appreciate the power of social media, and suffered prolonged reputational damage.

In late 2008, careless United Airlines baggage handlers at Chicago's O'Hare airport broke the $3,500 Taylor acoustic guitar of Canadian singer Dave Carroll. Following nine months of run-around and refusal by United to reimburse his $1,200 repair bill, Carroll wrote a song called "United Breaks Guitars," which he posted on YouTube in July 2009 as part of a humorous video (http://www.youtube.com/watch?v=5YGc4zOqozo). Within two weeks the clip had been seen by more than 3 million viewers, and millions more were exposed to criticism of the airline when Carroll appeared on TV talk shows across America. By mid-2011 the YouTube clip had accumulated well over 10 million views.

United Airlines belatedly changed its mind and agreed to compensate Carroll, though he refused the money and the airline instead made a $3,000 donation to the Thelonious Monk Institute of Jazz. But this modest goodwill gesture was dwarfed by the wider reputational and financial impact of the incident. The _Times_ of London reported: "Within four days of the song going online, the gathering thunderclouds of bad PR caused United Airlines' stock price to suffer a mid-flight stall, and it plunged by 10 percent, costing shareholders $180 million. Which, incidentally, would have bought Carroll more than 51,000 replacement guitars" (Ayres 2009). Furthermore, the respected business website _Fast Company_ commented, "Can United's $180 million loss be chalked up entirely to a song on You-Tube? Probably not. Did the song have a very real and very negative effect on United's brand equity? Absolutely" (Sawhney 2009).

Hindsight is a powerful perspective, yet analysis of the case shows that the airline had many early opportunities to rectify the situation. Moreover, paying the repair bill was a viable option only before millions accessed the singer's YouTube protest. After that, agreeing to pay for the repair appeared as little more than a valueless gesture.

However, while such high-profile examples may be unusual, experience and the headlines every week show that organizations of all sizes are just as vulnerable to management failure and reputational damage.

Conclusion

To achieve reputation management and crisis prevention during the pre-event stage there are four broad areas where issue management can contribute.

1. _Proactively addressing underlying systemic causes of potential crises._
   This involves openly and honestly identifying and dealing with the full range of potential issues, not just the natural risks associated with particular industries, but also more generic issues such as sexual or racial harassment or discrimination, executive or employee dishonesty, or management misbehavior. While some of these latter risks may be sensitive, management action or inaction is a major cause of crises and reputational damage.

2. _Establishment of effective signal-detection mechanisms._
   The fact that crises are so often preceded by red flags that are ignored highlights the importance of recognizing and acting on such warnings. It is essential that management systems are put in place that actively encourage upward reporting of concerns and problems, and there is no culture of "shooting the messenger." When senior executives refuse to hear bad news and listen only to people who agree with them, the organization and its reputation are seriously at risk.

3. *Properly identifying stakeholders and their perspectives.*
   When organizations set out to identify and prioritize potential risk issues, it is very natural to assess such risks from the organization's own viewpoint. But effective assessment demands properly identifying external stakeholders and seeing issues from their perspective. For example, while an NGO or activist group may have a view that is entirely different from the organization, their viewpoint can easily drive public opinion and determine what is perceived as "an issue."

SELECTING AN ISSUE

When a company chooses to defend an issue its considerations include whether arguments against the issue are plausible, any connection to other company issues, risk of adverse media exposure, strength of the activist opponent, and how easy a solution might be.

By contrast, activist considerations in selecting an issue include having a clear aim or goal, being easily understood by the public and the media, having a high symbolic or emotional value, potential reputational damage to the target, and whether it's easy for the public to get involved.

---

4. *Learning and unlearning on an ongoing basis.*
   There is, sadly, an extensive literature about how managers fail to learn from crises that have previously struck their organization or that have struck other organizations. In fact much has been written about the specific barriers that prevent managers learning (see, e.g., Elliott, Smith, and McGuinness 2000). To prevent crises and protect reputation, organizations need to honestly evaluate what has happened in the past, and be prepared to change themselves and their systems.

When crisis management is seen as a reactive process to get ready for a damaging event when it occurs, the best possible outcome is harm minimization. By contrast, when crisis management is seen as a proactive, integrated part of management aiming at preventing adverse events, issue management becomes the optimal tool to prevent crises and protect reputation.

Key Takeaways

1. The single greatest threat to reputation is a crisis, and real steps can be taken to reduce both the likelihood and the impact of a crisis.
2. Because most crises are preceded by red flags, it is critical to have an effective process in place to recognize and respond to warning signs from both inside and outside the organization.

3. While well-managed organizations typically have tactical processes in place to deal with emergencies and operational crises, true crisis prevention requires a much more strategic approach and greater involvement of senior management.

4. Issue management is a proven effective tool to prevent crises and protect reputation, and with proper planning it can be implemented at a basic level without deployment of extensive resources. The key requirement is management commitment to make a change.

Glossary

Crisis: A low-probability, high-impact event or development likely to endanger health or the environment, or seriously impact the reputation or viability of an organization, characterized by ambiguity of cause, effect, and means of resolution.

Crisis management: Coordinated action to prevent, prepare for, and respond to a crisis in order to minimize physical and reputational damage, to protect the organization, and to capture postevent learnings.

Crisis prevention: A suite of strategic and tactical activities intended to reduce the likelihood of a crisis, or to minimize its impact.

Event approach: The concept of treating crisis management with the main focus on preparing for and responding to a triggering event.

Issue: Any development, real or perceived—usually at least partly external to the organization—which, if it continues, could have a significant impact on its financial position, operation, reputation, or future interests and requires a structured response.

Issue management: A coordinated effort utilizing resources across the organization to identify, prioritize, and actively manage issues toward planned, positive outcomes.

Natural risks: Familiar or obvious risks usually associated with a particular industry, where organizations feel most comfortable and where sector-specific experience increases the feeling of control. Natural risks are frequently technical problems related to mechanical or physical failures, which are relatively easy to fix.

Process approach: The concept of treating crisis management as being one part of an integrated continuum of activities beginning long before the triggering event and continuing through the postcrisis phase.

Reputation: The overall estimation of a person or organization held by the public or key stakeholders, often formed on the basis of perception or expectation as well as performance.

Risk: The possibility of harm, loss, or danger to the organization, or to achievement of its objectives, caused by internal or external threats or uncertainties, often characterized as potential issues or potential crises.

Strategic issue management (SIM): A commonly used synonym for issue management. Sometimes also called strategic issue management system (SIMS).

References

AMA. "Crisis Management and Security Issues Survey." American Management Association. August 2002. http://www.amanet.org/research/pdfs/2002_Crisis MgmtSurvey.pdf.

Ansoff, H. Igor. "Strategic Issue Management." *Strategic Management Journal* 1, no. 2 (1980): 131–48.

AON. "Australian Risk Management Benchmarking Survey 2010/2011." 2011. http://www.aon.com.au/australia/thought-leadership/risk-survey.jsp.

Argenti, Paul A. "Collaborating with Activists: How Starbucks Works with NGOs." *California Management Review* 4, no. 1 (2004): 91–116.

Ayres, Chris. "Revenge is Best Served Cold, on YouTube: How a Broken Guitar Became a Smash Hit." *The Times,* July 22, 2009. http://www.timesonline.co.uk/tol/comment/columnists/chris_ayres/article6722407.ece.

Baylis, Mark. "Reputation the Top Risk as Insurer Solvency Worries Diminish." *Association of Insurance and Risk Managers,* June 15, 2010. http://www.airmic.com/press-release/Reputation-top-risk-manager-concern-insurer-solvency-worries-diminish.

Beal, Andy. "Half of Corporate 'Risk Managers' Ignore Reputation Risks." *Marketing Pilgrim,* March 19, 2009. http://www.marketingpilgrim.com/2009/03/half-of-corporate-risk-managers-ignore-reputation-risks.html.

Bissell, John. "Invoking the Lessons of Edison in the Great 'Frankenfoods' Dispute." *Public Relations Strategist* 6, no. 2 (2000): 10–14.

Boe, Archie R. "Fitting the Corporation to the Future." *Public Relations Quarterly* 24, no. 4 (1979): 4–6.

Buchholz, Rogene A., William D. Evans, and Robert A. Wagley. "Public Issues and Strategic Management." In *Management Response to Public Issues,* 38–69. Englewood Cliffs, NJ: Prentice Hall, 1989.

Camillus, John C., and Deepak K. Datta. "Managing Strategic Issues in a Turbulent Environment." *Long Range Planning* 24, no. 2 (1991): 67–74.

Canadian Investor Relations Institute. "Few Companies Are Prepared to Manage a Crisis." *Business Wire,* April 12, 2011. http://www.businesswire.com/news/home/20110412005462/en/Survey-Companies-Prepared-Manage-Crisis.

Catania, Thomas F. "Whirlpool Integrates Issue Management for Strategic Gain." *Corporate Public Issues and Their Management* 24, no. 1 (2002): 1–7.

Chase, W. Howard. *Issue Management: Origins of the Future.* Stamford, CT: Issue Action, 1984a.

Chase, W. Howard. "Issue Management Conference—A Special Report." *Corporate Public Issues and Their Management* 7, no. 23 (1982): 1–2.

Chase, W. Howard. "No Matter How Well Packaged, Corporate Fads Fade Fast." *Wall Street Journal,* November 12, 1984b.

Chase, W. Howard. "Objectives of CPI." *Corporate Public Issues and Their Management* 1, no. 1 (1976): 1.

Chase, W. Howard, and Jones, Barrie L. "CPI Presents." *Corporate Public Issues and Their Management* 2, no. 14 (1977): 1–4.

Clark, Nicola. "Société Générale Posts Record Loss on Trading Scandal, Subprime Exposure." *International Herald Tribune,* February 21, 2008. http://www.iht.com/articles/2008/02/21/business/socgen.php.

Coleman, Les. "The Frequency and Cost of Corporate Crises." *Journal of Contingencies and Crisis Management* 12, no. 1 (2004): 2–13.

Coombs, W. Tim. "Protecting Organization Reputations during a Crisis: The Development and Application of Situational Crisis Communication Theory." *Corporate Reputation Review* 10, no. 3 (2007): 163–76.

Coombs, W. Tim, and Sherry J. Holladay. *It's not just PR: Public Relations in Society.* Malden, MA: Blackwell, 2007.

Darmon, Keren, Kathy Fitzpatrick, and Carolyn, Bronstein. "Kafting the Obesity Message: A Case Study in Framing and Issues Management." *Public Relations Review* 34, no. 4(2008): 373–79.

Demetrious, Kristin. "People, Power and Public Relations." *Asia Pacific Public Relations Journal* 3, no. 2 (2001): 109–20.

Ebersole, J. Glenn. "Crisis Management Planning—What's Happening Where We Work?" *The Business Coach,* 2005. http://www.evancarmichael.com/Business-Coach/223/Crisis-Management-Planning—Whats-Happening-Where-We-Work.html.

Ehling, William P., and Michael B. Hesse. "Use of 'Issue Management' in Public Relations." *Public Relations Review* 9, no. 2 (1983): 18–35.

Elliott, Dominic, Denis Smith, and Martha McGuinness. "Exploring the Failure to Learn: Crises and Barriers to Learning." *Review of Business* 21, no. 3 (2000): 17–24.

Fearn-Banks, Katherine. "Starkist Tuna and 'Save the Dolphins'." In *Crisis Communications: A Casebook Approach,* 157–67. Mahwah, NJ: Lawrence Erlbaum, 1996.

Ferguson, Sherry D. "Strategic Planning for Issues Management: The Communicator as Environmental Analyst." *Canadian Journal of Communication* 18, no. 1 (1993): 33–50.

Gaines-Ross, Leslie. *Corporate Reputation: 12 Steps to Safeguarding and Recovering Reputation.* Hoboken, NJ: John Wiley, 2008.

Greening, Daniel W. *Integrating Issue Management Activities into Strategic Planning: An Empirical Analysis of Inter-Industry Differences.* Leesburg, VA: The Issue Exchange, 1992.

Gregory, Anne. "Communication Dimensions of the UK Foot and Mouth Disease Crisis 2001." *Journal of Public Affairs* 5, no. 3/4 (2005): 312–28.

Heath, Robert L. *Strategic Issues Management: Organizations and Public Policy Challenges.* Thousand Oaks, CA: Sage, 1997.

Heath, Robert L., and Michael J. Palenchar. *Strategic Issues Management: Organizations and Public Policy Challenges.* 2nd ed. Thousand Oaks, CA: Sage, 2008.

Henderson, Alison. "Activism in 'Paradise': Identity Management in a Public Relations Campaign against Genetic Engineering." *Journal of Public Relations Research* 17, no. 2 (2005): 117–37.

Heugens, Pursey P.M.A.R. "Environmental Issue Management: Towards Multi-Level Theory of Environmental Management Competence." *Business Strategy and the Environment* 15, no. 6 (2006): 363–76.

Ihlen, Oyvond, and Mike Nitz. "Framing Contests in Environmental disputes: Paying Attention to Media and Cultural Master Frames." *International Journal of Strategic Communication* 2, no. 1 (2008): 1–18.

James, Erika H., and Lynn P. Wooten. "Leadership as (un)usual: How to Display Competence in Times of Crisis." *Organizational Dynamics* 34, no. 2 (2005): 141–52.

Jaques, Tony. "Activist 'Rules' and the Convergence with Issue Management." *Journal of Communication Management,* 10, no. 4 (2006): 407–20.

Jaques, Tony. "Embedding Issue Management as a Strategic Element of Crisis Prevention." *Disaster Management and Prevention* 19, no. 4 (2010): 469–82.

Jaques, Tony. "Integrating Issue Management and Strategic Planning: Unfulfilled Promise or Future Opportunity?" *International Journal of Strategic Communication* 3, no. 1 (2009a): 19–33.

Jaques, Tony. "Issue and Crisis Management: Quicksand in the Definitional Landscape." *Public Relations Review* 35, no. 3 (2009b): 280–86.

Jaques, Tony. "Issue Management and Crisis Management: An Integrated, Non-Linear, Relational Construct." *Public Relations Review* 33, no. 2 (2007): 147–57.

Jaques, Tony. "Issue Management as a Post-Crisis Discipline: Identifying and Responding to Issue Impacts beyond the Crisis." *Journal of Public Affairs* 9, no. 1 (2009c): 35–44.

Lipton, Eric, and Scott Shane. "Homeland Security Chief Defends Federal Response." *New York Times,* September 4, 2005. http://www.nytimes.com/2005/09/04/national/nationalspecial/04fema.html.

Knight, Rory F., and Deborah J. Pretty. "Corporate Catastrophes, Stock Returns and Trading Volume." *Corporate Reputation Review* 2, no. 4 (1999): 363–78.

Mitroff, Ian I. "Crisis Learning: The Lessons of Failure." *The Futurist* 36, no. 5 (2002): 19–21.

Mizell, Amanda N. "Sweet Surprise: A Case Study of Argument about High Fructose Corn Syrup." San Diego State University Digital Research Collection, 2010. http://hdl.handle.net/10211.10/320.

Pearson, Christine M., and Judith A. Clair. "Reframing Crisis Management." *The Academy of Management Review* 23, no. 1 (1998): 59–76.

Pendleton, Susan C. "Man's Most Important Food Is Fat: The Use of Persuasive Techniques in Procter and Gamble's Public Relations Campaign to Introduce Crisco, 1911–1913." *Public Relations Quarterly* 44, no. 1 (1999): 6–14.

Renfro, William. *Issues Management in Strategic Planning.* Westport, CT: Quorum
    Books, 1993.
Roux-Dufort, Christophe. "A Passion for Imperfections: Revisiting Crisis Manage-
    ment." In *International Handbook of Organizational Crisis Management,* edited by
    Christine M. Pearson, Christophe Roux-Dufort, and Judith A. Clair, 221–52.
    Thousand Oaks, CA: Sage, 2007.
Sawhney, Ravi. "Broken Guitar has United Playing the Blues to the Tune of $180
    Million." *Fast Company,* July 28, 2009. http://www.fastcompany.com/blog/
    ravi-sawhney/design-reach/youtube-serves-180-million-heartbreak.
Schwarz, Jan O. "Linking Strategic Issue Management to Futures Studies." *Futures
    Research Quarterly* 21, no. 3 (2005): 39–55.
Select Bipartisan Committee. *A Failure of Initiative: Final Report of the Select Bipar-
    tisan Committee to Investigate the Preparation for and Response to Hurricane Ka-
    trina.* Washington, DC: US Government Printing Office, 2006.
Sheehan, Mark. "Super Size Me: A Comparative Analysis of Responses to a Cri-
    sis by McDonald's America and McDonald's Australia." In *Public Relations Is-
    sues and Crisis Management,* edited by Christopher Galloway and Kwamena
    Kwansah-Aidoo, 67–79. Melbourne, Australia: Thomson, 2005.
Shrivastava, Paul. "Ecocentric Management for a Globally Changing Crisis Soci-
    ety." Paper presented at *National Conference, Academy of Management.* Vancou-
    ver, BC, Canada. August, 1995.
Smith, Denis. "Business (Not) as Usual: Crisis Management, Service Recovery
    and the Vulnerability of Organizations." *Journal of Services Marketing* 19, no. 5
    (2005): 309–20.
Smith, Denis. "For Whom the Bell Tolls: Imagining Accidents and the Develop-
    ment of Crisis Simulation in Organizations." *Simulation and Gaming* 35, no. 3
    (2004): 347–62.
Stout, David. "Report Details How Madoff's Web Ensnared SEC." *New York Times,*
    September 3, 2009. http://www.nytimes.com/2009/09/03/business/03madoff.
    html?pagewanted=all.
Tannen, Andy. "What's Reputation Worth? Just Ask Toyota, Goldman and BP."
    Forbes magazine online, June 14, 2010. http://www.forbes.com/2010/06/14/
    bp-toyota-reputation-markets-goldman-sachs.html.
Titley, Simon. "How Political and Social Change Will Transform the EU Public
    Affairs Industry." *Journal of Public Affairs,* 3, no. 1 (2003): 83–89.
Toohey, Brian C., Matthew Dailida, and Linda C. Bartholomew. "Intersection of
    21st Century Technology with 20th Century Laws: A Case Study in Proactive
    Issues Management." *Journal of Public Affairs* 3, no. 3 (2003): 232–44.
Walton, Sara. "Site the Mine in Our Backyard: Discursive Strategies of Community
    Stakeholders in an Environmental Conflict in New Zealand." *Organization &
    Environment* 20, no. 2 (2007): 177–203.
Wartick, Steven L., and Robert E. Rude. "Issues Management: Corporate Fad
    or Corporate Function?" *California Management Review* 29, no. 1 (1986):
    124–40.

Wiebner, Michael. "The Battle of Bull Run: How Insurgent Grassroots Lobbying Defeated Disney's Proposed Virginia Theme Park." *Campaigns and Elections* 16, no. 1 (1995): 44–48.

Williams, Jody. *The International Campaign to Ban Landmines: A Model for Disarmament Initiatives?* Nobel e-Museum, 1999. http://www.globalpolicy.org/ngos/campaign/landmine/1999/0804nobel.htm.

CHAPTER THREE

The Art of Business Presentations: Communicating Effectively before Various Stakeholders

Mary L. Kahl

Steve Jobs and the Problem-Plagued Product Release

Every speaker can encounter technical difficulties during a presentation, but when your job is speaking about technical products those difficulties can only be exacerbated when unanticipated glitches occur. On January 7, 2010, the late Steve Jobs, then CEO of Apple Corporation, set out to deliver a major rollout address about the benefits of the iPhone 4.

Jobs was still in the introduction of his speech when he attempted to connect the iPhone 4 to the conference facility's wireless-fidelity (Wi-Fi) hotspot. Suddenly something unthinkable occurred: he couldn't connect. There Jobs stood, in front of a few hundred computer technicians and media representatives, and one of the most basic features of the iPhone 4 wasn't working.

In front of this live audience the Apple guru muttered, "Our networks in here are always unpredictable, so I have no idea what we're going to find. They are slow today." Jobs spoke these words with his body half-turned away from his audience, as he continued his attempts to connect his phone to the Wi-Fi. He then jokingly added, "You know you could help out if you're on Wi-Fi. If you're on Wi-Fi, if you could just get off." These remarks prompted a wave of nervous laughter from the audience. He next tried to connect to AT&T's 3G network, which has caused many iPhone users headaches, only to see the dreaded "'Cannot Open Page' Safari cannot open this page because it cannot connect to the Internet," which is an unfortunately common sight for many iPhone users. Of course, this further technological problem led to more laughter in the auditorium.

Apple representatives quickly rushed to the rescue. Ultimately, Jobs's tech team determined that the auditorium contained 570 separate Wi-Fi base stations that were jamming Jobs's phone, preventing it from finding and connecting to a single Wi-Fi hotspot. The iPhone 4 simply couldn't cope. Jobs ultimately told the audience, "We have two choices, either . . . I've got some more demos that are really great that I'd like to show you. So we either turn off all the stuff and see the demos or we give up and I don't show you the demos. Would you like to see the demos or not?"

Jobs continued for a few minutes with the promised demonstrations, but when he showed the video communication functions on the iPhone 4, everything froze again. With growing frustration, Jobs remarked, "This never freezes up, so you guys haven't turned off all your Wi-Fi. Come on, let's get it off please."

While Jobs smiled throughout the entire presentation, he clearly became increasingly agitated as his speech was plagued by more and more problems. His cool demeanor saved a disastrous set of circumstances, but other less-skilled speakers might not have fared as well.

The vital importance of effective business communication skills cannot be emphasized enough. These abilities are crucial to creating a productive work environment, employing sound management techniques, and promoting overall organizational success. Effective communication involves a set of complex skills; skills that are recognized as being among the most important characteristics that people can possess in any type of organization. Oral communication skills rank first among all attributes that are sought by potential employers and that contribute to long-term employee performance, according to decades of research (Donnangelo and Farley 1993; Hafer and Hoth 1983). In fact, the higher up the organizational ladder one climbs, the greater the emphasis on communicating effectively and the more time spent on engaging directly in communicative activities. As Andrews and Baird observe: "To get to the top [of an organization] requires communication skills; to perform effectively once you get there requires even greater skill" (2000, 3).

This chapter discusses several of the important types of speeches that you will encounter in a business context. These include technical briefings, proposal presentations, speeches of introduction, manuscript speeches, and extemporaneous presentations. While you may encounter other, more idiosyncratic, speaking situations, the ones explained here are the most common kinds of speeches that organizational members and leaders deliver.

Technical Briefings

Briefings are usually defined as short informational speeches delivered in a business setting. Sometimes scheduled at the beginning of the work day, briefings might be given on a wide range of topics. A technical briefing is a short speech which explains specialized or complex information that a speaker knows well. If you understand how to approach this kind of speaking situation, you will likely have confidence in giving other types of briefings that involve less-complex material. Obviously, briefings should be short because time constraints weigh heavily in many organizational contexts (Gamble and Kelliher 1999). A briefing is not the occasion for detailed explanations or instructions (Hostetler and Kahl 2012). Instead, concentrate on providing your audience with essential information that is clearly organized, keeping in mind the following guidelines.

Make the Abstract Concrete

Abstract theories, ideas, and terms demand concrete examples, illustrations, or definitions. Consider this example. In the romantic comedy film, *Other People's Money*, Danny DeVito plays the part of a Wall Street corporate raider trying to take over a small company. In his speech to the company's stockholders he says, "You know the surest way to go broke? Keep getting an increasing share of a shrinking market. Down the tubes! You know, at one time there must have been dozens of companies making buggy whips. And I'll bet the last company around was the one that made the best god dammed buggy whip you ever saw! Now, how would you like to have been a stockholder in that company?" (Warner Brothers, Inc. 1991).

The idea that it is bad to "get an increasing share of a shrinking market" is an abstraction of economic theory. It remains an abstraction until the speaker gives an example that transforms the higher-order principle into something concrete and memorable. This is not to say that good speakers never talk about abstract concepts. On the contrary, good speakers embrace complex ideas, but they recognize when those ideas need to be explained in concrete terms.

Beware of Statistics

Statistics—a general term encompassing all manner of numerical evidence—are a ubiquitous feature of discourse in our culture. Leaders are expected to invoke statistics in their communication, whether in business, politics, or education. Even though we read and speak of them all the time, skilled speakers realize that statistics are more likely to start an argument than to settle one. Further complicating our reliance on statistics is widespread ignorance and discomfort with mathematics itself. The mathematician John Allen Paulos has called this problem "innumeracy," defined as "an inability to deal comfortably with the fundamental notions of number and chance" (Paulos 2001, 3). When it comes to statistics, public speakers face a dilemma. Audiences have come to rely on and expect statistics even though most people—even educated ones—live and think in a mathematical fog.

Numbers are by nature abstract. For example, the word "one," as a noun, indicates nothing until it becomes an adjective as in "one car." But even as adjectives, numbers indicating very large or very small quantities are so abstract as to become meaningless. You probably have a fairly good idea of what $100 is, but how about one trillion dollars? Such a number is utterly abstract. Good speakers should help their audiences navigate through the fog of numbers. To say that $1 trillion would be equivalent to so many hundred dollar bills attached end to end to go the moon and back so many thousands of times is not much help. Don't explain one abstraction with another. Instead of verbally reciting numerical data, emphasize only the most significant or interesting numbers, explaining why they are particularly important. When using statistics for comparisons and contrasts, be sure to magnify the point of comparison or contrast. Keep in mind that numbers are not self-explanatory.

Slow Down

Complex subject matter demands a deliberate, measured rate of speaking targeted to the audience's familiarity with the material. A deliberate rate is connected to careful preparation. One of the most common reasons speakers find themselves rushing their delivery is a failure to prepare the appropriate amount of information for the time allotted for the speech. If there is too much information to give, the speaker often feels pressure to hurry. A well-prepared speaker never has to say, "I'm sorry, I'm running out of time." Trying to speed through complex information is a recipe for miscommunication and audience misunderstanding.

Avoid Jargon

People who have to attend lots of briefings often complain about the mindless use of acronyms and jargon. Of course, the impulse to use jargon or acronyms is a common one, especially when time is a factor. A speaker may naturally revert to this kind of "shorthand" to keep briefings within acceptable time limits, but it is not always wise to do so. Use acronyms and jargon if you know for sure that everyone in your audience understands the specialized meanings attached to your language. If not, explain the jargon sufficiently or cut it completely (Hostetler and Kahl, 2012).

Use, but Do Not Abuse, PowerPoint

The proliferation of Microsoft's PowerPoint software has had a substantial influence on informational speaking, particularly in business and academic settings. Speaking situations that at one time would not have had enough visual reinforcement now often have too much. One of the most outspoken critics of PowerPoint has been Edward R. Tufte, a Yale University professor who specializes in analytical design. He argues that PowerPoint has a distinctive "cognitive style" that leads to a host of problems: "foreshortening of evidence and thought, low spatial resolution, an intensely hierarchical single-path structure as the model for organizing every type of content, breaking up narratives and data into slides and minimal fragments, rapid temporal sequencing of thin information rather than focused spatial analysis, preoccupation with format not content, incompetent design for data graphics and tables, and a smirky commercialism that turns information into a sales pitch and presenters into marketers" (2001, 4).

Even though it has serious limitations, PowerPoint has valid uses such as the projection of photographs or simple graphic lists such as meeting agendas. For complex or technical data, paper handouts may be the best choice for communicating with your audience. Tufte argues that an 11 × 17 inch piece of paper "can show images with 1,200 dpi resolution, up to 60,000 characters of words and numbers . . . or 1,000 sparkline statistical graphics showing 500,000 numbers." ("Sparkline," meaning "intense, simple, word-sized graphic," is a term invented by Tufte and is discussed in his book, *Beautiful Evidence,* 2006.) "That one piece of paper shows the content-equivalent of 50–250 typical PP slides" (2001, 30). So, business speakers should use PowerPoint sparingly, despite the prevailing practice of doing precisely the opposite. The bottom line for using any presentation software is to prevent your content from being distorted or diminished by forcing it into an inappropriate visual format that is unnecessarily distracting.

Proposal Presentations

When you present an oral proposal you are formally recommending and defending a specific plan or course of action that is carefully developed. Often the impetus for presenting a proposal may be your own: you have a good idea that you would like to have adopted. Other times, however, you may be called upon to develop a proposal at the request of your immediate superior. Just as the reasons for making proposals vary, so too do the possible audiences for these presentations. Audience members may be a small group of your peers, or a group of higher-level corporate decision makers, or a board of directors. In most cases, you can usually count on the fact that your auditors have some amount of status and that they possess the authority to accept or reject your ideas. Because your audience will often be composed of leaders who manage their schedules carefully, you may find that you must make a solid case for your proposal within a particular time limit.

Proposal presentations should be constructed to organize and articulate a large amount of information in a relatively short length of time, often a period of no more than 10 or 15 minutes. In practical terms, your primary objectives will be to explain an idea and to report on as many ramifications of that idea as possible. Your ultimate goal is to persuade your listeners to adopt your proposal. In this regard, you are functioning as a persuasive speaker who "pitches" your idea in a comprehensive—yet compact—package to a small group of decision makers (Hostetler and Kahl, 2012). Almost all of the principles of persuasive speaking may be used in designing oral proposals. Here are some of these considerations.

Understand Your Audience

Prepare your proposal with the characteristics of your audience in mind. Learn whatever you can about your auditors before you begin to compose your presentation, including an estimation of their existing beliefs, values, and attitudes regarding your topic. Learn the knowledge specializations of your listeners, understand how members of this decision-making group function as a team, and determine who usually performs leadership functions within the unit (Andrews and Baird 2000). If your proposal is made in an organizational setting, find out about the structure of the company and about any problems it may be facing, especially if these things may have a bearing on the reception or acceptance of your ideas. Being audience centered will increase your chances of gaining a positive hearing for your proposal, as you will be speaking directly and realistically to the needs of your auditors and/or of the organization.

Focus on Solving Problems

As you compose your oral proposal you should focus clearly on the problem or the need that your idea addresses. You will most likely want to spend a few minutes demonstrating your understanding of the problem's significance and its effect on the current situation. You may want to speak briefly about other attempts to solve the problem, if any, and about the positive outcomes you envision resulting from your plan. Fairly early in your presentation you will want to offer a concise statement of your major idea. Do not keep your audience guessing about what you are proposing: using suspense in these situations is not to your advantage. The early artic-ulation of your idea functions as a thesis statement, allowing your listeners to begin processing your proposal more quickly and thoroughly (Sprague and Stuart 2008).

Organize the Oral Proposal Carefully

Because you are imparting a substantial amount of information in a rel-atively short period of time, you will want to make sure that your presenta-tion is well organized. Certainly your speech should have an introduction, a body, and a conclusion. Beyond this, there are specific patterns of orga-nization that are especially well suited to persuasive speaking and so are easily adapted to making proposal presentations. Three patterns that work well for oral proposals are: (1) the deductive approach, often called "state the case and prove it pattern" that focuses on solutions; (2) the inductive approach, often called the "problem-solving pattern" that grows from John Dewey's reflective thinking agenda (Dewey 1910); and (3) the motivated sequence, based on the work of pioneering communication scholar Alan Monroe (Monroe 1935). Regardless of which organizational pattern you adopt for your proposal, you should make sure that your speech is unified by a central theme, that it demonstrates logical coherence between points, that it emphasizes your most important arguments, and that it is as com-prehensive as time allows.

Address Decisional Criteria

You should also determine if there are any criteria by which your pro-posal will be judged and make sure to address these decisional guidelines directly in your presentation. If you maintain your focus on solving a prob-lem or need, it will be easy for you to incorporate decisional rules into your presentation: simply tell your auditors how your plan measures up to any criteria they must follow. If your audience is not using any decision-making criteria, mention some guidelines of your own choosing and em-ploy them to highlight the merits of your proposal. For example, you might state that any worthy proposal must not result in downsizing within the organization, and then you might offer some projections about how to make this happen.

Answer Potential Objections

Skilled persuaders often anticipate audience objections and answer them in the course of their speeches, before listeners have a chance to ask questions. If time allows, you may choose to do this in your proposal presentation. Your understanding of audience attitudes, leadership dynamics, or decisional criteria may give you the knowledge to foresee potential objections and to address them directly. You may want to use some two-sided arguments in your proposal—developing claims in which you assert your positive position, articulate a weakened version of anticipated objections, and then refute those objections forcefully.

Plan for a Polished Delivery

If at all possible, determine how to conduct yourself during your proposal presentation by learning about your audience's past practices and preferences. Do most presenters sit or stand? Are there institutional expectations for the use of PowerPoint or Smart Boards? Do decision makers prefer low-tech handouts or high-tech CD-ROMs? Adjust your use of presentational aids and your general demeanor to the culture of the organization. Also, be sure to familiarize yourself with all the facts of your talk so that you can speak extemporaneously. Make eye contact with your listeners frequently: this is especially helpful to achieving your persuasive goals in a small group setting.

Finally, there is the matter of time. Adhere to any time limits that have been imposed or suggested for your talk, being careful to leave sufficient time for questions and answers. You will likely want to prepare answers for certain questions that you suspect may be asked. If you call for questions and none are posed, you can then use these prepared questions and answers to extend your remarks, if necessary. On the other hand, if the question-and-answer period threatens to exceed your allotted time limit, ask the individual who is running the meeting if the discussion can be extended briefly. As you prepare your proposal presentation, consider the use of time in one additional context—that of timeliness. Make sure that you choose a propitious time to pitch your proposal: a strategic understanding of the "right time" is often a key component in successful persuasion.

Speeches of Introduction

Organizational leaders often encounter occasions in which they are called upon to introduce another speaker to an audience. This common speaking situation may be lightly regarded as a routine presentation, but a little reflection on the speech of introduction reveals that there is more to this type of communication than one might suppose. A starting point for preparing a speech of introduction is to consider how the introducer situates her or himself in the overall rhetorical transaction. In other words, where does the introducer stand in relationship to the participants in the event? Do you see yourself as speaking *on behalf of the audience* in welcoming the speaker? If so, some of your remarks will be directed to the speaker. Or do you see yourself speaking *on behalf of the event's sponsor* in welcoming both the speaker and the audience? In these cases, it may be necessary to introduce the topic as well as the speaker. Perhaps the most common approach is to see the introducer as speaking *on behalf of the speaker* to the audience. Regardless of how you view your role in the overall event, it is important to keep in mind that when you give a speech of introduction, it is not about you, it is about others. Your job is to draw attention to the speaker, the topic, or the audience in ways that frame the speaking event to the greatest possible extent for all those involved. The speech of introduction is performed as a service to others (Hostetler and Kahl 2012).

A primary purpose of the speech of introduction is usually to elevate the *ethos* or credibility of the speaker. There are several ways to go about this. The most common method, citing the speaker's accomplishments or awards, is a starting point. Most audiences, however, do not appreciate the recitation of a long list of academic degrees, corporate titles, or professional awards. Instead, choose to magnify two or three major accomplishments of the speaker that are clearly relevant to the topic or situation at hand. Another way to enhance a speaker's credibility is to tell an anecdote that puts the speaker in a favorable light. Make sure that the speaker is comfortable with the anecdote and is not planning to use the same story in his/her speech. Sometimes a speaker's standing in the eyes of an audience may be enhanced by seeing the speaker in an unexpected light. For example, if the speaker is a research scientist or corporate giant, a story about their interpersonal qualities or avocation might be telling and effective. Yet another way to build up a speaker's credibility is to share some of your own. In situations where you are introducing a protégé or someone who is subordinate to you in the organizational hierarchy, your own endorsement and positive comments will likely carry weight with the audience.

By speaking first, the introducer has the opportunity to exercise leadership and create a positive climate for the whole event.

From a practical standpoint, speakers should remember these tips when they are preparing a speech of introduction. First, keep your introductory remarks short. Your brief commentary should set the tone for the speaker who is to follow: you are not the main event. Speeches of introduction rarely last longer than three minutes. Second, be certain that you know how to pronounce the name of the person you introduce. In addition, find out if the person prefers to be called by a nickname or by a particular title. The surest way to appear unprepared is to make an error in pronunciation or in honorific address. Third, unless you have specifically set out to introduce the topic to the audience, avoid offering substantive commentary about it. Anything you say about the topic should be stated in such a way as to defer to the speaker and should not—even inadvertently—preempt the speaker's remarks. Finally, conclude your introduction by repeating the speaker's name and perhaps the title of the speech. This shows respect for the speaker and sets a tone of respect for the audience to model.

Manuscript Speeches

As James Winans, a Dartmouth University speech professor, remarked pointedly, "A speech is not merely an essay standing on its hind legs." Although there are no clear statistics to prove it, it is fair to assume that most of the speeches given in the United States every single day, whether in business, civic, religious, or educational settings, are delivered extemporaneously. That is, the speeches are prepared and then given in a conversational style from notes (Hostetler and Kahl 2012). By contrast, manuscript speeches, those that are written out and then delivered word for word from the written text, are less common, but they are often given in the most important speaking situations. Inexperienced speakers sometimes erroneously believe that manuscript speeches are easier to give than extemporaneous speeches. This is only partially true, at most. Almost anyone can stand in front of an audience and read words off a piece of paper. The communication that results, however, is hardly an engaging speech; it is merely someone reading words from a piece of paper. It is, in a word, sterile.

Most standard public-speaking textbooks advise using a manuscript when "specific wording is critical" (Zarefsky 2011). Which situations call for such careful wording? A situation in which you are delivering a speech that will be subject to extensive press coverage is one such occasion requiring thoughtful composition. Legal contexts also come to mind. If your words might be brought to bear on a civil or criminal proceeding or even be introduced as evidence in court, you must be very careful about what you say. Similarly, speeches given in the midst of various kinds of negotiations need to be worded specifically. Another setting where a manuscript would be advisable is when audience emotions are running high and where even a slight extemporaneous misstep could easily provoke a negative reaction. Crisis situations also call for manuscript speaking, lest the details of the conflict escape a speaker's grasp. Finally, many business speakers use a manuscript when speaking time is constrained. You should know exactly how long a manuscript speech will take to deliver by reading it aloud prior to the actual speaking event.

Good speakers do not take lightly the difference between an essay and a manuscript speech. Manuscript speeches require what is sometimes called "oral style." This means we must write like we talk, which most of us do not do automatically. Instead, we write as we have been educated to write, following the conventions of written prose. That is why an essay read to an audience does not sound like a speech. Very few people naturally write in the style in which they speak. Such writing is a learned skill, one that is developed only with practice.

Here are four primary qualities of oral style that should be incorporated into manuscript speeches. First, oral style sits loose to the rules of grammar. This does not mean that oral style is ignorantly ungrammatical, but that the rules are applied with a light touch. For example, sentence fragments—clauses lacking a subject or predicate—may be used to simulate ordinary conversation. Contractions are also more natural to spoken discourse than to written. Second, oral style often employs a more limited vocabulary. Our reading vocabulary is usually always more extensive than our speaking vocabulary. Manuscript speakers often employ the words and phrases common to oral discourse. Next, oral style features various types of repetition. What would be considered redundancy in a written composition seems natural in spoken communication. Moreover, repetition is a recognized means of reinforcing ideas so it is often useful for promoting audience recall and persuasion. Finally, oral style frequently employs personal pronouns. Unlike a writer addressing a "universal audience," a speaker, face to face with live human beings, can speak to them directly and personally through the use of carefully selected pronouns.

The secret of good manuscript speaking is delivering the speech exactly as it is written without appearing to be reading. This is why it is often claimed that preparing to deliver a manuscript speech is more demanding than preparing for an extemporaneous presentation. Audiences do not like to be read to and most listeners will recognize the difference between a manuscript and an extemporaneous presentation. If you over-rehearse the speech, it will come across as a memorized recitation—one that is unnatural and stilted. If you under-rehearse you will look down at the text too much and appear to be reading. So not only is writing a manuscript speech difficult, delivering it is also fraught with potential problems. You may want to compensate for these difficulties by doing the following: When preparing a manuscript, use a large type font and a spacious page layout. Make notations to yourself on the manuscript, such as where to pause or what to emphasize. Bracket sections that you may need to add or omit in order to conform to time constraints. Manuscript speeches tend toward inflexibility, so build some wiggle room into your address through the use of extra content that may be inserted as needed. And, finally, use the same manuscript to deliver the speech that you used in rehearsal. Practice until you are completely familiar and comfortable with your ideas, words, and the very pieces of paper you carry to the podium.

Extemporaneous Presentations

It is indeed the case that most speeches delivered today are extemporaneous in nature. This does not mean that the extemporaneous speaker is lacking in preparation. On the contrary, an extemporaneous speech is very often planned and structured with great care. The extemporaneous speaker addresses the audience using written notes—often an outline— but her/his presentation is neither read nor memorized. The ultimate goal is to achieve a conversational style of delivery, combined with solid content and the flexibility to respond to audience feedback.

In order to make an effective extemporaneous presentation, you should form a clear sense of the main ideas that you wish to cover in your speech and how you wish to organize them. Excellent extemporaneous speakers do not rely solely upon their own knowledge base to support the arguments they advance; they research their topics and often quote other authorities to support their own assertions. Examples from daily business activities or from corporate history may also enliven extemporaneous presentations, making it easy for audience members to identify with what you are saying. Further, by choosing to deliver remarks extemporaneously you are free to respond to audience feedback: you can alter the amount of time or the degree of emphasis that you place on certain sections of your speech. You may even feel free to take questions from your audience at the end of your remarks. Steve Jobs's remarks during the i-Phone 4 rollout debacle demonstrate the power of extemporaneous presentations: they are flexibly focused on content, on ideas rather than on specific phrases, and can therefore be adjusted as circumstances warrant.

Becoming a good public speaker in a business context is an ongoing process rather than a fixed goal. As speakers grow in experience, they typically feel increasingly more comfortable in the wide variety of public contexts in which they are required to perform. Business leaders speak well when they are knowledgeable about the functions and approaches that their discourses require, whether addressing corporate shareholders, boards of directors, formal employee gatherings, divisional meetings, or important external audiences.

Key Takeaways

1. There are five common speech types that executives are often called to deliver: technical briefings, proposal presentations, speeches of introduction, manuscript speeches, and extemporaneous speeches.
2. Each of the five common speaking types involves their own unique attributes and rules, so knowing how to differentiate among the five and what contexts to use them in is extremely important.
3. Making sure that a manuscript is consistently formatted is very important because it simplifies and accelerates both the editorial and production processes.

Glossary

Extemporaneous speeches: Speech where the speaker addresses the audience using written notes—often an outline—but her/his presentation is neither read nor memorized. The ultimate goal is to achieve a conversational style of delivery, combined with solid content and the flexibility to respond to audience feedback.

Innumeracy: An individual's inability to deal comfortably with the fundamental notions of number and probability.

Manuscript speeches: Speeches that are written out and then delivered word for word from the written text.

Proposal presentation: Speeches that formally recommends and defends a specific plan or course of action that is carefully developed.

Sparkline: Concept associated with visual representations of evidence that are intense, simple, and/or word-sized graphics.

Speeches of introduction: Speeches in which an individual is charged with introducing a primary speaker to an audience.

Statistics: A general term encompassing all manner of numerical evidence.

Technical briefing: Short informational speeches that explains specialized or complex information delivered in a business setting.

References

Andrews, Patricia Hayes, and John E. Baird, Jr. *Communication for Business and the Professions*. 7th ed. Boston: McGraw Hill, 2000.

Dewey, John. *How We Think*. Boston: Heath, 1910.

Donnangelo, Frank P., and Catherine Farley, "The Attributes of Job Applicants: Employer Expectations versus Perceptions of Minority Students." Educational Resources Clearing House, 1993. http://www.eric.ed.gov/ERICWebPortal/detail?accno=ED357805.

Gamble, Paul R., and Clare E. Kelliher, "Imparting Information and Influencing Behavior: An Examination of Staff Briefing Sessions." *The Journal of Business Communication* 36, no. 3 (1999): 261–79.

Hafer, John C., and C. C. Hoth, "Selection Characteristics: Your Priorities and How Students Perceive Them." *Personnel Administrator* (March 1983): 25–28.

Hostetler, Michael J., and Mary L. Kahl. *Advanced Public Speaking: A Leader's Guide to Communication*. Boston: Allyn and Bacon, 2012.

Monroe, Allan H. *Principles and Types of Speech*. New York: Scott, Foresman, 1935.

Paulos, John Allen. *Innumeracy: Mathematical Illiteracy and Its Consequences*. New York: Hill and Wang, 2001.

Sprague, Jo, and Douglas Stuart. *The Speaker's Handbook*. 8th ed. Belmont, CA: Thomson Wadsworth, 2008.

Tufte, Edward R. *Beautiful Evidence*. Cheshire, CT: Graphics Press, 2006.

Tufte, Edward R. *The Cognitive Style of PowerPoint: Pitching Out Corrupts Within*. 2nd ed. Cheshire, CT: Graphics Press, 2001.

Warner Brothers, Inc. *Other People's Money*, 1991.

Zarefsky, David. *Public Speaking: Strategies for Success*. 6th ed. Boston: Allyn and Bacon, 2011.

CHAPTER FOUR

Customer Service with a Smile: Creating a Climate Where Customers Come First

Tina A. Coffelt

Regional Grocers Use Customer Communication as a Competitive Advantage

Nestled in the small, manufacturing and university town of Maryville, MO, resides a great example of customer service—Fred Mares. Fred is a greeter at the local Hy-Vee store, which has survived the infringing competition from Wal-Mart when other local and regional grocers could not. There are several reasons Hy-Vee has survived and even expanded its Maryville food center, one of which is Fred Mares. Fred is no ordinary grocery store greeter. Fred excels at extending a warm, genuine greeting to every customer who enters the store. He remembers people's names and important events in their lives. I left this town over seven years ago, yet he frequently asks my mother how I'm doing. He reads the local newspaper and remembers information. He remembers where I live and my profession. When I am in town, Fred immediately recognizes me and calls me by name. My story is not unique. Countless local citizens make this same claim. What else does Fred do that makes him extraordinary? His presence is felt throughout the store. He offers hugs, sings songs, and gives flowers. When one customer made her first visit to Hy-Vee after the passing of her husband, Fred sang "One Day at a Time, Sweet Jesus" to her in the store! Years later, when this woman passed away, her granddaughter ventured into the store. Fred sang the same song to the granddaughter and gave her a red rose. The store director in 2010, Ben Conway, said, "In all my years with Hy-Vee, I have never worked with an employee who has a true passion and sincerity for customer service like he does. Fred makes a difference in people's lives every day." In 2010, Fred was recognized for his outstanding service when he received one of nine Hy-Vee Legendary Customer Service awards.

Could outstanding customer service be the competitive advantage that keeps local and regional grocers afloat in the midst of price-cutting Wal-Mart? What are the exemplary communication practices that help an employee achieve such legendary status and transcend average customer service? The focus of this chapter is to highlight the communication skills necessary to meet and exceed customer expectations. The chapter begins by introducing key definitions and concepts, then proceeds to suggesting how to get customer service right the first time. Comments on listening and nonverbal communication skills will be offered, followed by a discussion of challenging customers and service recovery. The chapter closes by mentioning the emerging trends of customer call centers, globalization, and technology.

Key Definitions and Concepts

Customer service is (1) usually provided by all industries and is the service provided in support of an organization's core products (Gronfeldt and Strother 2006); (2) the ability of knowledgeable, capable, and enthusiastic employees to deliver products and services to their internal and external customers in a manner that satisfies identified and unidentified needs and ultimately results in positive word-of-mouth publicity and return business (Lucas 2005). Servicing customers involves many different functions. For example, products and services need to be designed to meet customers' needs; logistics need to be coordinated to deliver products on time or before; managers need to hire, train, and reward employees to value customer service and to communicate with them in appropriate and effective ways; and price points need to coincide with perceived value. These different functions operate in tandem and are integral to the overall customer experience. One specific element of customer service is customer communication, which is the focus of this chapter.

> ### CUSTOMER COMMUNICATION
>
> Customer communication focuses on the points of intersection between the customer and the service provider.

These interactions are often face-to-face. However, organizations' shift toward the use of technology means that customers interact with mediated channels such as online support systems or smartphone applications with increasing frequency. Advantages and disadvantages of the use of technology will be addressed in a later section. The majority of this chapter will focus on face-to-face interactions because of their importance and complexity even though many of the same principles apply to mediated forms of communication. The aspects of customer communication introduced in this chapter include strategies to deliver positive customer experiences, listening, nonverbal communication, service recovery, technology, call centers, and culture. A few key concepts follow, specifically customer relationships, customer and industry types, and naming customers.

Customer Relationships

The term *customer* encompasses a broad range of relationships and levels of interdependence between organizations and those they serve. A client represents a repeat customer who has considerable interdependence with the organization and/or service provider. The client relationship alters the communication needed because the interactions will be frequent and involve considerable depth. A lawyer, for example, talks to a client on several occasions, discusses sensitive information, and the client relies heavily on the expertise and actions of the lawyer. Or, take ACME Industries, for example, a small contract manufacturer with only 10 customers ("Rustbelt Recovery" 2011). Ten customers who buy large industrial equipment are likely to be highly interdependent and operate more like business partners than a service provider–customer relationship. By contrast, a salesperson for Nordstrom may have one interaction with a customer or multiple interactions with repeat customers. The topic of clothing and accessories does not preclude a high level of disclosing personal information. The client relies on the salesperson for assistance, but can find similar services from many other clothing providers. Consider also the Wal-Mart associate who completes a transaction for hundreds of customers who have very little dependence on the associate. The length of the transaction is quick and the quality of the interaction is impersonal.

Another way to think about the types of interactions between customers and service providers is to review the distinctions made by Gutek et al. (2000). These scholars described the interface between customers and service providers as service encounters, service relationships, or pseudo-relationships. Service encounters are brief and occur only once with no expectation for repeat interaction with the same person. Examples of service encounters include a ticket teller at a sports or concert venue or associates who work for airlines. Service relationships are more involved with expectations of seeing the same service provider on future interactions. These could include a hairdresser or doctor. Pseudorelationships are characterized by repeat interactions with the same organization but the customer could interact with various service providers. Customers of large organizations such as AT&T, Target, or Burger King are examples of organizations who would engage in pseudorelationships. This chapter is geared toward the communication in service encounters, although many principles apply to service or pseudorelationships. While some of the same communication principles apply, the interdependence and frequent, repeat interaction will require additional communication skill sets that exceed the intent of this chapter.

Customer and Industry Types

Communication with customers also varies by the type of customer and by the type of industry (Yim, Tse, and Chan 2008). Customer and industry type must be given consideration when developing service strategies and communication norms because customers have different expectations for different types of service providers. For example, customers have higher expectations of professional service providers such as physicians, mechanics, and hairdressers (Ford 2003). The importance of customer type can be seen by contrasting Wal-Mart with Nordstrom's. Wal-Mart serves all cross-sections of the population and must therefore be prepared to communicate in general, broad ways. Their service encounters are brief and impersonal, as well, so the investment of the service provider in the customer is very low. Customers expect courteous service and someone to be available when help is needed. However, they rarely expect in-depth explanations of products or an overview of different product offerings available. Nordstrom, by contrast, deals with a specific target market—the high-end section of the population. Further, the product offerings are confined to clothing and accessories. The clientele possess and expect a level of sophistication in their transactions with service providers. Most Nordstrom's clients want personalized attention and expect to have an associate remember their name and clothing preferences. Nordstrom's sales staff are more interdependent with their customers than Wal-Mart associates. Berry (1995) refers to this distinction as relational services or transactional services. Yim et al. (2008) found that relational services are characterized by more affection and are more commitment driven than transactional services.

The industry also impacts the communication norms. For example, funeral home directors, hospitals, adoption agencies, or youth camps require social support, sympathy or empathy, and compassion when interacting with their customers. Dell, AT&T, or DirecTV need to be resourceful and knowledgeable when talking with customers. And, bill collectors must be firm and direct when interacting with their customers. When reviewing the information in this chapter, the reader must consider the ideas in relation to a specific industry and customer type.

Naming the Customer

Naming the customer can have meaningful consequences for customers. It is well known that Walt Disney World, Ritz Carlton, and many organizations in the hospitality industry refer to their customers as guests. This change in language shifts the mentality of the service provider to think of the customer as a guest in one's home, someone who is extended the best hospitality possible, who is catered to and cared about. Guests also sense a greater connection to the organization by seeing themselves as "more than" a customer, but rather a visitor who has come to a special place. Other examples include patients in the medical profession or patrons at libraries. Regardless of the label used, customers have expectations about how they will be served. These expectations are met or exceeded by organizations who understand the importance of providing excellent customer service.

> ### THE AMERICAN CUSTOMER SATISFACTION INDEX
>
> The American Customer Satisfaction Index (ACSI) gathers and analyzes data from over 225 companies and 47 industries in the United States. View their reports at www.theacsi.org.

Importance of Customer Service

Customer service is important for at least three reasons. First, the universal principle of the Golden Rule warrants treating others with respect and civility. The golden rule—do unto others as you would have done to you—exists in many cultures around the world and has permeated cultures throughout much of civilization. Plato, Socrates, Native Americans, Taoism, the Bible, and the Qur'an, among many other sources, have quoted some version of the golden rule, "Do unto others as you would have them do unto you." This apparent universal principle serves as an undercurrent for the treatment of customers. In general, when customers are treated with respect, have important information, and are cared about, they will be satisfied with their service encounter, make referrals, and/or repurchase products or services.

Second, repeat business and customer loyalty are more likely with outstanding customer service. Satisfied customers are, in general, more likely to return to the organization for future purchases (e.g., Helgesen 2006). Organizations experience higher profitability from these repeat customers by keeping marketing costs low.

Third, the financial benefits of superb customer service are well documented. As customer satisfaction scores increase, so, too, do stock prices (Fornell et al. 2006) and shareholder value (Anderson, Fornell, and Mazvancheryl 2004). In fact, investors who select firms with high and increasing customer satisfaction scores are likely to experience stronger returns than investing in the S&P 500 index (Aksoy et al. 2008). Companies such as Publix, USAA, Lexus, or Ritz-Carlton remain in business and maintain strong financial performance because of their commitment to customer satisfaction.

The reasons to emphasize customer service introduced in this section underscore the attention needed to be given to all facets of the customer experience. With this chapter's focus on communication, we now turn to a discussion of best practices to deliver outstanding communication with customers.

Getting It Right the First Time

A global survey conducted by consulting firm Accenture confirmed that superior customer service is characterized by the quality and competence of service personnel (Sprague 2009). How-tos for customer service are well documented in a multitude of sources, including generic training books and manuals, textbooks, organizational case studies, and company specific materials. However, this content is fitting for the current chapter for a review and comprehensive understanding of customer communication. When customers are communicated with in a respectful, cordial manner from the beginning of the interaction to the end, many problems can be alleviated and customers will have a positive experience. This section addresses several aspects of communication that boost service providers from average to exceptional by following an interaction from greetings to the transaction, then shifting to discuss (1) specific words and phrases to use, (2) words and phrases to avoid, and (3) stylistic ways to deliver messages.

Greetings

The greeting is the first point of contact between the customer and service provider, and it sets the tone for the rest of the interaction. Therefore, it is important that every customer be extended a greeting as soon as possible. The greeting should be friendly, prompt, and sincere and guide the customer to the next step in using the organization's services. The words used could include hello, welcome, or some other company specific wording. Follow this greeting with a lead such as, "How can I help you today?" or "What can we do for you?" Here, the customer is invited to share with the service provider and convey his/her needs.

Service providers face a dilemma when they are serving one customer and another one approaches. In these situations, service providers should excuse themselves from the current customer, acknowledge the new customer, and return to the original customer. When additional service providers are available, initiative should be demonstrated by the service provider with two customers by asking for assistance. When customers call on the telephone while the service provider is with a customer, the service provider has the option to let the call go to voicemail or take the call. Managers should evaluate their respective client base and discuss expectations so service providers will know how to juggle this situation.

Using customers' names can be powerful, as well. Carnegie (1936) said, "Remember that a person's name is to that person the sweetest and most important sound in any language" (83). It is the service provider's responsibility to take the initiative and ask for the customer's name when the industry warrants this personal touch. A cashier at Walgreen's would not be expected to ask for a customer's name but a mechanic or hairstylist would have this expectation. Repeat customers at any type of organization appreciate being known by name. So, if the Walgreen's cashier notices the same shopper every Wednesday morning, the shopper would likely appreciate being known by name. When service providers forget customers' names, an easy phrase to get the information again is, "Tell me your name again." This phrase requests the information and acknowledges that you have received it previously. People are usually flattered to be called by name and by efforts to remember the name. The greeting gradually progresses to the actual transaction where the service is provided.

The Transaction

After the greeting has been extended to the customer, the transaction will proceed.

HARRAH'S CASINOS

Harrah's Casinos evaluates service providers in three phases of guest interaction: welcome, build relationships, and bring them back.

Customers should be asked what they need and the service provider then proceeds to meet that need. As the transaction evolves, there are at least eight basic principles to follow:

1. Remain focused on the positive. Statements to customers should be about what the organization can do and how the customers' needs will be met.
2. Be specific by using the 5W1H approach. Use questions beginning with who, what, when, where, why, or how as appropriate to get information from the customer that the provider needs to complete the transaction. There are times when customers have a need, but they aren't aware of the steps involved or the choices they have to get their needs met.

ASKING QUESTIONS

When I purchased a dishwasher from Lowe's recently, my need was to get one that worked. The service provider asked me questions about the color options, plumbing connections, installation services, and dishwasher disposal, four aspects I had not thought about before setting out to replace my old dishwasher. These questions helped me see there was more involved with the purchase. As a result, I was a satisfied customer when I had a color that matched my other appliances, the right connector hoses, an installer set up through Lowe's, and the disposal of my old dishwasher.

---

3. Paraphrase back to the customer to confirm that the request has been understood. Restating an order at a restaurant or drive-through window is one way to confirm that orders are correct.
4. Use positively phrased questions. Lucas (2005) provides these examples of positively phrased questions (Table 4.1).
5. Ask the customer's permission before you make any change in the conversation. For example, ask a customer if you can place him/her on hold. Some customers might not have the time to hold and elect to call back.
6. Find opportunities to state "I agree" when interacting with customers. This simple phrase lets customers know their ideas are valid. For example, a customer who is decorating a living room may need to hear "I agree that you want to have three objects in a grouping."
7. Ask questions to get feedback. Ask customers if an item you found meets their needs.
8. Close the transaction professionally. Thank customers for their business, let them know you are glad they chose you, and invite them to return again or to refer you to others.

Table 4.1 Positively Phrased Questions

Instead of	Try
Why do you feel that way?	What makes you feel that way?
Why don't you like . . .?	What is it that you don't like about . . .?
Why do you need that feature?	How is that feature going to be beneficial to you?
Why do you want that color?	What other colors have you considered?
Don't you think . . .?	What do you think . . .?
Aren't you going to make a deposit?	What amount would you like to deposit?

The eight items in this list provide an overview of what to say during an interaction with a customer. Additional details of what to say follow.

What to Say

The messages delivered by service providers can follow a script or flow freely and spontaneously. This section discusses the advantages and disadvantages of using scripts, then addresses other aspects of what to say during a service encounter. Specifically, you-centered language is introduced and how to translate company jargon is mentioned.

Many organizations will prepare scripts for service providers to use, which are both beneficial and detrimental to customer communication. Advantages of using scripts include consistency and quality control. Consider the customer call center with dozens of customer service representatives (CSRs) fielding hundreds of calls in a day. The sheer volume of calls increases the probability for service issues. Further, most of these calls are made by dissatisfied customers to begin with. When organizations prepare scripts for these CSRs, they have a unified way of training CSRs to respond to customers and present a consistent, uniform approach to responding to customers' concerns. The disadvantage of scripts is the lack of spontaneity noted in the voices of the CSRs. Many of them are focused on getting the words right and following a protocol, which consequently miss the connection with the customer. The Starbucks approach to service deviates from scripted communication by using the "Five Ways of Being": be welcoming, be genuine, be considerate, be knowledgeable, and be involved. Employees are encouraged to communicate in ways that reflect the "Five Ways of Being" that suit each employee's personality and unique communication style.

Whether an organization chooses to use a script or not, you-centered language can enhance interactions with customers. You-centered communication shows listeners that their needs and wants are being attended to. It is achieved by literally using "you" language in phrases such as, "You can find that brand in aisle 8." You-centered language is one way to show customers that service providers are interested and concerned about their well-being and experience. Phrasing sentences with you-centered language is simple, subtle, and powerful. Notice the comparison between these phrases in Table 4.2.

You-centered language should be reflected throughout the entire service transaction. In addition, words that customers understand will be important because company jargon can create barriers between the customer and the service provider.

Organizations develop their own unique language or vocabulary referred to as jargon. These words or phrases help internal members of the organization conduct work in meaningful ways that reflect the mission and unity of the organization. However, these words and phrases do little to help the customer. Service providers have one of two options. First, change the language used. Speak in terms that customers understand, even if organizational members use different terms. Second, use the jargon and then explain this terminology to the customer. This option would be helpful if you anticipate the customer will have future correspondence regarding the same product or service. For example, if an attorney suggests a retainer, but the client has never worked with an attorney before, this word could be unfamiliar and require explanation. Or, first-time home buyers are inundated with new processes and procedures that have their own set of terms that realtors are quite familiar with. A conscientious real-

Table 4.2   You-Centered Language

Typical Messages	You-Centered Language
I'll get that right out to you.	Your order will be ready in five minutes.
I can show you these alternate styles.	You might like these alternate styles.
When I'm finished with this customer, I'll be right with you.	You are the next customer to be served.

tor will spend time explaining the process and corresponding terms with a first-time home buyer.

In brief, getting it right the first time means extending a greeting, attending to the transaction, and using you-centered language with terms customers understand. There are also phrases and words that should be avoided during customer interactions.

What Not to Say

What not to say can be categorized in three ways: (1) avoid negative information, (2) avoid small, yet powerful words, and (3) eliminate customer pet peeves. Customers rarely like to hear negative information and there are certain phrases to avoid to minimize the negativity. First, customers don't want to hear what the service provider can't do. Responding to a customer's request by saying "I can't do that" even if the intention is to be helpful irritates most customers. Customers aren't interested in what can't be done. They are seeking results. Instead, focus on what can be done. For example, the service provider could say "Manager X can help you with that. If you'll wait here for just a moment, she/he will be with you."

Second, avoid global terms such as always, everyone, or no one. These words, found to be used by pessimists (Seligman 1998), sound absolute or inaccurate, which create doubt in the minds of customers. Is it really true that "everyone" follows the incorrect procedures?

Third, patronizing speech should be avoided. Patronizing speech is characterized as slow, oversimplified, polite, and overly warm (Nussbaum et al. 1996). This form of speech has also been called baby talk because of the high pitch and rising intonation at the end of a statement. The elderly are often spoken to in this way by nursing home or assisted care service providers and the elderly report low levels of satisfaction and disrespect (Giles, Fox, and Smith 1993; Ryan, Hamilton, and See 1994) when talked to in this manner. Other customers, too, are likely to feel belittled and talked down to when service providers use patronizing speech.

Fourth, avoid verbal finger pointing. When a service failure has occurred, customers do not want to hear who made the mistake. The customer sees the entire organization and pointing fingers at other people/departments diminishes the credibility of the organization and shows a lack of communication within the company. While the individual service provider may be trying to save face, the whole organization suffers. Organizations should devote time to understand where and why service failures occur, but this information is usually not appropriate to share with the customer.

While negative phrases should be avoided, there are also some words that are short, yet emotionally charged. This section discusses four of these small but powerful words and pointers on how to use them in the customer communication context: should, but, they, and why.

Should. Avoid telling customers what they *should* have done. When a product or service failure has occurred, the customer knows about the failure and does not want to be told how he or she made the failure occur. What has happened is in the past and customer satisfaction does not benefit from telling customers what they should have done. There are ways to correct operator error without "shoulding" the customer. For example, the service provider could say, "The next time you use the product, try following this procedure."

But. Yes, *but* statements are designed with the best of intentions, but the *but* negates the original statement. Telling a customer, "that outfit looks fantastic on you, but you need a different pair of shoes" tells the customer that the outfit does not look great after all. Therefore, substitute the word *and* for *but.* Tell the customer, "That outfit looks fantastic on you, and these shoes would go great with it!" This simple change in wording also creates opportunities for upselling!

They. Who is *they?* This word is used a lot in everyday language and has carried over into business communication. Be specific with customers to show competence and convey confidence. When service providers say "they added on another surcharge" to explain an item on a bill, the vague "they" leaves the customer uncertain about the service provider and the organization. Rephrase this statement by saying, "The airline added another surcharge."

Why. Another small but powerful word is *why,* spoken as the accusatory question. Asking why a customer is interested in a particular product or feature is helpful. Asking a customer why he didn't use primer when painting a wall sounds accusatory and puts the customer on the defensive. These simple changes in wording can have a positive impact on the perceptions of customers' experiences with service providers.

While avoiding negativity and small, powerful words, service providers should also strive to avoid customer pet peeves. Customers don't like excessive wait times, service providers who have an unprofessional appearance or are chewing gum or tobacco products. The attitude of the service provider is important, as well. Customers have a disdain for service providers who seem disinterested in serving altogether and those who are blatantly rude. Customers also want to have the phone answered in less than four rings and they get annoyed when they are abruptly placed on hold. Service providers who do not have the requisite knowledge or authority to serve the customer are also annoying to customers. Finally, overfamiliarity can be a pet peeve. The server who calls her customers "honey" or "sweetie" may seem to be friendly and cordial, but many customers find this too personal and invasive.

Thus far, getting the service encounter right the first time has focused on the greeting, the transaction, what to say, and what not to say. The last component of the transaction includes stylistic characteristics of how to deliver messages.

How to Say It

How to deliver messages to customers can be summarized by discussing sociality communication and communication climate, turning first to sociality communication.

Communication researchers have analyzed sociality communication, defined as "performance that encourages a cooperative, social smoothness, void of intense interactions with others" (Pancanowsky and O'Donnell-Trujillo 1983, 139–40) as a means to interact with customers. Implementing sociality requires emphasis on four types of messages: courtesies, pleasantries, sociabilities, and privacies. Courtesies include greetings and thank yous and are characterized by warmth and friendliness. Pleasantries are synonymous with small talk. Sociabilities extend beyond small talk into joking, gossiping, or complaining. Privacies include sharing personal information as well as demonstrating support, consolation, or confession. Analysis of these four categories of service communication reduced them to two overarching types of service called personal connection (pleasantries, sociabilities, and privacies) and courteous expressions (Koermer, Ford, and Brant 2000). Personal connection and courteous expressions are both associated with customer satisfaction across different types of service industries, although courteous expressions were more important to predicting customer satisfaction with professional service providers (i.e., doctor and hairstylist-barber; Koermer 2005). Further analysis of physicians confirms that courteous expressions contribute to satisfaction more than personal connections (Koermer and Kilbane 2008). Courteous expressions and personal connection have also been found to be associated with customer loyalty (Koermer and McCroskey 2006). These studies indicate that being courteous is very important to ensuring customer satisfaction and loyalty. Making personal connections is associated with satisfaction and loyalty, and does not appear to be evaluated as heavily by customers.

Communication climate is the second concept that can be used to describe how to deliver messages to customers. Communication climates were described by Gibb (1961) as either supportive or defensive. Getting along with others in organizational settings can be achieved quite well in a supportive communication climate. Gibb (1961) observed employees in several national organizations and observed general tendencies among people to create a work environment that was either supportive or defensive. In a supportive communication climate, individuals are valued, cherished, and respected. Supportive climates are important for many contexts, including customer service. By contrast, a defensive communication environment is marked by individuals who feel rejected, disrespected, and invalidated. To describe these tendencies, Gibb contrasted sets of communication behaviors to show how supportive communicators convey their messages when compared to those who speak defensively. Table 4.3 shows six sets of these characteristics with the supportive qualities on the left and the defensive qualities on the right. Characteristics are understood best when compared with the quality in the same row. For example, descriptive language is understood best when compared to evaluative language.

Supportive communicators use descriptive language and make genuine requests for information. They are willing to experiment, investigate issues and solve problems. Their comments are honest and spontaneous without complication. Collaboration, gaining input, and extending reassurances and understanding are also invoked by supportive communicators. Those who are supportive also attach little significance to differences in status, talent, or ability.

Defensive communicators speak in an accusatory tone and blame others when bad things happen. They are often arrogant and stubborn, act like know-it-alls, and have to win arguments. Their motivations for communication are deceptive or ambiguous. Control is evident in defensive communicators as they assume inadequacy among those they are talking to. They might also suggest highly restrictive policies and pay too much attention to detail. Emotionally, they seem detached and clinical in their interactions. Defensive communicators will also one-up the person they are speaking with and believe they don't need help.

These qualities of supportive and defensive communication climates are not all inclusive. People are likely to exhibit some attributes of all these descriptors at one point or another. The best way to use these descriptions is to focus on the supportive communication characteristics and apply them to interactions with customers.

This section emphasized the qualities of service interactions that are important for consistent, high-quality customer service. In addition to the verbal messages that service providers offer, they also need to attend to their listening and nonverbal communication skills.

Table 4.3 Comparing Supportive and Defensive Communication Climates

Supportive	Defensive
Descriptive	*Evaluation*
Genuine requests for information	Accusatory tone, blame
I language, you seem	Place others in categories
	Too, very, you should
Provisionalism/flexible	*Certainty/rigid*
Willing to experiment	Arrogant, stubborn
Investigates issues	Know-it-all
Solves problems	Has to win an argument
	Low tolerance for opposite opinion
Spontaneity/genuine	*Strategy/manipulation*
Straightforward, honest	Ambiguous motivations
React spontaneously to situations	Withhold information
Uncomplicated motives	Deceptive
Problem orientation	*Control*
Collaborate, get input	Try to change with hidden motives
What do you think about . . .?	Assumes target is inadequate
	Too much attention to detail
	Restrictive policies
Empathy	*Neutrality/detached*
Convey worth of listener	Detached, clinical
Reassuring, understanding	Lack of concern
	"Don't feel bad"
Equality	*Superiority*
Attaches little importance to differences in talent, ability, status, etc.	One upper
	Won't jointly solve a problem
	Resistant to feedback
	Doesn't need help

Listening Skills

Listening skills are also vital to customer communication. These skills are essential to ensuring accuracy and achieving shared meaning between the customer and service provider. Listening was one of four deficient communication skills rated serious and frequent in a study of auditors by their clients (Golen, Catanach, and Moeckel 1997). The first step in discussing listening is to distinguish between hearing and listening. Hearing is the physical ability to receive sounds. Here, service providers need to ensure that distracting noises are reduced as much as possible. It is the service providers' responsibility to turn down music, close doors, or quiet other patrons to adequately serve customers. By contrast, listening is the cognitive process of interpreting information received and trying to understand the needs and wants of the customer. After securing the physical ability to hear, service providers need to attend to their customers by making and maintaining eye contact and using facial gestures that convey genuine interest. Then, the customer needs to process the information received and respond to the customer accordingly.

One of the challenges with listening is that people speak on average 125–150 words per minute but the brain can process 4–6 times that amount of information. It is easy to get distracted or prepare a response while the customer is still talking. Therefore, a good listener will be focused, responsive, alert, understanding, caring, empathetic, interested, patient, cautious, and open.

Good listeners also work to minimize barriers to effective listening. These barriers are either internal or external. Internal barriers include personal biases, psychological issues going on with the service provider, physical issues such as sickness, circadian rhythm, preoccupation, or hearing loss. External barriers include information overload, other people talking, ringing tones, speakerphones, or equipment.

To improve listening, service providers can stop talking, prepare, listen for concepts, be patient and open, take notes, and ask questions. Further, they can strive to engage in active listening or mindful listening.

Active listening is "an attempt to demonstrate unconditional acceptance and unbiased reflection. Active listening requires that the listener try to understand the speaker's own understanding of an experience without the listener's own interpretive structures intruding on his or her understanding of the other person" (Weger, Castle, and Emmett 2010, 35). Service providers can use active listening to convey to customers that they are being listened to carefully. To demonstrate active listening, service providers can smile, minimize interruptions, use good posture, lean toward the customer, paraphrase, nod, and use affirming language.

Mindful listening is "the ability to receive the spoken word accurately, retain information, sustain attention, attend to your own responsive speech, and encourage the speaker" (Shafir 2009, 219). This skill is important for service providers, particularly those who hear repeated questions over and over again. It is understandable that a service provider would become complacent with customers after hearing the same questions or concerns repeatedly. Customers will need to be trained well and receive frequent reminders that each customer is a person with individual wants and needs. While products or services are second nature to organizational members, the client may be experiencing the product or service for the first time and needs reassurance, validation, or information. Thus, maintaining an attitude of service and desire to help others are crucial skills for service providers in these types of service roles. For example, employees at colleges and universities who work in student support areas such as admissions, transfer centers, financial assistance, or cashiering hear repeated inquiries from thousands of students and their parents. These staff members should strive for mindfulness and awareness that each student comes from a different background and is unfamiliar with university processes and jargon.

Nonverbal Communication

Nonverbal communication messages arguably comprise the majority of a receiver's understanding of a given message (Birdwhistell 1970; Mehrabian 1972). For example, Starbuck's manager Lisa Lenahan commented on the importance of observing nonverbal communication when she said, "There's an art to knowing if your customers are displeased. You can read their body language, and you should be able to take care of concerns before you are even asked. If [customers] are tapping their foot or crossing their arms, you should already know that something is not quite right" (Michelli 2006, 145). This section reviews the major categories of nonverbal communication behaviors and provides suggestions for how to display these cues when interacting with customers: proxemics, kinesics, oculesics, facial expressions, chronemics, vocalics, haptics, and physical appearance.

Proxemics

Proxemics are nonverbal communication behaviors that refer to the physical distance between those who are communicating. Hall (1959) described four zones of interpersonal distance that are generally maintained by people in the United States. These zones include the intimate zone (3 to 6 inches), the personal zone (8 to 20 inches), the social/work zone (20 inches to 5 feet), and the public zone (5½ to 8 feet). Service providers should be aware of these social norms and strive for the personal or social zone, whichever is most appropriate for the industry and physical space where the interaction occurs. Standing too close to a customer while checking out new electronic devices at the local Best Buy will likely make the customer feel uncomfortable and perhaps leave the store.

Kinesics

Kinesics are those nonverbal gestures that involve body motion. These include posture, head nodding, gestures, and the handshake, among others. Movements service providers should avoid include fidgeting, crossing arms, and holding hands near the mouth (this gesture leads to distrust). The ways in which kinesic movements are performed is important for above-average customer communication. For example, the posture should be straight with a forward lean toward the customer. The head should nod in agreement when the service provider is in agreement or to signify acknowledgment of information. Gestures should be open and inviting. For example, a service provider could span his/her arms when a customer enters the organization. A handshake is important in particular situations. When you work in an industry where you shake hands with the customer, make sure the handshake is initiated by the service provider and firm.

Oculesics

Oculesics is another term for eye contact. Eye contact is a powerful way to connect with a customer. Generally, maintain eye contact for 5–10 seconds, then glance a way. Any more eye contact is perceived as staring, which makes others uncomfortable. Any less eye contact is perceived as lack of caring or distrust.

Facial Expressions

Facial expressions include movement of the eyebrows, eyelids, nose, and mouth. These parts of the face move in conjunction with each other to send messages, many of which are emotions (Eckman 2003). Further, these facial expressions that convey emotion are argued to be innate and universal (Eckman 2003). Therefore, service providers need to be aware of their emotions and do their best to be genuine. Counterfeit emotions attempted during a service interaction could be noted by the customer and the insincerity diminishes the attempt at positive customer communication.

The smile is a specific facial expression that has tremendous impact with customer communication. Smiling is perceived as welcoming, courteous, friendly, and helpful (Muir 2008). Customers will appreciate the service provided by those who genuinely smile. In fact, smiling is so powerful that service providers on the telephone are encouraged to smile while talking. Even though the customer cannot see the service provider, the positive changes to the voice that accompany a smile can be detected by the customer.

Chronemics

Chronemics encompass all aspects of the use of time. While wait times and throughput time are key indicators of performance for responses to customers, the aspect most closely related to communication includes how wait times are expressed to customers. For example, the restaurant industry frequently tells customers that the wait is longer than anticipated. Then, when the wait time is shorter than they were told, they are pleasantly surprised and have a positive reaction. However, when the doctor's office tells patients there is a 20-minute wait and the actual wait time is 1 hour, patients become agitated. Realistic wait times are important to communicate for positive customer reactions.

> **COMPARISONS OF ACCEPTABLE WAIT TIMES IN A PHYSICIAN'S OFFICE**
>
> A survey of physicians and patients found that 86 percent of patients believed the maximum wait time should be 30 minutes. By contrast, 27 percent of physicians believed the maximum wait time should be 30 minutes whereas 18 percent believed it should be 45 minutes and 54 percent believed the maximum wait time should be 60 minutes (as cited in Ford and Snyder 2000).

Vocalics

Vocalics or vocal cues include any aspect of sound delivered from the mouth without forming words. Several vocal cues impact customer communication. First, the tone of voice needs to be positive, upbeat, sincere, and friendly. Second, the tone needs to convey strength and confidence. Third, the volume should be loud enough so the customers can hear, but not so loud so as to draw unnecessary attention to the customer. Fourth, the rate of speech should also be set to meet customers' expectations. Fast speakers, especially when their voices are amplified through microphones, can be difficult to understand. Fifth, vocal quality can be important, as well. Matching service providers' voices to the industry and customer type will be valuable. A forceful voice at a spa would not be well received, but a soothing, calm voice would do little to build the confidence of a customer at a hardware store! Sixth, articulation is another vocal cue to consider. People who mumble or do not open their mouths articulate poorly and are difficult to understand. In brief, these vocal elements seem to be simple yet how many of the readers can recall an interaction with a service provider when one or more of these vocal elements diminished your ability to understand a service provider? Managers have a responsibility to train, coach, and correct these aspects of the voice to ensure customers can understand the messages given by service providers.

Haptics

Haptics refers to touch. Touch used by service providers can be helpful when used appropriately. The doctor who gives a reassuring pat on a patient's arm shows genuine concern. The funeral home director who puts her arm around grieving family members shows comfort and compassion. However, the cashier at a mall store who touches the hand of a customer when giving a receipt would be violating the customer's expectation, or the appliance salesman who puts his arm around a customer could likely be headed for a sexual harassment lawsuit! Some people are very comfortable with touch and have positive intentions. However, their expressions, when used with strangers, can make customers uncomfortable. Therefore, this aspect of nonverbal communication warrants a specific discussion with service providers about the expectations of the industry and customers.

Physical Appearance

Appearance is another aspect of nonverbal communication that is highly context specific as well as controversial. Whether organizations use uniforms or have a dress code, the overriding elements expected by customers include neat and clean grooming, attention to personal hygiene, and appropriate hairstyles, make-up, jewelry, body piercings, tattoos, or facial hair. Industry and safety standards vary for each of these characteristics of appearance. Have clear expectations for service providers. Make them aware of the appropriate standards for appearance and why these standards are important for customer service.

Despite the efforts of managers to train service providers to get it right the first time by emphasizing what to say, what not to say, how to say it, listening, and using nonverbal communication skills, there are some customers who create challenges for the best-trained service providers. The next section introduces difficult customers, followed by a section on service recovery.

Difficult Customers

Not all customers are alike, and this variety can create challenging situations for service providers. Some customers are cooperative and will seek a solution to a problem. Some are indecisive and don't know what they want. Some are angry and demanding. This segment discusses strategies to use with different types of customers, specifically angry, indecisive, demanding, and rude customers.

Angry customers need to be acknowledged and reassured that they are heard and will be attended to. Service providers need to remain calm and objective with angry customers and ask questions to determine the cause of the problem. Active listening (see description earlier in the chapter) is particularly important with angry customers and can help reduce frustration. Angry customers may need to feel as if they are part of the problem-solving process and may appreciate negotiation during resolution. Follow-up will be especially useful with angry customers to continue to diffuse their dissatisfaction with the organization.

TALKING WITH ANGRY CUSTOMERS

The customer is trying to get help with a computer problem he's experiencing. He's been through a number of "phone menus" and has been unable to reach a human or voicemail. (The mailbox is full.) He finally figures out how to speak to a live human being and he's exceedingly annoyed.

Customer:	What the heck is wrong with you people? I've been going around and around in your voicemail system and I haven't been able to leave a voicemail so I can get some help. I should be able to contact you without having to spend all my money on long-distance charges.
Service Provider:	I am going to help you and I apologize if you've been having problems with our phone system. You're right that this shouldn't happen. Since you've already spent so much time on the phone, can I ask you a few questions so I can help you?
Customer:	Damn right this shouldn't happen! I need help and I need it right away, and I don't deserve to be going around in circles.
Service Provider:	You're right. I'm sure you want that help now, so let me ask you some questions. Are you calling about a technical problem with a computer?
Customer:	Yes.
Service Provider:	OK . . . (Bacal 2005).

Some customers may not be dissatisfied, but they aren't satisfied either when they are at an impasse and cannot make a decision. The indecisive customer knows the overall need as in, I need a new couch, but has difficulty making an actual selection. Indecisive customers look and often ask a lot of questions. They may leave and deliberate and come back or call and ask more questions. They may fear making a mistake or not liking something after their selection has been made. When communicating with these customers, patience will come to the foreground as an important attribute. Asking open-ended questions or making suggestions will guide the customer in the decision-making process. Provide detailed information to confirm how the product or service works. Allow the customer to try samples where possible. Combine you-centered messages and reassurance to the customer using statements such as "You will find that this product . . ." "You will be pleased with the support you will receive after you make your purchase . . ." To guide in the decision making, you can ask "Have you considered . . ." "Have you thought about . . .?" Or stating your opinion, "I think you would like . . ." "It seems you want this one. I think that's a good choice for you."

Demanding and/or domineering customers can be particularly difficult for service providers who have a strong service orientation and want to be helpful. These customers require service providers who remain professional and show respect to the customer. Balancing firmness and fairness is the great challenge with demanding customers. Focusing on the customers' needs and reinforcing what the service provider *can* do for the customer will be helpful.

TALKING WITH DEMANDING CUSTOMERS

The customer is upset because her auto insurance company has offered her much lower compensation for damage to her vehicle than she wanted. After the employee informs her of the settlement offer, she becomes exceedingly angry and, after arguing her case unsuccessfully, starts demanding to talk with the president of the insurance company, who is actually located in another city.

Customer: I've been paying these ridiculous premiums for over 20 years, and this is the third time I've ever made a claim, and you're trying to screw me. I'm through wasting my time with you underlings. I want to speak to the president and I want to speak to him now.

Service Provider:	It's clear you're disappointed in the figures, Mrs. Jones, and I can understand you want to speak to someone you think might be able to help.
Customer:	Damn right! And you aren't going to help much. So, let me speak to the president.
Service Provider:	That would be Maria Pollock, the president of Loveme Insurance. If you want to go that route, instead of something that might be faster and easier for you, I'd be glad to help you get in touch with her. Before I do that, do you want to consider other options first?
Customer:	No, I don't want any "options." I want this Maria Pollock person.
Service Provider:	OK. That's up to you. Maria Pollock is located at the head office in Lubbock. You have a few options that I can help you with. You can phone her office, send her a fax, or write a letter outlining your concerns. If you tell me what you'd prefer, I can give you the information.
Customer:	I want to speak to her *now,* right *now.*
Service Provider:	OK. I understand you want fast action. I'm going to write the president's name and toll-free number down for you, along with your file/incident number and related information. That way you won't have to pay for long distance and you'll have the information you'll need when you speak to her office.
Customer:	Why can't you just call now and give me the phone?
Service Provider:	I'm sure you would prefer to have some privacy for your conversation and be able to call at your convenience.
Customer:	Well, OK.
Service Provider:	If you decide you'd like additional information, please feel free to get in touch with me. And also, if you'd let me know how it goes, I would appreciate that. Anything else we need to do right now?
Customer:	No, I guess not.
Service Provider:	OK. I'm sorry we couldn't come to some agreement. Good luck! (Bacal 2005).

Rude/inconsiderate customers, like the demanding customer, create difficulties for service providers. Service providers should remain professional, avoid retaliation, and rise above the inconsiderate behavior of the customer.

When Things Go Wrong, as They Sometimes Do

Despite careful hiring of service-oriented staff members followed by customer service training, service failures are inevitable. The ability of service providers to respond to these issues is critically important. Sometimes it is through service recovery that customers become highly satisfied or loyal.

A typology of dissatisfied customers helps organizations understand the different responses dissatisfied customers are likely to take after a service failure. Four different types of dissatisfied customers were suggested by Singh (1990; see Figure 4.1): passives, voicers, irates, and activists. *Passives* accounted for 14 percent of Singh's ample ($n = 465$). These dissatisfied customers tell very few people about their dissatisfaction, not even their own network of friends. *Voicers,* who made up 37 percent, complain to the organization without the intent to switch service providers. *Irates* made up 21 percent of the sample. These dissatisfied customers complain to the organization, tell their friends, and switch to another service provider. *Activists* comprise 28 percent of the dissatisfieds. They complain *and* take action outside the organization such as contacting the Better Business Bureau, the media, or a website.

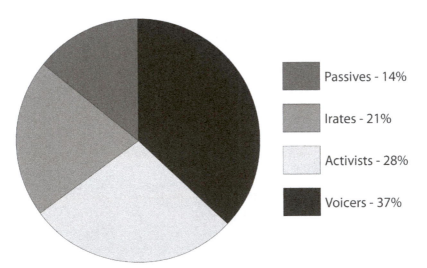

Figure 4.1 Summary of Tables

There are also customers that organizations don't want. The for-profit sector can strategically target its desired customer and find ways to let unwanted customers go. Some argue, "The customer is always right." Southwest Airlines CEO Herb Kelleher has a different perspective. He argues, "No, they [customers] are not. I think that's one of the biggest betrayals of employees a boss can possibly commit. The customer is sometimes wrong. We don't carry those sorts of customers. We write them and say, 'Fly somebody else. Don't abuse our people'" (Freiberg and Freiberg 1996, 268). Managers need to balance the dignity of service providers with keeping customers. If some customers cause too many problems, take some time to evaluate the return on the customer. Perhaps the organization can let a customer go and invest its energy and resources into other customers.

Soliciting Complaints

The idea of soliciting complaints sounds counterintuitive. However, when organizations treat a complaint as a gift (Barlow, Moller, and Hsieh 2008), the organization receives information that can help them make improvements to their processes and services. Customer relationship management (Fitzgerald and Doerfel 2004) is a "business strategy aimed at building and maintaining long-term relationships with customers through two-way communication, gathering and storing information regarding consumer preferences, and using the information to meet both parties' goals" (232). By contrast, customer handling refers to placating unhappy customers. It is therefore important to provide avenues for customers to share their complaints and for the customer to get feedback indicating the appreciation and value of the information. Organizations need to let customers know they want feedback. JCPenney associates regularly ask customers for feedback by asking the customer to fill out an online survey, circling the web address on the receipt, and handwriting their names on the receipt so that customers will remember who served them. This practice lets customers know that JCPenney is interested in their opinions about the service. Other ways to solicit feedback from customers include providing toll-free numbers, web addresses with places to submit information, or the direct question to the customer during a face-to-face interaction. Asking a customer, "What do you think of our service?" with a genuine tone lets the customer know his/her ideas are wanted. The standard "How is everything" asked by the servers at restaurants conveys the right idea, but the tone seldom invites a sincere dialogue about the quality of the food or service. Other options to solicit feedback include customer comment cards placed in strategic locations in the organization's facilities that customers can pick up and fill out. Providing a convenient location to send completed forms makes it easy for the customer to get the information to the respective person at the organization.

Staff members also need to be aware of what they can do when they receive feedback from customers. Service providers can be trained to respond favorably to customer complaints, but are they empowered to take the next step and alert management about the opportunity for improvement? Ritz Carlton employees are trusted with $2,000 per guest per day to engage in service enhancement or recovery efforts (Michelli 2008). Service providers are often good at fixing a problem in the short term. However, an organization that is highly responsive will also make sure service providers can voice their concerns and share customers' experiences to look for ways to make improvements in the product or service that meet customers' needs. Calling customers after a purchase or interaction with the organization is another way to solicit information. Lowe's calls customers after they have had an appliance installed to gauge the quality and professionalism of the installer. Short surveys can be used, especially if the organization serves many customers. Small business owners may be able to have an informal conversation to get input. The phone call also has an advantage over e-mailed surveys because of the personal contact and opportunity for the customer to provide explanations to answers. Customer informants are another way for managers to evaluate service providers. Mystery shoppers have been utilized in the retail and hospitality industries for years and are a way to gather evidence about the service provided. This approach needs to be done multiple times because one person's experience may not provide the depth of information needed to understand systemic issues in the organization. One cashier may provide outstanding service because of prior training with another organization, not because of specific training offered by the current organization. When possible, visiting the customer while using the product can be helpful. John Deere service technicians schedule ride-alongs with new tractor owners to serve the dual purpose of training the farmer to operate the equipment and to get information from the farmer about the functionality of the equipment. Finally, an organization will need to repeatedly ask customers to provide feedback. Just as marketers repeatedly send messages to prospective clients, existing customers also need repeated messages to understand the seriousness and value placed upon getting information from customers.

Service Recovery

There are several ways to respond to dissatisfied customers. The response has important consequences for customer satisfaction and loyalty.

For example, when customers' problems are fixed, they report very high customer satisfaction but when service providers blame others for problems, customer satisfaction is low (Punyanunt-Carter, Planisek, and Cornette 2006). Further, organizations that have decreased their customer defection rate by 5 percent increased their profitability by as much as 20 percent (Reichheld and Sasser 1990). Here is a suggested eight-step approach to service recovery:

1. Say thank you—tell the customer you are glad to receive the information and know about their issues. Remember, a complaint is a gift.
2. Explain why the complaint is appreciated.
3. Apologize. The apology should focus on the experience and not make the service provider feel personally responsible. For example, tell the customer, "I'm sorry to hear your new water heater isn't working properly" instead of "I'm so sorry." The personal I'm sorry statement makes the service provider sound accountable for actions he or she had no control over and can diminish credibility. However, the customer expects to hear an apology and being specific about the issue focuses on the incident, rather than the people. However, if the service provider did make a mistake and is with the customer, then personal responsibility is expected by extending a personal apology for a mistake or service failure.
4. Promise to do something immediately. Customers expect problems to be solved quickly. At a minimum, they expect to know that their issue is being attended to. Telling a customer who returned with a radiator that still isn't fixed that it will be two more weeks before the car can be looked at again is not going to make the auto owner happy. Perhaps the car cannot be fixed today, but it should be started as soon as possible and the customer should know the car will be looked at soon. Of course, these promises should be honest answers, not information the customer wants to hear. Giving a customer known misinformation to string them along makes customers angry.
5. Ask for necessary information. Taking the time to gather relevant information will increase the likelihood that the issue will be resolved accurately and to the customer's satisfaction.
6. Take action. The customer may need to provide specific information about the service failure so asking for necessary information may be warranted. However, if the customer has been passed through multiple service providers, minimize the repetitive questions by documenting information or telling the next service provider what the issue is. When customers tell several members of an organization the same story about their faulty product or service, they relive their frustration with the service failure and increase their frustration by retelling the story.
7. Correct the mistake as quickly as possible ensuring accuracy and safety. One participant in a research study noted that when her food order was

improperly prepared, she received an apology, a free replacement meal, and a gift certificate to return (Punyanunt-Carter, Planisek, and Cornette 2006).

8. Check customer satisfaction by following up with the customer to make sure the service recovery was successful. Then, take preventive measures to prevent future mistakes. Fixing a problem one time does not keep the issue from happening again. Organizations must be proactive by identifying areas of service failure and correcting issues to keep them from happening again.

This eight-step approach provides an overview of considerations for service recovery. When conflict escalates, particularly with clients who have a high degree of interdependence with the organization, an approach called "the script" provides one suggested pattern of statements to make. After reading *Why Am I Afraid to Tell You Who I Am?* by psychologist John Powell (1969) and *Nonviolent Communication* by Marshall Rosenberg (2005), the script emerged as a communication skill I've used personally and recommended to interpersonal communication students. The script also has useful applications to organizational environments when modified appropriately. The script includes a series of four statements that guide a person through disclosing his/her needs or wants during a conflict or difficult situation. Each statement begins with a particular I-statement and is introduced in the following text:

"*I Noticed.*" The I noticed statement is designed for the speaker to tell the recipient about an observed behavior. The focus with this statement is that it relies on evidence such as observed statements or behaviors. It does not rely on assumptions or opinions. This approach is particularly helpful for conflict communication because it diminishes hostile mind reading (Gottman 1994) and focuses on actual events. For example, a service provider might say to a customer, "I noticed you were very angry when you came into the store." You could modify this statement by saying "You seem . . ." Here, you are focused on your own perception without accusing the person or making an assumption about his or her behavior, which could put the person on the defensive and escalate the person's anger. For example, the service provider could say, "You seem angry" or "You seem dissatisfied." This allows the service provider to state his/her observation or perception, which conveys to the recipient the basis for subsequent statements.

"*I Thought.*" The I thought statement allows the speaker to express what his/her understanding or expectation for the behavior was. For example, a service provider might say, "I thought you understood the procedures for using the product after our discussion yesterday." This usage of the word "thought" is a literal interpretation. It is not intended to convey an opinion as people commonly say "I think" when expressing an opinion or idea.

"I Feel." The I feel statement gives the speaker the opportunity to convey his/her feelings about the situation, to show the effect of the person's behavior as identified in statement one. For example, a service provider might say, "I feel uncomfortable talking to people who are this angry." In reality, the use of feeling statements is often discouraged in work settings. Therefore, this statement can be modified by stating, "I am (insert adjective)" to convey the speaker's reaction to the expressed behavior. For example, the service provider might say, "I'm uncomfortable with your anger."

"I Need." The I need statement gives the speaker the opportunity to ask for what he or she needs to continue with the conversation. For example, the service provider could say, "I need you to step aside and calm down for 20 minutes."

Some customers will respond to this approach and realize that their anger is diminishing their ability to continue the transaction and get their needs met. The key to asking an angry customer to step aside is to reassure the customer how important he/she is and how committed you are to solving the problem. The service provider needs the customer to calm down to be of assistance. However, not all customers will react favorably to the script. Therefore, other strategies will be needed to give the angry customer a "time out." Sometimes, speaking to a manager can calm down an angry customer.

There are many facets to customer communication from the verbal message, to the nonverbal communication behaviors, to the strategies to use for different types of customers and situations. This chapter introduces many elements to show ways to talk with the customer in every transaction, which reduces the number of service failures. In addition, information has been introduced that discusses how to recover when service failures occur. In addition, there are at least three trends that impact customer communication and the ways in which service is provided to customers. These trends are technology, call centers, and globalization. Each of these aspects could be a chapter of its own, so highlights of these three trends are introduced here with the recommendation to seek further reading on these trends.

Technology, Call Centers, and Globalization

Call centers are arguably "the most important single source of customer contact in the developed information economies" (Russell 2008, 195). Call centers emerged as a prominent component of business operations in the early 1990s. They continue to increase in utilization, as much as 1,200 percent from 2000 to 2003 (Mirchandani 2004), and geographic reach to India, Ireland, Canada, and Australia (Granered 2005), among others. FedEx alone has 16 call centers in the United States and 35 overseas processing 500,000 calls each day (Xu 1999–2000). At the heart of these call centers operate a multitude of communications technologies, including "integrated voice recognition systems, predictive dialing capacity, blended in-bound and out-bound call functionality, web articulation, and drop-down call and screen capture systems" (Xu 1999–2000 197). This convergence of technology, call centers, and culture creates a new dynamic for executing extraordinary customer communication.

In the global business environment, CSRs who work in call centers receive extensive training on both customer communication and cultural differences. For example, employees in many Indian call centers watch U.S. sitcoms to learn more about the language and culture and take on an alternate identity, most notably by taking an American name (Pal and Buzzanell 2008). CSRs are also trained to change their accent and modify their grammar and vocabulary to conform to the English spoken in the United States (Mirchandani 2004).

These call centers offer advantages and disadvantages for U.S. organizations and customers. While there are several considerations businesses must make when deciding to outsource customer service and use a call center, those factors that impact customer communication will be the factors introduced here. It is important for all decision makers to be at the table and discuss cost, staffing, logistics, and customer impact. Customer communication considerations weigh in on this discussion.

Advantages of call centers include employees who specialize in customer service, a large supply of English speaking employees with low labor costs, and employees who are willing to work hours when customers are most likely to call, despite the local time. The disadvantages of call centers include employees' accents that clearly identify them as non-U.S. employees, negative stereotypes of non-U.S. English speakers, rigid scripts that make employees sound unnatural, high context communication, distinguishing between British and American English, and the pragmatics of language use.

Technological innovations are another trend and are quickly increasing to provide customer service. Shifting customer service to online support systems or service providers available by instant messaging, among other platforms, have advantages and disadvantages. Advantages include low cost and immediate customer feedback. Disadvantages include trying to service customers who do not have the requisite technological tools or expertise, complex problems that cannot be answered with basic troubleshooting, and customers' desires for the human connection. Organizations will need to continue to investigate emerging technologies and evaluate the advantages and disadvantages of using technology.

It is important to note that the suggestions made in this chapter revolve around organizations in the United States communicating with customers in the United States. The dominant culture in the United States favors individualistic, high uncertainty avoidance, low power distance, masculine communication characteristics (Hofstede 1980). However, two possibilities emerge that challenge this status quo. First, those in the United States who are not in the dominant culture have different communication characteristics. Second, foreigners will also be customers. The hospitality and tourism industry has long catered to this norm by hiring staff who speak other languages. As foreigners and immigrants travel, work, and move to the interior of the country and/or to less urban areas, more and more English speakers will need to understand the nuances of intercultural communication, a subject too extensive to review here. However, business managers would be wise to study and examine the communication characteristics of specific cultures that tend to live, work, or travel in their respective region.

Conclusion

Communicating with customers in ways that show respect, courtesy, and helpfulness can alleviate many service issues. As the opening vignette highlighted, exceeding customer expectations at Hy-Vee, an organization that has always emphasized customer service, has helped this regional grocer compete with large retailers such as Wal-Mart. As this chapter has shown, outstanding customer service has a positive result on financial performance and customer loyalty.

Key Takeaways

1. Customer service has a positive influence on financial performance.
2. Customer type and industry type must be considered when creating customer communication expectations.
3. Courtesy rates higher than small talk, being sociable, or sharing private information.
4. You-centered messages and I-centered messages are each important at key moments during interactions with customers.
5. Verbal communication skills include greetings, using positive language, avoiding customer pet peeves, and creating a supportive communication climate.
6. Listening and nonverbal communication are critical aspects of customer communication that service providers need training on.

7. Treat customer complaints as gifts; reinforce to customers the value of their feedback; communicate avenues for customers to provide their comments.
8. Follow the eight-step approach or the script as models for responding to dissatisfied customers or clients.
9. Technology, call centers, and globalization impact customer communication in both positive and negative ways; make sure someone who advocates for the customer is involved with decisions about each of these topics.

Glossary

Active listening: An attempt to demonstrate unconditional acceptance and unbiased reflection by a therapist of a client's experience.

Appearance: An aspect of nonverbal communication that includes what they wear, hygiene, and other artifacts worn on the body.

Chronemics: All aspects of the use of time.

Client: A repeat customer who has considerable interdependence with the organization and/or service provider.

Courtesies: Greetings and thank yous characterized by warmth and friendliness.

Customer: The recipient of the goods and/or services provided by an organization.

Customer communication: Focuses on the points of intersection between the customer and the service provider.

Customer handling: Placating unhappy customers.

Customer relationship management: A business strategy aimed at building and maintaining long-term relationships with customers through two-way communication, gathering and storing information regarding consumer preferences, and using the information to meet both parties' goals.

Customer service: The service provided in support of an organization's core products; the ability of knowledgeable, capable, and enthusiastic employees to deliver products and services to their internal and external customers in a manner that satisfies identified and unidentified needs and ultimately results in positive word-of-mouth publicity and return business.

Defensive communication climate: Individuals feel rejected, disrespected, and invalidated.

Facial expressions: Movement of the eyebrows, eyelids, nose, and mouth.

Haptics: The study of how touch impacts human communication.

Hearing: The physical ability to receive sounds.

Jargon: Unique language or vocabulary used within a specific organization.

Kinesics: Nonverbal gestures that involve body motion.

Listening: The cognitive process of interpreting information received and trying to understand the needs and wants of the customer.

Mindful listening: The ability to receive the spoken word accurately, retain information, sustain attention, attend to your own responsive speech, and encourage the speaker.

Oculesics: The study of how eye behavior impacts human communication.

Patronizing speech: Slow, oversimplified, polite, and overly warm.

Pleasantries: Synonymous with small talk.

Privacies: Sharing personal information, demonstrating support, consolation, or confession.

Proxemics: Nonverbal communication behaviors that refer to the physical distance between those who are communicating.

Pseudorelationships: Characterized by repeat interactions with the same organization but the customer could interact with various service providers.

Service encounters: Brief and occur only once with no expectation for repeat interaction with the same person.

Service relationships: Seeing the same service provider on repeat interactions.

Sociabilities: Extend beyond small talk into joking, gossiping, or complaining.

Sociality communication: Performance that encourages a cooperative, social smoothness, void of intense interactions with others.

Supportive communication climate: Individuals feel valued, cherished, and respected.

Vocal cues: Any aspect of sound delivered from the mouth without forming words.

References

Aksoy, Lerzan, Bruce Cooil, Christopher Groening, Timothy L. Keiningham, and Atakan Yalçin "The Long-Term Stock Market Valuation of Customer Satisfaction." *Journal of Marketing* 72 (2008): 105–22.

Anderson, Eugene W., Claes Fornell, and Sanal K. Mazvancheryl. "Customer Satisfaction and Shareholder Value." *Journal of Marketing* 68 (2004): 172–85.

Bacal, Robert. *Perfect Phrases for Customer Service*. New York: McGraw Hill, 2005.

Barlow, Janelle, Claus Moller, and Tony Hsieh. *A Complaint is a Gift: Recovering Customer Loyalty When Things Go Wrong*. San Francisco: Berrett-Koehler Publications, 2008.

Berry, Leonard L. *On Great Service: A Framework for Action*. New York: The Free Press, 1995.

Birdwhistell, Ray L. *Kinesics and Context.* Philadelphia: University of Pennsylvania Press, 1970.

Carnegie, Dale. *How to Win Friends and Influence People.* New York: Pocket Books, 1936.

Eckman, Paul. *Emotions Revealed.* New York: Holt Paperbacks, 2003.

Fitzgerald, Glynis A., and Marya L. Doerfel. "The Use of Semantic Network Analysis to Manage Customer Complaints." *Communication Research Reports* 21 (2004): 231–42.

Ford, Wendy S. Z. "Communication Practices of Professional Service Providers: Predicting Customer Satisfaction and Loyalty." *Journal of Applied Communication Research* 31 (2003): 189–211.

Ford, Wendy S. Z., and Olivia J. Snyder. "Customer Service in Dental Offices: Analyses of Service Orientations and Waiting Time in Telephone Interactions with a Potential New Customer." *Health Communication* 12 (2000): 149–72.

Fornell, Claes, Sunil Mithas, Forest V. Morgeson III, and M. S. Krishnan. "Customer Satisfaction and Stock Prices: High Returns, Low Risk." *Journal of Marketing* 70 (2006): 3–14.

Freiberg, Kevin, and Jackie Freiberg. *Nuts! Southwest Airlines' Crazy Recipe for Business and Personal Success.* Austin, TX: Bard Press, 1996.

Gibb, Jack R. "Defensive Communication." *Journal of Communication* 11 (1961): 141–48.

Giles, Howard, Susan Fox, and Elisa Smith. "Patronizing the Elderly: Intergenerational Evaluations." *Research in Language and Social Interaction* 26 (1993): 129–49.

Golen, Steven P., Anthony H. Catanach, and Cindy Moeckel. "The Frequency and Seriousness of Communication Barriers in the Auditor-Client Relationship." *Business Communication Quarterly* 60 (1997): 23–37.

Gottman, John. *Why Marriages Succeed or Fail.* New York: Simon and Schuster, 1994.

Granered, Erik. *Global Call Centers: Achieving Outstanding Customer Service across Cultures and Time Zones.* Boston: Nicholas Brealey International, 2005.

Gronfeldt, Svafa, and Judith Banks Strother. *Service Leadership: The Quest for Competitive Advantage.* Thousand Oaks, CA: Sage Publications, 2006.

Gutek, Barbara, Bennett Cherry, Anita D. Bhappu, Sherry Schneider, and Loren Woolf. "Features of Service Relationships and Encounters." *Work and Occupations* 27 (2000): 319–52.

Hall, Edward T. *The Silent Language.* New York: Anchor Books, 1959.

Helgesen, Oyvind. "Are Loyal Customers Profitable? Customer Satisfaction, Customer (Action) Loyalty and Customer Profitability at the Individual Level." *Journal of Marketing Management* 22 (2006): 245–66.

Hofstede, Geert. *Culture's Consequences: International Differences in Work-Related Values.* Beverly Hills, CA: Sage, 1980.

Koermer, Chas D. "Service Provider Type as a Predictor of the Relationship between Sociality and Customer Satisfaction." *Journal of Business Communication* 42 (2005): 247–64.

Koermer, Chas D., Wendy S. Z. Ford, and Curtis Brant. "Toward the Development of a Service Provider Sociality Scale and its Relationship to Customer Satisfaction and Loyalty." *Communication Research Reports* 17 (2000): 250–59.

Koermer, Chas D., and Meghan Kilbane. "Physician Sociality Communication and its Effect on Patient Satisfaction." *Communication Quarterly* 56 (2008): 69–86.

Koermer, Chas D., and Linda L. McCroskey. "Sociality Communication: Its Influence on Customer Loyalty with the Service Provider and Service Organization." *Communication Quarterly* 54 (2006): 53–65.

Lucas, Robert W. *Customer Service: Building Successful Skills for the Twenty-First Century.* Boston: McGraw Hill, 2005.

Mehrabian, Albert. *Nonverbal Communication.* Chicago, IL: Aldine Atherton, 1972.

Michelli, Joseph A. *The New Gold Standard: The Ritz-Carlton Hotel Company.* New York: McGraw Hill, 2008.

Michelli, Joseph A. *The Starbucks Experience: 5 Principles for Turning Ordinary into Extraordinary.* New York: McGraw Hill, 2006.

Mirchandani, Kiran. "Practices of Global Capital: Gaps, Cracks, and Ironies in Transnational Call Centers in India." *Global Networks* 4 (2004): 355–74.

Muir, Clive. "Smiling with Customers." *Business Communication Quarterly* 71 (2008): 241–46.

Nussbaum, Jon F., Mary Lee Hummert, Angie Williams, and Jake Harwood. . "Communication and Older Adults." *Communication Yearbook* 19 (1996): 1–47.

Pal, Mahuya, and Patrice Buzzanell. "The Indian Call Center Experience: A Case Study in Changing Discourses of Identity, Identification, and Career in a Global Context." *Journal of Business Communication* 45 (2008): 31–60.

Pancanowsky, Michael E., and Nick O'Donnell-Trujillo. "Organizational Communication as Cultural Performance." *Communication Monographs* 50 (1983): 126–47.

Powell, John J. *Why Am I Afraid to Tell You Who I Am?* Niles, IL: Argus Communications, 1969.

Punyanunt-Carter, Narissra M., Angela Planisek, and Sara Cornette. "Repairing Relationships when Customers have Complaints: A Focus Group Study of Organization Strategies." *Ohio Communication Journal* 44 (2006): 79–94.

Reichheld, Frederick F., and W. Earl Sasser, Jr. "Zero Defections: Quality Comes to Services." *Harvard Business Review* September/October, 1990, 105–11.

Rosenberg, Marshall B. *Nonviolent Communication: A Language of Life.* Encinitas, CA: PuddleDancer Press, 2005.

Russell, Bob. "Call Centres: A Decade of Research." *International Journal of Management Reviews* 10 (2008): 195–219.

"Rustbelt Recovery." *The Economist,* March 12, 2011, 35–36.

Ryan, Ellen B., Janet M. Hamilton, and Sheree K. See. "Patronizing the Old: How do Younger and Older Adults Respond to Baby Talk in the Nursing Home?" *International Journal of Aging and Human Development* 39 (1994): 21–32.

Seligman, Martin E. P. *Learned Optimism.* New York: Pocket Books, 1998.

Shafir, Rebecca Z. "Mindful Listening." In *Bridges Not Walls,* edited by John Stewart, 219–25. Boston: McGraw Hill, 2009.

Singh, Jagdip. "A Typology of Consumer Dissatisfaction Response Styles." *Journal of Retailing* 66 (1990): 57–99.

Sprague, Brian. "Customer Service is Crucial in a Downturn." *Businessweek,* May 15, 2009, http://www.businessweek.com/print/globalbiz/content/may 2009/ gb20090515_384778.htm.

Weger, Harry, Gina R. Castle, and Melissa C. Emmett. "Active Listening in Peer Interviews: The Influence of Message Paraphrasing on Perceptions of Listening Skill." *The International Journal of Listening* 24 (2010): 34–49.

Xu, Weidong. "Long Range Planning for Call Centers at FedEx." *The Journal of Business Forecasting* 18 (1999–2000): 7–11.

Yim, Bennett, David K. Tse, and Kimmy W. Chan. "Strengthening Customer Loyalty through Intimacy and Passion: Roles of Customer-Firm Affection and Customer-Staff Relationships in Services." *Journal of Marketing Research* 45 (2008): 741–56.

CHAPTER FIVE

Selling Yourself or Your Product Starts with Communication

Jackson Hataway

ProLife Insurance

At ProLife Insurance, things were looking bleak for Steven Rogers. He had worked for the company for one year and was seeing little progress in his sales numbers. Despite his incredible knowledge of the company's products, he felt like he was bouncing from one customer pitch to the next without seeing any results. Steven would visit several offices everyday ready to make his case and then not receive any commitments despite his best efforts to highlight the company's competitive prices. He was at a loss. The older sales-people at ProLife seemed to have no problem generating business, but he could not seem to get a client to say yes. He would leave phone messages asking for a response, send e-mails reminding people of his products, and follow any lead he was given. Nothing seemed to be working. Why wasn't Steven able to make a sale?

Note: To ensure confidentiality of the organization and/or people within the organization, names have been altered.

Introduction

If you ask someone outside of the profession what they know about sales, many will answer you with one phrase: follow the ABCs ("always be closing"). This mantra, which though popularized in the 1980s can be traced all the way back to the 1950s, has served for decades as a strategic sales philosophy used to drive home, for all salespeople, the importance of keeping sales goals at top of mind during every client conversation. Every interaction should be driven by the salesperson's ability to speak as if the deal is already done, as if the only thing left to determine is when the buyer will take possession of the goods. The sales conversation is constantly driving downward to a point of positive conclusion, making it an entirely transactional communicative event.

Of course, there are a number of reasons why the earlier mentioned philosophy is no longer applicable. First (and most importantly), any good sales professional will tell you there is much more to excelling in sales than just "knowing how to close." The product itself is only a small piece of a much broader and complex transaction. In the modern sales environment, "sales representatives must identify, create, develop, and propose ways to integrate the objectives of both buyers and sellers while reducing their differences" (Hunter and Perreault 2007, 16). In other words, a salesperson's role is no longer focused solely on pushing their own product, but instead on their ability to be creative in the ways that they relate to a buyer.

Because of this, a great salesperson knows their products inside and out, understands their own and their clients' margins with incredible specificity, and recognizes the importance of building relationships with clients that will spur future sales—meaning they must sell themselves as much as they sell their products. In many respects, the modern sales environment actually requires the salesperson to manage relationships more than they manage their products (Storbacka et al. 2009). Taken together, all of these elements can indeed create a formula that makes a successful close possible. But all of these pieces, including the ABCs of sales, are entirely reliant upon the salesperson's ability to communicate clearly, competently, and compellingly with their audience.

The second reason that the ABCs of closing are no longer applicable is much larger and much more convoluted: new economic dynamics. For better or worse, the Great Recession that began in 2008 has fundamentally altered business models throughout almost every industry. In every economic downturn, one of the natural short-term outcomes is that consumers begin to reduce their spending and save more of their annual income (Yerex 2011). As consumer spending decreases, businesses begin to hoard more capital and cut costs in order to create a cushion that will prevent continued loss. The Great Recession of 2008 took these results to an extreme, the effects of which are still being felt today in the business environment. Companies are holding on to more liquid capital than any time in recent history rather than engaging in investments, hiring, or major purchasing (Farzad 2011). This has created markets that are, in a sense, relatively frozen and decidedly unpredictable.

So what does that mean for sales? In general, it means that the tried and true system of sales that was particularly present during the economic boom of the 1990s and early 2000s—a system in which products almost sold themselves—no longer works. Salespeople have to be able to navigate a modern economic environment in which goods are caught in a volatile pricing system and in which consumer expectations are changing. This places more pressure on the salesperson to differentiate their products or services not just through cost or characteristics but through communication with the buyer or client.

To be fair, even before the financial crisis research had demonstrated that the loyalty a customer has to a specific salesperson is the most important predictor of sales growth and effectiveness (Palmatier, Scheer, and Steenkamp 2007). The Great Recession, however, only served to heighten the need to focus on building long-term relationships with customers (Homburg, Muller, and Klarmann 2011)—relationships that develop based upon the communication competency of the salesperson. The relational model of sales, in which communication is the key to sales success, relies on a salesperson's ability to understand their own communicative style, the communicative expectations of the buyer, and the situational context of the interaction.

Complicating Factors

Saying that communication is the key to sales is, of course, a little like saying water is the key to a stream; the statement is true, but it doesn't take a scientist to reach that conclusion. What complicates that principle is the fact that we tend to think of communication as an innate ability rather than as a complex but modifiable skill. For instance, many of us will say things like "I'm no good at talking to people," "She's a very good communicator," or "I wish I could talk like him." These methods of describing the ability to communicate inherently undermine our capacity to change our communication behaviors because they imply that change is impossible—and, as a result, they place very real limits on our ability to sell ourselves or our products. We become walking self-fulfilling prophecies of either success or failure with no real control beyond the competitiveness of our products and price points.

Are there components of communication that some people have natural predispositions toward? Certainly. Are those that we think of as "naturally gifted communicators" always going to win in the world of sales? Not at all! Are there ways that we can improve our own communication competency? Absolutely! Communication, like any other skill or talent, is only as useful as the effort and direction that is placed into it. Without purpose and preparation, the most naturally gifted communicators can accomplish very little in the professional sales world. At the same time, the most prepared salesperson cannot reach their potential without understanding how to alter their own communication patterns and behaviors to meet the expectations of potential buyers.

An example may be helpful in illustrating this point. Our company was recently working with a midsized financial institution that was attempting to implement a more "sales-oriented" culture among frontline staff. For years prior to this point, management had pressed the message to staff that the most important element of interacting with customers was high-quality service. However, this company, like many financial institutions, had experienced serious upheaval over the past three years and, as a result, had chosen to implement a strategic initiative to begin actively cross-selling financial products. A training program was introduced for staff that outlined all of the products offered by the company as well as means for identifying opportunities to offer a new product to an existing customer.

After a few months of little program success, management began to review that training process to ensure that staff understood all of the various financial products; what they found instead was that the program was hamstrung by the fact that staff interactions with customers were beginning to lack the service quality the company was known for as staff attempted to drive sales numbers. Customers were not responding to the sales system because it emphasized a script rather than a legitimate connection.

The example earlier is intended to illustrate two points:

1. Successful sales communication cannot be based entirely upon a scripted performance; customers want meaningful interactions with sales staff that are not just a "hard sell."
2. From a strategic communication standpoint, it is always critical to have a sales plan—but that plan has to incorporate a long-term, developmental view of the relationships that a salesperson must create with their clientele.

Even in sales settings where relationships with clients seem impossible to build (such as a retail shop) this approach to sales will produce positive results.

What Will Be Covered

In line with those two points, this chapter's focus is the importance of communication in selling yourself and your products. We will examine the role of communication in relationship building and maintenance, the necessity of identifying with potential buyers, and various strategies for adapting your communication style to meet the needs of the sales setting. A variety of examples and theories will be discussed in order to make these points clearer. At the end of this chapter, you will:

- Be familiar with general communication principles;
- Understand the importance of adaptation in sales communication;
- Be comfortable adjusting or improving your own communication skills;

- Be capable of managing the impression you make as a professional;
- Understand the importance of helping improves the customer's image; and
- Have an understanding of relational sales communication.

The Evolution of Communication and Sales

A brief review of some basic communication theory is necessary to begin discussing best practices in sales communication. Theories of communication have evolved over time to reflect our changing understanding of how communication works. As a result, the way we have thought of sales communication has changed as well. This section will discuss:

1. Linear model of communication,
2. Nonlinear model of communication,
3. Multifaceted model of communication, and
4. Implications for sales communication.

Models of Communication

The first theories of communication treated communication as a one way, linear flow of information from sender to receiver. Someone would create a message (sender), pass it to someone else (receiver), and the receiver would then have the information (Harris and Nelson 2008). If we apply this model to a sales setting, sales communication is little more than salespeople giving buyers information about products and prices—and based on this model, buyers then simply make their decisions. Although this pattern holds true in some settings, we know that there is much more to the majority of sales conversations. This way of thinking about communication in sales leaves no room for negotiation, adaptation, or differentiation among buyers.

In short, these initial communication models lacked *feedback*, the process of information making its way back to the sender from the receiver. Over time, communication theories evolved to incorporate feedback messages flowing from the receiver to the sender. This nonlinear, process view of communication for the first time made both parties important in communicating rather than just the sender (Narula 2006). Each person in this model is responsible for sending and receiving messages at different moments. From this perspective, sales communication became a two-way interaction, with a salesperson passing along information and a potential customer responding. Again, though, this view of communication was limited because it treated communicating as a one-off act; one person said something, then the person listening responded and then the first person might say something back. That may seem fundamentally true, but it is more accurate a description of e-mail exchange than of communication in its broadest sense. Conversations with customers involve a much more complicated interchange between salesperson and buyer.

Because communication is *dynamic,* modern models of communication describe communication as an ongoing, ever-changing expression of meaning among people (Littlejohn and Foss 2008). What that means is that communication is constant; we are almost always engaged in the act of communicating with people and, because of that, must always be aware of the communicative cues we and others are expressing. Think of a poker game. The best poker players in the world are always trying to watch *everyone* at the table because they know that we are constantly sending messages as we react to the world around us, even if we haven't spoken a word.

> Communication is now considered to be a dynamic process. It is always occurring and any number of variables influence how, why, and what we communicate. If you are interested in a more detailed explanation of the evolution of communication theory and its various components, read Julia Wood's *Communication Mosaics: An Introduction to the Field of Communication* (Wood 2010).

According to some research, nonverbal cues account for anywhere from 65 percent to 93 percent of what we communicate (Wood 2012). In many cases, even our lack of reaction to something that happens around us sends a message that can be interpreted by others. Think of some basic nonverbal gestures, and the value of nonverbal communication will become clear. When we smile, nod our heads, and make eye contact, we convey that we are attentive and interested. When we yawn, close our eyes, or tap our fingers, we seem bored. Now think of the impact those nonverbal gestures have when you are in the process of making a sale. If the buyer is beginning to yawn and shuffle their feet, should you continue to make your case as you have been, or should you change your approach? Obviously, the answer is you need to change your strategy. This example highlights the incredible power of recognizing nonverbal cues. Those cues tell you in an instant to adapt your sales message long before any verbal signals are sent—and by the time verbal signals are given (such as "no thanks") it is often too late.

As a salesperson, it is crucial to understand that communication is not a one-time event or a pure back-and-forth exchange. Instead, it is a constant process of interpretation that requires us to be *as aware* of the tendencies, behaviors, and preferences of buyers as we are of our own. But we must also understand that communication is situational; every person has their own, unique style of communicating, which means that similar words and gestures can have dramatically different meanings from one client to the next. We must work to establish frames of reference that are particular to a given client in order to determine how best to adapt our sales message to their expectations—and we must be do our best to manage the client's ongoing impression of us as credible, knowledgeable professionals.

Reassessing Our Beliefs

Understanding the progression of basic communication theory over time helps to illustrate how our own assumptions about communication, including when and how it takes place, are often underdeveloped or simply false. Communication takes place regardless of our intention to communicate with others. This has several important implications for salespeople.

First, salespeople are constantly engaged in the sales conversation no matter the topic or setting they are in with a customer. You are always "on" as the saying goes. Whether you are at a convention, in a restaurant, or at a coffee shop, you must consciously consider how and what you are communicating. One example illustrates this point very clearly. In 2006, Xiamen University in China began requiring law and business students to take golf lessons because so many business deals are made on golf courses (Wong 2006). Though this requirement generated criticism, it is an excellent example of considering communication from the broadest possible perspective. In the minds of these school officials, simply having a basic understanding of the principles, rules, and techniques of golf communicates that someone is a competent businessperson capable of "fitting into" the business world.

Second, reassessing our ways of thinking about communication helps us to realize that selling ourselves and our products is an *iterative process,* a process that evolves to become more accurate as it is repeated in different forms. Make no mistake, we engage in sales communication that, at its core, remains focused on compelling someone to purchase a good or service; our approach to those interactions, however, must constantly be changing and improving. We must be aware of communication cues, be sure we are acting and reacting appropriately, and be prepared to listen and learn as the conversation takes place because we will share the outcome of the sales conversation with the buyer.

Finally, knowing that we are always playing the roles of both sender and receiver means that we must pay attention to the various nonverbal and verbal communication signals we express. There is no faster way to ruin a potential sales opportunity than to create *dissonance* in the mind of the buyer. Dissonance occurs when we cause someone to experience mental tension or discomfort by forcing them to reconcile contradictory messages (Galinsky et al. 2008; Moshe 2010). This can easily take place in the minds of our audiences when our words and actions are not aligned.

> Dissonance occurs when we cause others to experience mental tension or discomfort by forcing them to reconcile contradictory messages.

For instance, in one simple case, a medical technology salesperson was in a meeting with a doctor trying to convince the doctor to begin using their company's surgical devices. The sales representative had spoken with the doctor on numerous occasions and had emphasized how focused they were on the doctor's needs. However, during the meeting, the salesperson continually glanced at a watch making the doctor feel rushed and as if his time was not appreciated. In reality, the salesperson was concerned about delaying another meeting set for later that afternoon—but the damage was already done. The dissonance experienced by the doctor made it impossible for the salesperson to make a successful pitch despite the salesperson's preparation and polish. In short, recognizing that communication is a constant, multilayered process will help you to identify ways that you can become a better sales communicator as well as ways to prevent a sale from falling apart.

Making an Impression

The previous section spoke generally about the relationship between communication, behaviors, and sales. An equally important component in selling oneself is recognizing and controlling the impression that you make upon others. You are probably not surprised by the fact that we spend a great deal of our time and energy attempting to manage the impressions others have of us. Depending on the setting we are in—a formal business presentation, a casual cup of coffee, attending a sporting event—we dress and act in a certain way to make people believe very specific things about us. This is referred to as *impression management* (Goffman 1959; Schlenker 1980). Impression management is a vital tool in the salesperson's toolkit because it deals with the ability of a salesperson to intentionally control the *context* of conversations with clients or buyers. Context refers to the surrounding conditions and setting of a communication event. If a salesperson has successfully constructed a desired image of themselves in the mind of a customer or client, then they have already begun to define the types of information that will be included in the conversation.

> Impression management is a vital tool in the salesperson's toolkit because it deals with the ability to intentionally control the *context* of conversations with clients or buyers.

What distinguishes impression management from the communication theory we have already discussed is that impression management begins well before you ever meet a client or buyer. We choose to emphasize certain elements of our identities for certain audiences. That does not mean we falsify anything about ourselves; instead, we simply highlight those attributes of ourselves that we believe an audience will appreciate most (Sallot 2002). From the moment you begin to plan the clothing you will wear, the places you will go, and the people you will see during a day, you begin to engage in impression management. For instance, if you know you have a presentation for a client, you will likely wear formal business attire to communicate the image of yourself as a credible sales professional. This act alone affects the way that buyers and clients will think of and speak to you; they will treat you as a subject matter expert and expect you to be capable of answering their questions.

The Difficulty of Building an Impression

The reason impression management is more complex than simply painting your face the colors of your favorite sports team is that creating an impression requires a person to envision a desired self-image and then act out that self-image, often on a continual basis (Seiter et al. 2009). For salespeople, these efforts often begin with our product knowledge. Salespeople are expected to have an incredible amount of knowledge about their own product as well as competitors products, leading some to conclude that the modern salesperson must maintain the image of "knowledge broker" to be successful (Verbeke, Dietz, and Verwaal 2011). A knowledge broker is a person who serves as a resource for others because of the incredible amount of information they have attained on a topic.

If clients and buyers view you as a knowledge broker, you are far more valuable an asset to them because of the breadth of industry knowledge you are able to demonstrate. However, putting that knowledge-broker impression to meaningful sales use requires a salesperson to be able to communicate what distinguishes their product from others, why those characteristics are significant for buyers, and how they will add value to a buyer or client in the long term.

To illustrate that point, another one of our clients in the financial industry was attempting to increase loan sales among staff. Because loans are a somewhat complicated and technical commodity, it was important that staff be capable of discussing the variety of loan products offered by the financial institution in comparison with their competitors. The management's goal was to make as many members of their front line staff knowledge brokers about lending as possible. However, they quickly realized that simply providing staff with loan product information was not enough; the staff needed to understand how lending plays into the overall success of a financial institution and the value loans can add to the lives of customers. In a sense, they needed front line staff to be able to see the whole picture of lending in order for staff to successfully convey the impression that they were loan experts. Simply put, the financial institution helped front line staff flesh out the particular impression that was necessary for the sales strategy to be effective.

In organizational settings, impression management is often a part of the job itself. For instance, a classic example of impression management can be seen in the role of flight attendants (Hochschild 1983; Murphy 2001). Flight attendants are expected to smile while on duty, make passengers feel comfortable, and act calmly at all times—all while working at 30,000 feet. Southwest Airlines in particular is famous for its flight attendants who really "show the love" to passengers by telling jokes and making the otherwise tedious experience of flying fun. The role of the flight attendant is clear: they must appear to be the professional on board keeping the passengers relaxed and safe. And they must do that on every single flight that they work, placing incredible strain on them to consistently communicate a certain impression.

Similarly, sales professionals are expected to construct an image of themselves in the minds of clients and then (ideally) manage that image over a long period of time. Research in impression management has shown that the more likely it is that our behavior will be examined by others, the more likely we are to put more effort into all facets of impression management (Leary and Kowalski 1990). As was mentioned earlier, when you make a presentation to a client, you will likely choose to wear business professional attire. However, that is only one piece of a larger effort to manage a buyer's impression of you. Knowing that our potential buyers will be watching us closely means that we will likely engage in any number of actions and behaviors that will show us to be intelligent, likeable, and generous. We strive to create an image in our clients' minds that will encourage them to trust and remain loyal to us, and we are expected to always maintain that image once it is established. Typical behaviors in this vein include:

- Being early for every client appointment.
- Exhibiting a deep knowledge of the clients business or situation.
- Exhibiting a deep knowledge about our own products.
- Creating unique offers for each potential buyer.
- Buying meals for clients.
- Talking with a client about hobbies or interests.
- Sending thank you notes for a client's time.
- Sending holiday gifts of appreciation.

Perhaps the best example of the impact of that impression management in sales that we have witnessed is what is known in the sales world as "the ride along." The ride along typically involves sales managers accompanying representatives to meetings with clients and observing every behavior of the sales representative from the moment they sit down in the car until the moment they arrive back at the office. The sales manager keeps a list of everything the sales representative does that is not consistent with the image the representative is trying to convey and then debriefs the representative at the end of the day. Although this may seem slightly overbearing and critical, the purpose is simply to ensure that the image the salesperson is *trying* to convey to customers matches the image that others are *perceiving* of them. For that reason, the sales manager watches the salesperson from the moment the day begins until the moment the day ends because the salesperson is supposed to be playing a very defined role.

For some salespeople, this level of observation is not always necessary. There are individuals who have a natural ability to fully self-monitor the image they are presenting to others. Those people are more naturally inclined to successfully engage in impression management (Turnley and Bolino 2001). However, for those who are not adept at self-monitoring, the role of the outside observer or sales coach is an integral component to becoming a more capable salesperson. And, regardless of your natural abilities, none of us are capable of completely monitoring every verbal and nonverbal signal we convey. What does that mean? Whether or not you excel at self-monitoring, having someone serve as a coach and observe your professional behavior will help you better communicate the impression that you believe is necessary to succeed in your industry. Creating a positive, lasting impression with buyers means constantly being attentive to the image you present, from your depth and breadth of product knowledge to the clothing you choose to wear.

Creating Meaningful Sales Relationships through Communication

Most salespeople will agree their favorite clients are those that "re-sign" every time there is an opportunity to do so. These are the buyers who want a particular product or service, prefer the version your company offers and, most importantly, seem to like you. What all salespeople will tell you, however, is that building those kinds of relationships is time consuming and difficult. They require commitment to the client through good times and bad, legitimate interest in the client's continued wellbeing, and a willingness to sacrifice your own profitability to ensure the client's satisfaction. Most importantly, you rarely know at the outset which of your clients may eventually develop loyalty to you as a salesperson, which can make accepting short-term deals seem much more appealing than working on long-term relationships (Gronroos 1995). It becomes the salesperson's job to use relationship-building communication in almost every client interaction if they hope to have sustained sales success.

Creating Loyal Customers

Relationships with customers that are based in loyalty to the salesperson are generally powerful predictors of sales effectiveness (Palmatier, Scheer, and Steenkamp 2007). As a client or buyer places greater amounts of trust in the salesperson, they will seek out more products and services from the salesperson despite, in many cases, pricing differences. However, these types of relationships demand relationship-building efforts on the part of the salesperson that take place over time. Some of these activities have already been mentioned in this chapter, such as attending social engagements with clients; almost all are focused on creating strong interpersonal bonds with the customer (Leonard 1995).

RELATIONAL SELLING

Larson (2001, 43) lays out the following characteristics of relational selling:

- We-oriented, not me-oriented.
- Selling is a service, not a contest.
- Follow-through is number one, not the close.
- Selling is helping, not just persuading.
- Great sellers truly care and are not manipulators.

In some sales settings, this approach does not seem necessary at first glance—but even in those situations, adopting this long-term perspective for sales growth is critical. Take, for example, retail sales. In work with a midsize, family-owned retail clothier, we have become very familiar with their philosophy on sales. The owners believe that even though many of their sales will be to people who simply stop in for a one-time visit, their associates should attempt to get to know as many clients as possible. Building a rapport with customers encourages them to come back and ask for the same sales associate time and time again. Some sales associates have customers who have been coming to them for years, and those clients receive extra attention and adapted product offerings. Though it requires a high up-front investment of salesperson time, the payoff in terms of long-term profitability makes the effort well worth it.

Open Communication and Customer Relationships

As a salesperson, working to build and maintain a solid relationship with a client often requires almost as much energy and effort as keeping up to date on changes in your products and industry. Some of the most successful salespeople we know go so far as to keep databases of client birthdays in order to guarantee that they communicate a commitment to their customers that goes beyond business. The takeaway from this point is simple: the more you can do to communicate your genuine care for a customer, the better.

This expectation, however, is actually two-sided. Just as a great salesperson gathers a great deal of interpersonal information from a client, they also are willing to reveal an equal or greater amount of interpersonal information. In fact, buyers have been found to see disclosure from a salesperson as indicative of the salesperson's trustworthiness (Crosby, Evans, and Cowles 1990). Remember—communication is not a one-way interaction. It is a multifaceted, ongoing exchange of meaning. Taking part in that exchange means revealing the interpersonal details necessary to build a relationship with a customer. All relationships are based in sacrificing some personal privacy for the sake of building trust; relationships with customers are no different.

Managing the Impressions Others Have of Your Customers

Along the lines of our discussion of impression management earlier, it is also important for salespeople to realize that we attempt to manage the impressions of others as well as ourselves. This form of impression management, however, plays directly into the ways we build relationships with clients and buyers. In general, we manage the image of others by praising or criticizing others in public settings (Seiter 1999). Specifically, we, as salespeople, must make sure we are managing the impressions others have of our clients by sharing positive image-building communication as often as possible.

In many respects, the key to building a relationship is making your customer feel as if he or she is the most important customer. That statement is not meant to imply that a salesperson should be disingenuous; indeed, if anything it simply means salespeople should fully express their gratitude and appreciation for each and every customer they have. Showing gratitude can be as easy as devoting ample time to each client or as complex as making referrals to certain buyers without sacrificing the interests of others.

From an impression-management standpoint, however, the most important facet for keeping the client relationship strong is to always communicate positive information about customers in order to keep their impression, in the eyes of others, positive. The more a salesperson helps to manage a customer's impression to others, the more appreciative the customer will be of the salesperson's efforts and the more faith they will place in the salesperson. Think of this as a "third party" approach to relationship management. You want other people and businesses saying good things about the way you talk about your customers.

In our work with one client, the notion of creating a business ecosystem became a crucial piece of the client's strategy. They decided not to just offer goods and services to their customers—they chose to connect customers with each other based on common interests and goals. As their customers came together to work on various projects because of recommendations from our client, they began to turn to our client to be their primary servicer. Simply put, this client enacted a brilliant method of managing the impressions their customers had of one another and, as a result, created even stronger sales ties to the entire business network.

It is not enough to simply come off as a knowledgeable professional—a great salesperson knows that making the customer's life better in a multitude of ways will result in more sales over a longer period of time. Creating relationships with your clients that are fruitful therefore requires you not just to communicate *with* your client but to actively communicate *about* your client whenever the opportunity arises to improve their standing. Relational communication that takes place on both of these levels and that is focused on establishing long-term bonds with customers and clients will dramatically improve your viability as a salesperson.

Conclusion

This chapter's purpose was to outline the importance of communication in selling yourself and your products. No matter what the industry, bringing an understanding of impression management and relational communication to the sales equation increases the likelihood that you will move the sales dial in the right direction. Success cannot be determined by short-term gains or exceeding your monthly quota; it must be viewed through the lens of sustainable sales relationships that will serve you for years to come. As you reflect on ways that you can better manage the impression of yourself and your clients to create strong interpersonal ties, remember Steven from the case study at the beginning of this chapter.

Steven (who is based on a real insurance salesperson) was constantly focused on the product and the bottom line. Steven did not take time to consider that he needed to take the time to create relationships with his potential clients, particularly given the economic climate. Few people are interested in a sales representative coming in and pushing insurance products when there is less money to spend. The success Steven noticed in the older salespeople had little to do with their ability to pitch products and more to do with the long-term relationships with customers those salespeople had at their disposal.

Perhaps more importantly, the ability of the experienced sales representatives to bring in new clients was almost universally driven by their understanding that the impression they conveyed had to be carefully crafted and repeatedly examined. Steven's immense knowledge of the products and services of ProLife meant little compared to the loyalty the older salespeople had generated with customers over time. A great salesperson understands that sales is not just a job that involves moving from one pitch to the next; it is a career that requires you to build an image of yourself as a credible professional in the minds of others. That image, along with the relationships you develop as you craft that image, will make the difference between short-term gains and long-term profitability.

Key Takeaways

1. Communication is a dynamic process that is constantly taking place. You must be aware that you are sending and receiving messages even when you do not intend to do so.
2. What nonverbal cues should you be sure to express in a sales setting and which ones should you absolutely work to avoid?
3. Give serious consideration to the impression you would like others to have of you as a salesperson. Have someone work as your coach to ensure that is the image you convey.
4. A long-term, relationship drive sales strategy is the most important factor to sustainable profitability. Try to improve your relational communication with customers whenever possible.
5. Work as hard to manage your clients' and customers' impressions of one another as you do to manage your own.

Glossary

Context: The surrounding conditions and setting of a communication event.

Dissonance: Mental tension or discomfort caused by forcing an audience to reconcile contradictory messages.

Feedback: In early communication models, messages that make their way back from receiver to sender. In modern communication models, ongoing, evaluative communication cues in a communication event.

Iterative process: A process that evolves to become more accurate as it is repeated in different forms.

References

Crosby, Lawrence A., Kenneth R. Evans, and Deborah Cowles. "Relationship Quality in Service Selling: An Interpersonal Influence Perspective." *Journal of Marketing* 54, no. 3 (1990): 68–81.

Farzad, Roben. "The Stress of Carrying Cash." *Bloomberg Businessweek*, August 15, 2011: 43–44.

Galinsky, Adam D., Joe C. Magee, Deborah H. Gruenfeld, Jennifer A. Whitson, and Katie A. Liljenquist. "Power Reduces the Press of the Situation: Implications for Creativity, Conformity, and Dissonance." *Journal of Personality & Social Psychology* 95, no. 6 (2008): 1450–66.

Goffman, Erving. *The Presentation of Self in Everyday Life.* Garden City, NY: Anchor/Doubleday, 1959.

Gronroos, Christian. "Relationship Marketing: The Strategy Continuum." *Journal of the Academy of Marketing Science* 23, no. 4 (1995): 252–54.

Harris, Thomas E., and Mark D. Nelson. *Applied Organizational Communication: Theory and Practice in a Global Environment.* 3rd ed. New York: Lawrence Erlbaum Associates, 2008.

Hochschild, Arlie Russel. *The Managed Heart: Communication of Human Feeling.* Berkeley: The University of California Press, 1983.

Homburg, Christian, Michael Muller, and Martin Klarmann. "When Should the Customer Really be King? On the Optimum Level of Salesperson Customer Orientation in Sales Encounters." *Journal of Marketing* 75, no. 2 (2011): 55–74.

Hunter, Gary K., and William D. Perreault Jr. "Making Sales Technology Effective." *Journal of Marketing* 71 (2007): 16–34.

Larson, Brian. "Relationship Selling: Finding a Revolution or Findings of a Re-Evolution?" *Journal of Promotion Management* 7, no. 1/2 (2001): 41–53.

Leary, Mark R., and R. M. Kowalski. "Impression Management: A Literature Review and Two-Factor Model." *Psychological Bulletin* 107 (1990): 34–57.

Leonard, Berry L. "Relationship Marketing of Services—Growing Interests, Emerging Perspectives." *Journal of the Academy of Marketing Science* 23, no. 4 (1995): 236–45.

Littlejohn, Stephen W., and Karen A. Foss. *Theories of Human Communication.* 9th ed. Belmont: Thomson Wadsworth, 2008.

Moshe, Mira. "Dissonant Political Discourse." *Journal of Language and Politics* 9, no. 2 (2010): 174–95.

Murphy, Alexandra G. "The Flight Attendant Dilemma: An Analysis of Communication and Sensemaking during In-Flight Emergencies." *Journal of Applied Communication Research* 29, no. 1 (2001): 30–53.

Narula, Uma. *Handbook of Communication: Models, Perspectives, Strategies.* New Delhi: Atlantic, 2006.

Palmatier, Robert W., Lisa K. Scheer, and Jan-Benedict E. M. Steenkamp. "Customer Loyalty to Whom? Managing the Benefits and Risks of Salesperson-Owned Loyalty." *Journal of Marketing Research* 44, no. 2 (2007): 185–99.

Sallot, Lynne M. "What the Public Thinks about Public Relations: An Impression Management Experiment." *Journalism & Mass Communication Quarterly* 79, no. 1 (2002): 150–71.

Schlenker, Barry R. *Impression Management.* Monterey, CA: Brooks/Cole, 1980.

Seiter, John S. "Does Communicating Nonverbal Disagreement during an Opponent's Speech Affect the Credibility of the Debater in the Background?" *Psychological Reports* 84 (1999): 855–61.

Seiter, John S., Harry Weger Jr., Harold J. Kinzer, and Andrea S. Jensen. "Impression Management in Televised Debates: The Effect of Background Nonverbal Behavior on Audience Perceptions of Debaters' Likeability." *Communication Research Reports* 26, no. 1 (2009): 1–11.

Storbacka, Kaj, Lynette Ryals, Iain A. Davies, and Suvi Nenonen. "The Changing Role of Sales: Viewing Sales as a Strategic, Cross-Functional Process." *European Journal of Marketing* 43, no. 7/8 (2009): 890–906.

Turnley, William H., and Mark C. Bolino. "Achieving Desired Images While Avoiding Undesired Images: Exploring the Role of Self-Monitoring in Impression Management." *Journal of Applied Psychology* 86 (2001): 351–60.

Verbeke, Willem, Bart Dietz, and Ernst Verwaal. "Drivers of Sales Performance: A Contemporary Metanalysis. Have Salespeople Become Knowledge Brokers?" *Journal of the Academy of Marketing Science* 39, no. 3 (2011): 407–28.

Wong, Stephen. "China's Poor Take a Swing at Golf." *Asia Times Online.* November 18, 2006. http://www.atimes.com/atimes/China_Business/HK18Cb04.html.

Wood, Julia T. *Communication in Our Lives.* 6th ed. Boston: Wadsworth, 2012.

Wood, Julia T. *Communication Mosaics: An Introduction to the Field of Communication.* 6th ed. Boston: Wadsworth, 2010.

Yerex, Robert P. "The Consumer-Driven Economy at a Crossroads." *Business Economics* 46 (2011): 32–42.

CHAPTER SIX

Marketing for the 21st Century: Thinking through Current Marketing Trends That Will Effectively Position Your Organization

Erin E. Gilles, Shannon M. Brogan,
Doreen M.S. Jowi, and Jason S. Wrench

H&R Block and Adventures in Social Media

Starting in 2007, H&R Block realized that it needed to compete electronically in the tax business. Too many people saw the company as just the people who offered tax advice from various retail sites. In actuality, H&R Block owned a number of digital products including TaxCut, which was designed to eat away at the market dominated by TurboTax, and Tango a recently developed new online tax-filing program.

Paula Drum, vice president of digital marketing for H&R Block, realized quickly that she needed an integrated marketing strategy that included both traditional and new social media avenues. Drum and her team developed a multipronged campaign that marketed H&R Block to the social media generation specifically by having a strong presence on YouTube, Second Life, Twitter, MySpace, and Facebook became prime channels.

One of their more innovative approaches was the *Me & My Super Sweet Refund* video contest on YouTube. Entrants were asked to submit a YouTube video explaining what they would do with their tax refund. All entrants had to mention TaxCut as part of their three-minute video montage, ensuring that the new products would be center stage. The winner was given $5,000, and the winning video was featured on the YouTube home page for an entire day. Furthermore, H&R Block allowed YouTube users to vote on the winning video. Ultimately, the 130 videos submitted received more than 1.6 million views.

Second, H&R Block created an island in Second Life, the interactive metaverse. The island was populated with real H&R Block representatives to help users and answer tax questions. The island also contained an auditorium where visitors could watch a video about the new tax-filing software, Tango. Visitors to the island also received a coupon for free access to the software. In line with the fun parts of Second Life, visitors could ride virtual scooters while touring the island or put on special shoes that allowed the users to dance the tango while visiting the island.

Third, in both MySpace and Facebook, the company set up pages and encouraged users to link to their pages. On Facebook, users could give a free "gift" that entailed a "bag of money" to their friends on Facebook. A total of 250,000 people gave the "bag of money" to their friends, which both informed people that it was tax season and kept the H&R Block brand front and center in people's minds. Lastly, the company created a series of videos featuring the actor Truman Greene who was hired to be the face of the H&R Block brand (http://www.youtube.com/user/TrumanGreene). The videos were posted on YouTube, but spread around Facebook and MySpace fairly rapidly.

Overall, the attempt at creating a multipronged marketing campaign was a gamble in attracting younger consumers.

The purpose of this chapter is to examine the intersection of communication and marketing. Marketing is fundamentally an act of communication that attempts to influence another person or person's purchasing habits in some fashion. However, the field of marketing has definitely broadened and the boundaries between the behaviors of marketing professionals and public relations professionals often are highly intertwined. Many organizations do not even distinguish between the two types of behaviors at all. In this chapter, we are first going to focus on what is marketing, communication and marketing, and best practices for marketing. After this discussion of the more traditional aspects of marketing, we will switch gears and examine Internet-based marketing and social media marketing specifically.

What Is Marketing?

Although marketing is a complex set of processes, which is often invisible to consumers, marketing is a part of our everyday lives. According to the American Marketing Association (AMA), marketing is defined as "the activity, set of institutions, and processes for creating, communicating, delivering, and exchanging offerings that have value for customers, clients, partners, and society at large" (www.marketingpower.com 2011). This definition was revised as of 2007, which indicates that the AMA is striving to create a definition of marketing that keeps pace with our changing culture. From the corporate perspective, Joep Cornelissen (2008) defines marketing as "the management process responsible identifying, anticipating, and satisfying customer requirements profitably" (260).

Marketing seeks to understand how companies can best serve their customers. Marketing professor Jerome McCarthy (1960) identified four key elements of a successful marketing campaign, which were later spread through the work of Philip Kotler (1967). The "four Ps" of marketing, also known as the marketing mix, are: product, price, place, and promotion. Product refers to products, which exist in a tangible form such as a laptop, soft drink, or a pair of jeans. Product can also refer to nontangible items, such as services, which could be a trip on a cruise, child care, or health insurance. Every organization has a product, and most offer a range of different types of products. The key task for companies is to determine which product lines should get the most marketing attention. According to Kotler and Armstrong (2001), the "four Ps" of marketing is an outmoded concept, which should be replaced with the "four Cs." The Cs are: customer solution, customer cost, convenience, and communication. Regardless of which method you choose, these elements of marketing overlap and all have relevance for marketing success.

Marketing in the 21st century is moving at an accelerated pace while experiencing many changes. Many companies or corporations must focus their attention on global forces that affect stakeholders; technological advances that are required in effective and efficient advertising; and deregulations of world economies (Hill and Rifkin 1999). The concept of marketing also allows organizations to examine their corporate marketing strategies that focus on the organization's vision and mission statements (Brunot 2011). To be successful corporate marketing, companies must understand their identity, branding, and image.

> Due to declining sales, in 1993 California's milk processors elected to use three cents from each gallon sold to spend on the marketing of fluid milk. The California Milk Processor Board hired Goodby, Silverstein & Partners to develop their campaign. This partnership resulted in the now-famous "Got Milk?" campaign, which debuted on television in 1994. The campaign instantly popular, and swept the industry awards. The marketing firm continues to keep the "Got Milk?" campaign fresh and updated the website in 2008 with interactive games, recipes, and new content.

Return on quality refers to the concept that "(1) the quality being delivered is the quality desired by the target market and (2) the added quality must have a positive impact on profitability" (McDaniel and Gates 2008, 7).

This means that companies strive to find innovations or add improvements to areas that customers find important. For instance, if you are marketing a GPS unit, some features will be more attractive to customers than others. Recognizing voice commands would be a valuable feature of this product, whereas being waterproof may not add value for customers.

Communication and Marketing

Marketing communication (MC) is a subcategory of the concept of marketing. MC includes all the approaches utilized by corporations to communicate with all company stakeholders. These approaches include marketing public relations, direct marketing, personal selling of products or goods, advertising, and sales promotion. In other words, MC is integrated because it is a combination of all forms of marketing procedures put together to provide stakeholders with a comprehensive understanding of the message (Cornelissen 2008). It is imperative to note that MC enables companies to convey a single message to stakeholders given that different messages tend to confuse stakeholders and may damage the corporate branding. A case in point: Kenya Breweries Limited's major brand is Tusker whose logo is an elephant, and their Swahili language catchphrase *Baada ya Kazi Faraja* means "reward yourself after hard work." This has been a very popular brand both locally and in international markets. In fact, Tusker Export has won many international awards. However, when the company decided to introduce two new brands in honor of the then Senator Obama (the senator) and now President Obama (the president), the company did not use the same logo and message even though the two beers were very popular among the average Kenyans just because they were associated with the name "Obama." The company had trouble marketing the lagers because stakeholders felt that the brands did not fit the same theme. The two beers were associated with glamour, politics, and freedom according to the civil society and yet, the company made the sale price to be cheaper than Tusker in order to cater for the common *Mwananchi* or citizen.

In the past, marketing has taken a product-driven approach. This means that companies focus on the product attributes, often without reflection upon the consumer. For example, Animal Crackers were created in England in the late 1800s and later trademarked by Nabisco in 1902. The early marketing focused on the Christmas holiday. The circus-themed box was designed with a string handle to be used to hang on Christmas trees. For over 100 years, the bright blue, red, and yellow colors have remained the same. However, the animals have changed over the years. There have been 54 different animals, but lions, tigers, bears, and elephants have always been included in the box. In 2002, the cookie's 100th anniversary, consumers chose koala bears to add to the cookie collection.

Current marketing takes a more comprehensive approach. There are three elements in the marketing concept. The first is the consumer orientation (also known as a market approach), which focuses on the target market and aims to understand how the product can best meet their needs. The second component is a goal orientation, which often has profit as a key motive. While the goal orientation may focus on the consumer, the company's main objective is to reach their goal. For example, the goal may be to increase website traffic or sales. The third component is a systems orientation, which focuses on the internal corporate structure and competitor activity. Companies often change their tactics to keep up with trends in the market place. For instance, many restaurants offer free Wi-Fi to accommodate busy professionals. This market segment may choose one locale over the other based on easy Internet accessibility.

> After years of customer requests, Starbucks unveiled free Wi-Fi in their coffeehouses on July 1, 2010. Since 2008, Starbucks has partnered with AT&T to provide Internet access in the United States. Bell has provided Canada's Starbucks with Wi-Fi since 2005. In 2011, Starbucks updated Starbucks Digital Network in cooperation with Yahoo! This service, which was introduced in 2010, offers current information from websites such as *The Economist,* ESPN Insider, and Marvel Digital Comics.

In order to be successful, marketing must rely upon a foundation of research. Companies create a marketing plan to guide their marketing campaigns and help them achieve their goals. According to Buttell (2009), "An effective marketing plan defines and organizes your marketing efforts, so that you are focused on implementing the vision of your practice through targeted efforts, rather than trying to be all things to all people and ending up being nothing to anyone" (6).

Although there are only six steps in the creation of a marketing plan, companies devote a lot of time and money to the development of a thorough and well-researched plan. The following list outlines steps in the creation of a marketing plan (Moriarty, Mitchell and Wells 2009).

Step 1: Research Consumers, the Product or Service, and Competitors

Most organizations conduct either a situation analysis or SWOT (strengths, weaknesses, opportunities, threats) analysis. The SWOT analysis examines internal (strengths and weaknesses) and external (opportunities and threats) factors. The examples in the following text are real companies and the factors that they might include on their own SWOT analyses.

- Strengths: Burt's Bees has a strong reputation for social responsibility and environmentalism.
- Weaknesses: After Toyota recalled cars after brake failures, their reputation for consumer safety was tarnished.
- Opportunities: Whole Foods can take advantage of the recent organic food trend.
- Threats: McDonald's is facing criticism for their character Ronald McDonald because advocacy groups dislike the marketing of fast-food to children due to rising child obesity rates.

Step 2: Create Marketing Objectives

Companies must create specific goals that their marketing plan must accomplish. These goals will help steer efforts throughout the implementation of the marketing campaign. Marketing objectives should include four criteria: the target market, the desired outcome, a timeline, and they should be measurable.

Step 3: Divide Audience into Market Segment

Even if a product is designed to be used by a wide range of people, such as a toothbrush, marketing efforts still need to be concentrated to a narrower range of people. This range is known as a market segment. By dividing your target audience into smaller groups, companies can tailor their message to best serve customer needs.

Step 4: Separate Your Product from the Competition

Every product seeks to create a position in the marketplace. This position gives consumers another way to think about products relative to their competitors. There are two common ways that companies can distinguish themselves. First, you can try to situate your product or service as having the best quality for the best price. In this case, you try to stand out from other products and services in the environment by making yourself the cheaper product. Second, you can try to position yourself as a luxury product in the same market. In this case, your goal is to sell fewer units of your product or service, but your goal is to be seen as a luxury item that costs more. Ultimately, you make your money from being perceived as the luxury niche.

Step 5: Develop the Marketing Mix Strategy

In this step companies determine product design, pricing, how the product will be sold, and which marketing channels to use (i.e., television or radio ads). One of the biggest mistakes that novice marketing professionals can make is to over rely on one marketing channel. For example, if you are only marketing on radio stations, you'll miss the majority of people who now listen to iPods or satellite radio in the car. At the same time, if you're only marketing on television, you'll miss those individuals who DVR everything and never watch commercials. In today's day and age, we are bombarded by marketing messages, so the more times an individual can see your message the more likely it will stick out.

Step 6: Evaluation

Evaluate your marketing plan. In this step, companies review the success or failure of a marketing campaign and decide changes to implement in future marketing efforts. Remember, we often learn as much from a failed marketing attempt as from a successful one. Highly innovative marketing organizations must be willing to take risks and fail in order to key on the best marketing strategies.

Best Practices for General Marketing

When designing a marketing campaign, managers must decide how to allocate funds between various products. Some products have the potential to be more profitable than others. The "growth-share matrix," developed by the Boston Consulting Group in the 1970s, is designed to help managers evaluate a product's profitability (see Figure 6.1). The matrix divides products into four categories: cash cows, dogs, question marks, and stars. Cash cows are products with high market share and slow growth rate. These products generate a lot of income, but the slow growth rate means that the profits should not be reinvested in these products. Dogs have a low markets share and a slow growth rate, which means that they are not desirable. Often, products become dogs after they have been on the market for a while. Question marks are a low market share, high-growth product. These products need cash support to thrive. Unless the product takes off, they can become a financial drain on the company. Stars, the most desirable products, are high-share, high-growth products. This potential may be short lived; however, and stars may fade into cash cows if their popularity continues.

Successful marketers understand that there is a difference between the terms consumer and customer. While consumer denotes that one is a user and purchaser of products and services, a customer is one who has bought

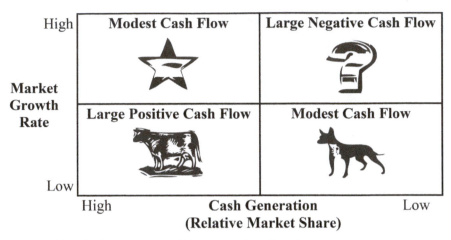

Figure 6.1   Cash Generation (Relative Market Share)

products from a specific brand or company. Therefore, everyone who has bought a computer is a computer consumer, but only those who have purchased a Mac are customers of Apple.

Over time customers can develop loyalty to a particular brand. A brand is a particular association to a product that companies work hard to cultivate. In fact, when companies are sold or merged, a lot of the value comes from equity built into the brand's name. Some brands carry an emotional meaning for customers, and they may refuse to buy products from another company. For instance, loyal Verizon customers refused to switch to AT&T to purchase the iPhone. Therefore, Apple agreed to allow Verizon to be a carrier of the iPhone.

Social Marketing in the 21st Century

Marketing has rapidly evolved over the past two decades as a result of Internet technologies. From the early days of simple banner advertisements on popular websites to Twitter feeds, how we approach marketing has been radically changed. In this section, we are going to first discuss a basic model for understanding social media marketing, discuss some tips and tricks for helping you with social media marketing, and then we'll discuss how to evaluate your basic attempts at social media marketing.

Marketing and Web 2.0

Since the earliest days of the United States's Defense Advanced Research Project Agency's invention of the Internet, people have been using the technology to socialize with other individuals. Individuals involved in the Internet project started using the technology to interact with peers around various hobbies as early as the mid-1970s. Of course, the real social aspects of the Internet really didn't completely take hold until the late-1990s after the U.S. Congress enabled public access to the Internet, service providers provided unlimited access to the Internet, and the World Wide Web and web browsers made finding information and socializing via the Internet user friendly. The culmination of all three of these events in the late-1990s opened up a completely new digital frontier and marketing professionals quickly realized that there were numerous opportunities to bring their products and services to their potential customers. However, in these early years, the majority of the content accessible through the Internet was organizational generated. In this case, organizations would create a corporate website and purchase banner ads on popular websites in an attempt to jump on the Internet bandwagon. Quickly, those old marketing tricks were either shown to be effective or ineffective in the new digital frontier.

The 21st century continued the development of the Internet, but instead of the content being created by highly specialized website developers, more and more of the content on the Internet is developed by individuals with no technological skills but a whole vast array of opinions. This later Internet development is commonly referred to in tech circles today as Web 2.0. Web 2.0 refers to the second generation of web development and web design that facilitates information sharing, user-centered design, user-generated content, and collaboration on the www. Because of the development of these new user-focused technologies, the early years of the Internet where organizations created content and you needed a web developer to get anything on the Internet is now referred to as Web 1.0, which is said to have originated in 1993 and still has some footholds in how marketing professionals approach the Internet today.

To help us understand how marketing occurs on the Internet in the 21st century, we developed a basic model looking at the types of marketing behaviors occurring today (Figure 6.2). This model has at its center the traditional consumer. The notion of a consumer has not changed with the advent of the Internet, but how we approach consumers has changed. In today's world, there are two different marketing forces that affect a consumer. First, we do have traditional marketing on the web. From advertisements that resemble television commercials before you watch a YouTube video, to banner ads, to Google ad word placement, there are a number of strategies that Internet marketers can utilize that resemble traditional marketing strategies. However, as people become more and more accustomed to these advertising strategies the more likely they are to ignore them or, worse yet, come to despise them.

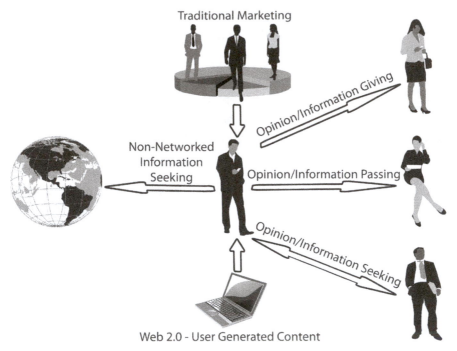

Figure 6.2   Social Marketing Model

Below the traditional consumer in the model are forms of online content that resemble traditional marketing content but have been created by users. User-generated content refers to "any material created and uploaded to the Internet by non-media professionals, whether it's a comment left on Amazon.com, a professional-quality video uploaded to YouTube, or a student's profile on Facebook" (Sathish, Kumar, and Bharath 2011, 14). For example, in spring 2011 in conjunction with Fox's hit television series *Glee,* the cast of *Glee* recorded a commercial for Chevy using their classic song "See the USA in Your Chevrolet." The cast then invited users from around the world to record their own versions of the Chevrolet's theme song. Ultimately, the winner Bruce McLamore won a Chevy for his a cappella version of the song. The contest produced around 500 different entries, so that's 500 different pieces of user-generated content all singing about Chevrolet that can now be found on YouTube. In July 2009, the Nielsen Global Online Consumer Survey of over 25,000 Internet consumers from 50 countries examined what types of advertising people trusted. While recommendations from people they know had a 90 percent trustworthiness score, consumer opinions posted online came in second at 70 percent tied with brand websites. More traditional media didn't fare as well: television 62 percent; newspaper 61 percent; magazines 59 percent;

billboards 55 percent; radio 55 percent; search engine ads 41 percent; online video ads 37 percent; online banner ads 33 percent; and mobile phone texts 24 percent (*NielsenWire* 2009). Overall, these websites show us that some of the most influential of the user-generated content comes in the form of product reviews placed by individuals who have purchased a product. In fact, many people today see Amazon.com's customer reviews as the go-to outlet for learning about a product or getting a general review of a product.

Obviously, one of the biggest problems with the high trust rate is that the majority of people who actually purchase a product will never submit a review for that product. General estimates would predict that about 10 percent of product reviewers account for 90 percent of the products reviewed online. As such, one factor marketing professionals may want to consider is how to influence these types of reviews. Obviously, it would be highly unethical to pay people to place product reviews. For example, in 2009 the vice president of marketing along with other Carbonite employees were caught red-handed when they posted reviews for the product on Amazon.com. While Carbonite was hardly the first company to attempt to sway online content, it is a good case of why you shouldn't attempt to fix the content. The story spread like wildfire over the Internet and the company went into full crisis mode, which included a public rebuke of the employees involved and the development of new online policies.

So, how can you impact this type of user-generated content in an ethical manner? First, if you provide people with a quality product or service, they are going to be more likely to go online and rate the product or service as such. You may want to send a reminder e-mail or letter asking them to write a review after the fact. These subtle reminders will increase the number of responses. Second, to avoid bad reviews, watch and respond. If you see that someone has poorly rated your product or service, try contacting that person and see how you can make her or his experience better. While there are always some consumers you can never change, many will alter their posts after the fact with "updates." Showing other consumers that you are watching and engaging is a very important facet of handling your online marketing. Remember, we call this form of marketing "social marketing" because you are building social relationships with your consumers. The more active you can be socially, the more positive the responses will be from your consumers.

In addition to traditional marketing and user-generated content, the left side of the model is referred to as nonnetworked information seeking. Nonnetworked information seeking occurs when individuals go out of their way to locate information that does not exist within their immediate social network. This form of marketing is hard to influence because most consumers now spend a great deal of time looking at products and services online before they ever purchase a product itself. According to Sathish et al. (2011), "89% of consumers pre-shop and conduct research online, but less than 7% of retail sales actually take place online. Online advertising drives $6 of in-store revenue for every $1 online. In today's marketplace, in-store sales start online for 89% of consumers" (11). As a marketing professional, your goal should be to predict how potential consumers' online experiences would look. Constantly run Internet searches for not only your product or service but similar products or services. You need to know what types of content exist both about your product or service and your competitor's products and services.

Where the left side of the model is all about the factors that influence a specific consumer, the right side of the model is how the consumer then acts after he or she has been influenced within her or his own social networks. On the right side of the model is really where we examine the social effects of Internet and what is called electronic word of mouth (eWOM) advertising. According to Henning-Thurau et al. (2004) eWOM is "any positive or negative statement made by potential, actual, or former customers about a product or company, which is made available to a multitude of people and institutions via the Internet" (39). As more and more people join various social networking sites such as Facebook, Twitter, LinkedIn, etc., marketing professionals are spending increasing amounts of money trying to influence purchasing decisions in these networking sites. In fact, according to Williamson (2006), marketing within social networking sites is expected to top $2.15 billion by 2010. With this amount of money streaming into social networking sites for marketing, the real question has become how to influence consumer behavior. However, much of what we've learned in social network marketing is that consumers are more likely to influence each other's behaviors. According to Chu and Kim (2011), consumers typically enact three different types of eWOM within their own social networks: opinion/information giving, opinion/information passing, and opinion/information seeking.

Opinion/Information Giving. The first type of eWOM behavior that consumers engage in within their own social networks involves giving opinions and information. Some consumers are constantly posting their opinions about various products or services they come in contact with online. From posting on various review sites, such as Amazon.com, to posting updates on Facebook about how much they love the latest book they've read, opinion givers are constantly sharing with their social networks information. While there are some opinion givers who can be influenced directly by marketers, ensuring that a consumer has a positive experience with a specific product or service is the fastest way to get positive results. One tactic that has been shown to work modestly is to locate those opinion givers who have wide circles of influence and target your marketing efforts at those individuals.

Opinion/Information Passing. A secondary behavior that many engage in relation to eWOM is what is referred to as opinion or information passing, which occurs when a consumer passes on someone else's opinions (either those learned from information seeking, traditional marketing, or user-generated content) to those individuals within her or his immediate social network. For example, if an individual reads an interesting tweet related to your product and then retweets that information, he or she is engaging in opinion passing. In the world of Twitter, many organizations have found this form of opinion passing to be highly important when spreading information.

In 2009 Starbucks started a purely social media campaign to reward its social media followers called "Free Pastry Day." After tweeting a free coupon via Twitter and creating a free pastry day group on Facebook, the amount of Internet traffic devoted to the event skyrocketed. Quickly, the Twitter coupon quickly accounted for 1 percent of the total tweets on the day of the event, which corresponded to a 10-fold increase in the number of mentions of Starbucks on a given day via Twitter. On Facebook, the event garnered more than 600,000 confirmed "attendees." According to Chris Bruzzo, Starbucks's vice president of brand, content, and online, the event drove more than one million people to stores. The event is now an annual event taking place in March. Overall, this example demonstrates that when people engage in opinion passing or information passing, the effects can be very large. Of course, it is ultimately in the hands of the marketing communication professional to determine how to create information that someone is willing to pass on to her or his social networks. In the case of Starbucks, it was something free.

Opinion/Information Seeking. In social networking communities, it is commonplace for individuals to post questions expecting someone in her or his social network who has experience with a specific product or service to provide her or his opinion to those questions. For example, when one of our coauthors was considering buying an iPad he tweeted and posted a question on Facebook to his social network asking about the pros and cons of buying an iPad. Within hours numerous individuals within his social network had provided their insight and he eventually made the decision to make the purchase. This give and take of information is one of the reasons why platforms such as Facebook and Twitter are so popular. As noted earlier, 90 percent of people trust the information and opinions they receive from people in their social networks, so this give-and-take is perceived as more credible as a whole because it is not coming from an organizational spokes person or an organization who is perceived as "having an agenda," which is one of the problems many Internet users have with traditional marketing on the Internet.

Tips and Tricks of Social Media Marketing

In the previous section, we discussed a basic model for understanding the types of influence that occur via the social web. In this section, we're going to briefly discuss 10 keys to creating powerful and effective online marketing campaigns.

1. *Go Where Your Customers Are.* One of the first things any good marketing communication professional must determine is where her or his customers are located. If you attempt to target all of your possible consumers using one social networking site, you may end up missing three-fourths of your potential demographic. As such, you must learn where your potential customers are online and then target them where they already are. While many marketing professionals attempt to drive people to their websites, most people do not eventually land on your website for information.

2. *Connect with Influencers.* In any social networking community, there are people that have more influence than others. One of the best strategies you can utilize is to find these top influences and attempt to get them on board with your product or service. This could involve anything from sending sample products to these influencers or providing them special deals. While many marketers will actually pay these influencers to mention products or services within their sphere of influence, this strategy can be problematic if it is detected for both your company and the influencer.

3. *Provide Assistance to Your Customers.* One of the smartest first steps you can take in social media is to provide customer service. BestBuy is notorious for allowing anyone within the company, who has gone through training, to help customers via social media. BestBuy employees constantly scour Twitter feeds looking for problems or concerns that customers have and then actively reach out to those individuals. This form of specialized customer service can definitely have a strong, positive boost in customer satisfaction. Furthermore, when people receive this kind of specialized attention, they are very likely to informally mention how impressed they were that a representative from a company reached out to them on such a personal basis.

4. *Promote Exclusive Offers Through Social Media.* Just as we saw in the Starbucks example earlier, one of the easiest ways to use social media is to offer exclusive offers for products and services via social media. First, it shows that you are taking your social media outreach seriously. Second, people love getting good deals, so showing people that you are willing to give something extra to people who are connected to your company via social media will make those people more likely to stay connected and tell others to become connected.

5. *Promote Products and Services.* It's definitely appropriate to promote your company's products and services via social media. You can do this through traditional press releases or videos on YouTube. Often creating videos of people using products or how to put together products can be a simple way of promoting what it is that your company does.

6. *It's Not Just About Products and Services.* Although it is appropriate to promote your products and services in social media, your focus should be on the development of relationships with the people you connect with. In the realm of social media, people who feel that they are being "advertised at" will become disgruntled and turn on you quickly. Instead, you need to balance the need to promote your company's products and services, but you need to create interpersonal relationships with the people connected to you. One easy way of doing this is to balance the professional with the personal. There are many CEOs on Twitter. The ones who typically have the largest followerships are those who talk about their daily lives, their families, trips they take, and so on. These mundane, everyday aspects of their lives are what keep people interested in reading their tweets. While these CEOs do throw in information about the company and their products and services, they make sure to keep the focus on self-disclosing information necessary in building interpersonal relationships.

7. *It's Not Just a Marketing Add-On.* One of the biggest mistakes that many marketing communication professionals make is to think of social media as an "add on" to traditional campaigns. Social media marketing must be an integrated part of any campaign. For example, in the Chevy "See the USA in Your Chevrolet" and *Glee* campaign, the campaign effectively tied in a combination of both traditional marketing (the *Glee* cast television advertisement) and the social media contest. One of these without the other would not have been as effective as the combination of both together.

8. *Monitor What Your Competitors Are Doing.* In our hypercompetitive world, you need to know what strategies and techniques your competitors are using in the social media world. While we do not recommend copying or mimicking your competitors, we do recommend knowing where their social media dollars are being invested. If they are investing huge amounts of money and time in Facebook, you have two decisions you could make. You could decide to compete with them in Facebook, or see if there are other social media markets they are completely forgetting by their singular focus. Ultimately, if you do not know what your competition is doing, it's hard to truly take progressive stances toward your own marketing niche.

9. *Stay Ahead and On-Top of Your Brand.* One of the biggest mistakes any company can make today is to be unaware of how others are viewing your brand and talking about your brand online. One of the simplest ways to handle this is to sign up for an RSS (really simple syndication) feed with your company's name or the names of your company's products or services. This way any time your company's names or the company's products or services are mentioned online, you can know what people are saying. By constantly

monitoring your Internet presence, you can more quickly respond when rumors arise on the Internet.

10. *Stay Informed of Trends, Tools, and News.* In the past few sections, you'll notice that we primarily mentioned only three social media tools: Facebook, Twitter, and YouTube, which was done on purpose. The reality is we are writing this chapter in late 2011, and by the time you read this section the newest tech trends and tools could have changed and probably have changed. There is no way for us to truly say what the future will hold. It's been our experience that anytime someone tries to say that X social networking site is the next big thing, that site is usually gone six months later. What we can say is that current trends are combining both the online experiences and the mobile experience. As more and more people own smart phones, the mobility of various online applications has become increasingly more important. People can now post Facebook updates, Tweet, and upload YouTube videos all from their smart phones, which was unheard of just five years ago. As this technology improves and as we become increasingly more mobile with our technology, how people interact with that technology and companies is going to alter along with the technology. We hope we've made these tips and tricks general enough to apply to whatever is coming in the future.

Evaluating Social Media Marketing

In the first part of this chapter, we discussed the social media case study of H&R Block who created a multifocal approach to social media marketing in 2007. According to Mcilroy and Klaassen (2008) the social media blitz led to 171 percent boost in Internet-ad awareness and a 52 percent increase in overall brand awareness. More than 600,000 people watched the Internet videos with the brand evangelist. Overall, the promotional campaign was ruled a gigantic success by H&R Block. All of this came from an expenditure that represented only 0.5 percent of H&R Block's total marketing budget for the year. But they're hardly the only organization that has found the return on investment (ROI) from social media campaigns to be highly profitable. For example, in research reported by Paine (2011) Sodexo spent $50,000 in a social media buy to vamp up its corporate recruitment efforts. The company filled all of its vacancies and decided to cut the $350,000 it was spending annually on Monster.com. Ultimately, this led to a savings of $300,000 or a net ROI of 6,000. Paine (2011) then discusses how Dell Computers used Twitter to increase their sales from 2007 to 2009. In this particular campaign, Dell offered special Twitter-only deals and then tracked the click through and purchase rates of those tweets. This Twitter campaign brought in roughly $3 million in revenues.

While the three examples earlier clearly show that social media marketing can be very beneficial to one's bottom line, Paine (2011) does caution about the over emphasis some companies may make on clear profits, "For decades, most companies have measured success in terms of volume of activity. Sales, marketing, hiring and pricing decisions were all made based on how many units you sold or needed to sell" (21). The problem with this approach to marketing is that it doesn't really take into account the world of social marketing. Instead, Paine recommends that companies "now need to factor relationships and reputation into your metrics. We've known for years that organizations only do business with the permission of their publics" (2011, 22). So how then does one approach measuring and evaluating social media marketing. As discussed in volume 1 of this set in chapter 15, the ROI is a very important metric that most communication professionals need to account for today. As such, the strategies and tips discussed in that chapter definitely are applicable here as well. Paine recommends six basic steps to measuring your social media ROI.

1. *Define Your Goals and Objectives.* Before you can really set out to determine the ROI of a marketing campaign, you really need to know what the basic goals and objectives of both the campaign and of the evaluation of the campaign will be. Unless all stakeholders are on the same page, you may end up with information that either does not satisfy the C-Suite or you'll end up missing what you should be measuring. Unfortunately, this chapter cannot possibly go into all of the possible social media metrics that can be evaluated, so we recommend reading Jim Sterne's (2010) book *Social Media Metrics: How to Measure and Optimize Your Marketing Investment* for more on this information.

2. *Define Your Environment, Your Audience, and Your Role.* As discussed previously in this section, you need to know who your potential consumer base socializes online. Furthermore, you need to understand your role in that online environment. Different online environments call for different mediated marketing tactics. For example, you should not handle your Facebook updates in the same way you handle your Twitter posts. First, Facebook allows for longer posts than Twitter (only 140 characters). Second, you need to understand what potential readers will do with your posted content. On Facebook, people can "like" what you've written or post comments, which is more passive and less directly influencing on their immediate social network. On Twitter, people can "retweet" what it is that you've written to their list of followers, which is more active and can be more impacting on their social network because of the emphasis halo effect.

3. *Define Your Investment.* You need to know how much you are willing to spend on social media marketing campaigns. As with any investment, there is always a certain amount of inherent risk. You also need to consider the

salaries and benefits of those people who will be directly responsible for managing or creating social media content as you determine the ultimate level of investment.

4. *Determine Your Benchmarks.* As generally discussed when talking about ROIs in business, it's very important that you know what your ultimate benchmarks should be. You should also know if your goal is to raise brand awareness, increase the number of people coming to your website, or actually increasing the sales of products and services. Depending on what your ultimate goal is for social media marketing, the benchmarks you need to set will differ. For your first foray into social media marketing, we recommend not over elevating your benchmarks artificially. While the examples discussed earlier had extraordinary ROIs, these are clearly not the norm. As such, you should research what similar types of social media campaigns in other sectors have done and what types of ROIs they achieved, so you can have a more realistic outlook when setting benchmarks.

5. *Select the Right Measurement Tools.* In addition to selecting appropriate benchmarks, you need to determine how you will collect your benchmark data. If your goal is determining how many people follow a link from a Twitter account to your home page and make a purchase, you're going to need to have a team of IT professionals help you in designing the mechanisms for measurement. If you're goal is to create a Facebook group with 10,000 "friends," then this type of measurement will not involve IT professionals. Again, the more forethought you can put into the measurement aspect of a communication marketing campaign, the stronger and more reliable your results will be.

6. *Turn Data into Action.* Lastly, you need to learn from your data. Whether a social media marketing campaign returns a large ROI or a negligible ROI, you still need to be open to learning from the campaign. While most people just want to say marketing was successful or unsuccessful, we learn as much from our mistakes as we do from our success. In the long run, you can use your data to find out what really works and what doesn't work in order to make future marketing campaigns stronger.

Key Takeaways

1. The "four Ps" of marketing (product, price, place, and promotion) is an outmoded concept, and should be replaced with the "four Cs" (customer solution, customer cost, convenience, and communication).

2. In order to be successful, marketing must rely upon a foundation of research.

3. There are six steps to creating an effective marketing plan: (1) research consumers, the product or service, and competitors; (2) create marketing objectives; (3) divide audience into market segment; (4) separate your product from the competition; (5) develop the marketing mix strategy; and (6) evaluation.

4. When thinking about a product's profitability, one must think of cash cows, dogs, question marks, and stars.

5. Social media marketing is about balancing the need to market products and services with developing relationships with various stakeholders.
6. In the traditional marketing model, the marketing professional has more control over how information is spread. In the social media marketing model, there is a lot more user-generated marketing that impacts people's purchasing power.

Glossary

Electronic word of mouth (eWOM): Opinion or information passing, which occurs when a consumer passes on someone else's opinions (either those learned from information seeking, traditional marketing, or user-generated content) to those individuals within her or his immediate social network.

Marketing: The activity, set of institutions, and processes for creating, communicating, delivering, and exchanging offerings that have value for customers, clients, partners, and society at large.

Marketing plan: Guide that enables an organization to ensure that their marketing campaigns help the organization achieve its goals.

SWOT analysis: An analysis of the strengths, weaknesses, opportunities, and threats in a given situation.

User-generated content: Material created and uploaded to the Internet by nonmedia professionals.

Web 1.0: The state of the World Wide Web, where the content was created by highly trained web designers and computer programmers.

Web 2.0: The second generation of web development and web design that facilitates information sharing, user-centered design, user-generated content, and collaboration on the www.

References

Brunot, Trudy. "What is Corporate Marketing?" August 2011. http://www.ehow.com/print/about_7350325_corporate-marketing-plan.

Buttell, Amy E. "4 Steps to an Effective Marketing Plan." *Journal of Financial Planning* (2009): 6–8.

Chu, Shu-Chuan, and Yoojung Kim. "Determinants of Consumer Engagement in Electronic Word-of-Mouth (eWOM) in Social Networking Sites." *International Journal of Advertising* 30, no. 1 (2011): 47–75.

Cornelissen, Joep. *Corporate Communication: A Guide to Theory and Practice.* 2nd ed. Los Angeles, CA: Sage, 2008.

Henning-Thurau, Thorsten, Kevin P. Gwinner, Gianfranco Walsh, and Dwayne D. Gremler. "Electronic Word-of-Mouth Via Consumer-Opinion Platforms: What

Motivates Consumers to Articulate Themselves on the Internet?" *Journal of Interactive Marketing* 18, no. 1 (2004): 38–52.

Hill, Sam, and Glenn Rifkin. *Radical Marketing.* New York: Harper Business, 1999.

Kotler, Philip. *Marketing Management: Analysis, Planning and Control.* Englewood Cliffs, NJ: Prentice-Hall, 1967.

Kotler, Philip, and Gary Armstrong. *Principles of Marketing.* 9th ed. Upper Saddle River, NJ: Prentice Hall, 2001.

McCarthy, E. Jerome. *Basic Marketing: A Managerial Approach.* Homewood, IL: Richard D. Irwin, 1960.

Mcilroy, Megan, and Abbey Klaassen. "What Accountants can Tell You about Using Social Media." *Advertising Age* 79, no. 20 (2008): 38.

McDaniel, Carl, and Gates, Roger. *Marketing Research Essentials.* 6th ed. Hoboken, NJ: John Wiley & Sons, 2008.

Moriarty, Sandra, Nancy Mitchell, and William Wells. *Advertising: Principles and Practice.* 8th ed. Upper Saddle River, NJ: Pearson, 2009.

NielsenWire. "Global Advertising: Consumers Trust Real Friends and Virtual Strangers the Most," (blog), July 7, 2009. http://blog.nielsen.com/nielsenwire/consumer/global-advertising-consumers-trust-real-friends-and-virtual-strangers-the-most/.

Paine, Katie Delahaye. "Measuring the Real ROI of Social Media: Organizations Need to Understand Not Just the Volume of Stuff They Sell, But the Social Context in which They Do It." *Communication World,* January–February (2011): 20–23

Sathish, M., V. B. Prem Kumar, and S. Bharath. "Impacts of Online Advertising on Sales." *Journal of Marketing & Communication* 7, no. 1 (2011): 11–17.

Sterne, Jim. *Social Media Metrics: How to Measure and Optimize Your Marketing Investment.* Hoboken, NJ: John Wiley & Sons, 2010.

Williamson, Debra Aho. "Social Network Marketing: Ad Spending Update." eMarketing White Paper, October 2006. http://www.emarketer.com/Reports/All/Em_soc_net_mktg_nov06.aspx.

CHAPTER SEVEN

Facebook, Twitter, LinkedIn, and Blogs Oh My! Social Media and Web 2.0: Using Today's Cutting-Edge Social Technology to Enhance Your Organization

Catherine Karl Wright

Organo Gold Embraces Technology; But Is that Enough?

Organo Gold is an organization that uses the network distribution system to introduce people to a healthier way to live through their products, as well as the ability to earn money while doing it. Given that this organization relies heavily on independent representatives who are part of a larger organizational chain, it would appear that Organo Gold would rely heavily on social media and advanced computing technology to maintain a strong presence in the mind of present and future customers and distributors.

Many distributors, especially those at the higher levels of the company, have embraced technology and are using it to reach out to people through text messaging, conference calls to hundreds, and through video on websites. However, there are better ways that the lower level independent representatives might reach out to people as they begin their venture into multilevel marketing.

Thus, the ability of the higher echelons of Organo Gold to reach out to the new or recently established representative becomes of most importance. As technology has expanded, independent representatives have sought ways to adapt and to use these tools to better facilitate their networking and their sales. However, with a diverse population and the propensity for network marketing to grow quickly without guidance for some, it is important that Organo Gold finds out what kinds of technology can be used so they can better incorporate Organo Gold's mission and vision statements.

There are a significant number of things that Organo Gold does now; however, there are some things that they might do in order to encompass their entire fleet of representatives from the brand new to the well established. As the company grows and seeks to reach its half-million representative goal for North America, Organo Gold needs to ask itself how can they use technology to aid their new reps? What kinds of technologies will be available to these new reps? What support can they expect from their upline? What training will be made available to new reps with lower than average computing skills? How will Organo Gold embrace the new stream of technologies to build their company to the next level? And, most importantly, what technologies are out there that they are not using, but should.

In the nascent days of the Internet, people had the ability to write e-mails and receive them and to browse through the graphic-bare websites. The fact that this technology existed was exciting to many because it allowed people to communicate instantaneously.

This original structure is known today as Web 1.0. Tim Berners-Lee created this protocol in 1991 and it became widely used over the following years. Dial-up modems were equipped to handle this kind of usage and were not, at that time, an impediment. Web 1.0 remained the constant throughout the 1990s and at the beginning of the new century; technology had evolved enough to support the change to Web 2.0.

Web 2.0 is the platform with which today's Internet users are most familiar. It relies on lightning-fast broadband connections to support its heft. This is the interactive, media-rich environment that supports programs such as Twitter, Facebook, YouTube, and millions of other graphic and video sites.

In today's world, the use of technology is essential for success in the workplace. With numerous avenues for information dissemination, it is important that organizations facilitate effective communication in order to best inform their workers.

How do organizations keep up with the constant need of information by consumers and employees? Do they focus on a specific set of platforms (Twitter, Facebook, and Blackboard) or do they try to use them all? This chapter will discuss these questions and challenge the reader to think about how he or she uses organizational technology in the form of social media in their everyday life. This chapter will look at what social media technology is, who uses social media, and the 10 most common activities online and how they relate to organizations. It will also address the kinds of social media available, will explain how they can be used, will address the ways in which organizations, including Organo Gold independent distributors, actually do use social media. Last, it will discuss ways in which all organizations might improve their uses of social media.

Social Media Technology

What Is It?

Originally, the Internet was designed to directly exchange information with others (Moore and Hebeler 2001). The Internet's purpose, primarily designed in the 1960s, was to provide military and academic institutions with the ability to share information from different networks in virtually real time (Barkai 2001). This is called peer-to-peer (P2P) exchange and was the building block of the first version of the Internet. Although computer technology was still young, the dreams were big. By the end of the 1960s, four universities joined together in the ARPANet in a successful effort to share information and communicate with others.

Two examples of how education and government, as well as those who understood technology, used the nascent Internet, were Usenet and Fido-Net. In the late 1970s, Truscott and Eh created Usenet so that people on different types of computers could converse with each other. Users had not been able to do so until Usenet was created (Beckett 1996). Fido-Net could best be described as a rudimentary e-mail system. This allowed users to post private and public notes in cyberspace for the first time (Balas 1993).

The use of P2P networking was the dominant way to share information through the 1970s and 1980s. During the mid-1980s when Apple introduced the first Macintosh, its creator actually envisioned it being used mainly as a communication tool (Cherry 2004). With P2P, computers "talked" directly to one another, without the use of a central server. Prior to Napster, the sharing of information directly between two or more people was the purview of people with intricate knowledge of the Internet. Toward the end of the 1980s, the Internet became something that was more easily accessible by "regular" people who became attuned to the chirping, whistling, and screeching of the 2400 baud modem. However, it was not until web browsing became available in the early 1990s that the Internet became easily accessible to the masses, thus dramatically decreasing the technological savvy needed to use the Internet.

When Andreessen created the Mosaic browser in 1993, the Internet again took a giant leap forward. The Mosaic browser enabled people to not only view text on their computers via the Internet, but to also view graphics. Through the 1990s, Netscape was the dominant browser used. In the late 1990s, Microsoft created Internet Explorer, which eventually became the standard because it was bundled with all Windows products. While Netscape no longer exists in its original form, it evolved into Firefox Mozilla browser, which many consumers still use.

The dot-com boom from 1995 to 2002 saw a revolutionary increase not only in the way people used the Internet, but also in the way organizations/corporations used the Internet (Callahan and Garrison 2003). The Mosaic browser was revolutionary and corporate America grasped at this opportunity to create online business portals where they could sell their products and services.

Take a look at the dates from the last few paragraphs and track how computer-mediated communication (CMC) technology grew. In the late 1980s and early 1990s, the computer became a household fixture rather than a work fixture. Children born during these years were introduced to computer technology, if not at home, then in schools. These years in which today's traditional college students and new, first-time employees were born and grew up have helped to shape the way technology is used in education and corporate America today (Efimova and Grudin 2007).

People who grew up in these years never knew a life without computer technology combined with communication technology. By the time they were old enough to hold a mouse, they had Internet. They have always used a mosaic browser. They have always been able to download music, watch movies, and e-mail their friends. They grew up playing Oregon Trail on their computers. They grew up with cell phones and text messaging. They grew up downloading music and movies. They grew up with Facebook and MySpace and Twitter.

Who Uses Social Media?

Given the numerous ways that organizations can keep in touch, it is not surprising that they use these media and embrace them. According to Mullan (2008) and Silence (2008), there are four age groups in the workforce: traditionalists, Baby Boomers, Gen Xers, and millennials. Groups are categorized as follows: traditionalists were born between 1922 and 1945; Baby Boomers between 1946 and 1963; Generation X: between 1964 and 1980; and millennials: between 1981 and 1995 (Silence 2008).

Each brings a different set of workplace ethics. "Traditionalists generally consider loyalty, patience, mission, and respect as the main values they expect from their workplace, while the Baby Boomers place importance on teamwork, long hours, hard work, and recognition. Gen Xers consider competence, ongoing learning, informality, and feedback as important. Millennials, on the other hand, tend to think achievement, structure, collaboration, and mission are more significant work values" (Mullan 2008, 16).

As college students graduate and enter the workforce, employers are working with a population that is often times more media- and technology savvy than those who manage them, although Generation Xers are catching up.

> 1922–1945: Traditionalists
> 1946–1963: Baby Boomers
> 1964–1980: Generation X
> 1981–1995: Millennials

A 2011 study by Pew Internet and American Life Project (Zickuhr 2011) discovered that millennials are more likely to own a laptop than a desktop, making their computing experiences far more portable. Only 9 percent of the adult American population did not own computer-related devices. Thus, with technology being this prevalent across adults of all ages, the challenge for organizations is to keep on par with the pulse of both their employees and their consumers.

Blogs were created in 1998, RSS feeds in 2000, Wikipedia arrived in 2001, social networking sites (SNS) such as Skype in 2003, Facebook in 2004, podcasts in 2004, YouTube in 2005, and Twitter in 2006 (Rainie 2006). Even in the past decade, there has been an explosion of applications, technological feats, and media that support them.

The millennial generation currently entering the workforce for the first time grew up using myspace.com during elementary and middle school, transferring to Facebook.com when they went to high school. As they went through school, Twitter became a phenomenon when they were in high school or freshmen in college, and millennials are already used to abbreviating words as they text messaged (160 characters), so truncating down to Twitter's 140-character limit about their every thought and action wasn't difficult.

While it may seem hard to imagine a world without being able to download or stream music (think iTunes or Pandora), movies (e.g., Bit Torrents), data (e.g., USB drives), or e-mail instantly (think smartphones), the World Wide Web is only just over 20 years old. Many people of all ages rely on the instant technology. A 2011 Pew Internet Project recorded that "seventy nine percent of American adults said they used the internet and nearly half of adults (forty seven percent), or fifty nine percent of Internet users, say they use at least one of SNS (Social Networking Site)" (Rainie et al. 2011). Additionally, they found that over half of SNS users are over 35. Technology has blurred the lines between what would be nice to have or nice to know with the instant yeaning and demand for answers 24 hours a day, seven days a week.

Social Networking Sites (SNS) are used by almost 3 out of 5 American adults, while the Internet is used by almost 4 in 5 adults.

People under 30 expect to be able to instantly get in touch of friends or a coworker immediately. Waiting for an answer isn't something they think is normal. They have asked it, it should be answered. They are not rude, not impatient, not petulant; they are simply living in age of technological instant gratification.

Millennials expect this instant and constant access. Adults in their 30s and older are relying more and more on this same technology. However, what about those from whom they expect information from as consumers and employees? Are organizations keeping up with the trends? Are they responding quickly enough to their consumers and employees? Are they using technology and applications that people need, want, or expect them to use? Last, how can organizations cater to the needs of the population when applications and/or platforms change practically overnight?

How Is Computer-Mediated Communication Technology Used?

Miller (2001) noted there are 10 common activities online that allow people to communicate and exchange information: distributed computing, e-mail, file sharing/swapping, FTP (file transfer protocol), group collaboration/conferencing, instant messaging, Internet chat, Internet telephony, Usenet newsgroups, and web browsing. Over the past decade, each of these has grown and adapted as technology has improved and increased in capacity. Therefore, some of the categories will include newer terms, which reflect the category's growth. Each of these will be discussed in terms of usage today in organizations.

1) Distributed Computing (Cloud Computing)

In today's business environment, distributed computing is not so much used as is cloud computing. While the two are slightly different, they are combined here because cloud computing is the new trend in information, programming, and file sharing; a grandchild, if you will, of distributed computing (Chappell 2008). As Kang et al. (2011) stated, "Cloud computing is a new information technology trend that moves computing and data away from desktops and portable PCs into large data centers" (3596). This is reminiscent of the 1970s when organizations had a central server to which workers connected.

According to (Dong et al. 2010), "a cloud is defined as a large-scale distributed computing paradigm that is driven by economies of scale, in which a pool of abstracted, virtualized, dynamically-scalable, managed computing power, storage, platforms, and services are delivered on demand to external customers over the Internet" (448).

> This information can be easily accessed by any computer-based item, such as a laptop, a desktop or a smartphone. This is a tremendous boon for those who telecommute or who need to travel extensively for their job.

Cloud computing is flexible, has fast deployment, reliable service, and can also reduce costs and improve operational efficiency (Tian, Lin, and Ni 2010). With cloud computing, people only need to pay for the services they actually use and are not bound by the costly acquisition of physical hardware (Lee et al. 2011).

While this might prove very effective in a large corporation with multinational offices, the question to think about is how this might be used in a smaller organization, such as Organo Gold. While their goal is to have 500,000 distributors in North America, is cloud computing something that would benefit a geographically diverse population with no real-time offices for people to work from? Is cloud computing necessary or can distributors find what they need from the company-provided individual website? How could cloud computing work to make the exchange of information more efficient?

2) E-Mail

Electronic mail (e-mail) is a staple of organizational communication. It allows people within buildings and across the globe to communicate quickly and effectively. In late 1971, Ray Tomlinson, a pioneer in computer networking and communication, linked two protocols through which people would be able to send and receive messages. It was Tomlinson who randomly chose the @ symbol to delineate between the user's name and the name of the host computer.

> Ironically, when [Tomlinson] shared his new invention [e-mail] with his coworkers, they were not terribly impressed. "At the time, no one knew the extent to which e-mail would redefine business and personal communication" (Kaplan, 2002, 28).

In 2001, the International Data Corporation stated that "9.8 billion electronic messages are sent each day" (Hafner 2001). According to the web-monitoring service Royal Pingdom, in 2010, over 107 trillion messages were sent. Clearly e-mail is of vital importance to millions of people, arguably many of them in business.

There is no question that over the last 40 years e-mail has been of tremendous use. With the number of e-mails increasing so drastically over one decade, it is tempting to extrapolate the data and consider the number of e-mails will only increase considerably.

But, one might ask," in the age where social media are numerous and the desire to get one's message out to as many people immediately as is possible, how do e-mails fit into the fabric of today's communication structure?" If an Organo Gold distributor wants to send out information or promotional specials to people, is e-mail the best vehicle through which to do so? Are e-mails of vital importance to organizations in disseminating information or are other media more viable? Would it be more beneficial to use an SNS?

As technology has advanced, so have the devices through which one can use the technology. No longer must one rely on a computer to communication via e-mail with others. Pew Research estimates that about 85 percent of adults own a cell phone (Zickuhr 2011). In the same article, Zickuhr writes that millennials "use their phones also for going online, sending email, playing games, listening to music, and recording videos" (1). With the ability to access the Internet at almost any time, the ability to send e-mails increases considerably. This is something that organizations need to consider as they navigate social media and interact with the current and future generations of consumer.

3) File Sharing/Swapping

The first program that one might think of when talking about file sharing or file swapping is Napster. In 1999, Shaun Fanning created a revolutionary program that allowed people to share files in real time without using a central server to host the swapping. Numerous lawsuits between and among companies occurred during the early part of first decade of the 21st century as well as organizations such as the Recording Industry Association of America suing individuals who were found to have illegally downloaded music, movies, and other copyrighted materials.

Smith and Fowler (2011) stated that while music piracy has decreased, piracy with film and TV has become a growing problem. Eric Garland, who is the founder and chief executive of an organization that tracks online activity, said that their research found that on average, top box-office movies are downloaded millions of times. This costs media companies billions of dollars. Over the past decade, many laws have been put into effect to prevent this and numerous legal options, such as iTunes, have been made available so that people who wish to abide by the law can do so.

Going back to the case study that started this chapter, Organo Gold does not utilize this Internet function; they make information available to their distributors and clients through .pdf, through video, and through websites, among others. However, what this means for other organizations is that they will need to maintain a certain diligence regarding the information they collect and the information they pass on. When organizations create information that might be necessary to be shared, do they ensure that this information is safeguarded and protected from those who might wish to steal or otherwise misuse it? Regardless, organizations will need to create enough legal outlets for their information or be creative in the way they introduce their information in order that they will not be a part of the problem, but rather part of the solution.

4) File Transfer Protocol (FTP)

Sohail et al. (2005) wrote that FTP is a common application used to upload or download files of a very large size. The transfer of files often takes a long time and has contributed to delays when bottlenecks occur. Despite the length of time some files require, it has remained an efficient way for people to exchange information. It remains a convenient way for people to share files that cannot be sent via e-mail and it has the advantage over file sharing in that to exchange files, it does not have to synchronous.

El-Rakabawy and Lindemann (2007) recognized the problems with network congestion and proposed a way in which files could be "chunked" and sent in many different, smaller pieces, eventually winding up at the other computer(s) as a whole file. This way, numerous people could begin to download the file and the program would search for the parts the end file still needed from numerous other users. In this way, they stated, significant Internet congestion could be lessened or even possibly eradicated.

As technology advances, it is now possible to use one's mobile device such as a smartphone to exchange files using a mail client or some other application for that purpose. Bandwidth available through technology such as 4G has made it possible for larger files to be shared than in the past. However, there is still reliance on a program or application. A proposal by L. Dorai, L. K. Veerabadran, and R. Dorai (2010) proposed a more efficient communication technique for multimedia file transfer. They stated, "Organization [sic] can use their own servers for storing the files and [the] operator's server is utilized for peer to peer architecture. Such

[a] concept of file transfer will benefit mobile operators, companies, orga-nizations, and general users" (1).

What they suggested is very similar to cloud computing. Thus, it is pos-sible that cloud computing may make FTP less used; however, FTP is still an important way that organizations can share information within their organization and post information for those outside their organization.

5) Group Collaboration/Conferencing

When the Internet was first created, one of its primary functions was to allow a group of computers to share information, making group commu-nication a priority. The ability to link together several people in a group setting has blossomed into a thriving business for organizations. The abil-ity to video conference via the Internet has become valuable to organiza-tions, saving them both money and time on travel. Such groupware allows people who are not similarly geographically located to meet together in present time to complete organizationally bound tasks (Josefowicz 2011). Schultz (1999) wrote that "in many organizations today, working in groups is the primary means by which the tasks of the organization get done" (379).

As Booth (2010) discussed, "Collaboration environments and virtual meeting spaces are growing increasingly sophisticated and customizable, as Google Wave and other new platforms integrate dynamic features and create rich real-time and asynchronous networks" (21). Such platforms can be useful in many ways, not only between and among employees, but also when working with other publics, such as focus groups, insight com-mittees, and customers.

Additionally, if someone cannot travel to a location, yet needs to present information to coworkers, employees, future clients, the use of collabora-tion/conferencing technology is vital for success.

There are numerous companies that support and sell these kinds of products. Generally, a video telephony program creates an environment where more than one person at a time can communicate through both video and microphone. In some programs, multiple people can be confer-enced in, alleviating the need to be physically face-to-face. Other products have the ability to use a white board, chat, take control of others' comput-ers, and to show and share files with about 50 people. This can certainly be advantageous to a group that needs to visually see and to have physical access to files in a synchronous fashion. These programs negate the need to by face-to-face physically for more than a few, limited times.

Organo Gold does not currently utilize a program like this, preferring to use group telephone calls where people dial into a main number and hundreds can listen in to someone, often a top producer, speak. Would a group program be beneficial to an organization like Organo Gold? Would it be helpful to host new training sessions or to have a meeting of their downline in order to explain new and exciting promotions? How might Organo Gold be better poised to help others using this kind of group meeting technology?

6) Instant Messaging

One of the most familiar computing applications, other than e-mail, through which people exchange information is instant messaging (Fattah 2002). Haas, Carr, and Takayoshi (2011) wrote that "IM is one example of an increasingly ubiquitous phenomenon in contemporary culture, interactive networked writing (INW)" (277), and the researchers noted that this phenomenon occurs in real time for the most part and is done via a keyboard or keypad. A leader in electronic communication technology, in 1996, AOL (America OnLine) created AIM (AOL instant messaging). Other well-known platforms of instant messaging include Google Talk, MSN Messenger, and Yahoo! Messenger. As early as the turn of the century, Miller (2001) noted that people used instant messaging to send over a billion messages each day. That staggering number represented more than the total mail volume of the U.S. postal service.

When first introduced, people used instant messaging as a way to exchange text-only messages between two or more people. As technology advanced and bandwidth increased, people became able to exchange text-only messages, document files, pictures, video, and voice files (Barkai 2001). The introduction of Apple, Inc.'s iPhone in 2007 brought in a whole new way for people to expand their communication capabilities; they were well received, surpassing expectations. With the introduction of the iPhone, Blackberry, and other smartphones, people are able to IM from a huge number of locations.

Kamel Rouibah (2008) noted that "IM helps millions of people around the globe to easily communicate with friends, colleagues, and strangers to exchange information in real-time" (35). Rouibah also notes that an advantage of instant messaging programs is that people can show up online as available or unavailable, thus facilitating communication. A 2002 article noted that when Verizon began using IM, it saved up to "30 minutes per day for each user" (Vaughan-Nichols 2002, 42). Vaughan-Nichols believed this time-savings was because the worker could "simultaneously chat online while teleconferencing or working on another project on their PC" (42). Is IM useful or is it a distraction during working hours? Do workers use it for personal communication or do they, in fact, use it to communicate with others in their workplace? Would this kind of communication be something that clients might be interested in? Do you think that a small organization that relies heavily on interpersonal communication and interaction might find IM limiting or time-saving?

7) Internet Chat

When the need for a small group of people to gather and exchange information, Internet chat is a good solution. Facebook, AIM, Yahoo Messenger, and MSN Messenger all have the chat function, whereby several people, yet far fewer than in a group-collaboration setting, can share information.

Facebook, which self-reports that it has 750 million users, has a chat function through which friends can join and discuss events relevant to their current or future plans. As many people already use Facebook as a way to keep in touch, using that platform's chat program makes sense. However, it is not as easy to share files and pictures in this chat program unless they are linked to a website, making other platforms more useful for this process.

An example of the slight limitation of chat can be found when in late June 2001, Chicago's mayor, Rahm Emanuel, held a town hall meeting through the Internet. People interested in joining in did so via Facebook and Livestream. The Mayor's Press Office stated that "589 people were online at once watching live, 708 people participated online prior to the event, [and] 517 questions were submitted online" (Sardin 2011, 2). Although this was a video, the fact that people could participate via Facebook made this chat session a lot more attainable. However, while people did use Facebook, it might have been beneficial to use the Livestream application instead. These, however, are things that each organization must consider when using or considering using different programs/applications in their technological menu.

8) Internet Telephony

In the day and age where cost-cutting has risen as prices have risen, it is not surprising that organizations would seek to use existing technology to ease both cost and commitment. Current telephony is driven by older technology and the incurrence of individual fees for individual lines. Individuals who no longer have landlines still know people who have them and still use them, making it challenging to use Internet telephony or cell phones without incurring some additional cost. Lee Rainie (2011) discovered that almost a quarter of American adult Internet users have, at one time, placed phone calls online. This number totals almost one-fifth of all American adults.

A 2009 article by Cliff Kuang hypothesized that as wireless companies are faced with consumers who use broadband capabilities both with and without their cell phones, Internet telephony will reduce or eliminate high costs for overseas calls. Kuang believes that soon "it'll be just another service embedded in a holistic data plan" (59). Until that time, people who use Skype, ooVoo, or companies such as Rebtel.com who specialize in international phone calls via the Internet must be prepared to spend money to talk with loved ones at home.

It is not just international callers who are intrigued by the cost savings of Skype and Rebtel-type companies. Organizations who pay hefty user fees to landline telephone companies have sought unique ways to cut their costs. Organizations are driven by contracts that have been made and kept, but may not be in the best financial interests of a department or even the organization as a whole. When the University of California experienced significant budget cuts, UC Berkeley Library decided to pilot a Skype program among its employees to see if using this Internet telephony would be an acceptable change from landline phones (Booth 2010, 20). The savings, Booth found, were significant: $30 per year for Skype versus $44 to $54 per month for a landline telephone.

An organization like Organo Gold relies heavily on interpersonal communication and building relationships. Would it benefit by having their employees and independent distributors sign up to communicate via Internet telephony? Who would or should be responsible for the costs incurred? Is there a need for this kind of communication package to be made available?

9) Usenet Newsgroups

Usenet groups rely on user-generated content. More importantly, they do not have to be accessed through a web client. These important additions to the Internet's "voice" are sometimes confused with blogs. A newsgroup, such as a Usenet newsgroup, has been around since the beginning of information exchange between computers in the 1970s, and in some form, even prior to then. A newsgroup is a group to which a user subscribes because they are interested in the news on a specific subject that is posted there and their ability to comment on those particular posts. The focus of the newsgroup is the subject at hand. A blog is created by one person (or a team) that tells a story from their point of view. While users can subscribe and interact with a blog, one subscribes to a blog because of the author's point(s) of view rather than the specific topics. Thus, a newsgroup is supposed to be more rounded in viewpoints versus a blog. Of course, there are many levels of communication exchange and as the Internet has grown and continues to grow, there are many times when these distinctions are blended and may appear homogenous in nature.

The more modern form of newsgroups is knowledge management (KM). KM has been around since the early 1990s. It is a set of organizational elements such as corporate strategies or best practices that an organizations uses. This has helped organizations note what they need to do in order to best serve their employees and internal publics.

Through the 1990s and 2000s, KM has been taught in numerous fields and many organizations have allocated internal resources to increasing KM within their employee ranks. While KM often targets organizational objectives, it also focuses on the dissemination of information that will broaden the strategic focus of the organization itself. Thus, the exchange of information is still very prevalent, it has simply updated itself to reflect the changing technological needs of employees in a way that Usenet cannot.

The foundation of Internet information exchange is still widely used. People in organizations use listserv to disseminate information, use bulletin boards to post questions and seek answers, and engage in KM, and these formats are a comfortable platform. While KM helps the organization maintain internal information flow, blogs have become a savvy way for organizations to brand themselves with their external publics.

A newsgroup is meant to introduce to someone news specific to the organization. The information in newsgroups tends to be "hard" news or variations of that. A blog is meant to contain useful information to consumers, but it might be seen more as "soft" news. A blog is a place where pictures, video, links, text, and chat functions can be found. They are ubiquitous, as most organizations, especially those trying to maintain a youthful base, have a blog.

> Newsgroups tell people information about something to do with an organization, more newsy than PR. However, when we discuss blogs, it's more about the PR kind of news or what some might consider "soft" news.

What are the advantages of having a newsgroup? What are the advantages of having a blog? If an organization has one, should it have both? Organo Gold gives the individual the opportunity to have a blog if desired, but does not offer them the service. Is this a good business decision?

Should Organo Gold have a newsgroup too or is the website, e-mail, and other items used enough?

10) Web Browsing

Web browsing is perhaps, after e-mail, one of the most common uses of the Internet. A web browser is the way that users move from one area of the Internet to another. It is the way that organizations, individuals, and numerous other entities can put a "face" to their name in cyberspace. Not having a website is the kiss of death to a company, especially if they are trying to sell a service or a product.

When Google appeared, it became the dominant search engine through which people could find information they were seeking. There are numerous search engines, billions of websites, and an infinite number of ways in which people use the web. In order for organizations to be seen, they ideally should be on the first page of the search results. Thus, a complicated and highly competitive means through which organizations show up first developed.

Browsing through the web to discover information is one of the best aspects of using the Internet. If you enter your terms in any search engine, for example, Google, Yahoo!, or a library portal, you will be introduced to numerous (sometimes millions) of possibilities. The ability to browse through websites has brought the power of the encyclopedia, the bookstore, and the library into people's living spaces and has completely changed the way in which people gather their information.

In 2008, Nicholas Carr wrote about his concern that the Internet has changed the way people read and process information; and not in a good way. Carr discussed his discovery that he, as well as some of his friends, used to be able to concentrate on long pieces of prose, drinking it in. Now, Carr feared, people are so used to browsing the web that they are being taught to skim, to glance, and to engage in the kind of reading and processing that does not require much deep thought, if any at all.

While this may be true for some, other researchers have indicated that as with other forms of technology, people will adapt and adjust their intake and processing and retain their abilities to intellectually process information. Cascio (2009) wrote, "the focus of our technological evolution would be less on how we manage and adapt to our physical world, and more on how we manage and adapt to the immense amount of knowledge we've created" (96).

There is no question that in order to be successful in a business setting organizations must use the Internet and websites to their advantage. When you sign onto the web the next time, consider where you go, what you research, and how you read and absorb information. Do your actions surprise you? Are you more aligned with Carr or Cascio?

Technology and Organizations

This chapter so far has discussed the 10 ways in which people can and do use the Internet. The question now arises: Organizations have social media and other technological advances at their disposal. Should they be used? And if so, how? Booth (2010) wrote that "personal preference was an important factor in virtual productivity" (21). If this is true for workers, might it be true for clients and consumers of organizations? Common sense would dictate that is it so, as what works for one person might not work for another. Thus, it would seem wise for organizations to have an array of options through which nonemployees and employees alike might be able to find more information.

Mobile computing is a very popular form of activity between and among business employees. As corporations leave the first decade of the new century, technological devices have gotten smaller in physical size, with larger memory and hard drives, and most importantly, this technology has become mobile.

Introduced in North America in 2005, one of the more popular mobile technologies was 3G, which allowed users to gain access to voice telephone, Internet access, TV, and to use programs such as Skype, all in a mobile environment. This advanced technology allowed for a greater sense of security, although it was not without issue. In late 2008 and early 2009, 4G was introduced. Currently, 4G is the technology of choice, as it allows for seamless mobile application usage, such as instant messaging.

With technology like 3G and 4G, people are able to do their computing activities from a variety of locations. One only needs a "hot spot" (where a device can pick up a wireless signal) or an Internet key (that will directly access the Internet) to connect to the Internet and thus access an entire office from a remote location.

Tablet computers are a computer designed to be taken with you. They are smaller than most laptops and are operated by touching the screen to type or perform commands. The more recent ones are highly haptic, allowing users to perform multifunctional commands easily.

M-learning is another way in which organizations can use mobile technology. In an organization such as Organo Gold, where independent representatives are spread throughout the globe, having learning tools available through their tablet computers or smartphones will enable the organization to disseminate information while, at the same time, offering needed information to their reps in ways that are convenient for them to receive.

In this way, organizations will work with their employees, meeting them in their area of comfort, rather than offering information that is not convenient or easy for them to receive, especially if they are away from the office.

In addition, to decide which platforms might best serve both internal and external publics, organizational policies for security need to be established. As Fossi (2010) noted, "if organizational policies are not established (both from an end user and network perspective), it can create security issues for the organization and its employees" (15). He goes on to discuss the importance of protecting confidential information and the exposure of liabilities.

Other organizations, such as the U.S. Army and U.S. Marine Corps, have either issued guidelines for their personnel using social media (army) to banning it from their network (marines). For a long time, members of the U.S. House of Representatives were not allowed to use video-conferencing software because of previous attacks on federal networks. In June 2011, the House Administration Committee approved the official use of Skype and ooVoo (J. Smith 2011, ¶ 1). This was cited as one way in which Congress could save money while maintaining close contact with its constituents.

Cbeyond, an IT and communication services company, noted in July 2011 that "Small businesses are using social media tools in creative ways to promote their brands and connect with customers" ("Communication Equipment Companies; Cbeyond Announces Winner of Social Media Contest" 2011, 291). In the same month, Dr. Smith's "Baby Steps for March of Dimes" promotion began. This promotion donated $1.00 for each time the "like" button on Facebook was clicked, up to $50,000. "Social outreach efforts to support the campaign include educational blogs, dedicated e-mail distributions to March of Dimes supporters, Facebook and Twitter posts, promotion by Dr. Smith's Premium Parent brand ambassadors and Facebook ads" ("Dr. Smith's Diaper Ointment Deploys Social Networks to Launch New Campaign" 2011).

In addition to earning money for charities, social media is used to build interest or create hype for certain events. AMC Theatre uses Twitter, Facebook, and YouTube to share breaking news with interested people. "Conversations about AMC Theatres and about the movies in general are happening all the time within social media channels and we are there, actively participating in the discussion" ("AMC Theatres; AMC Theatres® Conjuring up Record Advance Ticket Sales for Harry Potter and the Deathly Hallows—Part 2" 2011, 104). In this way, AMC Theatre and other organizations can post information, include their external publics, and create a solid communication network through which they can market their services and goods.

Kara Allan, owner of the successful business Style by Kara, said that in order to maintain her success, she creates "daily fashion, beauty and glamour tips about four times a day to almost 5,600 followers on Twitter, 5,000 friends on Facebook, and 1,400 contacts on LinkedIn. I reach clients that I never would have an opportunity to interact with if it wasn't for social media. It allows me to give potential clients information about what I can offer them, to try 'before they buy' and positions me as an expert. Social media has revolutionized my business!"

> Twitter, Facebook, and LinkedIn have been a boon to Ms. Allan and her business. Using these social media platforms, she is able to reach thousands of people with numerous tips regarding fashion, beauty, and glamour.

One of the most important considerations that this chapter has not addressed is cost. Although there are many free platforms for people and organizations to use, they can often times be limiting. The old adage, "You get what you pay for" can be a very dangerous way for organizations to live. In order for an organization to be successful, time, effort, and money must be wisely implemented to create a solid foundation from which a successful marketing campaign can be built. There are many creative ways in which this can happen and social media sites are at the forefront.

Communication Platforms

This section will briefly touch on three of the larger programs used by people and by organizations to disseminate information to a large group of people. A study by Rainie et al. (2011) found that of those involved with SNS, 92 percent of them used Facebook, 18 percent used LinkedIn, and 13 percent used Twitter.

These programs each use many of the 10 CMC items mentioned previously. Thus, as the Internet has grown in size and power, organizations have been able to be more creative and have begun to adapt to these changes and to incorporate them into their marketing programs. How Organo Gold and other organizations use Facebook, LinkedIn, and Twitter will be addressed and smaller, lesser programs will be mentioned in one section.

Facebook

In February 2004, Mark Zuckerberg created a program that was in many ways a public bulletin board for people to post information about their lives. In September 2005, the high school version arrived and a year later, Facebook was opened up to anyone with a valid e-mail address. It has grown from a platform designed to target the college-aged student, to a platform where people of all ages and businesses of all kinds can post information about their lives and/or products, can post pictures, play games, can link to items on the Internet, can chat, and do a host of other things.

One of the most useful functions from an organizational standpoint is the "like" button. If you are an independent business owner, such as someone who works for Organo Gold, you can create a page, send the link out to others and ask them to "like" your page. When this happens, Facebook links their page to yours and your friends can now see who or what you "like." It is the technological version of the telephone game where you tell other people something; unlike the telephone game, the information shared stays the same no matter how many times someone goes from your page to the organization's page.

Another useful feature of Facebook is the ability to post things onto your wall. This is the place where a person or organization can post information as text, attach files, link to other websites, show pictures, and otherwise create a personalize bulletin board for the world to see. As an organization, for example, you can post promotions, pictures of your products, a link to your website, and motivational messages—all designed to promote your product while maintaining a collegial, friendly, and very personal atmosphere. Friends go to other friends' Facebook pages, thus when a company has a Facebook page, they are attempting to show others how friendly they are.

LinkedIn

LinkedIn is a business-related social networking website. It was launched in May 2003 and self-reports more than 100 million registered users as of March 2011. LinkedIn has an array of services one can use: e-mail, news, forums, search engines, and ways on connecting with others. It allows you to manage your profile and maintain a sense of ownership over your professional life.

Unlike Facebook, which focuses on the social aspect of networking, LinkedIn focuses on the professional aspect of networking. It enables people to create a profile and then create and maintain a list of contacts. These can be people they know directly (first-level connection), people they know through others (second-level connections), or even third-level connections, where they link with a person their friend's friend knows.

This platform can be very useful in terms of networking and there are some measures put in place that keep the level of security reasonably high. In addition to individuals joining, organizations can also join so that people interested in an organization can gain accurate information about it.

LinkedIn diversifies the way people can get information, yet attempts to keep the information within channels of trust. If you reach out to a third-level connection, all you need to do is mention the networking chain, and there is a greater chance of success than there would be with a random phone call or e-mail.

While LinkedIn is a professional networking site, there is also a solid organizational presence on the service too. This means that people can easily post information to others or ask questions about endless topics. Jansen (2010) reported 46 percent of Americans used Facebook or Linked-In when sharing product or service information. This makes it more important than ever for organizations to maintain a strong web presence, to use social media to their advantage, and to be vigilant about all information shared from one to another about their products and services.

Twitter

Twitter began in March 2006 with three founders. Globe and Mail reported in March 2011 that Twitter has almost 200 million users worldwide and that almost half a million new Twitter accounts are opened daily. More than 140 million tweets are sent daily, amounting to about 1,600 tweets per second (Picard 2011). A study done by the Pew Internet and American Life Project in May 2011 found that 13 percent of online adults use Twitter. Of those who use Twitter, half of them use their cell phones to access it (A. Smith 2011). This is no small feat for a social media platform that according to PEW, only 13 percent of adults use.

NASA planned a two-day marketing campaign where people could tweet to win an opportunity to participate in the launch of the twin lunar-bound GRAIL spacecraft. The NASA website encourages people to participate in an opportunity to win a tour of the Kennedy Space Center Visitor Complex, to speak with scientists and engineers from the project, to view the space launch, and to meet members of the NASA social media team.

While the NASA Twitter experience asks for people to respond to a particular campaign, other ways in which Twitter can be used is through "retweeting". A specific tweet can be resent to many different people. It is almost like a pyramid. One person hears about something and retweets it to their account and then everyone who reads that person's tweets can hear about it too. While numerous individuals use Twitter to pass on information to others about things they are feeling, information they want others to know, or miscellaneous bits of information, organizations use it in a myriad of ways.

Some of the retweets might be uninteresting to some, but the ability to raise money for a good cause is one side benefit of retweeting. In

July 2011, Charlie Sheen was approached, via Twitter, and challenged to help a charity win a contest. He tweeted his support and his help boosted Cherubs, the organization that asked, to a third place spot ("Cherubs; Charlie Sheen Takes on Twitter Challenge by Grieving Mom to Help Sick Babies" 2011). In this way, information about something can be spread quickly and efficiently via social media for a good cause. This allows organizations of all kinds to get the word out to others about different things with which they're involved. It also gives individuals the power to support causes efficiently. Telephone and mail solicitation are quickly becoming a thing of the past. As mentioned earlier, the wave of the future that exists now is called knowledge management (KM). KM is not a new concept; it is simply a one that has become a phrase that encapsulates the umbrella of all that it takes to gather, categorize, and make information available to people in organizations (Atwood 2009). Thus, when an organization wants to keep track of all social media and other information, KM allows an organization to do just that.

PPC (Project Performance Corporation) defined KM as "the concepts, practices, and technologies used within and between organizations to capture, manage, and distribute information and leverage knowledge" ("PPC's KM Solutions Selected as a Trend Setting Product for Second Consecutive Year" 2011). These technologies certainly include the information disseminated via social media such as LinkedIn, Facebook, and Twitter. Some companies, such as Knowledge Management Associates, focus solely on Microsoft applications; others, such as Root Learning, take on a broader approach.

The benefit of KM is that an organization can utilize social media and other tools such as learning visualization and game-based education, in order to reach both internal and external publics and create a situation whereby information is shared equally throughout. This ability will allow organizations such as Organo Gold to create a center of knowledge easily accessible to all, no matter their location or time zone. Used correctly, this could revolutionize the way both the company and its representatives use and exchange information.

Future of Social Media Use in Organizations

The subject matter of social media and organizations could fill several volumes; thus it is a limitation of page length that prevents a comprehensive look at the phenomenon of social media. However, these few pages have attempted to introduce the reader to an evolution of social media while at the same time offering some relevant examples of its current uses. The foundations of CMC created a strong base and the future of CMC through current and future platforms will only be limited by the imagination of people.

Organo Gold is a growing multilevel marketing organization with a strong reliance on social media and CMC methods. Their use of many of these technological aspects is strong; however, as with all organizations, there is room for growth. The inclusion of more elements of CMC, such as group collaboration programs, will certainly enhance the feeling of community and create an opportunity for growth.

Social media, such as Facebook, have been instrumental in the creation of a community within Organo Gold, as has their website, with the main purpose of offering information to clients and potential customers. When an organization does not have a bricks-and-mortar store and relies heavily on a virtual storefront, establishing a sense of community is paramount to its success. As Organo Gold is a growing company, it seems to be on the right track.

In the beginning, several questions were proposed. As this chapter ends, consider what parts were answered and which parts remain of intrigue. How can organizations use these computer-mediated methods to increase their profits or share their social consciousness? When a particular organization is mentioned or thought of, what kinds of social media do they use? What comes to mind? Should organizations focus only on one or two platforms or should the reach out to as many as is possible?

Key Takeaways

1. Do you think cloud computing is appropriate for smaller organizations such as Organo Gold? Why or why not? Defend your answers using specific examples.
2. Security issues were not discussed in this chapter. How important is it for organizations to have strong security plans as they work with social media? How might these plans be implemented? What kinds of security measures should organizations take?
3. If you could choose one thing that you wished social media could do what would it be?
4. Is there a hole in the social media landscape that has not been filled by organizations?
5. Are there too many social media outlets causing the messages get lost or be less effective?

Glossary

Cloud computing: Instead of using a local server or a personal computer to store information, a network of remote servers is hosted by someone (or organization) to store, manage, and process data.

Computer-mediated communication (CMC): communication that occurs between two or more computers connected to each other by the Internet.

Distributed computing: When multiple computers work together via the Internet or some other computer network to achieve a common goal.

File transfer protocol (FTP): A way for data and other information to be shared across a network.

Knowledge management (KM): The concepts, practices, and technologies used within and between organizations to capture, manage, and distribute information and leverage knowledge.

Peer-to-peer networking: Communication between two or more computers that are connected to each other by the Internet without need for a central server.

References

"AMC Theatres; AMC Theatres® Conjuring up Record Advance Ticket Sales for Harry Potter and the Deathly Hallows—Part 2." *Marketing Weekly News* (July 30, 2011): 104.

Atwood, Christee G., *Knowledge Management Basics*. Alexandria, VA: ASTD Press, 2009.

Balas, J. L. "Bulletin Board Systems: A Nostalgic Look Back." *Computers in Libraries* vol. 5 no. 13 (1993)1993: http://dl.acm.org/citation.cfm?id=183673.

Barkai, David. Peer-to-Peer Computing: *Technologies for Sharing and Collaborating on the Net*. Santa Clara, CA: Intel Corporation, 2001.

Beckett, J. "The Internet Phenomenon." *Engineering Science and Education Journal* no. 5 (1996), http://ieeexplore.ieee.org/stamp/stamp.jsp?tp=&arnumber=503131.

Booth, Char. "VoIP in Professional Communication, Collaboration, and Development." *Library Technology Reports* 46, no. 5 (July 1, 2010): 20–24.

Callahan, Gene and Roger W. Garrison. "Does Austrian Business Cycle Theory Help Explain the Dot-Com Boom and Bust?" *The Quarterly Journal of Austrian Economics* 6, no 2 (2003): 67–98.

Carr, Nicholas. "Is Google Making Us Stupid?" *The Atlantic Monthly* 302, no. 1 (July 1, 2008): 56–63.

Cascio, Jamais. "GET SMART." *The Atlantic Monthly* 304, no. 1 (July 1, 2009): 94–98, 100.

Chappell, David. "Cloud Platforms." 2008. http://www.davidchappell.com/CloudPlatforms—Chappell.pdf.

Cherry, Steven M. "The Network Not Taken." *IEEE Spectrum* 41, no. 6 (2004): 60.

"Cherubs; Charlie Sheen Takes on Twitter Challenge by Grieving Mom to Help Sick Babies." *Investment Weekly News* (July 20, 2011): 201.

"Communication Equipment Companies; Cbeyond Announces Winner of Social Media Contest." *Marketing Weekly News* (July 16, 2011): 291.

"Dr. Smith's Diaper Ointment Deploys Social Networks to Launch New Campaign." *Health & Beauty Close—Up,* July 14, 2011.

Dong, Hanfei, Qinfen Hao, Tiegang Zhang, and Bing Zhang. "Parallel and Distributed Computing, Applications, and Technologies." Paper presented at the 2010 International Conference, Chengdu, China (2010), 448–53.

Dorai, L., L. K. Veerabadran, and Dorai, L. K. "A Novel Architecture—Peer-to-Peer and Closed Network Mobile Multimedia File Transfer in 4G MIPV6 Network." Paper presented at the 2010 International Conference, Chengdu, China, (2010), 1–6.

Efimova, Lilia, and Jonathan Grudin. "Crossing Boundaries: A Case Study of Employee Blogging." Proceedings of the 40th Hawaii International Conference on System Sciences, 2007.

El-Rakabawy, S. M., and C. Lindemann. "Peer-to-Peer Transfer in Wireless Mesh Networks." *IEEE,*2007. http://www.mendeley.com/research/peertopeer-file-transfer-wireless-mesh-networks/.

Fattah, Hassan M. *P2P: How Peer-to-Peer Technology is Revolutionizing the Way We Do Business.* Chicago: Dearborn Trade Publishing, 2002.

Fossi, Marc. "Online Threats: What Governments Need to Know." *Summit* (November 1, 2010): 15–16.

Haas, Christina, Brandon Carr, and Pamela Takayoshi. "Building and Maintaining Contexts in Interactive Networked Writing: An Examination of Deixis and Intertextuality in Instant Messaging." *Journal of Business and Technical Communication* 25 no. 3 (July 1, 2011): 276.

Hafner, Katie. "Billions Served Daily, and Counting." *New York Times,* December 6, 2001. Late Edition (East Coast).

Jansen, Jim. "Attention Shoppers: Online Product Research." September 29, 2010. http://pewresearch.org/pubs/1747/e-shopping-researched-product-service-online.

Josefowicz, Matthew. "Sharing Alike: Insurers Need to Figure Out How to Use New Collaboration Tools." *Insurance Networking News* (June 1, 2011): 28.

Kang, Mikyung, Dong-In Kang, Stephen Crago, Gyung-Leen Park, and Junghoon Lee. "Design and Development of a Run-Time Monitor for Multi-Core Architectures in Cloud Computing." *Sensors (14248220)* 11, no. 4 (2011): 3595–610.

Kaplan, Simone. "E-mail Turns 30." *CIO* (April 1, 2002): 28.

Kuang, Cliff. "When Will International Phone Calls Be Free?" *Wired* (September 1, 2009): 59.

Lee, Jun-Ho, Min-Woo Park, Jung-Ho Eom, and Tai-Myoung Chung. "Multi-Level Intrusion Detection System and Log Management in Cloud Computing." *Advanced Communication Technology* (2011): 552–55.

Miller, Mike. *Discovering P2P: Everything You Need to Know about P2P—To Understand it, to Use It, and to Benefit from It.* Alameda, CA: Sybex, 2001.

Moore, Dana, and John Hebeler. *Peer-to-Peer: Building Secure, Scalable, and Manageable Networks.* New York: McGraw-Hill Companies, 2001.

Mullan, Eileen. "The Generational Divide: World of Work Survey Encourages Collaboration." *EContent* (November 1, 2008): 16–17.

Picard, Andre. "The History of Twitter, 140 Characters at a Time." *Globe & Mail* (2011), A2.

"PPC's KM Solutions Selected as a Trend Setting Product for Second Consecutive Year." *Business Wire* 1 (September 2011): 1.

Rainie, Lee. "Digital 'Natives' Invade the Workplace." September 28, 2006. http://pewresearch.org/pubs/70/digital-natives-invade-the-workplace.

Rainie, Lee. "Internet Phone Calls." May 31, 2011. http://pewresearch.org/pubs/2006/internet-online-phone-call-skype-vonage.

Rainie, Lee, Kristen Purcell, Lauren Sessions, and Keith N. Hampton. "Social Networking Sites and Our Lives." June 16, 2011. http://pewresearch.org/pubs/2025/social-impact-social-networking-sites-technology-facebook-twitter-linkedin-myspace.

Rouibah, Kamel. "Social Usage of Instant Messaging by Individuals Outside the Workplace in Kuwait: A Structural Equation Model." *Information Technology & People* 21, no. 1 (January 1, 2008): 34–68.

Sardin, Thelma. "Technology Let's Chicagoans Join in on Conversation." *Hyde Park Citizen,* July 6, 2011.

Schultz, Beatrice G., "Improving Group Communication Performance: An Overview of Diagnosis and Intervention." In *The Handbook of Group Communication Theory and Research,* edited by L. R. Frey, D. S. Gouran, and M. S. Poole, 371–395. Thousand Oaks, CA: Sage Publications, 1999.

Silence, Michael. "Employers Need to Bridge Generational Gaps in Work Force, Labor Expert Says." *McClatchy-Tribune Business News,* April 24, 2008.

Smith, Aaron. "Twitter Update 2011." June 1, 2011. http://pewresearch.org/pubs/2007/twitter-users-cell-phone-2011-demographics.

Smith, Ethan, and Geoffrey A. Fowler. "Ganging Up on Internet Pirates; Hollywood, Telecom Providers Unite to Target Those Who Share Copyrighted Films, Music." *Wall Street Journal,* July 8, 2011.

Smith, Josh. "House Approves Use of Skype, ooVoo." *National Journal Daily M. Update* 28 (June 2011).

Sohail, S., C. T. Chou, S. S. Kanhere, and S. Jha. "On Large Scale Deployment of Parallelized File Transfer Protocol." *IEEE,* 2005, http://www.cse.unsw.edu.au/~salilk/papers/conferences/IPCCC2005.pdf.

Tian, Li-qin, Chuang Lin, and Yang Ni. "Evaluation of User Behavior Trust in Cloud Computing." *Computer Application and System Modeling* 7 (2010): 567–72.

Vaughan-Nichols, Steven J. "Instant Mess(age); Business Acceptance Stalls, but IM Slowly Proves Its Worth." *Ziff Davis Smart Business* (June 1, 2002): 42.

Zickuhr, Kathryn. "Generation and Their Gadgets." February 3, 2011. http://pewresearch.org/pubs/1879/gadgets-generations-cell-phones-laptops-desktop-comupter.

CHAPTER EIGHT

You Are What You Brand: Managing Your Image and Reputation

Don W. Stacks

British Petroleum (BP) Oil Spill

On April 20, 2010, a deepwater oil rig, Deep Horizon, exploring for oil in the Caribbean for oil giant BP blew up during capping the wellhead, killing 11 rig workers; what followed was a disaster not only for the environment and surrounding Gulf Coast states, but also for BP's brand and reputation. Over the next several months, due to a variety of miscues and miscommunications, BP's brand and reputation were sallied and to a large degree almost beyond repair.

Not only did BP's actions hurt stockholders—the stock tumbled—but they also hurt some of their most important stakeholders: their customers, their gasoline stations in the United States, and, perhaps most of all, the residents of the Gulf states: Alabama, Florida, Louisiana, Mississippi, and Texas. Over a period of several months BP attempted to quell stakeholder discontent and outrage through advertising, local hiring, a social media campaign, and visits by BP's chief executive officer (CEO) Tony Hayward. Adding to the controversy, BP's chairman made an off-the-cuff comment about Gulf Coast residents that came out differently than was meant. Their attempts at controlling the oil spill through access to information, including the videotaping of oil at the wellhead only caused more problems.

Although the brunt of criticism and financial and nonfinancial impact was on BP, almost hidden were two other organizations that contributed to the disaster, Transocean (the rig's owner) and its supplier, Halliburton. Although criticized for their failures, the major brand and reputational damage impacted most heavily on BP.

Throughout the crisis BP's actions only served to isolate itself from its stakeholders and it then reached out to its primary stakeholder group, its employees. Over a series of advertisements and bringing in former and local employees BP attempted to rebuild its credibility, trust, and relationships with its other stakeholders. It has slowly regained its reputation that was in tatters but the brand has by late 2011 yet to recover.

It has become axiomatic in today's business world that brand and repu-tation are the major drivers. As famed investment broker Warren Buffett (1995, 409) noted, "Lose money for the firm, and I will understand; lose a shred of reputation for the firm, and I will be ruthless." Your reputation, however, is tied closely to your brand. As we examine the effect brand and reputation have on corporate image we will differentiate between the two and will examine how public relations is employed to create an impression of brand and hence reputation, the four *communication* factors that influ-ence brand and reputation, and how branding can be used to influence perceptions of corporate reputation.

> Branding refers to the value that stake- and stockholders place in an organization that yields a brand value or equity that can be "cashed in" in times of crisis or turmoil. Branding refers to the identity or per-sonality or image of the brand.

Branding and Reputation

Organizations use branding and reputation to manage the impres-sions that others have of them. Impression management is important to branding because stake- and stockholders have different impressions of an organization at any given time. Such impressions may be gener-ally positive, negative, or neutral (Moffitt 2005). Impressions then deter-mine how others perceive the brand and that perception leads to both *formal* (e.g., media coverage and evaluation by opinion leaders) and *infor-mal* (e.g., word of mouth transmission of messages through interpersonal contact).

An organization attempts to frame the public's impressions through communications that impact that organization's brand value or eq-uity. As a brand's value and equity increases, so too does its reputation; as reputation decreases, so too does brand value and equity. Hence, we see reputation and brand being highly correlated, and both can impact stake- and stockholder impressions of an industry, company, unit within a company, and even down to the individual employee. Often brand and reputation perceptions are tied closely to the senior management, and certainly the CEO. One has only to look at how we Americans see ourselves as a country and how that often contrasts with how others see us through the eyes of our presidents. George W. Bush's presidency yielded a different reputation, and hence brand, than Barack Obama's presidency. One could say the same with John F. Kennedy's and Ronald Reagan's presidencies.

While branding is fairly straightforward, reputation is more complex. Think of the brand as the outcome that has its own return on investment (ROI) as equated with brand value or equity. Reputation as a driver of brand perceptions has been suggested as an *integrative* view of reputation across six approaches (Fombrun and van Riel 2004): economical, strategic, marketing, organizational, sociological, and accounting. Each approach takes a different view of reputation and yields what might be a labeled a *collective* perception of the organization (Fombrun, Gardberg, and Sever 2000, 243). Don W. Stacks and Marcia L. Watson (2007) see reputation as the *historical* relationship between an organization and its publics—stake- and stockholders, employees, customers, the media, and so forth. As such, reputation can be seen as a state of awareness, assessment, and asset (e.g., Barnett, Jermier, and Lafferty 2006) that is interpreted through a historical understanding of the organization's reputation and that will yield different values or equity of its brand over time.

> Reputation is a perception that an organization's publics—stake-holders and stockholders—have of that organization that is built over time. It takes the form of a variety of views and can be reduced to a general state of awareness, an assessment or judging of the organization, and as an asset of value to the stake- and stockholders. Reputation yields images of an organization that produce perceptions of brand. Such images are generally positive, neutral, and negative.

These images are clearly cognitions and attitudes of an organization that can be shaped, changed, projected, and polished and found in people's long-term memory and, as James Grunig (1993, 135) noted, "and associate them [cognitions and attitudes] when they have reason to think about an organization. A 'reputation'. . . has a long life." Thus, as Fombrun (1996) suggests, reputation is partly organizational identity or image and partly persuasive. Hence, as Stacks (2011) has noted, the persuasive strategy in public relations focuses on three main objectives. First, information must be received, recalled, and understood—this is the informational objective of any communication campaign. Second, the information activates cognitions (attitudes and beliefs) that are positive toward the organization (or against a competitor) and motivate the receiver to act—this is the persuasive or motivational objective of any communication campaign and can be corrected through evaluation of cognitive, affective, and connotative attitudes toward the organization, thus serving a feedback and refinement function. And, third, the information must drive behavior—the behavioral objective demonstrates an ability to reinforce or change targeted public's perception of brand and reputation. As Stacks and Shannon A. Bowen (2011) note, these three campaign objectives must be clearly stated with measureable outcomes.

Reputation and Brand Management

How then can an organization's reputation and brand be managed? Since both reputation and brand are image driven, the influence of four communication variables can be manipulated to create, reinforce, or change those images. The four variables are organizational credibility, organizational relationship to its stake- and stockholders, the trust that these publics have for the organization, and the confidence they have in organizational decision making. Each is part and parcel of the persuasive process as found in any public relations or corporate communication function.

Stacks, Melissa D. Dodd, and Linjuan Rita Men (in press) have formally stated that reputation is a function of these four variables. Specifically, they formally state the relationship as:

$$\text{Reputation} = (B_{ij} \pm \text{credibility}_{ij}{}^x \pm \text{relationship}_{ij}{}^x \pm \text{trust}_{ij}{}^x) \times (\text{confidence})$$

where B is a constant that is modified by the four communication variables. Further, one could argue that the same formal relationship can be stated for brand value or equity as

$$\text{Brand} = (B_{ij} \pm \text{credibility}_{ij}{}^x \pm \text{relationship}_{ij}{}^x \pm \text{trust}_{ij}{}^x) \times (\text{confidence})$$

and that reputation $\leftrightarrow$ brand (i.e., they are highly correlated). Stacks, Dodd, and Men (in press) demonstrate the impact of these variables on stake- and stockholders as found in Figure 8.1a and Figure 8.1b.

As seen from Figures 8.1a and 8.1b, the relationships between credibility, relationship, and trust all impact each other. Confidence is historical and modifies the reputation or brand as influenced by the three variables. This in turn produces what Stacks (2011) argues is ROE or return on expectations. Since stake- and stockholders may perceive an organization differently, they have separate paths to influence outcomes such as

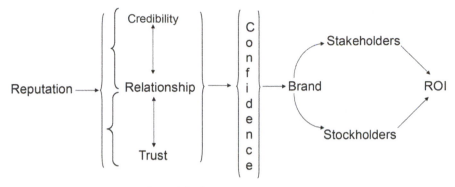

Figure 8.1a   Conceptual Model of Reputation

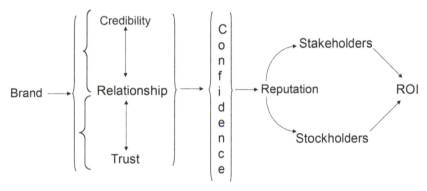

Figure 8.1b   Conceptual Model of Brand

Source: Don W. Stacks (2011). *Primer of Public Relations Research,* 2nd ed. New York: Guilford Press. Used with permission.

predicted by informational, motivational/persuasive, and behavioral outcomes. Indeed, it may be that stake- and stockholders mutually influence one another and a double arrow vertically between them.

According to Dodd (2011), one measure of reputation, then, could be if reputation matches branding (i.e., do stakeholders believe Coke = happiness?) and would likely fall within the credibility dimension of reputation. It is through impression management that we make this happen. In other words, if BP sought to brand itself as the most accident-free oil company (an identity), they would fail because of issues of reputation, specifically that of credibility, despite their best efforts at impression management. Thus, branding, in combination with reputation, results in the value that stake- and stockholders place in an organization, yielding brand value or equity as social capital that can be "cashed in."

Workplace Communication for the 21st Century

Message Variables

The function of any public relations and/or corporate communications department is to produce messages that will yield changes in an organization's brand or reputation. Such messages take the form of a number of different strategies that must be incorporated into the organization's business goals and objectives (Stacks, Dodd, and Men, in press). Thus, messages ("outputs") may evolve around corporate social responsibility, corporate capability, and effectiveness of communication as key messages. Outputs in turn influence the four key drivers ("outtakes") of credibility, relationship, trust, and confidence and do so to enhance the organization's intermediate outtakes of visibility, authenticity, and transparency or ethics; outtakes are perceptions and reside in the targeted audience. Outcomes that may be measured include public supportive behavior in terms of purchasing products, recommending the organization to potential customers, purchasing, or recommending the organization's stock. Stakeholder employee outcomes might include commitment to the organization, low turnover, engagement, and increased performance.

Employees also may be targeted as what Stacks (2011) describes as an "intervening audience" who might contribute to organizational reputation and branding by talking positively about the organization, its objectives, and its values. Other outcomes might include customer loyalty, positive media coverage, and community support. Stockholder investment in or encouraging others to purchase organizational stock is another outcome that can be measured in terms of stock price, sales, and revenue.

> Outputs are the actual communications created and sent through various communication channels such as print media, broadcast media, and social media. Outputs serve to meet informational objectives. Outtakes are the perceptions target audiences, opinion leaders, and others who influence an audience. Outcomes are what are expected at the end of an organization's campaign to enhance, bolster, or change its reputation and/or brand. For more, see Stacks (2011).

Credibility

Credibility is at the base of any analysis of reputation and brand. Stemming from the ancient Greeks, credibility or *ethos* is often the determining factor in any persuasive or informational message. As noted earlier, BP's credibility as a safe, efficient, and concerned company took major hits and its reputation and brand suffered greatly. Credibility then is a key determinate of organizational reputation and hence its brand. Although the concept of credibility has been noted for centuries, it has only been in the last 30 years that credibility has been seen as a key determinant of reputation and brand (see, for instance, Fombrun 1996; Newall and Goldsmith 2001).

If an organization is not seen as credible by an audience, its messages, regardless of how well crafted they are, will not be believed or will be believed as manipulative and may "boomerang" as they do not match the perceptions of the audience (c.f., Sherif, Sherif, and Nebergall 1965). Credibility, then, has a major influence on relationship, trust, and confidence. Further, the organization's credibility is rated in terms of believability in such a way as to interact with other stake- and stockholder expectations such as trust, relationship, and confidence, which, in turn, will impact organizational visibility, authenticity, and transparency (Stacks, Dodd, and Men, in press). Indeed, as Mark Hickson (2011, 22) noted, the public relations/corporate communication's basic function is "the management of credibility."

Relationship

A relationship is the association that stake- and stockholders have with an organization (Stacks 2011). Relationships are vital to an organization's reputation and brand identity. According to Linda Hon and James Grunig (1999), relationships can be distinguished by levels of commitment, power, satisfaction, and trust. Positive relationships are defined by *commitment* to serve stake- and stockholder needs such as employment, support of community projects, and return on stockholder financial investment in the organization. Relationships that result in mutual *trust* and *satisfaction* are also positive and should be indicative of a balance of *power* between the organization and its stake- and stockholders. As Yang (2007) noted, a close and quality relationship (i.e., positive) between an organization and its publics is highly associated with an organization's reputation.

Thus, looking back at BP's relationship with those affected by the Deep Water Horizon disaster it is clear that over time that relationship went from positive (BP was making money for investors, hiring local people to work on oil rigs, and participating in the local economy) to negative quite quickly. The change in relationship was a function of stake- and stockholder perceptions of a commitment to quickly stop the flow of oil, dissatisfaction with the progress being made, and a lack of trust associated with reporting of how much oil was flowing from the wellhead as it was controlled by BP's providing access to that flow to governmental regulators and others concerned with how much oil was actually flowing at the time.

As noted earlier, an organization's reputation and brand is often tied to its leadership and management. In BP's case the decision to bring corporate CEO Tony Hayward to the Gulf Coast cost BP its relationship with residents, businesses, and others struggling in the aftermath of the oil spill. Hayward's classic statement that he'd "like his life back," failed to resonate with those who were actually living through the disaster. This was further compounded by BP Chairman Carl-Henric Svanberg's misuse of "small people" when talking about those immediately affected by the oil spill. Thus, simple communication mistakes can and will impact reputation and brand.

Trust

Reputation and brand are highly associated with how trusted a company or its products are. Stake- and stockholder expectations of quality, reliability, and dependability help define their trust in an organization. From both stake- and stockholder perspectives BP's oil spill and its failure to control the wellhead diminished any trust held by them. Even more damning was the report that BP had secretly been part of a study of deep-water oil spills off the coast of Norway in 2000 by the U.S. government and other oil companies ("BP and MMS Secretly Rehearse Deep Water Oil Spill in 2000 in Norway" 2010). Thus, trust takes the form of what MacMillan et al. (2005) suggest must be maintained for reputation and brand to survive even in uncertain times.

Confidence

Confidence is what the stake- and stockholder has in an organization's ability to do what it says it will do, live by its values, and have a history of doing so. As noted in Figures 8.1a and 8.1b, confidence influences the interactive effects of credibility, relationship, and trust. For instance, an organization may be seen by employees as highly credible, have a good relationship, but trust in actually keeping its promises to employees is low will lead to low confidence and thus its reputation will take a hit, which may yield negative images of any of its brands.

Positive confidence will lead to what Dowling (2004) suggested is a combination of admiration, respect, and trust in an organization's actions. Thus, an organization being cited as one of the most admired companies, best places to work, a Top 100 company, or its CEO as a leader within an industry all build stake- and stockholder confidence in the organization and enhance its reputation and brands.

Key drivers are variables that can be used to enhance an organization's reputation and brand. Generally the key drivers are used to demonstrate the organization's communication (one- or two-way, symmetrical or asymmetrical), capability, and its social responsibility. From a message perspective, there are four primary key drivers: credibility, confidence, relationship, and trust. Each of these can be stressed as important or "key messages" when the focus is on reputation and brand.

Other Drivers

Aside from the four key drivers discussed, there are three intermediate drivers that impact reputational or brand outcome. The first is *visibility.* Visibility refers to stake- and stockholder familiarity with an organization (Fombrun and van Riel 2004). Visibility, however, is more than simple familiarity; it is dependent on a clear and visible image being communicated. When things are going well, visibility will enhance an organization's reputation and branding, as well as its branding process. When things are not going as well, visibility may hurt the organization's image and actually reduce perceptions of reputation and brand.

Visibility, then, is a two-sided sword. When reputation is high and the brand image is positive, any visibility through the traditional or social media will enhance the organization's reputation and brand. When things happen that impact negatively on the organization—such as technical or product failure, management misconduct, management deception, or management failure itself—any visibility will damage reputation and brand. Such damage may be brand-oriented—the product does not work, kills or injures people, makes stake- or stockholders victims (such as in a Ponzi scheme), and so forth—and the brand's "hit" yields lower organizational reputation. Conversely, a damaged reputation may lower the organization's brand image. Toyota's reputation was damaged when one of its brands had technical problems with the accelerator pedal and the floor mat in its Solara brand. In the same way Firestone's problems with one plant's tire brand, which led to tire failure in heated situations, also damaged its reputation; at the same time Ford, which used those tires as original products on its cars, had its reputation damaged by failure to disclose its knowledge of the problem when it knew of it several years earlier. Visibility does not have to be focused on just one organization; in today's world simply being "seen" with another brand or organization may enhance or reduce its reputation and/or brand.

Authenticity is a perception that an organization is real (Fombrun and van Riel 2004). As an intermediate driver of reputation and brand, authenticity refers the way that an organization represents itself to it constituencies. For instance, Johnson & Johnson's reputation and brand is held in highly positive regard because of its credo, a statement that all employees of the company learn and live. That reputation as an authentic company has helped it survive through multiple crises, beginning with the 1984 Tylenol crisis and continuing to date. What authenticity provides is an emotional appeal that is part of an organization's social responsibility (Dowling 2004; Fombrun and van Riel 2004).

Without authenticity an organization's image suffers. As noted by the *Arthur W. Page Society's* white paper, "The Authentic Enterprise Summary Report" (2011, 3), "authenticity will be the coin of the realm for successful corporations and those who lead them." Further, "an organization's values, principles, beliefs, mission, purpose or value proposition . . . must dictate consistent behavior and actions." The authentic organization focuses on establishing trust at the individual, enterprise, and societal levels and its core values are readily apparent to its stake- and stockholders.

Transparency is a term that in the general parlance has become overused. In helping to establish an organization's reputation, however, it is an important intermediate driver. According to Brad Rawlins (2009), *transparency* encompasses integrity, respect, and openness. According to Stacks, Dodd, and Men (in press) stakeholders' perceptions of reputation and brand are increased when the organization is transparent in its conduct of its affairs. Such affairs include, but are not limited to, disseminating truthful, accurate, and timely information that is balanced and substantial with stakeholder participation (i.e., communication is two-way and symmetrical) in helping identify the information they need (Rawlins 2009). How transparent an organization is can be measured in part by stake- and stockholder perceptions of its credibility, its relationship with them, the trust they have in it, and the confidence that it operates in an open and honest way with them.

Table 8.1 demonstrates how an organization's key drivers can be analyzed according to perceptions of key stakeholder audiences. Assuming a simple 1 (*low*) to 5 (*high*) met expectations on the key drivers by key stakeholder message strategies can be created and executed. Measurement over time can track the success or lack of success of the strategies. A quick examination shows that across key audiences, own management and customers' perceptions of key driver expectations are highly met (means of 4.43 and 4.29 out of a possible 5.00). As might be expected, union perceptions of expectations are lowest at 2.71, but employees are higher at 3.57. When looking across key drivers, all stakeholder perceptions range from a low of 3.00 (sort of neutral) for transparency to a high of 4.25 for visibility.

Table 8.1 Perceptions of Expectations of Key Stakeholders by Key and Secondary Drivers

	Credibility	Confidence	Relationship	Trust	Visibility	Authenticity	Transparency
Employees	4	3	3	3	5	4	3
Customers	5	4	5	5	4	4	3
Unions	3	2	3	2	4	3	2
Own Management	4	5	4	5	4	5	4

Applying Lessons Learned

So how does an organization manage its brand image(s) and reputation? Based on the preceding discussion brand and reputation management is a function of open and honest communication with stake- and stockholders. Further that communication, which should be a function of the public relations or corporate communication department, addresses the key drivers discussed earlier in reputational and branding messages. Understanding which outputs are most relevant to which stakeholder group or stockholders provides a way to get information to them that is accurate, timely, relevant, and substantive and which underscores the organizations' values and principles. These messages are constructed on a strategy that entails enhancing the organization's credibility, relationship, trust, and confidence in the organization.

Of importance to managing brand and reputation is the realization that the organization's own people—the managers, supervisors, and employees—are often the best ambassadors of organizational brand and reputational. As we saw in the BP case at the beginning of the chapter and allusions to it throughout, an organization's reputation and brand are more than just talking the talk, it must also walk the walk. Authentic, visible, and transparent organizations do just that.

Key Takeaways

1. Brand and reputation are interdependent on each other.
2. In many instances an organization's best opinion leaders are its employees.
3. Brand and reputation are highly influenced by an organization's credibility, level of trust, relationship with its stakeholders, and confidence in the organization's ability to do the right thing.
4. Visibility, authenticity, and transparency are important elements in building and maintaining trust.
5. In any organization the CEO is the brand's voice and care should be taken when he/she speaks.

Glossary

Authenticity: The perception that an organization is real.

Behavioral objective: A campaign objective that demonstrates an ability to change or reinforce stakeholder's perceptions of brand and reputation.

Brand: An image that others have of an organization or product.

Brand equity: The amount of influence a brand or reputation has.

Brand value: The equivalent of a brand's yield in monetary or reputational or social capital.

Commitment: The degree to which stakeholders see an organization living its values.

Confidence: The degree to which stakeholders believe they can depend on an organization or brand to do what it says it will do; to "walk the talk."

Credibility: The degree to which an organization is seen as believable by stakeholders.

Drivers: Variables that have impact an organization's brand and reputation; two kinds, key which are variables such as credibility, confidence, relationship, and trust that influence perceptions of brand and reputation and intermediate, which are secondary and often result from key drivers but important, such as visibility, authenticity, and transparence.

Impression management: The management of an organization's images through formal and informal communication.

Informational objective: A strategic objective that focuses on the measurement of how, when, and where communications are targeted to stakeholders.

Motivational objective: A strategic objective that focuses on stakeholder perceptions of an organization through its communications.

Outcomes: The outcome of a strategic campaign that is tied into ROE and ROI.

Outputs: Specific communication vehicles such as releases, VNRs, blogs, and so forth.

Outtakes: The intermediate effect of messaging whereby opinion leaders or specific stakeholders are targeted to carry the key messages to targeted audiences.

Relationship: The association that stakeholders have with an organization defined by commitment to serve stakeholders resulting in mutual trust and satisfaction with the organization.

Reputation: a perception by stakeholders of an organization that is built over time.

Return on expectations (ROE): The nonfinancial outcome that influences stakeholder perceptions of brand and expectations that will drive ROI for the public relations or corporate communication actions.

Return on investment (ROI): The financial outcome that influences stakeholders (and stockholders) to recommend a brand or purchase an organization's products and services.

Satisfaction: A factor that influences stakeholder perceptions of an organization.

Social capital: Nonfinancial outcomes that stakeholders perceive as an organization's equity value in its brand and reputation.

Transparency: A reputational driver that influences stakeholder perceptions of an organization's integrity, respect, and openness to stakeholders.

Trust: A perception that an organization will be dependable.

Two-way, symmetric relationship: A relationship in which stakeholders and an organization communicate openly, honestly, and respond to communications in a timely way.

Visibility: Stakeholder familiarity with an organization.

References

Arthur W. Page Society. "The Authentic Enterprise Summary Report." http://awpage society.com/images/uploads/AE_Summary_4.pdf.

Barnett, Michael L., John M. Jermier, and Barbara A. Lafferty. "Corporate Reputation: The Definitional Landscape." *Corporate Reputation Review* 9 (2006): 26–38.

"BP and MMS Secretly Rehearse Deep Water Oil Spill in 2000 in Norway." http://afterthepress.com/?tag=deepwater-horizon-2.

Buffett, Warren. *Buffett: The Making of an American Capitalist,* edited by R. Lowenstein. New York: Random House, 1995.

Dodd, Melissa D. (doctoral student at the University of Miami specializing in reputation social capital), in discussion with author, September 2011.

Dowling, Grahame R. "Journalists' Evaluation of Corporate Reputations." *Corporate Reputation Review* 7 (2004): 196–205.

Fombrun, Charles J. *Reputation: Realizing Value from the Corporate Image.* Boston: Harvard Business School Press, 1996.

Fombrun, Charles J., Naomi A. Gardberg, and Joy M. Sever. "The Reputation Quotient: A Multi-Stakeholder Measure of Corporate Reputation." *The Journal of Brand Management* 7 (2000): 241–55.

Fombrun, Charles J., and Cees B. F. van Riel. *Fame & Fortune: How Successful Companies Build Winning Reputations.* Upper Saddle River, NJ: Pearson Education, 2004.

Grunig, James E. (1993). "Image and Substance: From Symbolic to Behavioral Relationships." *Public Relations Review* 19 (1993): 121–39.

Hickson, Mark L. Cited in Don W. Stacks, *Primer of Public Relations Research.* 2nd ed. New York: Guilford Press, 2011.

Hon, Linda C., and James E. Grunig, *Guidelines for Measuring Relationships in Public Relations.* Gainesville, FL: Institute for Public Relations, 1999.

MacMillan, Keith, Kevin Money, Steve Downing, and Carola Hillenbrand. "Reputation in Relationships: Measuring Experiences, Emotions and Behaviors." *Corporate Reputation Review* 8 (2005): 366–84.

Moffitt, Mary Ann. "Corporate Image." In *The Encyclopedia of Public Relations,* Vol. 1, edited by Robert L. Heath, 202–5. Thousand Oaks, CA: Sage Publications, 2005.

Newall, Stephen J., and Ronald E. Goldsmith. "The Development of a Scale to Measure Perceived Corporate Credibility." *Journal of Business Research* 52 (2001): 235–47.

Rawlins, Brad. "Give the Emperor a Mirror: Towards Developing a Stakeholder Measurement of Organizational Transparency." *Journal of Public Relations Research* 21 (2009): 71–99.

Sherif, Caroline W., Mustafa S. Sherif, and Roger E. Nebergall. *Attitude and Attitude Change.* Philadelphia: W.B. Saunders Company, 1965.

Stacks, Don W. *Primer of Public Relations Research.* 2nd ed. New York: Guilford Publications, 2011.

Stacks, Don W., and Shannon A. Bowen. "The Strategic Approach: Writing Measurable Objectives." *PR Tactics* 21 (2011): 14.

Stacks, Don W., Melissa D. Dodd, and Linjuan Rita Men. "Corporate Reputation Measurement and Evaluation." In *Handbook of Communication and Corporate Reputation,* edited by Craig Carroll. London: Blackwell, in press.

Stacks, Don W., and Marcia L. Watson. "Two-Way Communication Based on Quantitative Research and Measurement." In *The Future of Excellence in Public Relations and Communication Management,* edited by Elizabeth L. Toth, 67–84. Mahwah, NJ: Lawrence Erlbaum Associates, 2007.

Yang, Su. "An Integrated Model for Organization-Public Relational Outcomes, Organizational Reputation, and Their Antecedents." *Journal of Public Relations Research* 19 (2007): 91–121.

CHAPTER NINE

Building and Maintaining Stakeholder Trust

Pamela Shockley-Zalabak and Sherwyn Morreale

Note: The authors wish to thank Adam Saffer, M.A. in Communication at the University of Colorado–Colorado Springs and a current doctoral student at the University of Oklahoma, for conducting and developing the case illustrations for the five drivers of trust.

Trust, Political Systems, and Turbulent Financial Times

The global financial crisis, beginning in 2008 continued into 2011 and 2012, can be traced to multiple ethical abuses as well as outright illegal behaviors. Although some of the most visible scandals could be linked to individual behavior, increasingly organizational structures and cultures were assessed blame (Shockley-Zalabak, 2012). The first in history downgrade of U.S. bonds occurred in August 2011 following global publicity of a contentious U.S. Congressional session that reached agreement only hours prior to a deadline for raising the U.S. debt ceiling. Trust in the government to make effective policy decisions was widely reported at an all-time low. Financial markets around the globe and in the United States reacted negatively signaling what many characterized as emotional reactions to the polarizing discussions of the future of the United States. Many claimed broad distrust in the American political process and called for massive changes in Washington, D.C. Few appeared worried about the actual default of America on its debt. Greece, Italy, and Spain experienced increasing unease as their economies faltered and few registered confidence in politician systems. The public, global partnerships, political parties, businesses of all sizes, the financial industry, and a host of special interest groups were increasingly vocal stakeholders. Many contended trust breaches were at an unprecedented high.

We know the stories. We know the pain. The early years of the 21st century have seen a rash of corporate and government scandals. From Toyota's massive recall, to Wall Street's mortgage and banking crises, to an oil spill in the Gulf of Mexico and a nuclear meltdown in Japan and revolution in the Middle East, these are but a few examples where significant trust breaches resulted in the loss of billions of dollars, unemployment for thousands, criminal charges leveled at leaders, and the toppling of governments. Deceptive messages, illegal accounting practices, taking corporate profits for individual gain, and a variety of strategies to conceal the truth, all were used to secure questionable and illegal advantage, resulting in scandal and public outrage. We know people got fired, fined, denied positions, and worse, imprisoned. We know organizations lost customers, harmed employees, and, in some cases, ceased to exist. Without question, highly publicized trust breaches now are both prevalent and profoundly negative in terms of their consequences for all stakeholders. Most organizational trust breaches do not make headlines. But whether visible or not, trust breaches are destructive for small and large organizations. And while certain breaches are never recognized, others steadily contribute to lowering organizational trust and overall effectiveness.

> Most breaches of organizational trust don't garner coverage in the media, but they are nonetheless destructive forces in organizations.

This essay discusses breaches of trust important for all types of organizational stakeholders and describes intentional actions for building and maintaining stakeholder trust. The essay describes an organizational trust model developed through extensive research and tested in numerous practical environments. We talk about major challenges to maintaining stakeholder trust and offer strategies for building that trust. We conclude with major takeaways about trust building, which can be utilized in almost any organization. We hope to make the case that high organizational trust positively transforms individuals and entire organizations. Importantly, trust building is a primary leadership responsibility. Leaders and communication professionals are central members of the trust team, helping organizations link intentions, behaviors, and bottom-line results.

What Do We Mean by Organizational Trust?

Trust definitions are numerous and varied. Based on our research and professional experiences, we offer the following: *"Organizational trust is the overarching belief that an organization in its communication and behaviors is competent, open and honest, concerned, reliable, and worthy of identification with its goals, norms, and values"* (Shockley-Zalabak, Morreale, and Hackman 2010, 12). This definition suggests five characteristics of organizational trust: trust is a multifaceted experience in organizations, is culturally determined, is communication based, is dynamic, and is multidimensional (behavioral, cognitive, and emotional).

When we say trust is multifaceted, we are referring to the variety of relationships individuals have with organizations, whether as employees, customers, donors, vendors, investors, regulators, or other types of stakeholders. We relate to organizations as individuals, in groups, and as part of a broad societal framework. Some of our relationships with organizations come from direct knowledge and personal interactions. Others are drawn from knowledge that is indirect, impersonal, and based on affiliations or reputations. We also know trust is culturally determined and therefore universal laws regarding organizational trust are elusive. Not only is organizational trust specific to an organization's culture, it also is part of the dominant society and culture in which the organization operates. Actions that build trust in one culture may have only a limited or even negative impact in another. When we say trust is communication based, we mean perceptions of organizational trust result from both direct communication behaviors and mediated communication experiences. Increasingly in contemporary organizations, we decide if we trust others, or not, based only on mediated experiences such as virtual communication; this somewhat new organizational reality underscores the role of professional communicators in building trust. The dynamic nature of trust refers to the fact that changing circumstances and experiences in or with an organization can move our evaluations from trust to distrust. Finally, when we claim trust is multidimensional we are acknowledging there are important relationships among actions of people in organizations (their behaviors), beliefs, intentions, motivations, expectations, and assumptions (their cognitions), and feelings (their emotions). Trust or the lack thereof in any organization is a direct result of the interaction of everyone's behaviors—what they do, cognitions—what they think, and emotions—how they feel. The "everyone" we are referencing here very much involves and affects the organization's stakeholders.

> Trust or the lack of it in any organization results from the interaction of what people do, think, and feel in any organization.

Who Are the Stakeholders?

Stakeholders are those individuals and groups who have an interest or "stake" in an organization and are able to influence the organization's ability to meet its goals. Stakeholders are employees, investors, customers, donors, clients, regulators, vendors, media, prospective customers, sometimes competitors, communities, governments, and others with special relationships to organizations. Sometimes referred to as the multiple publics of an organization, stakeholders are both influenced by organizations and influence a host of organizational outcomes. Stakeholders continuously make trust evaluations about organizations and those evaluations significantly influence overall organizational performance.

> High levels of trust are necessary for any organization to achieve real excellence.

Trust and Organizational Excellence

The evidence is clear: Trust is fundamental for achievement of organizational excellence. A broad range of studies and empirical evidence link trust to bottom-line economic performance and the achievement of goals. Restaurants, sales forces, NCAA teams, and nonprofit and for-profit organizations all experience more success with high-trust profiles. Stock market performance is significantly better in high-trust organizations and top and bottom innovators can be distinguished by organizational trust levels (Shockley-Zalabak, Morreale, and Hackman 2010). Conversely, distrust comes at a high cost. "We versus them" behaviors occur as organizational units and functions compete with one another. Distrust lowers employees' desire to contribute to productivity goals and even rewards, such as pay raises or promotions, will not easily restore trust. Distrust breeds fear and destructive behaviors, inability to deal effectively with crises, and is expensive in the need for increased surveillance, compliance, and low supervisor-to-employee ratios. Additionally, distrust limits the types of organizational forms that can be utilized and how organizations learn and renew themselves.

> It is a myth to assume there is little that can be done to become a high-trust organization.

A widespread myth suggests trust matters but there is little we can do about it. We disagree. We believe everything we do in organizations is about trust and there is much that we can do to build trust. But trust building must become more intentional and it is one of the fundamental responsibilities of both leaders and professional communicators. Trust with stakeholders requires this intentional approach. Interestingly, we know being a trustworthy person and being trusted by others are not the same. It is hard to face the fact that integrity does not equate to trust. Integrity and ethical behaviors are fundamental for trust, but organizational trust requires a more sophisticated alignment among intentions, behaviors, and interpretations of behaviors (Shockley-Zalabak, Morreale, and Hackman 2010). This intentional aligning is directly related to stakeholders' trust in any organization.

The Five Drivers of Trust

The question becomes how to develop this intentional approach to building and maintaining trust with stakeholders. We believe the model we present next and the strategies described later provide research- and practice-based guidance for those who seek to take a strategic approach to trust building.

> Our research-developed model consists of five drivers of trust—competence, openness and honesty, concern for employees/stakeholders, reliability, and identification.

We present a model with five drivers of trust—competence, openness and honesty, concern for employees/stakeholders, reliability, and identification—developed during a research project sponsored by the International Association of Business Communicators. The research was conducted in multiple languages with respondents in 53 organizations in eight countries on four continents. The results indicated the five identified drivers were strong and stable predictors of organizational trust across cultures, languages, industries, and types and sizes of organizations. The more positive the trust scores for an organization, the more effective the organization was perceived to be and the more satisfied with their jobs employees were. Low-trust scores had the opposite effect (Shockley-Zalabak, Morreale, and Hackman 2010). Figure 9.1 demonstrates this powerful effect of the five drivers of trust on both perceived effectiveness and job satisfaction.

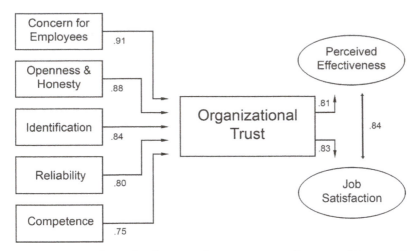

Figure 9.1   Relationship between the Five Drivers of Trust and Perceived Effectiveness and Job Satisfaction (These numbers indicate statistical significance. Standardized path parameters range from 0 to 1.0. The higher the number, the stronger the driver is as a predictor.)

Competence

The competence driver represents the ability of an organization through its leaders, strategy, decisions, quality, and capabilities to meet the challenges of its environment. Competence relates to the overall efficiency of the organization as well as to the quality of its products or services. Competence comes from the capabilities of employees at all organizational levels. Specifically, competence is measured by an organization's ability to achieve its objectives.

The Competence Driver of Trust in Action

On September 29, 2009, the Toyota Motor Corporation announced it would recall nearly 4 million vehicles to replace floor mats after reports that the accelerators in several models were becoming stuck while in operation. The company insisted that no vehicle-based problems were occurring. In the following months, concern mounted for the quality of Toyota's products and the decision-making abilities of the company's leaders. Ultimately a massive recall affected 16 million vehicles and their owners. Toyota's lack of efficiency in responding to the crisis and public perceptions of the quality of Toyota products is a prime example of a breach in trust based at least in part on a lack of competence.

Sources: http://www.msnbc.msn.com/id/35240466/ns/business-autos/; http://www.reuters.com/article/2011/01/26/us-toyota-recall-japan-idUSTRE70P1IE20110126.

Openness and Honesty

The openness and honesty driver is reflected in how organizations communicate about problems, engage in constructive disagreements, and provide input into job-related decisions. Openness and honesty are positively evaluated when managers and supervisors keep confidences and provide information about job performance and evaluation of performance. Employees evaluate an organization as open and honest when they are provided information about how job-related problems are handled and how major organizational decisions will affect them as individuals.

The Openness and Honesty Driver of Trust in Action

As events following the 2011 earthquake and tsunami in Japan continue to unfold, the handling of information concerning radiation levels at the Fukushima nuclear power plant provides an example of the openness and honesty driver of trust. The Tokyo Electric Power Company (TEPCO), operator of the nuclear power plant, has been under scrutiny about its procedures for handling and reporting incidents even before the most recent crisis. Between 1977 and 2002, the organization falsified nuclear safety data prompting widespread investigations. More recently, during the Fukushima crisis, the company reported readings of radiation levels around the crippled nuclear plant that were later deemed "not credible." Stakeholders literally around the world called into question TEPCO's failure to communicate openly and honestly about a serious problem with global ramifications.

Source: http://www.dailymail.co.uk/news/article-1370409/Japan-nuclear-crisis-Fukushima-plant-radiation-levels-10m-times-normal.html#ixzz1KDk2lr8G.

Concern for Employees/Stakeholders

The concern driver is squarely about communication and employment and stakeholder policies, processes, and practices. Stakeholders trust organizations if they believe they are heard. Trust is higher when leaders bring information to those affected by decisions. Safety procedures, health plans and benefits, family leave, vacation, performance evaluation, salary scales, promotional practices, customer policies, service requirements, vendor policies, and a host of other organization-wide processes determine whether an organization is concerned for its stakeholders.

The Concern for Stakeholders Driver of Trust in Action

The British Petroleum Company's oil spill in the Gulf of Mexico in 2010 quickly became America's worst environmental disaster in history as crude oil gushed for three months into the ocean and along the coast. The fallout from the disaster directly impacted the lives of fishermen, businesses, and families along the Gulf Coast. As a year's wages for many fishermen slipped away, the CEO of British Petroleum, Tony Hayward, made an untimely remark: "There's no one who wants this over more than I do. I'd like my life back." The fishermen and their families had a hard time feeling any sympathy for the wealthy CEO. His particular comment, whether intentional or not, clearly demonstrated a lack of concern for stakeholders.

Source: http://www.csmonitor.com/
USA/2010/0620/A-yachting-trip-The-10-worst-BP-gaffes-in-Gulf-oil-spill.

Reliability

The reliability driver is about keeping commitments and basic follow-through. It is about leaders doing what they say they are going to do. It is about describing why change must take place. It is about consistent behaviors from day to day and consistently listening to ideas, issues, and concerns. Reliability is responding whether the response is positive or negative. Reliability is a steadiness in behavior that builds the trust necessary for uncertain times.

The Reliability Driver of Trust in Action

To the misfortune of many individuals and organizations, Bernie Madoff has become a household name. The one-time Wall Street tycoon crafted together what appeared to be a successful investment company. For nearly 20 years, the financier shifted money among accounts and falsified trade documents all to end in a $64 billion collapse of his financial empire in 2008. The scandal that robbed many of their savings and livelihood also brings into question the reliability of the U.S. Securities and Exchange Commission, a national oversight organization that was aware of Madoff's Ponzi scheme two years before his demise. The Exchange Commission's response—or lack thereof—and Madoff's misalignment of words and actions exemplifies the reliability driver of trust.

Sources: http://www.businessweek.com/bwdaily/dnflash/content/mar2009/db20090312_431966.
hth; http://www.newsweek.com/2011/04/17/america-s-top-liars.html.

Identification

The identification driver is the connection between the organization and stakeholders most often based on core values. Identification is high when stakeholders believe their values are reflected in the values the organization exhibits in decisions, communication, policies, practices, and a host of other behaviors.

The Identification Driver of Trust in Action

The current state of the American political system serves to illustrate the identification driver of trust. During the 2008 presidential and 2010 midterm elections, candidates for national office became increasingly reliant on a growing group of voters known as the independents. The Pew Research Center reports that the number of people choosing to forego identifying with a particular political party has reached a 70-year high. Obviously, the values the Democratic Party and the Republican Party exhibit in their decisions, communication, policies and practices fail to connect sufficiently with these independent voters.

Source: http://www.npr.org/templates/story/story.php?storyId=104406480.

Table 9.1 presents the results of our research on the trust model and the work of others with regard to organizational outcomes for each of the five drivers. If the driver is present in an organization, the high trust and positive outcomes are listed; if the driver is not present, the distrust or negative outcomes are listed.

Table 9.1   The Organizational Trust Model with Trust and Distrust Outcomes

Trust Model Drivers	High-Trust Outcomes	Distrust Outcomes
Competence	Goal achievement and loyalty	Lower stakeholder loyalty
	Attracts and retains quality employees	Lower stakeholder effort and commitment
	Increased innovation	Fear of change
Openness and Honesty	Improved collaboration	Less sharing of information
	Reduction of uncertainty	Barriers to innovation
Concern for Employees	High employee satisfaction, retention, and loyalty	Stakeholder needs not met and unfair treatment
	Productivity goals met	Productivity goals not met and negative impact on bottom line
Reliability	Consistent results	Abuse of power
	Positive perceptions of effectiveness	Broken commitments
	High performance	Lower performance

(*continued*)

Table 9.1   (*continued*)

Trust Model Drivers	High-Trust Outcomes	Distrust Outcomes
Identification	Shared values and sense of purpose Promotes positive change Increased quality	Stakeholders pursue self-interests Job insecurity Increased absenteeism and intentions to leave

Source: Shockley-Zalabak, Pamela, Morreale, Sherwyn and Hackman, Michael. *Building the High-Trust Organization,* 2010, 172.

Challenges to Maintaining Stakeholder Trust

Before we describe how each of our trust drivers can be used to build and maintain stakeholder trust, we want to describe major challenges to stakeholder trust. These challenges, while not surprising in and of themselves, cannot be ignored when thinking about diverse stakeholders. The 21st-century challenges we will discuss are globalization; virtual organizations; innovation, creativity, and risk; conflict and crisis; and the future. We do not believe these are the only challenges but have selected those with particular significance for trust building.

> Challenges to building and maintaining trust in 21st-century organizations include: globalization; virtual organizations; innovation, creativity, and risk; conflict and crisis; and the future.

Globalization

Our global world both excites and challenges. Globalization has been described as promoting anxiety, excitement, anxiety, and opportunity. Most agree it is impossible to find clarity in these turbulent and uncertain times. We recognize the complexity of trust building in global environments with vastly differing cultural perspectives. That is one of the reasons we developed our model across several continents. We know there are significant cross-cultural differences in values around the globe. But, while cultural differences impact all groups of stakeholders, those differences do not have to create a negative impact on collaborating effectively. The key is to develop an understanding of the differences likely to influence stakeholders in diverse cultures and plan how to address the differences in specific relationships.

Cultural differences, while important, are not the only consideration when thinking about trust building in global environments. When working globally, national perceptions of trust, financial market conditions, and specific institutional considerations all contribute to trust perceptions among stakeholders. In these circumstances, trust relationships are related to trust in governments to honor multinational agreements; to legal protection of money flows, investments, and intellectual property agreements; and to confidence in institutional operations without any personal familiarity or similarity.

Virtual Organizations

Estimates vary but most agree nearly 90 percent of all organizations have significant aspects of their work performed virtually. Interactions with customers, investors, clients, or donors are common through electronic communications. Face-to-face interactions are replaced with working electronically across time and space. Technological connectivity is key. Control and monitoring systems based on physical location are replaced with technical systems permitting employees and customers to work together across time zones, language differences, and other significant local/global considerations. Leaders of today can utilize the potential efficiencies of the virtual organization only if they discover how to run organizations based more on trust than on control. Working effectively in virtual organizations is based as much on trust as it is technology.

Innovation, Creativity, and Risk

Trust is fundamental to stimulate innovation, creativity, and risk taking. The reason is simple. If employees or other significant stakeholders do not trust an organization they withhold the best of their thinking. They play it safe by staying with the status quo. Innovation, creativity, and risk taking suffer. Stakeholders innovate in environments in which it is safe to challenge and change the status quo. Mistakes are expected and supported when reaching for new solutions. Research and practical experience both support the finding that high-trust organizations are more creative, innovative, and able to engage in productive risk taking than their lower-trust counterparts. This creativity and innovation also involve planning for change in high-trust organizations. Effective change is based on trust in decision makers; openness about the rationale for change, its impact, and expected results; excellent execution of change; and continuous evaluation of results. In high-trust organizations, the communication strategy and plans for change are a shared responsibility of leaders and communication professionals (Shockley-Zalabak, Morreale, and Hackman 2010).

Conflict/Crises

Again, it is both practical experience and academic research that allows us to state that trust during conflict improves outcomes. When top management teams are in conflict, trust has been demonstrated to provide the glue important for productive resolution. We know leaders make better decisions when differing perspectives and conflicting ideas surface. We know decisions are generally better supported when personal attacks are avoided during conflict. But what is important and sometimes illusive is the underlying trust or distrust present in a leadership group, which literally shapes the conflict. When trust is low, leaders may silence important disagreements, refuse to agree based on low trust in individuals presenting ideas, or agree but not support key decisions. When trust is low, leaders often later engage in resistance behaviors that didn't surface in the decision meetings. Regardless of the behavior, the results lower decision quality (Korsgaard, Brodt, and Whitener 2002; Simons and Peterson 2000).

The choices made during crises affect organizations into the future. Poor crisis response damages reputations and lowers trust. The greater the magnitude of the crisis and the longer it lasts, the longer stakeholders will remember it. Stakeholders become angry and distrust increases if the organization denies responsibility or appears to be slow, inaccurate, or self-serving in its actions and responses. Employees, customers, clients, investors, and donors make decisions about continued relationships with organizations based on how a crisis is handled and how much trust they retain in the organization (Stocker 1997).

The Future

Leaders succeed in producing outstanding results only when they are trusted by their constituents and stakeholders to make changes during uncertain times that promise to lead to a better future. Increasingly, organizations are working with fluid and rapidly changing boundaries and parameters on their work world. For example, in many organizations in the future, there will be fewer managers with larger spans of control. Work teams will have higher degrees of autonomy and control over immediate work situations, and power and control will be dispersed across the organization. In these dynamic and changing organizations, professional communicators will have increased responsibility. Developing formal communication policies is the responsibility of professional communicators in collaboration with top leaders, which includes message development, dissemination, feedback, and evaluation. The spin doctors of the past are being replaced with trustworthy communication professionals who understand data collection and interpretation and the needs of diverse stakeholders, who develop credible message strategies, who utilize diverse technologies wisely, and who understand the demands of instant information in a virtual world (Shockley-Zalabak 2009).

Building Stakeholder Trust

Intentional trust building begins with understanding trust and distrust in particular contexts. Intentional trust building requires continued vigilance by leaders because gradual erosions of trust often go unnoticed. Intentional trust building becomes one of the "habits of excellence" of outstanding organizations.

We begin this section by describing an overarching approach for building trust. Next we describe specific strategies to enhance trust among stakeholders using each of the five drivers. These descriptions are meant to stimulate thinking for leaders and professional communicators to become more intentional about trust building for increased organizational effectiveness.

> A trust profile or picture of trust in any organization is essential to building or repairing trust.

Understanding the trust profile of a particular organization is fundamental to building trust or repairing distrust. This profile is simply a picture of the organization with regard to levels of trust. Several empirical measures of trust are available including the Organizational Trust Index (OTI), which was developed as a result of the research sponsored by the International Association of Business Communicators (IABC). The OTI measures and provides a picture of the organization regarding trust levels for each of the trust drivers we already described (Shockley-Zalabak, Morreale, and Hackman 2010). Although we support using empirical measures, relying on any instrument to profile organizational trust is insufficient to produce excellent results. Identifying productivity measures or outcomes to monitor trust can contribute to the usefulness of the results obtained using the organizational trust profile. Trust, in fact, can be reflected in a very diverse set of organizational outcomes. The outcome measures to be tracked along with an organization's empirical trust profile are organization specific and should be selected with care and understanding of the vision and objectives of the specific organization. Table 9.2 lists possible choices of outcomes for trust monitoring.

Finally, organizational policies and procedures provide important information to help understand an organization's trust profile. A wide variety of organizational policies and practices should be reviewed regularly for how they communicate the trust values of the organization. Generally speaking, the more detailed and prescriptive policies and practices become, the more distrust is communicated to stakeholders. The more policies and procedures empower people to "do what is right," the more trust is present. Even necessary compliance policies can communicate trust if they provide a strong rationale for their need and include an emphasis on the

Table 9.2   Organizational Outcome Measures for Monitoring Trust

1	Financial performance
2	Competitive positioning
3	Productivity compared to industry/sector benchmarks
4	Levels of collaboration and cooperation
5	Performance in strategic alliances
6	Flexibility and coordination costs
7	Employee commitments and morale
8	Customer/donor/other stakeholder loyalty
9	Innovation environment
10	Support for change initiatives
11	Leader effectiveness
12	Productivity in virtual teams
13	Employee turnover rates
14	Employee-absenteeism rates
15	Accidents and worker compensation claims
16	Litigation records
17	Ethical/legal abuses
18	Media coverage
19	Crisis management
20	Industry/sector reputation

Source: Shockley-Zalabak, Pamela, Morreale, Sherwyn, and Hackman, Michael. *Building the High-Trust Organization,* 2010, 210.

equity with which they will be implemented. Table 9.3 lists categories of policies and procedures that have the potential to help build trust.

Intentional trust building also requires the alignment of vision, strategic direction, and operations. Leaders should regularly review the organization's vision, strategy direction, and operational plans for their impact on trust. Instrumentation, productivity measures, and policy and procedure review do not replace top leaders regularly assessing vision and strategy for their impact in ever changing and evolving circumstances. Additionally, the communication strategy of the organization must begin with a solid leadership communication plan. All behaviors and organizational actions should be evaluated along trust dimensions. What we are saying is trust should drive the organization's behaviors and action, and communicating

Table 9.3   Categories of Policy and Procedures for Trust Building

1	Hiring policies and practices
2	Performance feedback and appraisal
3	Compensation policies and practices
4	Disciplinary processes
5	Termination processes and practices
6	Promotional processes and practices
7	Employment benefits
8	Vendor policies and practices
9	Sexual harassment policies and practices
10	Workplace harassment policies and practices
11	Conflict of interest policies and practices
12	Ethical standards
13	Customer/client relationships
14	Confidentiality of private information
15	Financial responsibility
16	Communication of information
17	Feedback processes
18	Media relations
19	Corporate/organization communication standards and practices
20	Organizational philanthropy

Source: Shockley-Zalabak, Pamela, Morreale, Sherwyn, and Hackman, Michael. *Building the High-Trust Organization,* 2010, 211–12.

clearly with all stakeholders is the best communication strategy for in-creasing trust and addressing the negative impact of distrust.

Now we move to the specific challenge of building stakeholder trust with emphasis on understanding and assessing each of the five drivers: competence, openness and honesty; concern; reliability; and identification. Some of the identified strategies recur across the drivers emphasizing the importance of understanding trust profiles as in an overall organizational profile.

> Assessing competence begins with examining and understanding the current state of the competence of the organization and the trust level of stakeholders in that competence.

Competence and Stakeholder Trust

Assessing competence begins with examining and understanding the current state of the competence of the organization and the trust level of stakeholders in that competence. Questions must be asked about the clarity and relevance of the current vision as well as the capability of leaders to support the vision. The core competence of individual leaders and leadership teams must be examined. Often distrust responses among stakeholders can be traced directly to the lack of competence and ethical behaviors of leaders. In addition to a current state assessment, understanding must be developed about how key stakeholders respond to the strategy and goals and the structure in place to achieve the goals. An assessment of competence rests on designing an organizational structure or architecture for results. Stakeholders trust organizations that produce high-quality results. Many organizations with strong purpose and vision fail to regularly examine whether their execution structures continue to make sense. Producing excellent results requires regular examination and updating of policies and procedures, ranging from hiring, performance review, and compensation to internal and external communication planning. Finally, and perhaps most important, competent organizations have leaders who can lead needed change. Competence is reflected in responses to change, crisis, and challenge.

> Assessment of openness and honesty begins with conducting a complete evaluation of the current state of this trust driver throughout the organization, including the extent to which stakeholders trust in the openness and honesty of the organization.

Openness and Honesty and Stakeholder Trust

Assessment of this driver begins with conducting a complete evaluation of the current state of openness and honesty throughout the organization, including the extent to which stakeholders trust in the openness and honesty of the organization. Although initially overwhelming, the next step or strategy calls for a comprehensive review of communication practices. This assessment relates to all regularly occurring communication events and practices, ranging from staff meetings to performance evaluations. It includes internal and external communication processes and departments as well as stockholder and regulatory relationships. The assessment should include a comprehensive review of various media including social media. The next strategy requires a thoughtful assessment of leaders with regard to communication. Many leaders who are technically outstanding do not understand their communication responsibilities nor do they have the communication competencies to execute those responsibilities with credibility. Once an understanding is developed of leader communication competency, it is important to develop core communication capabilities for those who have significant communication responsibilities. Finally, trust in openness and honesty is directly related to creating a compelling, comprehensive communication plan. Once values and expectations for communication responsibilities have been clarified, the plan moves to the specifics of:

1. Identifying themes and other types of information that need to be communicated and by whom;
2. Identifying audiences who should regularly receive information;
3. Identifying audiences who should regularly provide information;
4. Describing types of media to be utilized;
5. Assessing timing and frequency of various types of communication practices;
6. Assessing how the plan supports the development of relationships; and
7. Determining how the plan should be continually evaluated.

> Assessment of concern for stakeholders begins with a complete and thoughtful assessment of the current state of this driver throughout the organization, including the extent to which the stakeholders trust in the organization's concern for them.

Concern for Stakeholders and Stakeholder Trust

This driver directly addresses the diversity of stakeholders who determine the trust profile of the organization. As with the previous drivers, assessment here begins with a complete and thoughtful assessment of the current state of concern for stakeholders throughout the organization, including the extent to which those stakeholders trust in the organization's concern for them. Second, assessment of policies and practices for demonstration of concern is important. An audit of policies and practices (return to Table 9.2 for specific examples) not only reviews the technical aspects of policies and practices but analyzes "concern" messages embedded in each. A comprehensive audit goes beyond the most obvious policies and practices to include conflict resolution, financial controls, reward and recognition programs, medical benefits, leave policies, and a host of other processes. The audit is not designed to change organizational practices, policies, and procedures, but to understand their impact on trust. Sometimes change will be needed while, at other times, clear communication about what the organization is doing will improve the concern trust profile. Concern must be communicated clearly and directly and all communication planning should be assessed for its direct messages about concern for stakeholders.

> Assessing reliability begins with a complete evaluation of the current state of reliability throughout the organization, and the extent to which stakeholders trust in that reliability.

Reliability and Stakeholder Trust

As with the other drivers, assessing reliability begins with a complete evaluation of the current state of reliability throughout the organization, and the extent to which stakeholders trust in that reliability. Not to be confused with sameness, reliability comes from a culture of aligning words and actions and providing dependable responses even to the most difficult of circumstances. Reliability also is related to promoting accountability for results at all organizational levels. Promoting accountability requires examining performance expectations for top leaders and determining how those expectations are met and translated into expectations throughout the organization. Trust in reliability is enhanced when blame is avoided, and when individuals are encouraged to admit mistakes, offer solutions to problems, and work for positive change. Trust in reliability requires a transparency in communicating expectations, processes, and results. Trust in reliability requires an understanding of whether stakeholders understand expectations, have consistent information, know how problems and issues are handled and resolved, and have methods to provide input to the organization.

> Assessment of the identification driver emphasizes understanding how and whether stakeholders identify with the organization, and the extent to which their identification is the result of intentional relationship planning.

Identification and Stakeholder Trust

Finally, assessment of the identification driver emphasizes understanding how and whether stakeholders identify with the organization, and the extent to which their identification is the result of intentional relationship planning. Building trust in identification requires designing key processes and practices to support stakeholder identification. High-identification organizations communicate continually how stakeholders of the organization are connected to something special—the core mission of the organization. Internally, hiring processes seek not only appropriate technical skills for a job but a fit between the values of the organization and those of potential employees. Content for orientations and training programs assists employees and other stakeholders in connecting their values, needs, and goals to the organization. Promotional processes, compensation, and award programs all communicate how employees can or should identify with the organization. Organizational stories, history, celebrations, and use of language all support identification. External stakeholders are encouraged to relate to the organization through customer communication, messages about service, problem resolution, quality, and the achievement of organizational goals. Less visible but important are messages of trust and respect for all stakeholders. In other words, trust is built when organizations excel at communicating stakeholder value, trust, and connection to the organization. Such an organization lives by visible values and principles that resonate with an array of diverse stakeholders.

Key Takeaways

1. High organizational trust positively transforms individuals and entire organizations. By contrast, breaches in trust, like those we used to illustrate the five drivers in our trust model, result in disappointment, at best, and outrage on the part of any organization's multiple stakeholders. Therefore, building and maintaining stakeholder trust is a professional imperative for leaders and communication professionals.
2. Trust building should be intentional. Trust building should be part of strategic planning for all organizations.

3. Trust is not just a nice, illusive concept but the very bond and stimulant that produces lasting excellence.
4. Trust is capable of replacing certainty and control as our bridge to the future. We have choices about that future.
5. The choice to build trust is practical and will affect bottom-line organizational outcomes and bring measurable positive results.
6. Stakeholders value an organization in which they can place their trust and, in turn, that trust will propel the organization to success in the 21st century.
7. The choice to build trust also speaks to the best in all of us, our high ideals, and our dreams for the future.

Glossary

Competence driver of trust: Driver of trust representing the ability of an organization through its leaders, strategy, decisions, quality, and capabilities to meet the challenges of its environment.

Concern for employees/stakeholders driver of trust: Driver of trust concerned about communication and employment and stakeholder policies, processes, and practices.

Identification driver of trust: Driver of trust examining the connection between the organization and stakeholders most often based on core values.

Openness and honesty driver of trust: Driver of trust reflecting how organizations communicate about problems, engage in constructive disagreements, and provide input into job-related decisions.

Organizational trust: The overarching belief that an organization in its communication and behaviors is competent, open and honest, concerned, reliable, and worthy of identification with its goals, norms, and values.

Organizational Trust Index (OTI): Measure providing a picture of the organization regarding trust levels for each of the five trust drivers.

Reliability driver of trust: Driver of trust concerned about keeping commitments and basic follow-through. It is about leaders doing what they say they are going to do.

Stakeholders: Those individuals and groups who have an interest or "stake" in an organization and are able to influence the organization's ability to meet its goals.

References

Korsgaard, M. Audrey, Susan E. Brodt, and Ellen M. Whitener. "Trust in the Face of Conflict: The Role of Managerial Trustworthy Behavior and Organizational Context." *Journal of Applied Psychology* 87 (2002): 312–19.

Shockley-Zalabak, Pamela. *Fundamentals of Organizational Communication.* 7th ed. Boston: Allyn & Bacon, 2009.

Shockley-Zalabak, Pamela. *Fundamentals of Organizational Communication.* 8th ed. Boston: Allyn & Bacon, 2012.

Shockley-Zalabak, Pamela, Sherwyn Morreale, and Michael Hackman. *Building the High Trust Organization.* San Francisco: Jossey-Bass, 2010.

Simons, Tony L., and Randall, S. Peterson. "Task Conflict and Relationship Conflict in Top Management Teams: The Pivotal Role of Intragroup Trust." *Journal of Applied Psychology* 85 (2000): 102–11.

Stocker, Kurt P. "A Strategic Approach to Crisis Management." In *Handbook of Strategic Public Relations and Integrated Communications,* edited by Clarke L. Caywood, 189–203. New York: McGraw Hill, 1997.

CHAPTER TEN

Every Organization Faces Risk, but Effectively Communicating Risk Is a Skill

LaKesha N. Anderson and Daniel L. Walsch

A Campus under Siege: Crisis Management of Campus Shootings at Northern Illinois University

In 2008, Northern Illinois University's incident became the fourth-deadliest university shooting on an American campus. It occurred over a brief span of six minutes and resulted in six deaths, including the perpetrator's suicide. Within an hour of the shootings, university authorities decided to close the campus for the remainder of the day and the rest of the week. A number of local, regional, and even national agencies became involved in the handling and investigation of the incident. These ranged from the university's own police department and the Illinois state police to the local fire department and the Federal Bureau of Investigation (Peters 2009).

Not surprisingly, the students, staff, and faculty throughout the institution were reported to be in shock, distraught, and numb from the gravity of the horror that had been inflicted upon their campus. Like many people, they had held the notion that institutions of higher learning are safe and peaceful environments (Langford 2004). A study conducted several weeks after the deadly violence at the DeKalb campus found nearly 75 percent of the student body suffered from significant psychological distress (Vicary and Fraley 2010).

The institution's public relations office estimated receiving hundreds of media inquires and calls in the immediate aftermath of the shootings. Three weeks after the incident, however, university president John Peters urged the campus community and external publics, including the media, to focus on helping them "look forward" (Peters 2008) as plans were made to memorialize those who had been killed and as the institution carried on with the remainder of the semester. Citing the "bad taste" of some reporters, Peters finally announced that he would no longer conduct media interviews about the incident, stating, "There won't be a press release. I'm not talking to the press. I think the people of the state understand this. They have to give us a little room here, because this is such an emotional time" (Peters 2008, under "Letter from NIU President John Peters on Cole Hall").

The shootings at Northern Illinois University constitute an organizational crisis. The event was unexpected and unplanned, generated a high level of uncertainty for both internal and external publics, and was a significant potential threat to the university's reputation (Ulmer, Sellnow, and Seeger 2007). Occurring less than one year after the deadliest university shooting in history, the Virginia Tech shootings, the public was primed to respond with shock and outrage. Simply due to time and history, the shootings at the university set the stage for a public relations disaster. Perhaps due in part, however, to precedence, the shootings at Northern Illinois University were also a risk. With the increase in the number of school shootings over the past 15 years, and the Virginia Tech shootings in 2007, it is evident that campus shootings are a real and present, though minimal, risk associated with campus life.

Despite having a negative connotation, crises are not always bad. In fact, a crisis can be positive for an organization. Depending on how a crisis is handled, it can serve as an opportunity for organizational growth and improvement. Conversely, if handled incorrectly, a crisis can quickly become a threatening situation that can cause lasting harm to an organization's external reputation, internal effectiveness, and overall profits.

In the case of Northern Illinois University, a great deal of attention was immediately placed on the institution. Thus, any failure to handle the crisis appropriately could jeopardize the public's confidence in the university, negatively affecting donations, enrollment, and even state financial support.

Given the negative consequences associated with poorly managing crises, it is imperative that organizations are equipped with the knowledge and tools necessary to responsibly handle a crisis, and to appropriately manage a risk before it becomes a crisis. Crisis communication, from a limited perspective, is designed to be short term in that it primarily speaks to the crisis at-hand. However, that does not mean that crises cannot and should not be anticipated. In fact, strategic communication is a long-term effort designed to help an organization better understand how transformative events, such as crises, may impact the organization's overall mission, vision, culture, and environment. Thus, the central theme guiding this chapter is that to best communicate during a crisis, organizations must integrate their crisis and risk communication with their strategic-communication efforts, taking into account that there are ongoing risks that threaten an organization and transformative events that may represent short-term crises. Each, if managed poorly, has long-term impacts on organizational success.

Given the importance of effective risk and crisis communication on organizational outcomes, it is imperative that those charged with managing these efforts understand what risk and crisis communication really is and the best way to practice each. Thus, this chapter will explore risk and crisis communication, provide a model for effective risk and crisis communication, and explore the link between risk and crisis communication and an organization's strategic-communication plan.

Risk and Crisis Communication

While commonly used interchangeably, risk and crisis are different. The most immediate difference is that risk is unavoidable, while a crisis can be avoided. Regardless, both risks and crises must be well communicated to the various stakeholders public being affected and both require planning in order to be managed well. Communicating risk involves preparing publics for the risk while crisis communication speaks to dealing with an actual ongoing situation. The following pages will further explore the difference between the two while also introducing the CAUSE model, which serves as a bridge between preparing for disasters and managing them when they occur (Rowan et al. 2009).

Risk Communication

Risk communication is communication meant to provide laypeople with the information needed to make informed decisions regarding risks (Morgan et al. 2002). Risk communication, as mentioned, is so important because risk is unavoidable. Each day, people take risks simply by driving, walking, or bicycling to work. Some former risks have subsided in severity. There have been great advances in medicine that has led to decreased infant mortality rates and improvements in disease prevention and treatment, for instance. At the same time, there are always new risks emerging. While including more fruits and vegetable in one's diet is a positive decision, experts are now weighing in on the risk of genetically modified foods, which are laboratory-designed crops used to produce many of the fruits and vegetables, and even cotton products, seen in stores today. Risk is present in nearly every facet of one's life. Does the coffee we drink cause cancer? Is airline travel safer than auto travel? In order to answer those questions and weigh the risk/benefit of their choices, people turn to organizations for answers. Risk communication, then, serves an important role in the decision-making processes of people each day.

Unfortunately, often what people think is risky is not and vice versa. For instance, in 1995, mad cow disease incited fear in meat eaters around the globe when the first human cases of the condition were discovered. However, the actual likelihood of mere exposure to mad cow disease is low. In fact, there is no known risk of contracting the virus in the United States and a minimal risk of contraction outside the United States (Ropeik and Gray 2002). In the United States, however, there was intense response to the idea that humans could contract a bovine disease. It was even the issue at the heart of a Texas cattle owner's lawsuit against media mogul Oprah Winfrey, who famously said she did not want to eat beef after a guest on her talk show warned of an outbreak of human mad cow disease in the United States. Comparatively, there appears to be much less public fear, or at least vocalized fear, about sexually transmitted diseases. Unlike mad cow disease, more than 65 million Americans are living with an incurable sexually transmitted disease. Further, the likelihood of exposure to a sexually transmitted disease is high (Ropeik and Gray 2002). Yet, this information does not lead to protective measures for much of the potentially affected population. In fact, as one study found that two-thirds of the men in a monogamous relationship and one-third of those without a primary partner admitted to not using condoms. In addition, the study found that even after being treated for a sexually transmitted disease, men still refused to wear condoms to prevent future infections (Grimely et al. 2004).

While it is true that one's chances of dying from an asteroid impact are greater than the chances of dying from a fireworks discharge (Britt 2005), most people do not share the same concern for the rare risks that professional risk assessors consider each day. Instead, most people are concerned with the risks that most immediately impact them and those close to them (Morgan et al. 2002). These risks are also the ones people can exert the most immediate control over. Because of this, many people are simply unaware of other more exotic risks.

RISK COMMUNICATION

Communication meant to provide laypeople with the information needed to make informed decisions regarding risks.

Even more unfortunate is that many organizations do not put forth the effort to communicate these risks to their publics. Most organizational risk assessors are not trained in communication. As a result, these organizations adopt a magic-bullet approach to risk communication, assuming that by simply transmitting or disseminating the message they have done their job. In addition, these organizations tend to evaluate their success not by data, but by the creation of public relations documents such as websites, press releases, and brochures (Littlefield et al. 2010). However, true success can only be measured by outcome variables such as behavior change. Yet, as any communication professional knows, changing behavior is difficult and is a function of also tapping into the public's values, attitudes, preconceptions, and beliefs. As a result, for risk communication to be effective, it must be about more than simply creating and disseminating a message to a public. In fact, according to Perry (1979), in order for a risk message to be effective, a person must perceive there to be a high personal risk and a high reality for the risk to occur. In addition, the content of the warning message and the sheer number of times the message is received also play a role in the likelihood that a message will be attended to by the intended public. Effective risk-communication strategies not only help individuals, and organizations, avoid unwanted occurrences but also provide them with tools to successfully contend with the unexpected that comes in the form of a crisis.

Though many organizations rely on public relations professionals to manage their risk- and crisis-communication efforts, not all risks and crises fall into the spectrum of public relations. One key difference between risk communication and the more generic practice of public relations is that risk communication is geared more to a well defined, potentially realistic scenario. A fire or a tornado would be examples of this as such disasters are recognized as being within the realm of possibility. Public relations efforts, however, speak more to scenarios that are created or self-generated by communication officers. These would include introducing a new product to the public, promoting the presidential aspirations of a candidate, initiating an alliance with another entity, or reacting to external occurrences.

Lundgren and McMakin touch on ingredients that help set risk communication apart from its "family cousins": crisis communication and strategic communication (2004). The two identify three types of risk communication: care communication, census communication, and, interestingly, crisis communication. Collectively, the three types represent communication efforts designed to help publics contend with well-defined dangers, work together more easily, and face actual unwanted occurrences in a coordinated, relatively seamless manner. While these elements distinguish risk communication, they also reinforce the reality that all subsets of the overarching public relations are driven by one of two fundamental goals: persuasion and partnership (Grunig and Hunt 1984). Communicators strive either to persuade publics to take certain actions or adopt certain beliefs or attitudes they had not previously taken or contemplated or form or participate in alliances—short or long term—that are based upon shared interests or concerns.

Sandman (2002) also examines differences in risk communication, which he explains is comprised of four categories: public relations, stakeholder relations, outrage management, and crisis communication. Sandman supports the previous argument that immediacy and probability are factors in delineating between general public relations and crisis management, despite both being elements under the greater risk-communication umbrella. As Sandman explains, the difference is really in the levels of hazard and outrage generated by the hazard. Public relations activities, for instance, typically address issues that are high hazard but low outrage. Often, an organization's public relations efforts are aimed at attempting to reach an apathetic audience. In this case, higher levels of outrage may actually boost the chance of getting the message out; thus generating outrage may be an effective goal of public relations at certain times. On the other hand, crisis communication is both high hazard and high outrage. In this case, the organization is seeking to calm and reassure a scared and, often angry, audience that is highly involved in the outcome of the situation. Thus, as Sandman explains, while not all crisis communication is falls under the greater scope of public relations, both are part of effective risk communication. In short, to effectively reach an audience via risk-communication messages, an organization must prepare for the risk and for the management of the risk, which requires a thorough understanding of public relations, crisis communication, and risk communication.

The CAUSE Model

Rowan's (1991) CAUSE model originally provided a framework for examining the goals, risks, and principles associated with risk communication. Specifically, it looked at the establishment of five communicative goals: creating confidence, generating awareness, enhancing understanding, improving satisfaction, and motivating action, or enactment. These goals are not easy or quick to attain, and each must be continually communicated in order to ensure they remain in the minds of key publics should a crisis develop (Ripley 2008a). Since her 1991 article, Rowan's CAUSE model has been applied in various communication research contexts, even cancer research (see Rowan et al. 2003). The CAUSE model is ideal for dissecting the communicative issues facing organizations facing both crises and preparing for and managing risks. It serves as a strategic-planning guide for organizations, moving them step by step through an effective risk- and crisis-management process. CAUSE stands for: confidence, awareness, understanding, satisfaction, and enactment. Let's look at each of these steps in turn.

Step One: Confidence

The first step in the model is generating confidence. For there to be a chance that either internal or external publics would listen to, or adhere, to information communicated to them from an organization, the public must have confidence in the organization. According to Morgan et al. (2002), source credibility is the cornerstone of effective risk communication. Simply put, the more authoritative the source, the more likely the public is to heed risk warnings than if the message is passed on from peers or via media (Perry 1979). Yet, if a public does not trust the organization or person providing the information, this could lead to confusion and damage relations between an organization and its publics, while allowing less credible sources to reach these publics (Morgan et al. 2002). For internal publics, this confidence may come as a result of high morale among employees or a belief that company leaders are actively engaged in the well-being of their employees (Crozier 2010). Trust or confidence is the key to an organization's successful implementation of a risk or crisis strategy. It is the result of parties holding favorable perceptions of one another to the point that various outcomes can be and are achieved (Wheeless and Grotz 1977). Thus, effective or successful crisis communication depends upon long-term practices, such as building trust, confidence, and a high level of readiness with key constituencies. These characteristics are shared by effective strategic communication.

Step 2: Awareness

The second step in the CAUSE model is creating awareness. Messages can fail if their intended recipients are not aware of them; that is, a warning message is not seen, heard, or detected in other ways. In the case of Northern Illinois University, for example, there were reports that initially many students, staff, and faculty members were not even cognizant that deadly shootings were occurring on campus despite efforts by university officials to inform the campus community that shootings were occurring and that people were in danger. At Northern Illinois University, the administration utilized its web page as the primary vehicle for communicating its emergency to its numerous internal publics. The obvious obstacle in this case was that not everyone had access to the university's web page at the time of the crisis. It is vital, of course, that publics immediately understand when they are being notified of an actual danger or crisis. The obvious benefit of this is that they will give these messages serious attention. Rowan (1991, 311) describes this awareness as detectability, which she explains as the "ease with which a message may be heard or seen." As Rowan, Talkington, and Beck (2009) explain, however, making a message detectable does not mean an audience is aware. In addition to detectability, Rowan (1991) says that good informatory messages are also decodable and take the audience into consideration. A decodable message is one that can be easily understood and paraphrased by those intended to view the message.

Another obstacle organizations face when relaying information to publics is that, oftentimes, the concepts presented in the messages are simply difficult to understand. Rowan (2003) identified three primary barriers to understanding difficult concepts, which may help better explain risk- and crisis-related messages. These include (1) distinguishing essential and associated meanings, (2) visualizing unseen, unfamiliar, or complex phenomena, and (3) understanding counterintuitive messages (Rowan 2003, 419). An example of these concepts can be found by examining postpartum depression, one of the most serious maternal health risks during the first postnatal year and a condition that has garnered increased media attention in the past decade. Postpartum depression is often linked to changing levels of estrogen and progesterone (Kahn et al. 2008; Stone and Eddleman 2003) and serotonin (Null and Seaman 1999), chemicals produced naturally by the brain. In applying Rowan's principles, it is easy to understand how simply talking about postpartum depression can be frustrating for women. It can be difficult to understand how estrogen and progesterone, chemicals usually discussed when talking about birth control pills or menopause (associated meaning), is related to postpartum depression (essential meaning). It may also be difficult to understand how a chemical produced by the brain can invoke feelings of inadequacy and fears of harming oneself or her child (unseen, complex idea). As well, it can also be difficult to comprehend how a woman could feel like harming her child or herself when she is supposed to be enjoying new motherhood (addressing counterintuitive ideology). Omitting jargon and using simple language are basic strategies to help organizations manage similar problems associated with awareness.

Step Three: Understanding

The third step in the model, deepening understanding, focuses on moving publics "from minimal awareness . . . to fuller comprehension" (Rowan

2003, 240). Communicating in a way in which people can understand is a fundamental tenet of communication. Unless a public understands a message, they may not be able to accurately follow directions in a risk or crisis situation. It is a mistake for an organization to simply assume that a public understands a message. However, intended or not, it often happens that an entity assumes their publics to be as informed and understanding as the scientists behind the message.

One organization that experienced backlash when it failed to provide much more than minimal awareness to its publics is the Food and Drug Administration (FDA). In 2010 the FDA issued a warning that bisphenol A (BPA), a chemical commonly found in hard plastic and metal food-storage container bottles. In the warning, the FDA explained that while low level exposure to BPA was considered safe, the office had concerns about the potential effects of BPA on the brains, behaviors, and prostate glands of fetuses, infants, and young children (Food and Drug Administration 2010). This warning created alarm for parents as baby bottles contain BPA. These parents did not know what level of BPA, if any, was safe for their child. At the same time, what alternative did they have for feeding their baby? The FDA's warning said the agency supported industry efforts to remove BPA from baby bottles in the future; yet, the FDA did not suggest that parents stop using bottles currently produced with BPA (Hellerman 2010).

Speaking or communicating in a way in which people can understand is a fundamental tenet of communication. Furthermore, anticipating and preparing for your audiences' reaction is a fundamental part of crisis communication. Organizations cannot assume that in times of crisis or great risk that all publics will be rationale. Thus, more planning must go into ensuring that a message is fully explained so that it can be fully understood. Further, because people often take action based on what is communicated to them, how well they understand the messages is vital (Botan and Hazelton 2006).

Step Four: Satisfaction

The fourth step in the CAUSE model is satisfaction. This function involves recommending actions designed to achieve a positive outcome to a crisis situation and anticipating obstacles to the proposed solution. Ideally, these steps should be addressed as part of the planning stage so as to avoid confusion and possible tragedy when a real crisis occurs. One effective way to do this is to involve the public in crafting the solution. This process is designed to raise the level of satisfaction and decrease resistance in the message on the part of the public (McGuire 1961). In this method, the organization acknowledges other perspectives on the situation before introducing their reasons for making certain recommendations. This two-sided persuasion strategy reinforces the idea that the organization has been open to all suggestions before coming up with their own particular set of recommendations. Executed well, this type of strategic communication advances the effectiveness of the message (Hovland, Lumsdaine, and Sheffield 1949). Also, a message is more likely to be accepted if listeners believe it to be of value to them (McQuail 2010) and one in which they have a vested interest.

Step Five: Enactment

The final step of the CAUSE model is enactment. This step speaks to how well receivers of the information/messages implement the ideas being recommended to them. Do they merely agree that a proposal is a good idea or do they actually enact it? Rowan, Talkington, and Beck (2009) found that despite reading an emergency procedures poster and engaging in discussion about responding to emergency scenarios on campus, students felt less confident that they could handle an actual campus emergency. In this case, talking through the solution lowered the self-efficacy of the audience. As a result, students did not feel confident in their abilities to carry out the action. The enactment step, while at its core, is an action step, is also an evaluation tool. If the crisis-communication plan failed, or was not followed, it will become evident during this step. Lessons learned during the enactment phase will help strengthen and revise already existing plans, which aligns with the goals of strategic planning as well.

CAUSE MODEL

A framework for examining the goals and principles associated with risk and crisis communication through five communicative goals: creating confidence, generating awareness, enhancing understanding, improving satisfaction, and motivating action, or enactment.

Risk- and crisis-communication plans are essential parts of any organization's overall strategic-communication plan. At its most effective, crisis-communication efforts should be designed before a crisis occurs. Before a crisis ensues, it is essential that an organization already have a thorough understanding of their key publics, have in place effective communication tools or vehicles from which to work, and have a strong acceptance on the part of their publics to honor a crisis plan should it be implemented. This preparatory work should derive from, and align with, an organization's overall mission, values, and goals.

Crisis Communication

A crisis is a specific event with a potentially negative outcome that creates high levels of uncertainty and affects an organization or entity as well as its public, products, services, and reputation (Fearn-Banks 2007; Ulmer, Sellnow, and Seeger 2007). Crises possess three defining characteristics: (1) surprise, (2) threat, and (3) short response time (Hermann 1963). The circumstances, while occurring, often seem unexpected, or unpredictable, thus seeming to leave those caught up in it to be at the mercy of the occurrence itself (Heath and Millar 2004). Such was the circumstance at Northern Illinois University. As is typical during a crisis, the university saw a swell in interest by the public, fell under close media scrutiny, experienced interference in their normal operations, and even felt potential threats to their public image and financial stability (Fink 1986).

> **CRISIS**
>
> A specific event with a potentially negative outcome that creates high levels of uncertainty and affects an organization or entity as well as its public, products, services and reputation and has three defining characteristics: surprise, threat, and short response time.

Organizations are increasingly aware of the need for crisis-communication planning. Organizations understand, at least from a business standpoint, the harm that a crisis can have on its overall financial objectives and key stakeholder relationships. However, what organizations do not yet understand is how to effectively craft crisis-communication plans so that these plans work harmoniously with risk-communication plans in an effort to avoid crisis, as well as with strategic-communication plans, to ensure that the organization's mission and goals are not compromised should a crisis occur. Organizations, while understanding that crisis can wreak financial havoc on its bottom line, do not often put the resources behind supporting crisis management, or include public relations staff in strategic-planning efforts. However, as Fearn-Banks states, "crisis communication is a necessity, not a frill or a procedure or policy that is developed if a company has a skilled employee with spare time" (2001, 479). To adequately prepare for crisis, crisis management must be thought of as strategic planning, and the individuals charged with communicating the organization's strategic plans deserve a seat at the table with financial managers, program managers, and head executives. An organization cannot expect an employee to simply pick up the task of crisis management. Crisis management is an ongoing process that begins with research on risk assessment and communication, requires ongoing and positive relationships with news media, and segmented stakeholder messaging strategies. This type of two-way symmetrical communication cannot occur without long-term crisis-management efforts by knowledgeable and dedicated public relations practitioners who are constantly updated and informed by organizational leadership as well as allowed to participate in discussions and decisions made by an organization's top executives. By definition, a crisis poses a significant threat to an organization's stability and, in some cases, existence. Consequently, it is vital that its top public relations or communication officer play an important role in the conceptualizing and implementation of strategies to address any unexpected and unwanted situation (J. Grunig, L. Grunig, and D. Dozier 2002). This was the case at Northern Illinois University. The institution's president elevated the vice president for university relations to its executive council when a decision was made that it needed to strengthen its risk- and crisis-communication strategies. The result was the development of a comprehensive plan that incorporated many key elements found in the CAUSE model.

Risk, Crisis, and Strategic Communication

Risk, crisis, and strategic communication are growing areas within workplace communication. Organizations are devoting significant portions of their budgets toward strengthening their communication competencies in each of these areas. When crafted with the organization's strategic plan in mind, risk and crisis plans not only help avoid and manage risk and crises, but also help entities move toward fulfilling an overriding vision or carry out an organizational mission. Ideally, risk-, crisis-, and strategic-communication plans should be part of an integrative approach to management that benefits the direction of an organization (Dyck and Neubert 2010).

Despite the similar characteristics of risk, crisis, and strategic communication, often these are viewed separately as the implementation of each is seen as being largely appropriate only at particular times, and for specified lengths of times. Little research exist that link risk-, crisis-, and strategic-communication plans in an organizational context. A review of research, however, indicates that individually these plans represent an effort to maintain a continuum toward a specified goal. When risk-, crisis-, and strategic-communication efforts are more directly melded together, an organization's ongoing efforts to continue moving forward are greatly enhanced (Fombrun 1996). While a primary difference between crisis and strategic communication might be in the circumstance of their implementation and enactment, their overall integration would better serve the greater good of the organization.

As strategic communication speaks to an entity's overall mission or policy goals, it serves as an umbrella for all plans carried out in its name (Smith 2009). Such a less-encompassing effort would be a risk- or crisis-communication plan. Such plans are designed to address a potential or specific event or circumstance being faced by the organization and are meant to establish an ongoing dialog between an organization and its publics that is maintained while a particular risk is communicated or crisis is handled (Fearn-Banks 2007). The connection between these communication plans is further solidified by recognizing the common elements they share. These are: transparency of action, ongoing flow of information, targeted publics, specific message points, and measurements of evaluation (Sandman 1983; Smith 2009).

> When risk-, crisis-, and strategic-communication efforts are more directly melded together, an organization's efforts to continually move forward are greatly enhanced and their overall integration would better serve the greater good of the organization.

These points link risk-, crisis-, and strategic-communication plans in theory and in several examples indicate how more enmeshed planning would have helped several organizations avoid crises. Thus, risk, crisis, and strategic communication should be viewed as interdependent and complementary to one another. That is to say, each plan should seek to fulfill the organization's mission and long-term strategic goals and be considerate of the audience and message when communicating both risk and crisis. The CAUSE model provides several guidelines for how to ensure each plan aligns in a way to best serve the organization. This model is supported by decades of research on risk and crisis communication which finds that factors surrounding credibility, messaging, and ease of enactment are associated with risk- and crisis-communication compliance and successful risk and crisis management.

Conclusion

The information provided in this chapter speaks to the importance of both preparing for a potential crisis and properly managing an occurring crisis. In the case of Northern Illinois University, the university has been lauded for the way it handled the aftermath of the campus shootings. But, what exactly did it do well?

Success and Implications for the Future

First and foremost, the institution had already prepared a crisis-management plan to help prepare for unwanted events on the campus. Thus, the university has taken assessment of several risks and acknowledged the possibility that they may occur, with potentially negative outcomes. The university had gained valuable insight on how to handle the situation from officials at Virginia Tech, who were still managing the aftermath of the April 2007 shootings.

Next, the university utilized the CAUSE model effectively. Within two hours of the incident, the university's public affairs office held the first of a series of press conferences. These press conferences continued over the coming days. A website was established that provided up-to-date information on the incident. The public affairs office and university officials encouraged the public and the media to utilize this website for more information between press conferences. As a result, the website received nearly 14 million visits. Additionally, the administration worked to be transparent by responding to e-mails and sending mass e-mailings to its key stakeholders updating them on the incident and any related news, and by holding meetings with a number of meetings with faculty, staff, and various external constituents. By immediately providing an official spokesperson and making easily understandable information transparent and available several ways (both online, via media, and during press conferences), the university demonstrated an understanding of the confidence, awareness, and understanding steps of the CAUSE model. In addition, one university official explained that they were always upgrading and advancing their emergency plans (Buettner 2011). As a result, leaders of the crisis-management team knew what steps to take immediately. Due to this preparation, although the response was reactionary in nature, it did not lead to a communication breakdown among university leaders, thus enabling the internal public to work together as a cohesive unit to overcome the crisis and address the external public as a unit. This preparation and collaboration speaks to the institution's appropriate use of the model's satisfaction and enactment steps. In addition, and perhaps most telling, the university's public affairs official was included as part of the executive council, invited to serve in this capacity by the president. Recognizing, respecting, and understanding the role that public relations has in an organization's current and future success is an integral part of why Northern Illinois University succeeded in emerging from this crisis as a success story. For their work in helping the institution emerge from the crisis with its reputation intact, without threat of legal action, and an increase in admissions applications, Northern Illinois University's public affairs office was awarded a Silver Anvil Award by the Public Relations Society of America. Two years after the incident, university president John Peters was honored by the Student Affairs Administrators in Higher Education for his leadership during and after the tragedy. Today, the university has returned to the business of educating its students. However, despite its honors for effective crisis-communication management, the institution experienced a decline in admissions (Lagana 2010). Thus, the university's crisis-management efforts are honing in on their recruitment efforts. As a result of the shootings, admissions officers now find themselves dealing with questions from prospective students and their families as to the safety of the campus and whether it would be wise to pursue an education at Northern Illinois University. Therefore, the admissions office is working closely with the university's relations office to craft messages that will help address concerns expressed by potential students and their families. As a senior university administrator stated, "We try hard not to let it define us, but it is a very difficult thing to overcome" (Buettner 2011).

The efforts at Northern Illinois University illustrate the reality that risk and crisis communication are not stagnant enterprises. Much like any organization's strategic-communication planning, they must be living efforts that reflect any entity's evolution and constant set of challenges as well as the ever-changing nature of its surrounding environment. Risks and potential crises are ever-present. Consequently, the two require the same constant attention as strategic planning itself.

Summary

A fundamental question of a risk-communication strategy, or any communication strategy for that matter, is how its success is defined or determined. If all elements of a risk-communication strategy, such as the steps outlined in the CAUSE model, are implemented, what determines if it was a successful strategy? Perhaps another way to ask this is: Is it necessary for an actual crisis to occur and see how people react for the success of the risk-preparatory strategies to be adequately determined? Do we need an actual fire to happen before it can be truly determined whether employees in an office building, for instance, have learned what to do when such a crisis occurs?

Perhaps in a pure sense the answer is "yes." But fortunately there are enough tangible examples available that illustrate the vital and, ultimately, necessary role that risk-communication efforts play in preparing people for the reality of a crisis. A dramatic case-in-point is found in the person of Rick Rescorla, head of security for Morgan Stanley Dean Witter in New York City's World Trade Center between 1993 and 2001 (Ripley 2008b). Rescorla, a decorated war hero in Vietnam, was present at the time a man drove a truck full of explosives in the center's underground parking garage. When the bombs went off, vibrations were felt throughout the tower, including the spacious offices of Morgan Stanley Dean Witter. Rescorla positioned himself in the center and shouted for his coworkers to pay attention to what was going on. Initially, he was ignored. Eventually, however, he gained his coworkers' attention and was able to lead them to safety.

Following that, at the time, unprecedented incident, Rescorla vowed to ensure his company's employees would be adequately prepared should any similar acts of terror occur in the future. With the support of the company's executive officers, Rescorla implemented an ongoing, rigorous series of drills designed to prepare all employees on what steps to take should there be a crisis. The drills were held weekly and without fail and interrupted business calls, meetings, and other operational duties. Generally, employees were not happy to be interrupted from their routines on such a regular basis, but because the drills were mandatory, they participated. Years passed. The weekly drills continued. Employees continued to grumble because the possibility of another act of terror seemed so remote.

Unfortunately, that second act of terror eventually did occur on September 11, 2001. However, Rescorla's employees knew what do. Without fuss, hesitation, or resistance, Rescorla successfully led more than 2,687 Morgan Stanley Dean Witter employees out of the building to safety on that terrible morning. The company sustained one of the lowest causality counts at 13 deaths (Ripley 2008b). This number included Rescorla, who went back into the building to help others escape but never came out. Nevertheless, he is remembered as a hero for his determination, for implementing an effective risk program, and for instilling within each of his stakeholders the instinct as to what steps to take during a crisis.

Rescorla's effort is a stunning example of how to implement the CAUSE model. Rescorla, upon assessing the risk associated with his organization's location, immediately determined it was necessary to have an evacuation plan in place. Not only did he create a plan, he obtained support of the company's executive staff to implement and test the plan, which gave him the authoritative voice he needed to have his coworkers comply with mandatory drills. In addition, Rescorla's plan included detectable messages, clear instruction, and a rationale for why the drills were being executed. Further, Rescorla understood that, in the event of an actual crisis, his fellow staff members would not be a rationale audience. Thus, it was important that he clearly explained the drill so his coworkers would know what to do in an emergency situation. The mandatory nature of the drills continually reinforced Rescorla's messages, enabled him to discover and remedy any obstacles that would impede an evacuation, and served as a way to reach an audience that had grown complacent about terrorist attacks. As a result, amid the chaos when the World Trade Centers were attacked, Rescorla's office was prepared and his evacuation plan was a success. Because Rescorla and his organization's executives saw the benefit in risk communication and linked it to their overall organizational strategy, they were able to effectively manage a large and unexpected crisis.

Risk communication is not easy. As Sandman suggests, to effectively reach apathetic audiences and prepare them for crisis is difficult. Yet, it is more difficult to calm an irrational, scared, and outraged audience. Because of this it is important that organizations allocate the time and resources to effectively educate their stakeholders about potential risks, whether physical, financial, or otherwise. As can be learned by the cases of Northern Illinois University and Rick Rescorla, having risk- and crisis-communication plans integrated into the overall organizational strategic plan is essential to minimizing loss, reducing outrage, preparing stakeholders, and ensuring a quicker return to daily operations.

Key Takeaways

1. The best crisis-communication plans are those that are grounded in research, are timely, and are closely aligned with an organization's strategic-communication plan.
2. To best prepare for a crisis or avoid risk, organizations should practice tabletop exercises and delegate tasks to individuals able to carry out the plan.
3. Risk, crisis, and strategic planning include organization-wide actions, strong elements of persuasion, measurable goals, and ensuring connections with various publics.
4. Simple message dissemination is not enough. To be effective, risk and crisis messages must be personally relevant, probable or occurring, repetitious, and content specific.

5. The CAUSE model is an excellent tool for effective risk and crisis communication and is linked to important aspects of an organization's overall strategic plan, such as: understanding organizational stakeholders and their values, beliefs, and attitudes; strengthening organizational credibility and trustworthiness; and, generating support for organizational decisions.

Glossary

CAUSE model: A risk/crisis framework with five communicative goals: creating confidence, generating awareness, enhancing understanding, improving satisfaction, and motivating action, or enactment.

Crisis: A specific event with a potentially negative outcome that creates high levels of uncertainty and affects an organization or entity as well as its public, products, services, and reputation.

Risk: Communication meant to provide laypeople with the information needed to make informed decisions regarding risks.

References

Botan, Carl H., and Vincent Hazelton. *Public Relations Theory II*. New York: Lawrence Erlbaum Associates, 2006.

Britt, Roy. "The Odds of Dying." *Live Science,* January 6, 2005. http://www.livescience.com/3780-odds-dying.html.

Buettner, Kathryn (vice president for university relations, Northern Illinois University), in discussion with Daniel L. Walsch, January 24, 2011.

Crozier, Alan. "Engaged and Enriched." *Communication World* 27 (2010): 32–36.

Dyck, Bruno, and Mitchell Neubert. *Management: Current Practices and New Directions*. New York: Houghton Mifflin Harcourt Publishing Company, 2010.

Fearn-Banks, Kathleen. *Crisis Communication: A Casebook Approach*. Mahwah, NJ: Lawrence Erlbaum Associates, 2007.

Fearn-Banks, Kathleen. "A Review of Some Best Practices." In *The Handbook of Public Relations,* edited by Robert L. Heath, 479–86. Thousand Oaks, CA: Sage Publications, 2001.

Fink, Steven. *Crisis Management: Planning for the Inevitable*. New York: AMACom, 1986.

Food and Drug Administration. *Bisphenol A (BPA): Update on Bisphenol A (BPA) for Use in Food*. Washington, DC: Food and Drug Administration, January 20, 2010. http://www.fda.gov/NewsEvents/PublicHealthFocus/ucm064437.htm.

Fombrun, Charles. *Reputation: Realizing Value from the Corporate Image*. Boston: Harvard Business School Press, 1996.

Grimely, Diane E., Edward W. Hook, Ralph J. DiClemente, and Patricia Lee. "Condom Use Low among Low-Income African American Males Attending an STD Clinic." *American Journal of Health Behavior* 28 (2004): 33–42.

Grunig, James E., and Todd Hunt. *Managing Public Relations.* New York: Holt, Rinehart, & Winston, 1984.

Grunig, James E., Larissa Grunig, and David Dozier. *The Excellence Theory.* New York: Lawrence Erlbaum Associates, 2002.

Heath, Robert, and Dan Millar. *Responding to Crisis: A Rhetorical Approach to Crisis Communication.* Mahwah, NJ: Lawrence Erlbaum Associates, 2004.

Hellerman, Caleb. "Limit Infants' Use of Bisphenol-A Products, FDA Says." *CNN Health.* January 15, 2010. http://www.cnn.com/2010/HEALTH/01/15/fda.chemical.bpa/.

Hermann, Charles F. "Some Consequences of Crisis Which Limit the Viability of Organizations." *Administrative Science Quarterly* 8 (1963): 61–82.

Hovland, Carl I., Arthur A. Lumsdaine, and Frederick D. Sheffield. *Experiments in Mass Communication.* Princeton, NJ: Princeton University Press, 1949.

Kahn, David A., Margaret L. Moline, Ruth W. Ross, Lee S. Cohen, and Lori L. Althshuler. "Major Depression during Conception and Pregnancy: A Guide for Patients and Families." 2008, http://www.womensmentalhealth.org/wp-content/uploads/2008/04/mdd_guide.pdf.

Lagana, Brandon (admissions director, University of Illinois), in discussion with Daniel L. Walsch, December 28, 2010.

Langford, Linda. "Preventing Violence and Promoting Safety in Higher Education Settings: Overview of a Comprehensive Approach." *The Higher Education Center for Alcohol and Other Drug Abuse and Violence Prevention* (2004): 1–12.

Littlefield, Robert et al. "We Tell People. It's Up To Them To Be Prepared: Local Emergency Managers' Intuitive Public Relations Theories." In *The Handbook of Crisis Communication,* edited by W. Timothy Coombs and Sherry J. Holloday, 245–360. Malden, MA: Blackwell Publishing, 2010.

Lundgren, Regina, and Andrea McMakin. *Risk Communication: A Handbook for Communicating Environmental, Safety, and Health Risks.* 3rd ed. Columbus, OH: Battelle Press, 2004.

McGuire, William. "Resistance to Persuasion Conferred by Active and Passive Prior Reflection of the Same and Alternative Counterarguments." *Journal of Abnormal and Social Psychology* 63 (1961): 326–32.

McQuail, Denis. *Mass Communication Theory.* London: Sage Publications, 2010.

Morgan, M. Granger, Baruch Fischhoff, Ann Bostrom, and Cynthia J. Atman. *Risk Communication: A Mental Models Approach.* New York: Cambridge University Press, 2002.

Null, Gary, and Barbara Seaman. *For Women Only: Your Guide to Health Empowerment.* New York: Seven Stories Press, 1999.

Perry, Ronald W. "Evacuation Decision-Making in Natural Disasters." *Mass Emergencies* 4 (1979): 25–38.

Peters, John. "Letter from NIU President John Peters on Cole Hall." *Chicago Daily Herald,* March 4, 2008.

Peters, John. *Report of the February 14, 2008 shootings at Northern Illinois University.* Dekalb, IL: NIU Press, 2009.

Ripley, Amanda. "A Survival Guide to Catastrophe." *Time Magazine,* May 29, 2008a, http://www.time.com/time/magazine/article/0,9171,1810315–1,00.html.

Ripley, Amanda. *The Unthinkable: Who Survives when Disaster Strikes—And Why.* New York: Crown, 2008b.

Ropeik, David, and George Gray. *Risk: A Practical Guide for Deciding What's Really Safe and What's Really Dangerous in the World Around You.* New York: Houghton Mifflin Company, 2002.

Rowan, Katherine E. "Goals, Obstacles, and Strategies in Risk Communication: A Problem-Solving Approach to Improving Communication about Risks." *Journal of Applied Communication Research* 19 (1991): 300–29.

Rowan, Katherine E. "Informing and Explaining Skills: Theory and Research on Informative Communication." In *The Handbook of Communication and Social Interaction Skills,* edited by John O. Greene and Brant R. Burleson, 403–38. Mahwah, NJ: Erlbaum, 2003.

Rowan, Katherine E., Carl H. Botan, Gary L. Kreps, Sergei Samoilenko, and Karen Farnsworth. "Risk Communication Education for Local Emergency Managers: Using the CAUSE Model for Research, Education and Outreach." In *The Handbook of Crisis and Risk Communication,* edited by Robert L. Heath and H. Dan O'Hair, 170–93. New York: Routledge, 2009.

Rowan, Katherine E., Lisa Sparks, Loretta Peccioni, and Melinda Villagran. "The CAUSE Model: A Research-Supported Aid for Physicians Communication with Patients about Cancer Risk." *Health Communication* 15 (2003): 235–48.

Rowan, Katherine E., Brigit Talkington, and Tobin Beck. "Critical Thinking in Campus Emergency Response Situations." White paper, George Mason University, 2009.

Sandman, Peter M. "Four Kinds of Risk Communication." *The Synergist* (April 2002): 26–27.

Sandman, Peter M. "Responding to Community Outrage: Strategies for Effective Risk Communication." Paper presented at the meeting of the American Industrial Hygiene Association, Fairfax, VA, 1983.

Smith, Ronald D. *Strategic Planning for Public Relations.* New York: Routledge, 2009.

Stone, Joanne, and Keith Eddleman. *The Pregnancy Bible: Your Complete Guide to Pregnancy and Early Parenthood.* Buffalo, NY: Firefly Books, 2003.

Ulmer, Robert, Timothy Sellnow, and Matthew Seeger. *Effective Crisis Communication.* Thousand Oaks, CA: Sage Publications, 2007.

Vicary, Amanda M., and R. Chris Fraley. "Student Reaction to the Shootings at Virginia Tech and Northern Illinois University: Does Sharing Grief and Support Over the Internet Affect Recovery?" *Personality and Social Psychology Bulletin* 37, no. 11 (2010): 1555–63. doi: 10.1177/0146167210384880.

Wheeless, Lawrence R., and Janis Grotz. "The Measurement of Trust and Its Relationship to Self Disclosure." *Human Communication Research* 3 (1977): 250–57.

CHAPTER ELEVEN

Responding Effectively to Crises: Best Practices in Organizational Crisis Communication

Timothy L. Sellnow, Morgan Wickline, and Shari R. Veil

Domino's Crisis

In the spring of 2009, two Domino's employees concocted a scheme to post what they interpreted as a hilarious video on YouTube. The video, showing one of the employees disgustingly contaminating ingredients with his body and placing them on pizzas and sandwiches, "went viral" and was seen by more than a million alarmed viewers before it was taken down. The video created a reputational crisis for Domino's, sparking such questions as: Were Domino's products contaminated? Were Domino's employees depraved, foolhardy, or both?

Fortunately for Domino's, the company was prepared to manage such a crisis. Their vice president of communications, Timothy McIntyre, was well trained and experienced in effectively managing crises. When he discovered the video, he responded quickly and effectively. In consultation with Domino's USA president Patrick Doyle, McIntyre first verified that the video's creators had actually served no contaminated food. Second, he recorded and uploaded to YouTube a statement, read by Doyle, affirming Domino's ardent commitment to food safety. Doyle also verified in the statement that the previous video was a hoax. Once the Doyle video appeared on YouTube, the story quickly lost momentum and was resolved.

McIntyre and Domino's were successful largely because they followed many of the best practices of crisis communication. For example, they recognized the public's concern and responded with openness, honesty, and candor. They collaborated with the police and franchise owners in the city where the corrupt video was made and Doyle's response communicated genuine compassion for Domino's upstanding employees and for all consumers of Domino's products. Fortunately, many of these skills can be learned and practiced in advance of a crisis. In this chapter, we identify a comprehensive set of best practices that can empower managers to communicate responsibly during crises.

No organization is immune from crisis. By crisis, we mean "a specific, unexpected and non-routine organizationally based event or series of events which creates high levels of uncertainty and threat or perceived threat to an organization's high priority goals" (Seeger, Sellnow, and Ulmer 2003, 7). Crises encountered by modern organizations and agencies are actually intensifying in both frequency and severity (Sellnow et al. 2009). Industrial catastrophes, for example, occur with such increasing frequency that Perrow (1999) makes a compelling argument for viewing them as *normal* accidents. Thus, the question is not will our organization face a crisis, but rather, are we prepared to lead our organization through a crisis. Despite their regularity, however, the inherent nature of crises makes them difficult to manage. This difficulty arises from the three characteristics that are consistent in all crises: threat, surprise, and short response time (Ulmer, Sellnow, and Seeger 2011). Perhaps most challenging of all is the fact that crises erupt as a surprise. Every organization has to manage difficult issues on an ongoing basis. Crises are distinct in that they come as a shock, threatening the survival of the organization and demanding an immediate response.

Given the difficult challenge of responding to crises, why do some organizations emerge from calamities successfully, while others fail miserably in their crisis response? Scholars have endeavored to answer this question for decades. Their efforts have fostered a series of recommendations, typically described as best practices, for successfully managing crises. The goal of best-practice research and development is to learn from the experiences of the past, detect errors, correct them, then determine ways to apply learning and practical knowledge to foster continued improvements (Veil

Continuously Evaluate and Update Crisis Plans		
PLAN AHEAD	**COMMUNICATE RESPONSIBLY**	**MINIMIZE HARM**
Plan Ahead for a Prompt Response	Form Partnerships with the Public	Be Accessible to the Media
Establish a Crisis Communication Network	Acknowledge Public Concern	Communicate Compassion
Accept Uncertainty	Be Open and Honest	Provide Suggestions for Self-Protection
Acknowledge and Account for Cultural Differences		

Figure 11.1   The best practices established by the NCFPD serve as a guide for how to plan for a crisis, what to do in the acute phase of the crisis, and how to move forward from the event.

and Sellnow 2008). In this chapter, we summarize a comprehensive list of 11 such best practices for effectively managing crises. The best practices we provide span the crisis-planning process, crisis response, and postcrisis recovery (see Figure 11.1). In the following paragraphs, we provide an explanation of how we chose the best practices we present, a summary of each best practice, and an explanation of the opportunities and constraints organizations experience when applying the best practices.

Identifying the Best Practices for Crisis Communication

The Department of Homeland Security was founded in the United States as a response to the 9/11 terrorist attacks. In addition to many other responsibilities, the department sponsored several centers of excellence to encourage university research on preventing and responding to catastrophic events ranging from terrorist attacks to natural disasters. One such center, the National Center for Food Protection and Defense (NCFPD), was assigned the responsibility for creating a generalizable set of best practices for crisis communication. In response to this challenge, a group of crisis-communication scholars performed an exhaustive review of the existing literature on crisis communication. This review revealed a consistent set of recommendations. The NCFPD group then created an expert panel to review and critique the recommendations. Once the panel reached consensus on a set of recommendations, they established an agenda for testing the recommended practices using both qualitative and quantitative methods (Seeger 2006). Specifically, case study research was conducted to observe relationships among the presence and absence of selected communication strategies and the outcome of the crisis (Venette 2007). Simulations were also conducted in laboratory settings to evaluate the impact of various message strategies (Sellnow, Sellnow, Lane, and Littlefield, 2012). As a result of these efforts, the NCFPD group generated a set of 11 best practices for effective organizational crisis communication. We chose this list for our chapter for two reasons. The list is comprehensive and it has been rigorously evaluated to verify its accuracy (Palenchar 2009).

The best practices established by the NCFPD serve as a guide for how to plan for a crisis, what to do in the acute phase of the crisis, and how to move forward from the event. These practices can be summarized as: (1) pre-event planning, (2) establishing partnerships, (3) listening to the public's concerns and understanding the audience, (4) honesty, candor, and openness, (5) collaborating and coordinating with credible sources, (6) meeting the needs of the media and remaining accessible, (7) communicating with compassion, concern, and empathy, (8) accepting uncertainty and ambiguity, (9) disseminating messages of self-efficacy,

(10) acknowledging and accounting for cultural differences, and (11) taking a process approach to policy development (Seeger 2006; Sellnow and Vidoloff 2009). To better understand the value of each of these practices, we will explain the practicality of each and use examples to illustrate the value of following (or the harm in ignoring) these practices in real life scenarios.

(1) Planning Pre-Event Logistics

Crises are nonroutine events in an organization. Even small-scale events can escalate and bring an organization to its knees if there is not an appropriate response plan in place. Ulmer, Sellnow, and Seeger (2007) argue that organizations should prepare for the uncertainty, threat, and unique communication demands that accompany crises through training and simulations before the crisis hits. This preplanning allows an organization and its members to understand their roles during a crisis. This advanced planning and practice also serves to avoid adding uncertainty to an already ambiguous event because participants have knowledge of the crisis plan, and their responsibility within that plan.

One of the first steps in crisis management should be to create a crisis plan. A crisis-management plan is defined as a "strategic document carefully prepared and maintained as a master guide for framing, overseeing, and tracking a systematic crisis management and response process" (Seeger et al., 2003, 169). Organizations must first determine the goals for crisis response (Ulmer, et al. 2007). These goals are usually broad statements that guide decision making and are usually different for each organization. The response goals also serve to reduce ambiguity because, when faced with a difficult decision during a crisis, the organization can consistently turn to its goals as a guidepost.

(2) Establishing Partnerships

A second component of the crisis-management plan is to develop partnerships with other organizations and stakeholders important to the organization. As society becomes more complex, organizations, in turn, increase in complexity and interconnectivity. In this multifaceted system, a crisis for one organization has the potential to affect a myriad other organizations with which it is associated. These interorganizational relationships create the necessity for collaboration and communication among all entities. Ulmer et al. (2007) define partnerships as "equal communication relationships with groups or organizations that have an impact on an organization . . . established through honest and open dialogue about important issues for each group or organization" (35). Cultivating partnerships in advance is critical to effective crisis communication.

An example of a strong partnership that lead to a successful postcrisis fundraising campaign is the affiliation between the Red Cross and phone companies. After the Haiti earthquake, perhaps the strongest and most beneficial partnerships proved to be those between the Red Cross and mobile software company mGive. mGive partners with various telephone companies to promote text-messaging campaigns for nonprofit organizations. This campaign allowed cell phone users to text "Haiti" to 9099 and be billed an extra $10 on their next phone bill, which would go to Haiti relief. "Over the next 36 hours, the campaign raised more than $4 million, making it the most successful texting fundraising effort ever" (Bush 2010, ¶ 2). In fact, this text campaign surpassed text donations for all the causes in 2009 that used texting campaigns (Feldman 2010). Forming this partnership early after the crisis allowed for a broad launch of a campaign whose success in raising money to help rebuild the country was unprecedented.

(3) Listening to the Public and Understanding Audience Needs

The public can also be an integral partner in crisis response if the organization is willing to listen. Audience analysis is important for any form of public communication. Sensitivity to audience is absolutely essential during crises. The lives of those touched by a crisis are radically disrupted. Fear and outrage are common emotional responses to crises (Lachlan and Spence 2007). The public may even unfairly blame the organization for problems it did not cause. The temptation may be to deny responsibility and to assign blame to others. Doing so, however, is unlikely to diminish public outrage. A much more effective strategy is to listen to audience concerns, acknowledge that the concern exists, and provide some means of assisting the audience in dealing with the concern.

Tracy (2007) exemplified the importance of acknowledging public concern in her analysis of the public meetings held by a troubled school district. The district confronted "a multimillion dollar budgeting error" (419). Public alarm peaked as the school board sought to cut budgets as a means for managing the crisis. Public meetings hosted by the board were widely attended and public criticism and concern were openly expressed. Although the board was frustrated with the intense public outrage, the public meetings eventually empowered the district to create a solution that was acceptable to all parties. Given the public's level of outrage, this resolution would not likely have occurred without the board taking the time and effort to listen carefully to and acknowledge the concerns of the residents.

(4) Honesty, Openness, and Candor

Candor should be applied unwaveringly in all crisis situations and in all communication with all stakeholder groups for organizations. The organization must be seen as trustworthy. Intentionally giving false or misleading information is never a good alternative, even when there is little or no information to give. Being open about the lack of knowledge regarding the development of a crisis is a far better strategy than fabricating information, which will later be falsified.

One example of problems resulting from a failure to follow this practice occurred in the Exxon Valdez oil spill of 1989. Exxon's initial response included messages assuring the public that no environmental harm would come from the spill and that using chemical dispersants would allow them to clean up the spill quickly. Obviously, the reverse turned out to be true, as the spill became one of the largest industrial accidents of the 20th century causing enormous environmental damage and consequences still being felt decades later. Exxon and its officials were openly admonished for being poorly informed and reporting untrue information to the media. In a crisis situation, with the organization's reputation already on the line, it is important to ensure that the public and other stakeholders not be given any other reason to doubt the organization's credibility by presenting false or misleading information. Misconstruing the situation does more damage to the reputation than simply admitting, "we don't know."

(5) Collaborate and Coordinate with Credible Sources

While developing strong relationships with stakeholder groups such as employees and related organizations is essential, having good relationships with people whose opinion and support lend credibility to the organization is equally important. These people include technical or subject matter experts, department or agency heads, and others in respected, powerful positions (Wolf 2009).

When information is communicated through a well-respected source that the public sees as credible, there is an increased likelihood that the audience will acknowledge or accept the message (Arpan 2002). Perhaps one of the best examples of a lack of credibility was the performance of FEMA in the wake of Hurricane Katrina. The inability of FEMA to quickly organize a rescue mission and establish a functioning relief operation garnered the agency much criticism from the media and the public as their effectiveness and reputation were called in to question. The 2005 hurricane season was the first time Red Cross and FEMA worked as co-primacy agencies (Government Accountability Office 2005). While the communication chain was disputed, Red Cross had to request assistance through FEMA (Veil and Husted 2012). And yet, Red Cross became the primary source of information in media reports when FEMA was no longer considered a trusted source.

(6) Media Accessibility

The organizational relationship with the media is always important, but it becomes critical in a crisis situation. The media is the most viable resource for sharing essential information with the public (Littlefield and Quenette 2007). In turn, the media presses the organization for answers about how and why the crisis happened and what steps are being taken to remedy it. Being available to speak with the media as soon as the crisis becomes public is crucial. That being said, there are several lessons to follow when speaking with the media to ensure that the message is as accurate as possible, without over assuring or giving unconfirmed information.

Precrisis planning should help the organization determine who is to be the spokesperson during the crisis. Ulmer, Sellnow, and Seeger (2011) address the key points an effective spokesperson should understand before dealing with the media. This person should be familiar with the media and have developed good, working relationships with them ahead of time, per the instructions of best practice (2). Additionally, the spokesperson should understand that they should not allow the media to push them into saying things they do not want to say, nor should they get frustrated with the media. It is also important to express regret and concern for anyone harmed by the crisis. Avoiding the phrase "no comment" is key as this phrase gives the public the idea that the organization has something to hide. That being said, if there is a question for which the spokespersons have no answer, they are encouraged to admit that they do not know, but assure the audience that they are working to find the answer.

If spokespersons speak with certainty when they are in fact uncertain of the veracity of their statements, this most likely will come back to haunt the organization if the information is later found inaccurate. Hence, as described in best practice (4), being open, honest and candid about what is known and about what is unknown is crucial. Lastly, the spokesperson should be willing and able to coordinate and cooperate with other members of the crisis team when they do not know the answer. Once again, precrisis planning and developing strong partnerships before an incident occurs makes this easier when a crisis does happen. Knowing who will work with the media before a crisis, and knowing that they understand the best ways to communicate with the media allows for communication between the groups to flow more easily in the wake of a crisis.

(7) Communicate with Compassion

Coombs (1999) said it best when he said "crisis managers must provide crisis-related information to stakeholders and demonstrate compassion for victims" (126). This practice should be followed even if the organization feels it is not to blame for the incident. Even when the event is something completely out of the control of the organization (such as a natural disaster) acknowledging the pain and suffering of those experiencing the adversities caused by the event is advisable.

When a Chi-Chi's restaurant received a shipment of green onions that was contaminated with hepatitis A, they did not realize the food-borne illness outbreak that was to hit in the coming days. After several patrons and Chi-Chi's employees contracted hepatitis A, the restaurant was determined to be the source of the outbreak. Chi-Chi's released a statement apologizing for those who were sickened by their food and reassuring the public that they were doing everything in their power to ensure their patrons had a healthful dining experience and their employees had a safe working atmosphere. They took responsibility for the event even though it was later determined that the onions were infected by the ice in which they were packed by the supplier. Throughout their crisis response, Chi-Chi's did not attempt to lay the blame on their supplier; instead they focused on the well-being of their patrons and compensating those who became ill after eating at their restaurant (Veil et al. 2005). Overall, this was beneficial to Chi-Chi's, and patrons lined up to eat at the restaurant when the affected location reopened.

(8) Accept Uncertainty and Ambiguity

Crises involve the elements of surprise, threat, and a short response time. These are unique incidents in the life of an organization and no two crises will ever play out the same way. Because of this fact, organizations cannot foresee the full impact of a crisis. Thus, to manage a crisis effectively, organizations must accept the uncertainty that a crisis brings. By the same token, it is imperative for organizations to communicate to the public about the changing and uncertain nature of the crisis. Doing so gives them the information that is known and what questions still need to be answered. Some spokespersons intuitively believe that the credibility and reputation of the organization would be damaged if they did not speak in certain tones. In reality, being able to admit gaps in knowledge and display organizational honesty in a crisis situation can actually lead to increased trust by the public (Wolf 2009).

An example of this failure to accept ambiguity was experienced by Jack in the Box restaurants in 1993 when an outbreak of *Escherichia coli* (*E. coli*) was linked to the chain (Ulmer and Sellnow 2000). Initially the company refused to confirm or deny that its hamburgers were the cause of the outbreak, but once it was announced that they were indeed the source, they responded by destroying large quantities of meat while attempting to shift the blame to their supplier. However, the *E. coli* bacteria in the meat could have been killed in the cooking process as long as a certain temperature was reached. The restaurant was supposedly informed of new health department regulations requiring restaurant grills to reach a certain temperature, but Jack in the Box claimed they had no knowledge of this new regulation. A later search of their files produced the written notification that Jack in the Box had received informing them of the new higher required temperatures. Instead of accepting the ambiguity and admitting they were unsure, Jack in the Box took a defensive strategy that made them look foolish when the truth of their disregard for health department mandates came to light.

(9) Provide Messages of Self-Efficacy

Messages of self-efficacy provide instructions to the public about how to protect themselves from the dangers created by a crisis. These messages are vital and should be distributed widely if an organization wishes to mitigate harm for its audience and stakeholders. Failure to communicate effectively with the public during a crisis could only serve to heighten ambiguity and amplify the harm caused by the event.

While communicating messages of self-efficacy is important, listening to stakeholders and adjusting communication to fit their changing needs is equally important. As Ulmer et al. (2007) point out, "effective communication is not a one-way process" (38). This is especially true in a foodborne illness as vast as the *salmonella* outbreak in the egg supply, which occurred in August of 2010. A study conducted by researchers at the University of Kentucky sought to determine the frequency of self-efficacious messages disseminated through broadcast media during the acute phase of this crisis. Collaborating with subject matter experts at the NCFPD, three key messages (how to identify the contaminated product, how to safely prepare eggs, and how to clean hands and surfaces) were determined to be the most crucial for audience members to hear in order to avoid contracting salmonella through the contaminated eggs. Coding of over 500 broadcasts revealed that the key messages were mentioned in the broadcast at an alarmingly low rate, while the most frequent direction was for viewers to visit a website to get more information—the information that should have been given in the broadcast—including names of recalled brands, plant numbers on contaminated cartons, and cooking information (Wickline and Sellnow 2011).

Because the organizations involved, including Wright County Eggs, Hillandale Farms (the sources of the contaminated eggs) and government organizations (CDC, FDA, etc.), did not take into account the needs of their audience and make the pertinent information more easily accessible to them, they could have done permanent damage to their reputations. According to Ulmer et al. (2007), "information communicated to stakeholders about how to protect themselves—self efficacy—should be useful and practical and should suit their divergent needs" (44). This need for practical information was not met by the broadcasts that were aired in the initial phase of the outbreak.

(10) Acknowledge and Account for Cultural Differences

Sellnow and Vidoloff (2009) added acknowledging and accounting for cultural differences as a best practice in crisis communication following a series of studies demonstrating that stakeholders, particularly minority stakeholders, distrust government figures and have inconsistent access to and viewing of traditional media (Lachlan et al. 2009). Latinos and Asian Americans face similar barriers (Muniz 2006; National Council of Asian Pacific Americans 2005), "compounded by issues of language, culture, and their status as undocumented or uninsured residents" (Andrulis, Siddiqui, and Gantner 2007, 1270). Crisis communicators should make additional efforts to reach racial and ethnic minorities as well as other underrepresented populations, including those who are enduring poverty, are new to America, or others who have limited access to mainstream media. Understanding how messages may be interpreted in different cultures, ethnic groups, and socioeconomic groups is essential, as is determining the mass communication and interpersonal communication channels best suited to reach them (Veil and Husted, 2012).

In the wake of the anthrax attacks following 9/11, studies revealed distrust of government messages by racial minority groups (Quinn, Thomas, and McAllister 2005). Specifically, African American postal workers continuously compared the CDC's push for workers to get vaccinated to the Tuskegee syphilis studies. The CDC stressed that the vaccine was being given first to the workers because they had the highest chance of being exposed through the mail system, but because the vaccine was not recommended for the general public, the workers felt like test subjects. The CDC did not account for how the iniquitous history of medical studies with a minority group would affect their credibility in responding to the anthrax attacks.

(11) Continuously Update and Prepare Plans and Policies

Just as crisis situations are constantly changing, an organization must change and update its crisis plan to adjust to the changing needs of its stakeholder groups. Lagadec (1997) said "the task is not merely to induce reflexes; the task is to prepare, as an organization, to confront situations that are unimaginable and potentially highly destabilizing" (27). This statement makes the point that crises, by their nature, are nonroutine, and therefore the plan in place to respond to them cannot be routine and merely a "reflex." Rather, the plan should be changed and updated as organizational learning takes place (either through crises experienced firsthand by the organization, or through watching another organization experience a crisis) and fundamental lessons are learned from the way the incident was handled by the key figures (Lagadec 1997). The crisis plan must also adapt to the changing technological environment. For example, Veil, Buehner, and Palenchar (2011) provide an extensive application of how social media tools can assist organizations in following the 11 best practices listed here. In short, crisis plans must change as the organization changes. If this level of updating is not achieved, plans dilapidate over time, leaving the organizations ill prepared.

The 11 best practices have been honed and developed over many years of research and have proven to be of utmost importance in an organizational crisis. Failure to follow even one of these can have disastrous results, escalating the crisis rather than minimize its effects. After all, crises happen, but the way organizations respond can determine the level of harm and reputational damage suffered.

Opportunities and Constraints in Applying the Best Practices

Although the best practices of crisis communication greatly increase the likelihood that organizations will emerge successfully from crises, there are several opportunities and constraints that warrant consideration. Specifically, the organization's ability to learn, the ethical foundation of the organization, the resources available to the organization, and the organization's commitment to consistently enacting the best practices all influence the organization's ability to respond effectively during crises. We discuss each of the variables from the perspective of opportunities and constraints.

Organizational Learning

As we discussed at the beginning of this chapter, crises are an inevitable problem faced by organizations of all kinds. Experiencing a crisis does not necessarily mean an organization has failed in some way. Experiencing the same crisis a second time, however, is problematic. There is a public expectation that organizational leaders will learn from crises and prevent repeating the same mistakes. A pattern of failure causes the public to view the organization as "dysfunctional" (Birkland 2007, 29). The best practices function best when organizations are constantly engaged in learning and unlearning from failure.

Crises can actually create the impetus for positive change. Organizations often become so comfortable in their routines that they are unwilling or unable to detect minor failures and to change in response to them. This insensitivity to failure often precedes full-blown crises. For example, the Tennessee Valley Authority either willfully or inadvertently ignored consistent warning signs that a holding facility for coal ash was beginning to crumble. When the walls of the facility gave way in 2008, the toxic ash devastated an entire community in Roane, Tennessee. Veil (2011) labels this inability or unwillingness to change routines in response to failure mindlessness. She observes that the recalcitrance of crises actually enable organizations to break free from harmful routines and dysfunctional cultures to engage in meaningful change.

Organizational learning requires organizations to recognize failure, assess the causes, enact change, and maintain an organizational memory of the failure (Larsson 2010). Thus, organizational learning necessitates considerable dedication from an organization's leadership. Simply recalling a product, paying a fine, or cleaning up a spill does not constitute organizational learning. Organizations must engage in systematic changes based on the new knowledge acquired through the crisis experience. The best practices of crisis communication demand that organizations constantly learn. Their experiences, both negative and positive, must inspire constant updating in their relationships at every level. Equally important is the process of building an organizational memory that accounts for the wisdom acquired over time. The Tennessee Valley Authority admitted that its leadership had failed to adequately maintain its organizational memory. These lapses lead to the failure described earlier. As a result, the organization has rededicated itself to learning from and responding to even minor failures.

Ethical Foundation

To succeed over time, organizations must display both competence and character (Veil et al. 2005). In other words, organizations must provide a valuable service competently, but they must also meet society's expectations for good character. An organization cannot at once engage in the best practices of crisis communication and unethical behavior. In fact, no set of best practices can salvage an organization built on an unethical foundation. We realize that making judgments about an organization's character or ethics is a complex process. From the perspective of crisis communication, however, an organization's ethicality is often judged in the court of public opinion. Such verdicts are simplified to assessing whether or not the organization's intentions and strategies were "right or wrong, good or bad, and desirable or undesirable" (Ulmer et al. 2011, 200). If the evidence surrounding a crisis reveals unprincipled leadership, the organization cannot meet the best practice of openness and honesty.

Too often, organizations seek to absolve themselves of ethical failures by attaching blame to a single individual or small group of individuals and removing that person or group from the organization. For example, when Rupert Murdoch's News Corp group was accused of hacking into phones of 9/11 victims and British politicians, the organization initially fired several high-level employees. This strategy failed to resonate with an angry public. Sacrificing a few employees as scapegoats is not an effective strategy because the public realizes that the decisions preceding an organizational crisis are typically made in "collective ways" (Ulmer et al. 2011, 201). Thus, the public tends to view corporations themselves as moral agents. The inappropriate behavior of News Corp was so widespread that no single individual or even a small group of individuals could have been held solely accountable for the violations.

When a crisis is based primarily on clear ethical failure, the best practices cannot rescue that organization. Minor ethical lapses, accidental failures, or behavior by a few rogue employees are exceptions. When an organization's foundation is based on behaviors that consumers see as wrong, bad, or undesirable, they likely render a very negative verdict in the court of public opinion regardless of how the organization responds to the crisis. The best way to avoid this level of disdain is to make sure the organization operates with a base of sound ethical principles.

Adequate Resources

Sadly, organizations can follow the best practices in earnest, yet fail to recover from a crisis because they lack the necessary resources. Odwalla overcame an *E. coli* crisis by introducing a new form of juice pasteurization. Schwan's endured the largest *salmonella* outbreak to date by purchasing its own fleet of trucks and building a new pasteurization facility. In both cases, the organizations learned from the crises they faced and spent millions of dollars to prevent future crises. On the other hand, organizations such as Chi-Chi's restaurant and Topps Meat Company were both lost because they did not have the resources available to make the kinds of changes enacted by Odwalla and Schwan's. Chi-Chi's leadership wanted desperately to compensate the customers infected with hepatitis at its Beaver Valley Mall restaurant in Pennsylvania. The company followed the best practices described in this chapter until being forced into bankruptcy and foreclosure (Veil et al. 2005). Topps, a company with nearly 70 years of history, was undone after going through the second-largest beef recall in the history of the United States. Topps did not have the resources to sustain itself after such a massive loss (Sellnow et al. 2009).

Effective crisis communication does not occur independently from the bottom line pressures experienced by organizations. An organization's leadership may want to form partnerships and respond to public concern while responding to a crisis, but may not have the resources needed to say and do what they know is right. Crises are more likely to overwhelm companies that are relatively small and new (Sellnow et al. 2009). Such companies do not have the financial wherewithal to retool and refinance after major losses. Thus, using the best practices in such distressing cases can, at best, aid an organization in a graceful departure from the industry.

Commitment

An organization's commitment to consistently applying the best practices is another variable that can determine success or failure. The best practices for crisis communication require constant attention and regeneration. For example, organizations must constantly be planning ahead and building networks if they hope to successfully manage a crisis. In his foundational work, Lippitt (1969) coined the phrase "organizational renewal" to account for the development process intended to move organizations to "higher stages progressively, and to preclude a decline toward a lower stage" (28). By remaining vigilant in the precrisis planning process organizations can engage in a discourse of renewal that allows them to "point out fallacious assumptions or unforeseen vulnerabilities" while reestablishing core values and precipitating "consensus, cooperation, and support" (Toelken, Seeger, and Batteau 2005, 47). Thus, an ongoing commitment to the best practices of crisis communication can and should foster a spirit of organizational renewal.

By their nature, the best practices of crisis communication cannot be enacted fully without precrisis planning and commitment. If an organization wishes to communicate effectively during a crisis, it must be committed to the best practices before the crisis occurs. If an organization views the best practices as some sort of emergency manual that can be pulled down from a shelf, dusted off, and performed for the first time at the start of crisis, the organization is doomed to failure.

Conclusion

There is little hope or expectation that organizational crises will be any less prevalent in the foreseeable future. The shocking nature of crises along with the uncertainty they create make crisis communication a challenging endeavor. If, however, organizations develop crisis-management plans, update those plans frequently, and familiarize themselves with the best practices of crisis communication, they can greatly enhance their capacity to survive and learn from crises. The best planning efforts cannot, however, overcome challenges related to unscrupulous decision making and inadequate resources. In a world where catastrophic industrial accidents are reaching the level of normalcy due to their frequency, organizations of all types should dedicate significant resources to the intertwined efforts of planning and working to avoid crises.

Key Takeaways

1. *Plan in advance*—No organization is immune from crisis. Discussing a response strategy before a crisis occurs is essential. Anticipating problems, knowing who will lead the response team, and establishing a communication network linking all key parties are essential steps in any crisis response plan.

2. *Acknowledge public concern, including underrepresented populations*—An organization does not have the luxury of determining when or if a crisis has occurred. If the public, including all organizational stakeholders, is alarmed or outraged, the organization must acknowledge this concern with a crisis response. This sensitivity must be directed to *all* stakeholders, not just those with the most resources.

3. *Accept uncertainty, but always be open and honest*—Crises are complex events and should be treated as such. Oversimplifying the situation by providing definitive answers in ambiguous circumstances will eventually hurt an organization's credibility. Organizations should be open and honest by always explaining what they know, what they do not know, and what they are doing to gather more information.

4. *Update the plan*—Planning ahead is not effective unless organizations rehearse their plans and update them based on what they learn. Plans dilapidate over time. Thus, crisis planning should be an ongoing process in any organization.

Glossary

Best practices: Generally accepted strategies, techniques or processes that have repeatedly resulted in positive outcomes.

Crisis: A specific, unexpected and nonroutine event that creates high levels of uncertainty and threat or perceived threat to an organization's high-priority goals.

Crisis-management plan: A strategic document carefully prepared and maintained as a master guide for framing, overseeing, and tracking a systematic crisis management and response process.

Partnerships: Equal communication relationships with groups or organizations that have an impact on an organization.

Self-efficacy: A person's belief that they can take the appropriate actions to accomplish a goal or task.

Underrepresented populations: Racial and ethnic minorities and those enduring poverty, are new to America, or have limited access to mainstream media.

References

Andrulis, Dennis P., Nadia J. Siddiqui, and Jenna L. Gantner. "Preparing Racially and Ethnically Diverse Communities for Public Health Emergencies." *Health Affairs* 26, no. 5 (2007): 1269–79. doi: 10.1377/hlthaff.26.5.1269.

Arpan, Laura M. "When in Rome? The Effects of Spokesperson Ethnicity on Audience Evaluation of Crisis Communication." *The Journal of Business Communication* 46, no. 3 (2002): 362–403.

Birkland, Thomas A. *Lessons of Disaster: Policy Change after Catastrophic Events.* Washington, D.C.: Georgetown University Press, 2007.

Bush, Michael. "Red Cross Delivers Real Mobile Results for a Real Emergency." *Advertising Age* 81, no. 8 (2010): 38.

Coombs, W. Timothy. "Information and Compassion in Crisis Responses: A Test of Their Effects." *Journal of Public Relations Research* 11, no. 2 (1999): 125–42.

Feldman, Amy. "Haiti Earthquake Provokes Wave of Text Donations." *BusinessWeek,* January 4, 2010: 3.

Government Accountability Office. "Hurricanes Katrina and Rita: Coordination Between FEMA and the Red Cross should be Improved for the 2006 Hurricane

Season." GAO-06-712. Washington, D.C.: US Government Printing Office, 2005.

Lachlan, Kenneth A., Jennifer Burke, Patric R. Spence, and Donyale Griffin. "Risk Perceptions, Race, and Hurricane Katrina." *Howard Journal of Communications* 20, no. 3 (2009): 295–309. doi: 10.1080/10646170903070035.

Lachlan, Kenneth A., and Patric R. Spence. "Hazard and Outrage: Developing a Psychometric Instrument in the Aftermath of Katrina." *Journal of Applied Communication Research* 35 no. 1 (2007): 109–23. doi: 0.1080/00909880601065847.

Lagadec, Patrick. "Learning Processes for Crisis Management in Complex Organizations." *Journal of Contingencies and Crisis Management* 5, no. 1 (1997): 24–31.

Larsson, Larsake. "Crisis Learning." In *The Handbook of Crisis Communication,* edited by W. Timothy Coombs and Sherry J. Holladay, 713–18. Malden, MA: Blackwell, 2010.

Lippit, G. L. *Organizational Renewal: Achieving Viability in a Changing World.* New York: Appleton-Century-Crofts, 1969.

Littlefield, Robert S., and Andrea M. Quenette. "Crisis Leadership and Hurricane Katrina: The Portrayal of Authority by the Media in Natural Disasters." *Journal of Applied Communication Research* 35, no. 1 (2007): 26–47. doi: 0.1080/00909880601065664.

Muniz, Brenda. 2006. "In the Eye of the Storm: How the Government and Private Response to Hurricane Katrina Failed Latinos." National Council of La Raza White Paper, February 28, 2006. http://www.nclr.org/index.php/site/pub_download/In_the_Eye_of_the_Storm_How_the_Government_and_Private_Response_to_Hurrican.

National Council of Asian Pacific Americans. Katrina and the Asian American Community Congressional Briefing. http://www.navasa.org/PressReleases/2005/Katrina%20Congressional%20Briefing.doc.

Palenchar, Michael J. "Historical Trends of Risk and Crisis Communication." In *Handbook of Risk and Crisis Communication,* edited by Robert L. Heath and H. Dan O'Hair, 31–52. New York: Routledge, 2009.

Perrow, Charles. *Normal Accidents: Living with High-Risk Technologies.* Princeton, NJ: Princeton University Press, 1999.

Quinn, Sandra Crouse, Tammy Thomas, and Carol McAllister. 2005. "Postal Workers' Perspectives on Communication during the Anthrax Attack." *Biosecurity and Bioterrorism: Biodefense Strategy, Practice, and Science* 3, no. 3 (2005): 207–15.

Seeger, Matthew W. "Best Practices in Crisis Communication: An Expert Panel Process." *Journal of Applied Communication Research* 34, no. 3 (2006): 232–44. doi: 10.1080/00909880600769944.

Seeger, Matthew W., Timothy L. Sellnow, and Robert R. Ulmer. *Communication and Organizational Crisis.* Westport, CT: Praeger, 2003.

Sellnow, Timothy. L., Deanna, D. Sellnow, Derek Lane, and Robert, S. Littlefield. "The Value of instructional communication in crisis situations: Restoring order to chaos. *Risk Analysis* 32, no. 4 (2012): 633–43.

Sellnow, Timothy L., Robert R. Ulmer, Matthew W. Seeger, and Robert S. Little-field. *Effective Risk Communication: A Message-Centered Approach.* New York: Springer Science+Business Media, 2009.

Sellnow, Timothy L., and Kathleen G. Vidoloff. "Getting Crisis Communication Right." *Food Technology* 63, no. 9 (2009): 40–43.

Toelken, Kathryn, Matt Seeger, and Allen Batteau. "Learning and Renewal Following Threat and Crisis: The Experience of a Computer Services Firm in Response to Y2K and 9/11." Paper presented at the International Community on Information Systems for Crisis Response and Management. Brussels, Belgium, April 2005.

Tracy, Karen. "The Discourse of Crisis in Public Meetings: Case Study of a School District's Multimillion Dollar Error." *Journal of Applied Communication Research* 35, no. 4 (2007): 418–41.

Ulmer, Robert R., and Timothy L. Sellnow. "Consistent Questions of Ambiguity in Organizational Crisis Communication: Jack in the Box as a Case Study." *Journal of Business Ethics* 25, no. 2 (2000): 143–55.

Ulmer, Robert R., Timothy L. Sellnow, and Matthew W. Seeger. *Effective Crisis Communication: Moving From Crisis to Opportunity.* Thousand Oaks, CA: Sage, 2007.

Ulmer, Robert R., Timothy L. Sellnow, and Matthew W. Seeger. *Effective Crisis Communication: Moving From Crisis to Opportunity.* 2nd ed. Thousand Oaks, CA: Sage, 2011.

Veil, Shari R. "Mindful Learning in Crisis Management." *Journal of Business Communication* 48, no. 2 (2011): 116–47. doi: 10.1177/0021943610382294.

Veil, Shari R. and Rebekah A. Husted. "Best Practices as an Assessment for Crisis Communication." *Journal of Communication Management* 16, no. 2 (2012): 131–45.

Veil, Shari R., Tara Buehner, and Michael J. Palenchar. "A Work-In-Process Literature Review: Incorporating Social Media in Risk and Crisis Communication." *Journal of Contingencies & Crisis Management* 19, no. 2 (2011): 110–22. doi: 10.1111/j.1468–5973.2011.00639.x.

Veil, Shari R., Min Liu, Sheri L. Erickson, and Timothy L. Sellnow. "Too Hot to Handle: Competency Constrains Character in Chi-Chi's Green Onion Case." *Public Relations Quarterly* 50, no. 4 (2005): 19–22.

Veil, Shari R., and Timothy L. Sellnow. "Organizational Learning in a High-Risk Environment: Responding to an Anthrax Outbreak." *Journal of Applied Communications* 92, no. 1/2 (2008): 75–93.

Venette, Steven J. "Best Practices in Risk and Crisis Communication: Advice for Food Scientists and Technologist." International Union of Food Science and Technology—*Scientific Information Bulletin,* October 2007.

Wickline, Morgan C., and Timothy L. Sellnow. "The Ethic of Significant Choice as a Criterion in High-Risk Health Messages." Paper presented at the *2011 National Communication Association Conference.* New Orleans, LA, November 2011.

Wolf, Kelly E. *Risk and Crisis Communication Message Testing.* Fargo: North Dakota State University, 2009.

CHAPTER TWELVE

I Read It on a Blog: Combating Rumors in the Age of Constant Communication

Kristin Roeschenthaler Wolfe

Petrobras Case Study

Petrobras, Latin America's largest publicly traded company, located in Rio de Janeiro, established a corporate blog in 2009. According to the Petrobras's website, "Petrobras is driven by the challenge of supplying the energy that can propel development and ensure the future of the society with competency, ethics, cordiality, and respect for diversity" (http://www.petrobras.com). One way they hoped to fulfill their basic mission was to develop a corporate blog that would reach Brazilian society as a whole and, more specifically, the company's employees, the press, and the company's investors. The company started the blog to provide full access to the CPI- (parliamentary inquiry commission) related information after the Brazilian Senate set out to investigate perceived "irregularities" within the company. The blog allowed the public to make their own decisions regarding the case and to follow along if they so chose to, without the possible slant of the media.

The Petrobras Inquiry Commission was launched on May 15, 2009, in order to allow the company's stakeholders the ability to better scrutinize its image and corporate conduct during the CPI. The corporate blog initiative provided transparency to all communication. It showed the arguments in question, the company's responses, and, sometimes, the distortion that occurred through the media's reporting of the story.

Also, Petrobras provided information in a communication channel that was democratic—allowed many different audiences share their opinion on what was happening; had wide penetration among the youth—allowed an older, established company to reach a younger audience; and allowed participation by the general public—anyone who had Internet access could read the blog and post his or her own comment, allowing the conversation to begin. The blog was the perfect solution to provide unbiased information regarding the hearing. The blog allowed the 56-year-old state-run oil and gas company to revitalize itself through new media methods and open the company up for more opportunities to talk with their customers and any other interested parties.

During the hearing, all documents and communication related to the CPI were posted openly on the blog. Furthermore, the majority of the comments during the hearing were published whether they were positive or negative to the company. The only ones that were not published were those that went against the "policy of comments" that the company had established. It did not matter if the comments were positive or negative toward the company, but that they met the criteria previously established.

Note: This case study was an International Association of Business Communication Silver Quill Winner and was written by Gilberto Puig Maldonado (2010).

Join the conversation. Start the conversation. Do whatever you need to do to make your company more transparent, more accessible to your customers. As the corporate representative, you want to be the first person to announce new products, to answer any concerns a customer might have, to attempt to squash any rumors before they start and definitely before they get out of control. One way to achieve all of these initiatives is to start a corporate blog! Is blogging for every company? No. Should marketing and public relations handle the blog? Not really. Should an executive blog? Is he or she personable? If so, yes; if not, *no*. Also, the corporate blogger needs to be committed to the blog. Not only does he or she need to post frequently, usually daily, but he or she must also be able to respond to comments in a timely manner. Ignoring comments and not responding to people who take the time to provide feedback will kill a corporate blog, and possibly a corporate reputation very quickly.

Blogging has a reputation for being mostly a way for people to put their ideas and thoughts on the Internet for all to see and comment on. However, more and more corporations are joining in the blogosphere to keep in touch with their customers. *The Cluetrain Manifesto* advises that companies must join the conversation. Customers are on the Internet talking about you and your product. You can either join the conversation or get lost in the links. Customers everywhere are, hopefully, talking about your company and your product in a good way; however, if the message is not good, you need to be ready to combat it, and combat it quickly.

Joining the conversation, that is, starting a corporate blog, does not set you up for overexposure if it is done correctly. Starting a corporate blog can help your customers learn to trust you and feel like there are people who are available to answer any questions they may have. Feeling like they are dealing with people and not machines lets customers be more confident about buying from, and dealing with, your company.

What's Ahead?

In this chapter we will examine if a corporate blog is right for your company; the difference between a corporate blog and a personal blog dealing with business; and how to begin the blogging process. We will also examine the guidelines for corporate blogging and suggestions on setting up guidelines for your employees regarding the blog. The chapter then examines how to utilize the corporate blog in a crisis situation. Finally, the chapter provides the steps necessary to set up your corporate blog and join the conversation.

Is a Corporate Blog for You?

Granted, corporate blogging is not for everyone or every company. However, if you are a customer-facing company with a product or service and have an employee who has the ability to communicate clearly and honestly with others, you may want to consider starting a corporate blog.

Corporate blogging is not without risks, but with the proper guidelines in place, it can be a very beneficial, and relatively inexpensive, move for a company. How do you know if corporate blogging is right for your company? Answer these simple questions:

1. Does your company want to receive feedback from customers, whether it is positive or negative?
2. Is your company willing to take the time to post blog entries and respond to comments?
3. Is there someone at your company who can communicate in a human voice, not corporate speak, and interact well with others?
4. Is your company willing to share information with customers, competitors, etc., on the Internet?

If you answered yes to these questions, then you might want to consider starting a corporate blog. To clarify what is meant by a corporate blog, here are some divisive features: a corporate blog is different from a professional or executive blog in that the corporate blog represents the company as a whole, whereas a professional or executive blog relates an individual's opinion regarding corporate actions. Later in the chapter professional and/or executive blogs will be examined.

In order for a corporate blog to be effective, it must be updated regularly and honestly. The writing must be done in someone's "real" voice; not corporate speak. The readers must feel that they are dealing with a real person. *Do not* set up a corporate blog under the guise of marketing or public relations; bloggers will see right through that and will spread the fact that your blog is a marketing ploy throughout the blogosphere. This type of behavior will ruin your credibility in the blogosphere. One thing about the blogosphere is that the readers, the bloggers, etc., are all about honesty. Tell it like it is. If there is a problem, let them know; don't over promise; don't under deliver.

Who should write the corporate blog? Should it be the CEO, the head of marketing, or a random employee who truly understands the company's mission, products, and customers? The person should be willing to make the time and commitment to write daily, or more often, to read and respond to comments, to respond to posters via e-mail or on the blog for clarification. Some companies hire a person as the corporate blogger; others find an employee who is willing to do the job. Many technology companies had employees start blogs long before corporate blogging was the norm. Some have put rules in place as to what the blogger can and cannot say on their blog, what information is confidential, and what will happen if the blogger does not follow those rules. Most often, the resulting action of a blogger who does not follow corporate blogging guidelines is that they are fired.

According to Nancy Flynn (2006) in *Blog Rules: A Business Guide to Managing Policy, Public Relations, and Legal Issues,* "Unlike the web, which facilitates the one-way consumption of information, a blog is interactive, featuring the blogger's article, or *post,* and often encouraging comments from readers who are interested in weighing in on a topic to keep the on-line dialogue going" (8). Dialogue is what blogging is all about—getting into a conversation with your customers, finding out what they think of your product, your company, your competitors, etc. This is important information for businesses as they move forward in the 21st century. Businesses must adapt to a new way of doing business in the social networking era. Gone is the ability for a company to render one-way communication telling the customers what to think, what products to buy, and how to act. Customers want a voice; customers have a voice; and they are not afraid to use it! Why not listen to that voice? Your competitors most likely are already listening.

SIX PILLARS TO BLOGGING

Scoble and Israel identified six primary pillars to blogging: (1) publishable, (2) findable, (3) social, (4) viral, (5) syndicatable, and (6) linkable.

Scoble and Israel (2006) believe that there are six pillars to blogging. These are important to pay attention to as you begin and continue your corporate blog. These six pillars are:

1. Publishable,
2. Findable,
3. Social,
4. Viral,
5. Syndicatable, and
6. Linkable.

Going back to the case study, Petrobras managed to include all six pillars in their corporate blog. They had information that was definitely publishable and an audience that wanted to read what they had to say. The blog was found by many people over the course of the hearing and beyond. Petrobras made sure that the key players knew about the blog through e-mail blasts and press releases to interested parties. Petrobras responded to comments and addressed any concerns that the readers might have had. This made the blog very sociable and the company, by extension, seem very sociable. Through word of mouth and press releases, Petrobras made sure that interested parties knew where to find the blog, what its contents were, and because of this, the blog grew well beyond their imagination. Because of the nature of the blog, in the beginning, it was something that others wanted to read and wanted to comment on. Whether those comments were shared in the blog itself or shared through links from other sites, the blog was very much syndicated within days. And finally, because of the media interest in the hearing and the government tie with the company, this blog became very linkable as the country, and the world, watched in anticipation for the outcome. Since the hearing has ended, Petrobras has expanded the scope of the blog; it has allowed for interested parties to learn more about the company and its dealings outside of the hearing, allowing Petrobras to grab a stronger foothold on the market.

How to Have a Successful Corporate Blog

Why did Petrobras have such a successful first run with corporate blogging? How can you achieve the same results? Well, this chapter will not promise impossible results, but will allow you to have a solid ground on which to start your foray into corporate blogging. The first thing—as Petrobras did—that is recommended to all corporate bloggers is to be honest and not try to sell on the blog. The blog provides a two-way communication channel for the company and the customer to share ideas and provide feedback. Using your corporate blog as a sales channel will not go over well in the blogosphere. Utilize your blog to talk with your customers. Notice that it is *with,* and not *to.* A blog offers the unique opportunity for a company to talk with their customers, learn and understand their concerns or ideas, and respond openly and honestly. This does not mean that a company must take every idea that a customer puts on the blog as a "must do," but as a way to garner open feedback and possibly improve the products and services that the company provides. Isn't this what we are all after? Whether businesses or consumers, we just want the best-possible product for the task at hand. If you are the company, you want to produce it; if you are the customer, you want to use it. Companies should take the opportunity that a corporate blog provides to listen to and communicate with their customers regarding their products and services; after all, the customer uses the product in ways that it was intended for and ways that the company never thought of. Think of your corporate blog as *free* brainstorming and focus groups. However, taking the time to read and comment on the blog and also on the comments made by other readers does take time, so free may not really be free, but it is a lot cheaper than the older focus group alternative.

That last point brings up another tip for corporate bloggers. Blogging takes time. The blogger cannot just open up their window and type whatever comes to mind without thinking. After all, the corporate reputation is tied to the corporate blog. Does the blogger have something interesting or noteworthy to share about the company? Can the blogger write at a consistent level with some consistency to time? Will the blog be updated regularly? Will the blogger be able to respond to comments and, possibly, edit comments before allowing them to be posted? These are all questions that need to be addressed before putting up a corporate blog. After all, you don't want a corporate blog that no one goes to because the blog is only updated once every couple of months. That kind of consistency will have your blog fall off the map of the blogosphere before you can build a true following.

Blogging takes time; time costs money. Relationships build customer loyalty; customer loyalty builds buying power. You need to determine if the time needed to create a corporate blog is worth the upswing your sales and reputation will gain through your corporate blog. Like all good things, there is a trade-off. Many companies have found the trade-off to be a beneficial one. Having customer loyalty and trust is worth quite a bit to a company, but then everybody knows that.

One thing better than customer loyalty is customer evangelists. These are the people who are out in the world singing the praises of your products and your company. They have had a great experience with your company and want to share it with anyone and everyone who will listen.

Finding these evangelists can be difficult, but if you have a corporate blog, they will find you, comment on your blog, and possibly link to it or send others to the blog. Word of mouth is the best advertising because customers trust other customers. And, as Scoble and Israel (2006) state, "Yossi Vardi told us, 'Blogging is word of mouth on steroids'" (43). Although word of mouth is not always accessible to a company, comments on a blog are and those comments can begin the word-of-mouth cycle. If the comments are positive, other readers will see them and possibly want to try your product. After all, the comments are not from the company or the company spokesman, but from another person, an unbiased source, who has used the product and liked it.

The comments will also allow the company to combat any negative statements quickly and realistically. If the company has messed up, it needs to address the problem immediately, own up to the error, and tell how the problem will be or has been rectified. By the company acknowledging and addressing the problem, the rumor mill can be stopped before it even gets started and the word of mouth can be positive instead of negative.

Problems with Corporate Blogging

However, corporate blogging can also be dangerous! Established ground rules for corporate blogging must be shared with all employees, especially those who are in any way associated with the upkeep of the corporate blog. In fact, organizations should probably think through their social media policies as a general whole. While an individual within your organization may not have anything to do with the official corporate blog, you should have policies in place to regulate the type of proprietary content various employees post on their personal and professional blogs as well. If an employee creates a personal blog and mentions the company within that blog, there should be guidelines in place that are shared with employees. Just because it is a personal or professional blog does not mean that there should be no control when the company name is being mentioned. Heather Armstrong is the perfect example of this situation. After she posted on her blog, Dooce.com about her company, without using any names, another person saw the post and reported it to Heather's boss, she was fired immediately. That is why, today, if someone is fired for blogging they are said to have been "dooced" (Flynn 2006, 100).

> **PROBLEMS THAT MAY OCCUR WITH A CORPORATE BLOG**
>
> 1. A post not representing the company's philosophy accurately.
> 2. A disgruntled employee posting on the blog.

3. Trade secrets or legal documents being shared on the blog.
4. New product information being released to the public before the company is ready to release this information.
5. The blog being used for corporate-speak or marketing initiatives.

Problems that can occur with a corporate blog include a post not representing the company's philosophy accurately; a disgruntled employee posting on the blog; trade secrets or legal documents being shared on the blog; new product information being released to the public before the company is ready to release this information; and the blog being used for corporate-speak or marketing initiatives. These are all things that can happen and cause corporate blogging to be challenging. However, establishing guidelines for the corporate blog and assigning responsibility to one person or department can help to combat these problems. Let's examine each one separately.

Problem (1): A Post Not Representing the Company's Philosophy Accurately

This can occur if proper training was not done with the employee who is posting on the blog. Refresher training courses should always be conducted so that employees remember the company mission and purpose. Someone who has been with the company for 10 years may not remember their orientation; so any customer-facing employee needs to have refresher courses in the company philosophy, especially if they are to communicate daily with customers, and especially if they are going to have such a visible position as posting on the corporate blog.

Problem (2): A Disgruntled Employee Posting on the Corporate Blog

If there is a process in place where each comment is reviewed before it is posted, then this can be minimized or completely eliminated. Of course, the process and the explicitly written and posted blogging guidelines must be shared with all employees from the first day of employment and be posted where this information is easily accessible and can be referred to often. Work with the legal department and the public relations/communications department to set up the blogging and commenting guidelines. Of course, just as Petrobras did not deem all negative comments as unfit to publish, this should be a guideline for every corporate blog. Just because a comment may not praise the company, it does not make censoring comments acceptable. Setting up guidelines for the types of comments that will be censored prior to establishing a blog is important. For example, you may censor comments that are profane, use names and addresses of individuals, are discriminatory, etc. When you establish these guidelines prior to starting a blog, the guidelines help prevent knee-jerk reactions to comments that may be unflattering but also are important for others to read. Other posters may combat the negative comment for you, or your company can learn where the product or service needs to be improved. This is one of the benefits of blogging. This two-way conversation can help improve the company, the product, and the relationship with your customers. If your customers know that you are listening, they will be more connected to your brand. The company can only improve its product and its customer service if the company listens to their customers and is able to accept criticism.

Problem (3): Trade Secrets or Legal Documents Being Shared on the Blog

Once again, this is where the need for a clearly written blog policy comes into play. Release of information that could damage the company is definitely a danger; however, with proper training and guidance, this can be avoided. Legal documents, unless released by the legal department itself, should not be published. Trade secrets are just that, secret. Anything that is shared on a blog, or in a comment, is public. Anyone can access it. Removing the post or comment does not necessarily remove the information. Hyperlinking makes it possible for others to have already shared that information. Obviously, this is one of the biggest dangers with a corporate blog; but with proper training and a written blogging policy in place, this can be avoided.

Problem (4): New Product Information Being Released to the Public before the Company Is Ready to Release This Information

New product information should always be released by the marketing and/or public relations department. Previously, it was stated that the corporate blog should not be used as a marketing tool, and that bloggers and readers would not accept that. Therefore, no new product information should be released first on the corporate blog. If, once the new product is released, there were some discussions about the product on the blog that is acceptable; however, the blog should never announce new product information. Once again a written blogging policy should address this.

Problem (5): The Blog Is Being Used for Corporate-Speak or Marketing Initiatives

This is not the purpose of a corporate blog; this is the purpose of a press release. Customers do not go to your blog to read corporate-speak, they go to hear from real employees in their own voice about what is going on with the company. This type of communication on a corporate blog will kill your reputation faster than just about any other communication. If people wanted to read the marketing department's information, they would pick up your brochure or read your press releases; people go to the corporate blog to hear from real people in the company and to hear from other customers via the comments section.

What Is a Corporate Blogging Policy?

> **INFORMATION TO INCLUDE IN CORPORATE BLOGGING POLICY**
>
> - Blogging risks and liabilities.
> - Acceptable blog content.
> - Company policy on sexual harassment and discrimination.
> - Employee code of conduct and ethics.
> - Copyright law.
> - How to handle trade secrets and confidential information?
> - What is First Amendment Law?
> - Steps to monitoring the bog.
> - What information posted on the blog must legally be retained?
> - What regulatory rules affect the corporate blog?
> - What type of training the blog writers should receive?
> - How to handle spam comments?

What is the written blogging policy that keeps being brought up? Each company must create their own standard policy, but there are some general guidelines and departments that should definitely be followed and consulted. First, never put any corporate policy into place without consulting the legal department. After all, that department knows what can and cannot be enforced in terms of termination and legal action. This department is especially important if your industry happens to have government regulations that are imposed; such industries may involve healthcare, financial services, banking, drugs and tobacco, to name a few. Companies in these industries must be very careful about what is said on the corporate blog, even more so than many other industries. According to Flynn (2006), a corporate blogging policy might include some of the following areas of concern: blogging risks and liabilities; acceptable blog content; the company's policy on sexual harassment and discrimination; employee code of conduct and ethics; copyright law; guidelines on trade secrets and confidential information; First Amendment explanation and privacy issues; concerns with monitoring the blog; what constitutes a business record that must be retained; what regulatory rules affect the corporate blog; writers' training; and comment spam handling (78–80). Of course, this is not an all-inclusive list and each company should consult its attorneys and create the best policy for the company. However, it is most important to enforce the policy equally and to make sure that the blogging policy is not open to interpretation; in other words, that the policy is written very clearly and, when possible, specific examples are provided, and that the policy is available for all employees to access at any time, possibly on an internal website or through the human resources department. It is vital that this policy is readily available to all employees and that it is enforced quickly and to the letter in all cases.

What Are the Corporation's Blogging Risks and Liabilities?

Are there trade secrets that could be shared inadvertently? Are there legal documents that should never be posted on the blog? The corporate blogging policy should spell out exactly what are the risks of having the blog and also what liabilities the blog may open up for the company. By clearly delineating these concerns, the policy helps to enable employees to know what the concerns are and therefore be aware that they are not damaging the company in any way, even unknowingly.

What Is Acceptable Blog Content?

Creating a list of acceptable blog content begins to specify exactly what type of information should be shared on the corporate blog. For example, in Petrobras's case, the blog was originally set up for the sole purpose of keeping records and sharing unbiased information on the CPI. When the blog and the blogging policy were established the purpose of the blog was solely for the dissemination of information regarding the hearing. Therefore, employees knew that the only information to be shared on the corporate blog was information pertaining to the CPI hearing. Once the hearing was over, the blog's intent was expanded and new information was shared through this communication channel.

Why would the blogging policy need to include the company's policy on sexual harassment and discrimination?

Many times employees consider sexual harassment and discrimination to be something that is verbal or physical. The company's policy should reiterate that a joke or something derogatory that is written on the blog, or anywhere, can also lead to harassment and discrimination lawsuits. Remind employees that harassment and discrimination go well beyond just the spoken word or an action.

Include the company's employee code of conduct and ethics as a reminder. The more often employees see this information, the less likely they are to violate it. The blog is a very public forum and having an employee violate this code in such a public manner could damage the company's reputation throughout the blogosphere, and then throughout the community at large. By keeping this information front and center, the company demonstrates the seriousness of the code.

Explain and Define Copyright Law

What can be shared on a website without written permission from the original author? What information is necessary to include, what permission is necessary to get before posting information on a blog? This information is vital to have available for employee access, especially those employees who will share information on the blog. The company does not need a copyright infringement lawsuit because of an error in posting information without permission. This type of lawsuit would cause the company embarrassment and cost money if copyright law is violated. It is best to have the legal department tackle this section as they are experts on the law.

What Are Your Company's Guidelines on Sharing Trade Secrets and Confidential Information?

Very carefully, and clearly, document this section. Trade secrets can be accidently shared and, once they are in the blogosphere, they cannot be taken back because someone else may have already linked to the information or shared the information on their website. Therefore, it is very important that this information be clearly and succinctly shared with employees. It is also important that the company shares the consequences to the employee for sharing this type of information. After all, confidential and secret should explain that this information should not, under any circumstances, be displayed on the corporate blog.

First Amendment Explanation and Privacy Issues

The First Amendment does not protect bloggers! In order to clarify the law for your employees, specify the corporate interpretation of the First Amendment, explain clearly the corporate stance on privacy. By clearly stipulating these two areas, there will be little chance for misinterpretation from an employee regarding what is covered by the constitution under the right to free speech and, also, what information is not to be shared with others in any given situation.

What Are the Company's Concerns with Monitoring the Blog?

Who is responsible for monitoring the blog? Not just the posts generated by employees, but also the comments shared by others. Many companies insist on screening before any comment becomes "live" on a blog. This allows for any necessary editing or deletion based on content and/or inaccurate information. Remember Petrobras did not post several comments. This was not because the comments reflected negatively on the company—they let those through—but because the comments did not have anything to do with the topic of the post. It is important to remember that the blog is a conversation with customers and other interested parties. Do not withhold all negative comments, allow customers to comment and respond to others through the blog; however, if the comment has absolutely nothing to do with the post on which the comment is posted, it is probably good blogging policy to remove that comment.

What Constitutes a Business Record That Must Be Retained?

There are many laws and regulations in business about what constitutes a business record that must be retained in case a judge or court would ever request the documents. The blogging policy needs to specify which documents are necessary to hold on to; how long they need to be held; and where they need to be stored. E-mail and web pages have been subpoenaed in previous business lawsuits and, if they are not available, the corporation can be held in contempt and lose the lawsuit because the documentation is not produced. The blogging policy needs to specify exactly what types of blog files must be kept. Even comments that are posted on the blog by others can be subpoenaed so this section needs to be very specific on retention and time of retention. Having to look for a document on servers after it is subpoenaed can be a difficult, if not impossible, endeavor. A detailed listing of all documents that could be subpoenaed for any reason should be maintained and updated in the corporate blogging policy as rules and regulations are updated. There should be a department or position within the company that is responsible for keeping track of all of this material, should it ever be necessary to access and submit this type of record.

Know What Regulatory Rules Affect Your Corporate Blog

Does the industry have any specific requirements which need to be followed? For example, the health care industry must follow the HIPAA regulations and banking must conform to the rules established in the Gramm-Leach-Bliley Act. Knowing the requirements of your industry and following them to the letter is very important when it comes to corporate blogging. Your corporate blog is very visible and accessible so this is not the place to misstep when following regulations.

How Do You Plan on Training the Writers' Who Will Post on the Corporate Blog?

This needs to be determined and specified in the blogging guidelines. That way all of the training, from the very beginning, is consistent. By having a corporate standard for how to train the blog writers, there will be better consistency and control over the message that is shared through the blog. Also, it will assist in making sure that any message that is shared on the corporate blog is written in a way that provides a corporate voice to the website. By providing a singular presence or tone to the blog, it will be a more pleasant experience for the visitors. By having many different voices and messages displayed on the blog, a visitor might get conflicting messages and may not be sure which message is the one the company will stand behind.

What Is the Recommended Procedure to Handle Comment Spam?

Put a process in place to review all comments before they are posted to the corporate blog. Make sure that only comments that are directly related to the blog entry are posted on the website. However, do not delete any negative comments that are related to the blog entry; word that you are screening comments and deleting any negative ones will get around. This type of behavior will only hurt your reputation in the blogosphere, and word will more than likely spread to others as well. Removing comment spam is completely acceptable and recommended. People would wonder if the corporation ever looked at the blog if comment spam was not removed.

Information such as that listed earlier should be the basis of the corporate blogging policy, but each corporation will add their own guidelines to their policy. What is most important is that the corporation has a blogging policy in place and that the employees know what the policy is and have the ability to access it at any given time before they post or comment on the corporate blog. The clearer the blogging policy is written, the easier it will be to enforce. The blogging policy must be enforced equally across the organization. It must be strictly enforced or there will be consequences that could result in lawsuits against the company.

Content and Tone

What type of information should be included on the corporate blog? That depends on what the purpose of the corporate blog was determined to be. Nancy Flynn (2006) states that "[p]articularly skillful writers can use corporate blogs to build valuable relationships—and possibly avert public relations disasters—thanks to their willingness to be forthright, transparent, and brutally honest in their commentary" (7). The first rule of corporate blogging is to share information with those who visit the blog that might not be able to be found anywhere else. Give them a reason to come to the blog. Be honest. Be friendly. Be creative. Be yourself. As previously stated you do not want to use corporate-speak on a blog, it will drive people away. Let the blog have a voice all its own while maintaining a similar personality that customers and stockholders have come to expect from your company.

Blogs are inexpensive tools to build customer relationships. Being friendly, honest, and open allows your customers to feel like they know you; that your company has a personality; and that they can share feedback and information with your company without any concerns of repercussions. This is what the corporate blog can do. It can build relationships! And, it is much cheaper than a 30-second commercial or full-color print ad, which can only run a certain number of times . . . the blog is forever!

The blog is forever, which is a very scary thought for many organizations. The blogging policy is in place to help ensure that the information shared on the corporate blog is valuable, accurate, and understandable. Share information that customers would need or want, don't use the blog to sell your product, use the blog to enhance the customers' relationship with your product and company. What is meant by valuable information? Is it information regarding the product that the consumer can use such as new ways to use the product or a product recall? Marketing and advertising information is not valuable to the customer. Useful information will help the customer use your product in new ways and to use it correctly. Accurate information lets the customer know what a recall might be about and how to go about getting the product fixed. A blog provides all of the details about any information posted and verifies that the information provided is correct. Understandable information means that the customer can read the information and know exactly what it means. There is no corporate speak with the blog. The blog should be written in common language that all readers can understand. The blog should have a personality; the blog should be fun and interesting. Remember that your blog is your company's face to customers and stakeholders.

The corporate blog should be updated regularly—if possible, daily. However, do not post just to post; make sure that the post is of interest to the readers. Just putting something up on the blog to have a post for the day is going to turn readers off and drive them away from your blog. Keep the blog current, but also keep it interesting. Is there a news story that relates to your company? Link to it, tell the readers how it relates or how it affects them and then sit back and let the conversation happen. After all, blogging is about conversation, it is about having two-way communication with your customers. It is about sharing ideas and listening to what the customer wants or needs from your company. Take it seriously, but still have fun.

Corporate and have fun—can these terms really work together? These two phrases do not need to be completely separate; they can and should coexist on the corporate blog. If there is not some sense of fun or entertainment on the corporate blog; if there are mostly marketing messages on the corporate blog, no one will visit more than once. As mentioned earlier, the corporate blog should have a personality. Albeit a personality that fits with the corporate image that consumers and stakeholders have of the company; your corporate blog should not be extremely funny if your company deals in medical supplies or nuclear energy. Keep the tone of the corporate blog consistent with the tone of the corporation; it does not necessarily need to sync up completely with the marketing language, but the tone should seem like it fits with the company's image.

Remember the Petrobras case study? The purpose of the corporate blog evolved with time. What began as a communication channel to share information about the CPI evolved into a place for customers, stakeholders, and journalists alike to gather information about the company; and, it gave the company a new, unbiased communication channel to share information with its many publics about new products, promotions, and other information tied to the corporation. Allow your corporate blog to grow and evolve as your company evolves. Just because the blog was established for one purpose at its inception, five or ten years down the road or even less it may be time to revisit the corporate blog and determine that its purpose is outdated and needs a fresh look or a fresh angle to keep readers coming back for more information. This is one time that the corporate blog may become something else. Another time is during a time of crisis.

Crisis Management via the Corporate Blog

Whether the crisis is a natural disaster, such as Hurricane Katrina, or a man-made crisis, such as September 11, 2001, the corporate blog can serve as the central communication point for both employees and stakeholders. Imagine that your corporation had a warehouse facility in the path of Hurricane Katrina; how would you quickly let your customers know that product delivery would be delayed because the warehouse was hit by the hurricane? One way would be to post a message on the corporate blog. Of course, you would also need other means of communication because not all of those affected may read the corporate blog; however, those that do read the corporate blog, including the media, would get the information very quickly and could pass that information on to others. After all, word of mouth is sometimes the quickest way to get information, whether good or bad, spread to those that need to know. For crises that affect more than just your company word will spread quickly because the event will become a major news story very quickly; however, those crises that affect only your company may not become major news stories until your company drops the ball on customer service or product recall. At that point, the damage is done. If your company is able to share this information first and include a possible resolution, or at least let the stakeholders know that you are working on a solution, you can begin damage control before the damage is out of control. Not having damage control in place is how minor issues become major crises; not having a solution in place is how rumors about your company get started and how things can quickly spiral out of your control. Having a crisis-management plan in place, and including the corporate blog in that plan will greatly aid in stopping rumors and keeping your corporate image spotless by showing that your company can handle a crisis with grace and open communication.

Imagine that your corporation has the need to recall a product. Imagine that you work for a drug company that needs to recall the pharmaceuticals that you sell—people have become violently ill after taking the pills. How do you get this information out quickly? How do you tell the consumer where to return the pharmaceuticals for a full refund? How do you let the public know which pills were affected? Definitely, you want to get out a press release to the major media companies as quickly as possible. You want to send whatever notification you can to your customers as quickly as possible. And, if you have a corporate blog, you want to put the information on the blog quickly and in greater detail with the return address and possible reactions listed clearly. This will allow your company to work quickly to stop even more events from happening; it will show the media and your publics that your company is proactive and concerned about the public, as well as your corporate image. Also, placing this information on the corporate blog will allow for your employees to access the same information that your customers and stakeholders can access so that they are sharing the same information with the customers that the corporate blog shares. This will allow for the corporate message to be consistent across all communication channels. In a time of crisis your company wants to make sure that the information is clear, consistent, and comprehensive. Attempting to put together this type of communication at the spur of the moment when crises occur is difficult, at best. It is best for the corporation to have a crisis contingency plan in place, and to include the corporate blog in that plan. It also would be recommended and encouraged to include a crisis-management section in the blogging policy for a quick reference if this information is ever needed. Having a crisis-management plan in place and including the corporate blog in that plan can allow employees and management to have a common starting point for retrieving information regarding the incident and a depository for talking points that the corporation has put together so that the message shared by any member of the corporation is the same as any other member of the corporation.

Rumor Management through the Corporate Blog

The corporate blog is also the best place to respond to any rumors that might be spread about your company or product. The faster you can get the correct information out to your customers and stockholders, the easier it will be to control and possibly stop the rumor. Rumors are started for many reasons: lack of information, incorrect information, business rivalry, and many more reasons. No matter what the reason for the rumor, your company needs to combat it quickly and provide accurate information to your customers. The corporate blog can help you spread the correct information quickly and it can answer any questions or concerns that your customers or stakeholders might have regarding the rumor.

With rumor management, the last thing your company wants to do is to respond to the rumor by starting a rumor of your own. Always respond to rumors with facts and any solid and factual information that you can find. The more solid your argument is, the easier it will be to combat the rumor. Placing all of this information on the corporate blog makes the information accessible to anyone who might have heard the rumor or might hear the rumor in the future. In the second case, it would be a preemptive strike to clarify the rumor before it has even been shared with everyone. By providing information from the company it provides a way to combat the rumor quickly and to provide a voice in the conversation before the rumor gains a life of its own.

Averting a crisis through rumor management is important and your corporate blog can be your greatest tool. Many business and communications scholars discuss the importance of refuting a rumor and providing the facts as quickly as possible; your blog may be the quickest avenue for you to respond. Yes, you will still want to follow traditional public relations and customer relations venues but the corporate blog will allow many more consumers and industry experts to learn the truth before the rumor wreaks too much havoc.

Rumors can be very damaging for a corporation. If there is the slightest amount of truth to the rumor, your company needs to be the one to address that issue. Also, be prepared to answer any questions from customers, stakeholders, and the media. By having this information readily available, it will demonstrate to those interested parties that your company is paying attention to the conversation and taking an active role via responding in a prompt manner. These steps will allow the public to see that you are taking action and elevate you in their opinion.

Becoming an Industry Expert through an Executive Blog

If any of your executive staff has knowledge about the industry that is superior to others in the field, it would be beneficial for the company, and the executive, to share this information through a blog. Sharing his or her insight and information will provide an executive the opportunity to be seen as an expert, industry leader, or thought leader. In this position, media personnel and others who have questions about the industry or any area related to the industry would think of your corporation and that specific executive first when looking for someone to interview about a story or to use as a reference when citing information about the industry. This type of exposure for both the executive and the company is free exposure and places both in the position of industry leader and expert.

Setting up the Corporate Blog

Are you ready to join the conversation? Are you ready to set up a corporate blog? Great! Begin at the beginning—choose a URL that is easy for your stakeholders to remember and can be directly connected to your company. Make sure that your stakeholders can find your corporate blog; the blogosphere is crowded, the easier you make it for your stakeholders to find you the more likely they are to visit your blog, and to keep coming back. Once you have come up with the URL make sure that it is available and purchase it; purchase the URL in the company's name and not under an individual's name, just in case the individual would leave the company under undesirable circumstances and want to damage the company's reputation. Once you have the URL secured, start to advertise it on any communication that goes out from the company and place it on the letterhead and corporate website. Again, the easier you make it for people to find your corporate blog, the more likely that people are to visit and to keep returning.

Now that you have the URL for the blog, you need to determine how to set the blog up. Will the corporate blog be housed on the corporate servers and completely coded by the IT department or will your company take advantage of the various platforms available for blogging. Some of the more popular include Blogger, WordPress, Movable Type, TypePad, Drupal, and SquareSpace. Each of these platforms has their benefits and their drawbacks. It would be best to examine each platform to determine which one is the best fit for your company, and doing an Internet search is the best way to find all of your options. Also, Biz Stone in *Who Let the Blogs Out,* lists some of the benefits and drawbacks of each platform. This text is excellent reading for those just entering the blogosphere and will help to make the platform decision-making process easier.

Before beginning to share the URL, make sure the blog is ready to go live: know who the corporate blogger will be, have the blogging policy in place and approved by the legal team, and have the blog design approved by all corporate entities that must approve it. These steps will help to move the corporate blog quickly into production and not have the blog tied up in legal and corporate channels after it has been launched to the public.

The first post on the corporate blog should not be an apology for the fact that the blog was not available once the address was shared with the publics. Use the first blog post to welcome readers to the blog and encourage them to share comments regarding all posts.

Explain a little about the corporate blog policy related to comment moderation; by posting this policy on the blog itself there will be little question when a comment is edited or not posted because it does not fit the corporate blog policy. By posting this information and providing easy access on the corporate blog, there is less possibility of backlash from the blogosphere if a comment does not appear or if a commenter places a critique on their own blog stating that you didn't post their comment. Clearly available and posted blogging policies allow your company to have a fall-back position, as well as a legal leg to stand on if necessary. Again, the clearer and more transparent you can make the corporate blog, the less of a chance that your company will experience either reputation or legal repercussions from the blogosphere.

What should you do next? Start the conversation and/or join an already existing conversation. Your goal is to become an integral part of the conversation as it relates to your industry and your company. The more embedded you become in the conversation, the more your publics will look to your company for answers and for expert opinion about your industry. Not only will the media come to the corporate blog, as they do with Petrobras, looking for stories and looking for unbiased information regarding your industry, they will reach out to your company as an opinion leader in order to gain a better understanding of your business as an expert.

Engaging your customers and the media in a conversation allows your corporation to be transparent, to let these people and entities see into your corporation and how it works. The more transparent you are, the more likely your company is to be trusted. Being transparent may take time and may require a dramatic change in your corporate culture, but, in the long run it will help your corporation build stronger relationships with the media and with your customers. And, it is always better to be on the good side of the media and to have your customers become customer evangelists for your product and your company. Only a consistent message and regular updating of the corporate blog will allow for these relationships to blossom into something larger than just a consumer/product relationship and become an expert/evangelist relationship. Utilize the power of technology and the two-way communication model of the blogosphere to benefit your company in ways that only blogging can do! Join the conversation, start a corporate blog today.

So, how did Petrobras succeed in making the corporate blog a key part of its communication strategy? There were obviously some learning curves that were addressed as Petrobras was new to blogging. Originally, the company would post the questions from journalists, and the answers, before the journalists were able to report their story. This caused a lot of controversy. However, it was resolved when Petrobras reviewed its posting schedule and alerted the media to the specific time that the story would be published on the blog, allowing the journalist to have full disclosure of this information. Even after the CPI had come to an end, Petrobras added new features and revamped the blog as a company communication channel. Updates to the blog included expanded interactivity; increased informal posts on corporate activities such as cultural sponsorships. and added a series of interviews with the Petrobras executives.

Now, the press visits the blog for information regarding Petrobras; what was once a thorn in their side is now a great source of information for current and future stories. The outcome of the CPI was favorable, somewhat due to the use of the blogging channel and the opportunity it provided for the company to be honest and open about all its communications and allow the stakeholders to speak freely regarding the hearing. Open and honest communication between corporations and stakeholders . . . that's the ability of corporate blogging done right!

Key Takeaways

1. Determine if a corporate blog is a positive step for your company.
2. Do not make the corporate blog a marketing tool; let the blog have its own voice.
3. Be honest and open with stakeholders on the corporate blog; join the conversation.
4. Do your homework regarding the platform and URL for the blog.
5. Create and publish a corporate blogging policy that has been approved by the legal team to avoid any problems before they happen.

Glossary

Blogging platform: The programming or software used to create a blog with.

Blogosphere: The network of blogs that is created on the World Wide Web.

Corporate blog: A blog that is started by, and sanctioned by, a corporation as a communication tool with all posts being sanctioned by the corporation.

Customer evangelists: Customers who believe in your company and products so much that they are willing to endorse your product or company without any type of recognition or payment.

Dooced: Fired for blogging.

Gramm-Leach-Bliley Act (aka Financial Services Modernization Act of 1999): Requires financial institutions to explain how they share customer information to their customers and also requires them to safeguard all sensitive data.

HIPAA: The Health Insurance Portability and Accountability Act of 1996.

Professional or executive blog: A personal blog that has been set up by a member of a corporation, but who does not officially speak for the corporation. This type of blog is not corporate sanctioned.

Spam: Unwanted blog comments.

URL (Uniform Resource Locator): Address where a website can be located.

References

Flynn, Nancy. *Blog Rules: A Business Guide to Managing Policy, Public Relations, and Legal Issues.* New York: AMACOM, 2006.

Maldonado, Gilberto Puig. "Blog Facts & Data: Shifting the Source-Press Relationship Paradigm." In *Gold Quill Winner Case Studies published by the International Association for Business Communicators,* 2010. http://discovery.iabc.com/.

Scoble, Robert and Shel Israel. *Naked Conversations: How Blogs are Changing the Way Businesses Talk with Customers.* Hoboken, NJ: John Wiley and Sons, 2006.

CHAPTER THIRTEEN

Strategically Preparing for and Relating with the Media: Why Planning and Training Matter

Eric Bergman

Succinct Answers Solve Multiple Problems

In late August 2008, a media trainer arrived nearly an hour early to a full-day workshop, which was organized by the public affairs department of a large bank. Six people were scheduled to attend, all of them subject matter experts in their field. When he walked into the room, the trainer was surprised to find a participant already there.

After introductions, the trainer and participant starting talking.

"You're my last hope," the participant told the trainer, after a few minutes of chit-chat.

"Why is that?" the trainer asked.

"Because if you can't help me, I'm not doing any more interviews with journalists," the participant said.

The participant was a senior member of a foreign exchange trading desk at a major bank, which is a highly technical subject area. Earlier that year, at the encouragement of her employer, she started accepting interview requests from journalists, primarily newspaper reporters. She was somewhat disappointed after reading the article that resulted from her first interview. There were no large problems, but she felt that the journalist did not understand the intricacies of foreign exchange. As a result, she vowed to try harder to educate journalists in the future.

"The second article was even worse," she said. "There were a number of significant inaccuracies in the second article."

After that experience, she talked to a friend of hers, a former journalist. Her friend recommended that she prepare messages in advance and keep bridging to those messages during the interview. "Stay on message regardless of the question," was the advice.

"The third interview was a complete disaster," she said. "It was wildly inaccurate. Most of what I said was taken out of context. I even had a colleague at another bank—someone

I've been friends with for years—tease me by calling me up to ask if I know what I'm doing, even though he knows I do. Can you help?"

"Yes, I can," the trainer said. "I'm certain that your issues will be dealt with during the day, but please feel free to ask questions relevant to your specific situation as the training unfolds."

The day of training emphasized short answers to questions, particularly when dealing with print journalists. Pause, answer the question, and stop talking (P-A-S) was discussed and practiced numerous times, both as a form of protection by reducing the context from misquotes can be drawn and as a way of letting journalists educate themselves about issues on which they're reporting. Indeed, the first of four rounds of practice interviews conducted during the day was entirely devoted to P-A-S.

At the end of the day, the trainer checked to see if the issues earlier expressed by the foreign exchange trader expressed were addressed. "Yes, they were," she replied. "By keeping my answers short with print journalists, I can protect myself and the bank. I can be more strategic, because my messages will be more likely to be used as quotes in the article. And my interviews will probably be shorter."

The timing could not have been better. During the fall of 2008, global financial markets melted down and the foreign exchange trader received an average of three interview requests per week from local daily newspapers and national publications. After reading one such article, in which his client was quoted extensively, the trainer sent her an e-mail. "Excellent article today," it said.

"Thank you," she replied. "I had a good teacher. The interviews take very little time (compared to my past experience) and I can almost predict which quote the journalist will use because I give them very few from which to choose."

Note: To ensure confidentiality of the organization and/or people within the organization, names have been altered.

The case earlier illustrates a number of important media training issues. The first is risk management. The risk when dealing with journalists, particularly print journalists, is being misquoted or quoted out of context, whether inadvertently or deliberately. The simplest way to mitigate this is to keep answers as short as possible. Quite simply, when you reduce the context, you reduce the risk of being quoted out of context.

The second issue is the journalist's need to understand. Journalists are generalists by nature. They have to teach themselves about an issue before they can comfortably teach others through the articles they write. The best way for them to teach themselves is to ask as many questions as possible per minute. This also underscores the value of clear, concise answers. Shorter answers translate into more questions asked per unit of time.

Next, this case hints at the differences between dealing with print journalists and those who ply their trade in the broadcast media. While slightly longer answers are acceptable and somewhat desirable with broadcast media, succinct answers are preferable in print.

Finally, there is the issue of being strategic—of the spokesperson actively using exchanges with journalists to influence the attitudes, opinions, or behavior of specific audiences that support the organization's business objectives. There are two lines of thought here. One emphasizes bridging to messages whenever possible. The drawback to this approach is that it creates more context and more risk. It also creates longer answers that make it difficult for print journalists to educate themselves about the issue or subject area in question.

The second approach is a balance between the needs of the journalist and the needs of the spokesperson. Research shows there are many parallels between excellence in negotiation and excellence in communication (Grunig 1992). In negotiation, win-win outcomes are most sustainable. Both parties gain from the exchange. The same applies to communication in general, and to media relations specifically. To be successful, spokespeople should approach every interview with the goal of managing the process to a win-win outcome, in which both the spokesperson and the journalist gain from the exchange. Spokespeople should protect themselves at all times, but strive for win-win outcomes wherever and whenever possible.

This chapter advocates the latter approach, under the assumption that a strict focus on one's message is not how you build long-term, positive working relationships with anyone, let alone reporters. With increased emphasis on organizational transparency in today's world, organizations are facing pressure to listen carefully and answer effectively. If an individual or organization doesn't answer questions, those seeking the answers—whether journalists, employees, investors, suppliers, donors, voters, or others—have multiple sources from which to obtain the answers.

This chapter will cover a number of specific topics. First, we're going to examine what "the media" actually constitutes in our modern age. Traditional media still wield significant influence. But they are no longer the only players with a potential axe to grind or the means with which to hone an edge to a fine point. In a modern age, you must be prepared to deal with all forms of media, both traditional and social. Be aware that as they compete for readers, listeners, and viewers, media outlets of all types will create polarization to attract audiences.

That brings us to our second topic. We will introduce a model to help you strategically manage polarization. This model is a powerful tool to enable you to use someone else's hostility to change opinions in your favor. By applying it effectively, you increase your chances of strategic success.

The third topic we'll examine is the fine line between spin and sin. We'll take a brief philosophical look at lies and deception, and the areas in which the line between spin and sin is and is not breached.

We'll examine how to answer questions effectively. This is perhaps the least-developed skill in human interpersonal communication. We will specifically look at P-A-S and how that approach can be applied to a variety of situations to improve communication and manage risk.

Next, we'll examine how to strategically target your interviews. In a nutshell, strategic communication is less about inputs than it is about outcomes. In other words, what you say is less important than the way in which what's said influences attitudes, opinions, and behavior. This section provides a number of tactics to employ, depending on whether you're dealing with print or broadcast journalists.

Finally, this chapter will examine specific defensive strategies that you can apply with journalists, but which also can be used in any situation where it's important to defend yourself or your organization. We will outline four basic defensive strategies and provide examples of how they can be applied.

What Is "the Media"?

Traditionally, the role of the media has been to keep audiences informed—quickly, accurately, and to the best of their ability—on matters that significantly affect those audiences (Bergman 2006a). As newspapers, magazines, television stations, and radio stations evolved through the 20th century, emphasis was placed on objectivity in news reporting. Media outlets recognized that their long-term credibility, and therefore their ability to attract advertisers, depended on how they interpreted the word "accurately." Make no mistake, throughout history every media outlet has had a perspective and every story has had a slant. However, as we turned the corner into the 21st century, traditional mainstream media played by a similar set of rules. Most of the journalists working at these outlets received formal training in journalism and journalistic ethics, and the word "accurate" meant that facts included in stories tended to be true, or as true as the journalist developing the story could ensure that they were at the moment the story was filed, aired, or printed.

Many people believe the rules changed with the advent of social media, which began with the emergence of written blogs, podcasts, and video blogs, and evolved with networking sites such as Facebook and Twitter. Social media outlets often have to "shout" to be heard above the clutter and make a name for themselves. However, social media is simply following a trend, the seeds of which were sown during the last two decades of the 20th century with the rise of talk radio.

During the 1970s, radio listeners shifted their loyalty from amplitude modulation (AM) stations to frequency modulation (FM) stations. FM radio offered stereo sound and enhanced fidelity. Quite simply, music played on FM stations sounds significantly better than music played on AM stations. As consumers began purchasing FM receivers for their homes and offices, and automobile manufacturers began installing FM receivers in vehicles, loyalty shifted. To survive, AM radio needed to reinvent itself. It did so by relying on the sound that doesn't require high fidelity to be carried well: the human voice. With that realization came the rise of talk radio as a significant influence on the media landscape.

To attract listeners, talk radio created polarization. To varying degrees, polarization has been used by media outlets for centuries. As Randolph Hearst knew during the journalism muckraking era of the early 20th century, controversy sells newspapers. It also sells magazines, attracts viewers to televised news programs, and creates listening audiences for talk radio. Early in its evolution, talk radio set new standards for controversy. Hosts would make outlandish statements to attract listeners, often based in opinion or conjecture instead of fact. Some managed to attract large followings.

However, over time, talk-radio hosts realized they had to pay greater attention to concepts such as accuracy in order to survive. Long-term credibility became an issue. Talk-radio hosts would still attempt to create polarization, but would do so by the way they structured facts rather than by making outlandish, untrue statements.

Current Media Landscape

Today, the media are often divided into a number of broad categories: traditional, social, and emerging. For our purposes, however, we are going to pay less attention to distinctions such as traditional versus emerging. We are going to divide the media according to two traditions of human communication that have existed for thousands of years: literacy and orality.

Literacy is the written word or print media, which includes newspapers and magazines—words written on paper. However, literacy also encompasses blogs, words written on Facebook pages, and Twitter tweets. For our purposes, it doesn't matter whether written words appear on paper, or on a computer, or smartphone screen, they are part of a print story.

Print stories tend to need much more information than broadcast; the first two or three paragraphs of a newspaper article can potentially contain as much information as the entire story on radio or television. One or two computer screens of a blog can examine an issue to the same depth as a five-minute podcast. As a result, print interviews tend to be longer than those for broadcast, and print journalists tend to ask more questions. They need to teach themselves about the topic before they can comfortably and accurately teach others.

In print, whether for a daily newspaper or a neighborhood blog, a quote of yours may be used, but the path to the end audience is always indirect; you communicate with the reporter who, in turn, takes your information, combines it with other information, filters it, and communicates it to readers.

If the interview is with a print reporter, there is significant risk, because what you say can be taken out of context. This underscores the importance of being clear, concise, and focused. One of the most critical skills to learn is how to stop talking as soon as you've answered a question.

Orality is the spoken word. It includes television and radio, but it also encompasses podcasts, videocasts, YouTube, and any sights and sounds captured by anyone with audio and/or video capability on their smartphone. In broadcast, whether sound bites or live interviews, it is possible to send messages directly to the end audience.

Broadcast interviews tend to be shorter than their print counterparts, which is true of live interviews (in which the audience hears questions and answers together with minimal editing or no editing at all), but it is especially true with interviews for the purpose of obtaining a sound bite (in which the audience will not hear the questions asked and only about 8 to 12 seconds of any answer). There will be fewer questions. In this environment, it is still important to answer questions, and the direct answer to the question should probably be the first thing out of your mouth, but the answers need to be slightly longer than those provided during print interviews.

With broadcast media, there are two challenges: sound bites and live interviews. Sound bites are snippets from the spokesperson that vary in length from a few words to a maximum of 12 seconds. They are usually part of a newscast, although can also be used in investigational or public affairs programs. The key to preparing for sounds bites is discipline. Each time you're asked a question or series of questions, you create a self-contained piece of information that combines the question, answer, and a single message related to the topic. This structure is important because the audience rarely (if ever) hears the questions asked. You do not want what you say to be positioned against something other than what was asked.

Live interviews, by contrast, are interviews in which the audience hears questions and answers with minimal editing or no editing at all, regardless of whether the interview is "live to air," is recorded and played six months later, or has been sitting on a website for 10 years or more. Live interviews encompass everything from one-on-one interviews to panel interviews with multiple interviewers and/or guests, call-in programs, satellite interviews, and Skype interviews. While answering "yes" or "no" or "it depends" and stopping is perfectly acceptable for print interviews, as a general statement answers need to be a bit longer during live interviews. However, it is still important to answer questions. If you ignore the question and focus on your message, you limit your success by decreasing your ability to change opinions as a result of the interview. You will not effectively manage polarization.

Polarization is always an issue with journalists, but so is credibility. Journalists prefer to have two sides at opposing ends of the spectrum, but they want to maintain their credibility in positioning the story at the outer edges. Reporters and editors, whether a blogger developing an audience to battle 300 percent water utility increases or the international editor at CNN or CNBC, do not want to be marginalized by being branded as zealots. They understand that maintaining their credibility enables them to reach and influence audiences.

Managing Polarization

An intimidating element of media interviews is the fact that editorial staff often try to create polarization in their coverage of events and issues. In other words, the further apart the two sides of any dispute, the more dramatic the story. Drama sells newspapers and magazines. It also improves the ratings of television and radio programs. It drives traffic to blogs, wall posts, and tweets.

To understand polarization, it is important to examine the role of issues. By definition, an issue is an unresolved problem that has the potential of escalating into a dispute. In simple terms, it is a fight looking for a place to happen. When someone "takes issue" with your organization, they are mapping out the territory in which that dispute is likely to be fought. Battle lines are drawn. People choose sides. Figure 13.1 demonstrates this.

Every potential response to an issue can theoretically be mapped along a spectrum, from openly hostile on one side to openly supportive on the other. Those with no opinion can be found somewhere in the middle.

An example may help illustrate this point. Consider the issue of cutting government spending. On the openly supportive side will be those people who strongly believe that government waste is rampant everywhere and keeping a rein on the budget is the only way to keep the bureaucrats in line. On the opposite side are those who might not be able to visit a hospital if spending is reduced, or unions who know that less government

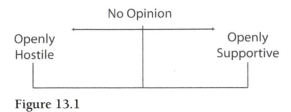

Figure 13.1

revenue means fewer government employees, and therefore less union revenue. Between these two extremes, you will find virtually everyone else. Some people may have no opinion about the issue, and sit somewhere in the middle.

Issues formulate opinions. The longer an issue is played out by the media, the more opinions it forms and the more polarization it can create. The further apart the two sides in a dispute, the more dramatic the issue and, by extension, the more newsworthy it becomes.

This is significant to you, as your organization's spokesperson. There may be some rare cases in which you or your organization may wish to occupy an extreme position at one end of the spectrum. In most cases, however, you will achieve better results by letting others occupy the outer edge. As you do, it's important to remember that middle ground is almost always better. If you can occupy this middle position—the "high ground" as it is often called—your media interview can become an integral component of your overall communications strategy.

Figure 13.2 demonstrates this. On the spectrum, as you move away from the center, the way that people respond to an issue goes from a logical, rational framework to an emotional one. Your challenge is to stay within the logical region of the dispute.

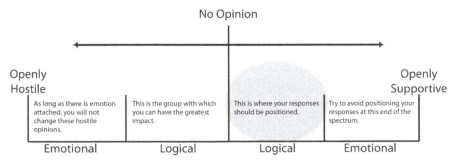

Figure 13.2

Positioning Your Responses

What does this mean to you? If you react to emotional hostility with open emotional support, you might have a tasty morsel for the evening news, but there is little chance that anything will be ultimately resolved by the information you convey. In watching the news item on television or reading about it in a newspaper, all those who started on the right-hand side of the spectrum—supporting your perspective—will end up there. Conversely, all those who started on the left-hand side of the spectrum—opposed to your viewpoint—will finish there. By feeding polarization with your response, you ultimately limit your potential for success. Nothing gets resolved; no opinions are changed during the exchange.

If, however, you can position your organization in the logical and supportive portion of the spectrum (and if you can keep your cool during media interviews, regardless of how tense the situation), you accomplish a great deal more. First, by conveying information that supports previously held beliefs, you reinforce all opinions that originally supported yours, whether based in logic or emotion. You do not need to feed supportive emotion directly; they will add all the emotion they need. On the other side of the spectrum, as long as someone has an emotional attachment to a perspective contrary to yours, you will never change their opinion, no matter how hard you try, so why try? It is appropriate to acknowledge that someone who disagrees with you has the right to feel the way he or she does, and to try to find middle ground wherever possible by treating her or his opinion with respect, but not to try to change her or his opinion through direct force. If your information is based in logic, fact, and reason, those with a logical opinion, but one that is opposed to your perspective, are the people with whom you can have the greatest impact. For this group, two forces are at work.

First, if you present a case based on logic, they can compare your logic to theirs and make a reasonable, rational decision. And second, they may not feel comfortable associating with those whose opinion is based in emotion, even if those people are on "their side" of the issue. By offering a reasonable, rational alternative, you may attract them to your perspective as a means of disassociating themselves from the dissidents and zealots at the outer fringe.

To accomplish this, however, your side of the story must be reasonable, rational, logical, ethical, responsible, and defensible. If your perspective does not meet these standards, the first step to preparing to meet with journalists is to make it so. Take responsibility if you're wrong. Find ways to make improvements moving forward. Make decisions that strengthen your logic. Once you do that, explaining your perspective to the inside and outside worlds is relatively easy, even within the context of emotionally charged issues.

Lies, Deception, and Spin

Before going any further, it's useful for us to examine the fine line that exists between deception, lies, and spin. In her book *LYING: Moral Choice in Public and Private Life,* philosopher Sissela Bok (1999) defines deception as that which occurs when "we communicate messages meant to mislead . . . meant to make them believe what we ourselves do not believe" (13). She defines a lie as "any intentionally deceptive message which is stated" (13). To lie, you must make some form of statement; you cannot lie by simply omitting facts. If you omit facts or arrange them in ways that create a false impression, you are practicing a form of deception.

DEFINITION OF "SPIN"

Spin is simply the process of linking facts together facts in a way that attempts to portray an individual or organization in the best possible light.

In a presentation to the American Political Association, John J. Mearsheimer (2004) provided a definition of spin that clearly delineates it from both lying and deception. Spin simply occurs when someone links together facts in a way that attempts to portray an individual or organization in the best possible light. Chances are that anyone who has sent out a résumé has practiced spin. Spin involves downplaying or ignoring certain facts that would create a negative perception. The emphasis is on making the individual (or organization) look as good as possible by focusing on information that creates a positive impression.

The thin line between spin and sin lies somewhere between the creation of a true impression and a false impression, resulting from which facts are included, which facts are omitted, and how the facts are structured. In other words, if the facts are true and the impression left by those facts is true, the overall approach has not crossed the line between spin and sin. However, if the facts are true but the impression left is false or misleading, the precise location of the ethical line needs to be discussed or reviewed by the decision makers involved. If the facts are untrue, and people in the organization know them to be untrue, the organization is lying (Bergman 2006b).

The way that human beings defend themselves against deception, lies, or spin is to ask questions. Indeed, the more questions they ask, the better their defense. By asking questions, it is possible to determine which facts are highlighted, which are ignored, and whether the person answering questions is engaging in some form of deception or lie. This is why interviews, not just résumés, are important to the hiring process. From a more formal perspective, this is what happens when prosecutors and defense attorneys (or plaintiffs and defendants) square off against each other in a court of law. This is also what occurs in the court of public opinion when reporters, employees, or other stakeholder groups ask spokespeople about the actions, activities, opinions, and behaviors of the organizations they represent.

The Skill of Answering Questions

Answering questions effectively is a critical skill to develop if you hope to be successful as a spokesperson. By nature, reporters ask questions to gather information. It is their primary tool. As a spokesperson, if you believe that win-win outcomes are important to building long-term relationships with journalists, your job is to answer those questions. It's the only way to help them get their win.

If you ignore the question, evade it, or waffle in any way, the reporter will notice. At the very least, their professional curiosity will be aroused. At worst, your inability to answer the question will affect your credibility as a spokesperson, and potentially absolve them of any responsibility in treating you fairly.

As a general statement, when someone asks you a question in your daily life, he or she is looking for one thing: *the* answer. If the answer is "yes," the person asking will want to hear it. The same applies if the answer is "no," "possibly," "absolutely," "eventually," "unlikely," or "only under specific conditions." How much more they want or need to hear will surprise you when you begin closely examining the question and answer process. Generally, the person asking you a question needs significantly less than you feel tempted or compelled to give.

In your daily life, if someone asks "What time is it?" you hopefully look at your watch and tell them. You don't tell them how the watch works. But if someone asks you a remotely complex question in your professional life, how tempted are you to provide extensive background information? To enhance your ability to answer questions, you should resist this temptation and simply answer the question asked, recognizing that if they want more information, they'll ask more questions.

The person asking a question is not looking for a speech or presentation. They are not looking for the answers to the next 20 questions that may or may not be asked. They want the answer to that specific question. If they want more, they'll ask, particularly if you facilitate a communicative environment in which they feel comfortable asking.

Reporters constantly face tight deadlines. They don't have a lot of time to waste. They do not want to wade through a mountain of information to get to the nuggets that fit their story, and they don't have a lot of patience for people who can't—or won't—answer their questions. If you're more focused on driving home key messages than finding a balance that allows the reporter do his or her job quickly and efficiently, you significantly decrease your chances of building a positive working relationship with that reporter.

Although there is sometimes no such thing as a simple question or even a simple answer, your role should be to simplify the process as much as possible. Theoretically, every question sits at the apex of a large pyramid of information. There can be simple answers, as long as you just answer the question being asked, not the 10 or 20 that may or may not follow it. Be accurate. And keep your answers short. The vast majority of questions you've ever been asked in your life can be answered in 10 words or less. For print reporters particularly, keep this 10-word limit in mind, and only breach it when you are attempting to influence audiences important to you that the reporter is also attempting to reach.

There is no way that you can reach into a reporter's mind and fully anticipate where he or she is headed with a line of questioning. Later we'll discuss how to negotiate the interview as a means of obtaining information from the reporter about topics to be discussed. By doing so, you should have an idea of what's coming. But you can't anticipate everything.

Rather's Rules

There are three acceptable answers to every question from a reporter, sometimes referred to as "Rather's rules," because they are believed to have been coined by television reporter Dan Rather.

- Yes, I have the answer to your question and here it is.
- No, I don't have the answer to your question, but I'll get it for you, or find you someone who can answer the question.
- Yes, I have the answer to your question, but I cannot provide it at this time.

> ## THREE ACCEPTABLE ANSWERS TO ANY QUESTION
>
> - Yes, I have the answer and here it is.
> - No, I don't have the answer but I'll get it for you (or find the right person for you to interview).
> - Yes, I do have the answer, but I cannot discuss it.

There are a few specific circumstances in which you would evoke the third of Rather's rules and choose to not answer a question because you cannot provide the information at this time. These are situations in which:

- Employees have not yet been notified about a specific issue; they shouldn't get the news through a newspaper article, or a television or radio report (but if a journalist is asking, you had better inform them as quickly as possible).
- Employee, patient, or client privacy may be breached by answering the question.
- A disaster or emergency has taken place, and next of kin have not been notified.
- Sensitive competitive information would be divulged, which would provide competitors with insight into your sales or market share.
- Securities legislation would be breached.
- Sensitive union negotiations are taking place and a news blackout has been imposed.
- The organization is being sued and legal counsel has advised against communicating with or through the media.
- Issues of national security.

In situations where you cannot answer, simply say that you cannot answer and briefly explain why. For example: "I cannot provide the names of victims because next of kin have not yet been notified."

Pause Before Responding

In general, especially during print interviews and all interviews for sound bite purposes (and, in fact, in your personal and professional life), you should pause before answering every question. The only case in which you can't pause much is the live interview because interviewers in that format do not like "dead air" during their interviews.

> ### THE FIRST PAUSE
>
> Pausing before answering enables you to:
> - Take the time to think; examine the question and understand it.

- Formulate the right answer (which is almost always the shortest possible answer).
- Determine if it is appropriate to weave your organization's message into the answer.
- Maintain control over the pace at which questions are asked.
- Maintain control over your emotions.
- Look confident.
- Establish a pattern in which difficult questions will not stand out.
- Become a better listener.

Once you've paused, the next step is to answer the question. But remember, you're not answering questions that the reporter may ask in the future. You're not answering questions that you hope the reporter will ask. You are simply answering each question as it is asked, allowing the reporter to steer the process. After all, he or she is responsible for developing the story.

After you've answered the question, stop talking. Let the reporter ask the next question. Chances are, you won't have long to wait. After all, reporters get paid to ask questions. By keeping your answers brief, you can manage the process and find ways in which to match your needs to theirs.

We want to be clear here. We are not advocating an approach in which you, as the spokesperson, passively lie back and accept whatever whim the journalist throws your way. If you have to adopt a defensive position because the circumstances dictate that you should, do so without hesitation. If you have to correct misinformation, do so. As we'll discuss later, your two top priorities are to protect yourself and your organization. However, you can often achieve both by simply answering and stopping.

Approach interviews from a collaborative perspective. Help the reporter do his or her job. Manage exchanges to win-win outcomes whenever possible. Answer questions clearly and concisely. Learn to stop talking. Adopt a defensive position if necessary. But above all, manage the process in an active and efficient manner.

Negotiating with Reporters

Creating win-win outcomes during exchanges journalists begins when the interview is first negotiated, whether the spokesperson negotiates directly with the journalist, or someone negotiates the interview on the spokesperson's behalf. It is essential to understand what the journalist hopes to accomplish and who the journalist is trying to reach, especially if your goal is to manage the exchange to a mutually satisfactory conclusion.

As general statement, therefore, you should always negotiate the interview with the journalist as a means of assessing risk and preparing your thoughts in advance of the interview. If a reporter calls you with an unsolicited interview request, ask the journalist a number of questions, then disengage and take time to get your thoughts in order. Try to understand what the reporter is trying to accomplish with the story, and who he or she is trying to reach. Based on this, who would you like to strategically influence as result of this interview, with this reporter, at this specific moment? Disengage to get your thoughts in order, but remember that the amount of time you have to prepare will be dictated by the reporter's deadline.

If you've contacted journalists with a news release or other outreach, you should be ready to conduct the interview as soon as journalists call. However, before answering their questions, you should understand who they are and where they're from, and ask them three quick questions:

- What aspect of the news release most interests you?
- How does the news release fit into your overall story?
- Who else are you planning interview for the story?

If the answers to these questions are consistent with the topic and intent of the news release, go ahead with interview. But if the scope of the story seems extend well beyond primary topic of the news release, or if you perceive significant risk on the basis of the reporter's answers, you may need to disengage to check with others.

On the other side we have situations in which a reporter contacts you directly for either positive or negative reasons with an unsolicited interview request. In these situations, it is important that you ask a number of questions to understand specifically what the journalist is seeking, whether there is undue risk involved with this interview, and how you can potentially influence specific audiences as a result of the interview.

To negotiate the interview, ask a number of questions. Who is the reporter and where is he or she from? What are the topics to be discussed? What is the issue to be addressed? Is the reporter talking to anyone else about the issue? If so, what is their perspective?

What is the space the story will need to fill? How many words for newspaper or magazine articles? How much time will it occupy on TV or radio? If it's for TV or radio, is the reporter looking for a sound bite? Are they looking for a "live" interview—not necessarily played directly to air but one in which the audience hears questions and answers together with minimal editing or no editing at all?

This information from the reporter helps you determine the amount of information you'll need to bring to the interview, and will give you a better idea of how to prepare. If you're being interviewed by a TV reporter for a newscast, you'll need to bring significantly less information than if your input is going to be a major component of an in-depth newspaper report.

Will the interview be conducted by telephone or in person? You must agree with the reporter on a location and/or time for the interview. As you're getting this information, also develop a contingency plan in case something comes up. How can the reporter contact you if there's a problem? Where can the reporter reach you? How can you contact the reporter if something comes up?

If appropriate, ask the reporter if you can send background information in advance. If you do, provide appropriate background information as early as possible, but be extremely selective with what you send. Less is always more.

As a final item, you may consider asking the reporter if he or she has enough sources on this issue. If not, can you recommend experts? Other sources? Other potential interview subjects?

Strategically Targeting Your Interviews

During this section, we're going to introduce the concept of weaving in messages. Keep in mind that there is a significant difference between weaving them in and driving them home.

Messages are integral to your success with any interview. They should be directly relevant to the topic under discussion (which was negotiated in advance) and the specific question asked. They are not arrived at with phrases such as "what's really important" or "what I'd really like to talk about is . . ."

Woven messages are designed to influence specific audiences important to the organization's success. Strategic media relations mean targeting your messages. There is no such thing as "the public" or "the general public." Each of these comprises smaller, specifically identifiable publics that have varying degrees of influence on an individual's and/or organization's success. Know who you would like to influence in advance and be prepared to strategically target those audiences as the interview unfolds.

Finally, woven messages are focused on creating desired outcomes, not hammering home inputs. The messages you selectively choose to include should be aimed at influencing the attitudes, opinions, and behavior of specific audiences you're targeting. You do not achieve this by blindly and mindlessly repeating precanned statements.

Perhaps the best way to explain this is through an example. Like most parents, I cannot count the number of times I've asked our son to turn off the light in his room. Today's children are exposed to information about the environment that should make it easy for them to connect turning off the light in their room to saving the planet. But repeating the key message simply does not work.

To get the outcomes you're seeking, sometimes it's important to change the input. This is what I learned with our son. Every May, when he comes home from university and leaves the light on in his room, I call out to him and ask him to please come upstairs and turn it off.

"But dad, you're right there," he will say.

"Yes," I reply, "but I'm not the one who left it on."

He will then have to unwind his large frame from in front of the television, where he's watching sports-something, walk up the stairs, and turn off the light in his room. It usually only takes once or twice before he modifies his own behavior, and I never have to ask again.

Remembering key messages is unimportant in communication. Applying information or taking action counts for everything. If someone applies your information to their decision-making process or takes action on it, key messages are, by definition, remembered. And you shouldn't need to beat people over the head to achieve that goal.

Print Interviews

As we discussed earlier, print reporters need more information than their counterparts in radio and television to complete their stories. They ask more questions. As a result, print interviews tend to take longer and go into greater depth than interviews for broadcast. And in a print interview, the path to the end audience (the readers of newspapers and magazines) is always indirect. Reporters and editors stand between you and the end audiences with whom you would like to communicate which is why you must be clear, concise, and focused during print interviews. Keep your answers short. Allow the reporter to ask more questions. As you focus on this, there are two basic tactics to keep in mind. The first is to P-A-S. The second is to pause, answer the question, weave in a message, and stop talking (P-A-W-S).

Your primary responsibility during print interviews is to answer questions clearly and concisely, and then stop talking. This is illustrated by the chart of interviews A and B (Table 13.1). Both interviews are 100 questions in length.

Spokesperson A pauses, answers, and stops 95 times. He or she pauses, answers, weaves in a message, and stops five times. Spokesperson B does the opposite. He or she is able to pause, answer, and stop five times, choosing to weave in a message 95 times. Of course, when someone weaves in messages that often, the case could be made that the spokesperson is not weaving in messages; he or she is driving them home.

Table 13.1   A Tale of Two Print Interviews

	Interview A	Interview B
P-A-S	95	5
P-A-W-S	5	95

Which of these two interviews will consume more of the journalist's time and the spokesperson's time? Interview B will, of course. Longer answers mean longer interviews for both the journalist and the spokesperson.

With which interview will the journalist be more confident about the information being included in the story? After the interview with spokesperson A, the journalist will be much more certain and secure including information in the story. Too often, spokespeople spend an hour or more on the telephone with a journalist, only to discover when the story is printed that they are not quoted and nothing they talked about was included in the final story. If this ever happens to you or your spokespeople, the first thing you should question is the length of the answers provided to the journalist.

Which interview has more risk? Interview B. The most significant risk with print interviews is being quoted out of context, even inadvertently. Because of the number of long answers during interview B, there is a significant likelihood of being quoted out of context. In risky or potentially hostile situations, it will be easy for the journalist to twist the spokesperson's words.

Finally, which interview is more strategically focused? Interview A. The spokesperson only gave the journalist five potential quotes. Hopefully, those quotes are aimed at influencing the attitudes, opinions, or behavior of specific audiences important to the organization's—and therefore the spokesperson's—strategic communication success.

As a spokesperson, you need to understand the difference between closed- and open-ended questions. Closed questions are those questions requiring a short answer. This could be "yes" or "no," but could also be "possibly," "potentially," "under certain circumstances," and "never." Open-ended questions—such as "why?" and "how?"—tend to require more explanation. But an open-ended question is not a license to talk nonstop. In weaving in key messages, you will, at carefully selected points (and probably more frequently while answering open-ended questions), pick appropriate moments in which to weave in those messages.

Above all, remember the value of stopping after answering the question. You will have difficulty protecting yourself and your organization if you cannot stop talking. This is particularly true if you talk nonstop to simple closed questions requiring a yes or no answer.

By keeping your answers short, you allow the reporter to steer the process. You can influence the interview and point out new directions as the process unfolds. But always remember that it is the reporter who has to satisfy his or her editor. If you can't answer questions and provide information in a clear and concise fashion, the reporter will keep looking until he or she finds someone who can. Of course, if that occurs, your opportunity to positively influence the direction of the story will be lost.

Broadcast Interviews

With broadcast, there are two basic challenges. The first is sound bites. The second is live interviews, which encompasses everything from one-on-one interviews to panel interviews, talk shows, satellite interviews, and call-in programs. The most significant distinguishing feature between the two (other than the fact that sound bites vary in length from a few words to a maximum of 12 seconds and live interviews can be two, three, five or ten minutes in length) is that the audience will not hear the questions asked during sound bite interviews.

To effectively manage sound bite interviews, spokespeople need to create self-contained snippets of information to respond to each question or series of questions asked by the reporter. Each of these snippets will contain the question, the answer, and the message in one tight package. This is represented by the Figure 13.3.

SOUND BITE

A sound bite is a short quote from a spokesperson that is inserted into a story for radio or television, most often in a newscast. Sound bites worldwide average 8 to 12 seconds in length.

Pause — Question, Answer & One Key Message — Stop

Figure 13.3

A sound bite is a short piece of information from a spokesperson that is inserted into a story for radio or television, either in a newscast or some type of feature program. Sound bites can be up to 12 seconds in length. They are rarely longer. Most often, they are shorter. If you really want to improve your perspective on how short sound bites can be, watch a couple of newscasts on television with your closed captioning feature switched on. Some are as short as five or six words.

You should approach sound bite interviews with the goal of creating self-contained units of information for each question or series of questions asked. These units of information should be complete to the point that they stand on their own. This is important because the audience will not hear the questions asked. They will only hear your answer.

To be successful with this particular challenge, you need to pause, re-state the question, and answer it (or vice versa), weave in one appropriate and directly related message, and stop talking (P-A/R-W-S).

In many cases, the reporter will ask you more than one question at a time before allowing you to answer. After asking one or more questions, the reporter will put a microphone in front of you and await your answer. Remember that the end audience, even in a media scrum, will probably not hear the questions asked. These are almost always left out of the final story. You must take the time to think before you talk.

Pausing before answering also helps from a technical perspective. In the editing suite, they will be looking for a clean sound bite, which they can insert into the story with minimal editing. Pausing helps this process. It also helps ensure that the microphone is in place before you start speaking. If the microphone is still moving toward you when you start talking, that sound bite will not be used.

How long can you pause? In reality, as long as you need to in order to think before talking. During that thought process, you're going to create the self-contained piece of information. You repeat this process for each question or series of questions asked.

It's important to recognize that you restate the question. You do not re-ask it. Here are a couple of examples to give you an idea of how this process can unfold:

Question:	Do you understand how to answer and restate the question?
A/R:	Yes, I understand how to answer and restate the question.
R/A:	I understand how to answer and restate the question, yes.
Question:	Aren't call centre jobs a bunch of low-paying, dead-end jobs?
A/R:	No, call centre jobs are neither low-paying nor dead-end.
Question:	Do you think it's fair that securities investigators have camped out at your institution?

A/R-W:	Yes, we do think it's fair that securities investigators have borrowed office space here (message) because this will help us balance the needs of their investigation while protecting client privacy.
Question:	Will you need to protect client privacy hamper the investigation?
A/R-W:	No, our need to protect client privacy will not hamper the investigation because we will ensure that investigators obtain the information outlined in the warrant they're serving.

As you can see, where sound bites are needed, the spokesperson restates and answers the question for each question or series of questions asked. Where the reporter uses prejudicial language while asking a question, the spokesperson has the right to change that prejudicial language while answering and restating the question (i.e., "camped out" became "borrowed office space"). However, in one example the negative phrase "low-paying, dead-end jobs" is actually repeated. In this case, it is repeated to reduce the reporter's ability to actually use the phrase in a negative connotation elsewhere in the story. The entire sound bite could be: "No, call centre jobs are not low-paying, dead-end jobs. In fact, a number of our vice presidents started their careers at our call centre."

In live broadcast interviews, whether played live to air or recorded and played back later, the audience hears questions and answers together with minimal editing or no editing at all. Whether for television or radio, this format is designed to emulate a conversation between the spokesperson and the interviewer and/or other guests and callers. It's important that you answer questions. If you don't, you won't fool anyone. If your decision making is reasonable, rational, and ethical (i.e., consistent with the concepts discussed in managing polarization), you should have no fear of the interviewer steering the shape, context, and dimension of that story. That is, after all, their job. Your job is to help them do their job while you do yours.

This is the most challenging of all interviews, and is slightly different from the other challenges we've discussed. The first difference is that you cannot pause much during live interviews. In fact, if you do, you'll antagonize the interviewer. He or she will not want much "dead air" after questions are asked. As the interviewer is asking the question, therefore, you must already be forming the answer. While you're doing this, you must still make sure you know what you're answering.

In general, a live interview is a situation in which the audience gains an entire perception of you and your ability to answer questions. This can potentially work for and against you. It can work for you because it is difficult to take any answer or remark that you provide out of context. Every aspect of the context is in plain view. However, therein lies the danger. If you sidestep, waffle, or evade, that is also in plain view. You may get away with it from time to time, but you can't fool everyone forever. Make no mistake, if you don't answer the question, the audience will recognize that fact and your ability to change opinions will be limited.

It is also extremely difficult to answer questions with one word during a live interview, but the answer to the question should be one of the first things out of your mouth. Be prepared to provide a bit of additional context to your answer. Having said this, however, keep your answers relatively short. When you've provided some context, stop talking. The interviewer will undoubtedly ask another question.

Strategically, your job is to find the balance that not only has you communicating through the reporter to the audiences important to your organization, but enables you to also communicate to the reporter and answer his or her questions. Indeed, the only time you should focus exclusively on key messages is when you are forced to take a defensive position and have exhausted all other options. In such situations, simply repeat your message, regardless of the question asked. In all other cases, however, balancing what the reporter is attempting to achieve with what your organization hopes to communicate will lead to enhanced, sustainable strategic outcomes.

Defensive Strategies

It is important to manage risk during exchanges with journalists. But before we can delve into that topic in greater detail, it is important to recognize that there are four specific priorities that all spokespeople should embrace. In descending order of importance, they are:

1. Protect yourself.
2. Protect your organization.
3. Answer questions.
4. Weave in messages.

It makes sense that the first priority should be to protect yourself. Nobody wants to commit a career limiting move as a result of an interview with reporters. Closely intertwined with this is the need to protect the organization the spokesperson represents. No organization accepts a media interview with the intent of damaging its reputation. In the vast majority of cases, protecting yourself and the organization are inextricably linked; when you do one, you almost certainly do the other.

> **FOUR PRIORITIES OF A SPOKESPERSON**
>
> 1. Protect yourself.
> 2. Protect the organization.
> 3. Answer questions.
> 4. Convey messages.

When it comes to the third priority, answering questions, it's interesting to note that this priority is P-A-S, which we discussed earlier, is actually your primary defensive strategy in all situations. Pausing, answering, and stopping actually enable spokespeople to protect themselves and their organization. This concept may seem counterintuitive, but to understand it, consider what happens when a lawyer prepares a witness to give evidence in a court of law.

The lawyer provides advice that has stood the test of time. When asked a question, the witness is counseled to pause and think before saying anything. In that pause, the witness will be encouraged to carefully examine the specific question that was asked. If the witness is unsure of what's being asked, he or she will ask for clarification before answering.

Next, the witness will answer that question and that question only. He or she will not consider the 50 or 60 questions that could precede the actual question asked, nor will the witness think about the 200 or 300 questions that could follow. Witnesses are taught to focus on one question at a time.

After answering the question, the witness will be taught to immediately stop talking and wait for the next question to be asked. In other words, the witness is told to pause, answer, and stop. This is the most important skill to learn prior to dealing with journalists, and is something we've discussed a number of times in this chapter.

P-A-S is important to helping journalists achieve their win, but it also serves double duty as a defensive strategy. Do lawyers suggest that witnesses pause, answer, and stop because the lawyer wants them to damage their credibility? No, lawyers want witnesses to protect their credibility. Do lawyers counsel witnesses to pause, answer, and stop because they want them to damage the case, in a bold attempt to increase billable hours? No, lawyers want their witnesses to protect the case and/or the organization.

Therefore, by pausing, answering, and stopping, witnesses can protect themselves and their organizations in a court of law, which is arguably one of the most difficult question-and-answer environments that exist. If this advice works well in that environment, wouldn't it also work well to pro-tect spokespeople and their organizations in the court of public opinion? It will and it does.

Your job as a spokesperson is to balance priority 3 and priority 4. In other words, answer questions and find places in which to weave in mes-sages. And remember, messages should be woven in, not driven home.

There are four basic defensive strategies of which you should be aware. Not every journalist is out to portray the spokesperson or organization in a negative light, but even the best journalists can inadvertently misquote a spokesperson in a way that causes anxiety for the spokesperson and/or their organization.

The first defensive strategy is P-A-S. This should be your first line of defense during any interview, regardless of whether with print or broad-cast journalists. With print reporters, P-A-S keeps answers shorter. This reduces the context provided to reporters, and reduces the risk of being quoted out of context. It also reduces the risk of being misunderstood. P-A-S enables the reporter to better understand the issue or topic under discussion during the interview.

With broadcast journalists, P-A-S is an excellent defensive strategy, re-gardless of whether the journalist is seeking a sound bite or you are en-gaged in a live interview. You can use it to influence the journalist's line of questioning away from dangerous or inflammatory subject areas.

If you're being interviewed for a sound bite and the reporter asks a particularly inflammatory question that is designed to goad a response, you can pause, answer, and stop, thereby reducing the risk of providing reporter something he or she can use to portray you in an unflattering light.

And you don't need to get caught up in finding a clever answer. The clas-sic example is something like: "When did you stop beating your spouse?" In reality, you could pause and say: "I never started." Another example is if the journalist asks: "Is there mismanagement at your organization?" Again, you can pause, answer "no" and stop talking. In both cases, the journalist cannot complain that you did not answer the question. They may com-plain that you did not provide a juicy sound bite for the six o'clock news, but that's their problem, not yours.

The same concept applies to live interviews, which includes panel in-terviews, call-in shows, and any other format in which the audience hears questions and answers together with minimal editing or no editing at all. By using short answers, you can modify the interviewer's behavior. If the interviewer asks an inflammatory question and you honestly answer it in less than five words, he or she will realize that to have an entertaining show, questions will need to focus on a different topic area.

A second defensive strategy is to challenge prejudicial language in the reporter's question. For example, suppose you are a petroleum refinery manager. A journalist drives out to your facility and, during an interview, asks: "Do you pollute?" This is a situation in which you do not want to pause, answer, and stop because the honest answer to the question is "yes." Every petroleum refinery pollutes, and so do its products, but you do not want to be quoted as the spokesperson who says so. In theory, however, a journalist who drives a vehicle out to a refinery to conduct an interview also pollutes (although you would not want to point that out during the interview!).

By challenging prejudicial language, you would simply ask the reporter: "What do you mean by pollute?" In most cases, the journalist will clarify the term in a way that you can provide an acceptable answer. Once that happens, answer the question, stop talking, and wait for the next question.

There is a caution here. If you challenge every word or phrase that the journalist uses, you will not develop a strong working relationship with that journalist. They will become frustrated, and their frustration could lead to them to think: "So you think I'm not precise with the language I use? Wait until the article is published. I'm sure you won't argue with my precision at that point."

DEFENSIVE STRATEGIES

1. P-A-S.
2. Challenge prejudicial language.
3. Ask and answer.
4. Stay on message.

The third defensive strategy you can apply is ask and answer. You simply turn the journalist's original question into a series of questions and ask and answer them yourself. For example, let's suppose you challenge the term pollute in the previous question and the journalist simply asks the same question again: "Do you pollute?"

"Does effluent leaves this facility? Yes. Is that effluent carefully monitored? Yes. Does the effluent leaving this facility ever exceed strict government regulations? No. Would we inform the community if it ever does? Yes."

The caveat with this approach is that the answers must be truthful. In the case earlier, you had better be certain that you would inform the community if effluent ever did exceed environmental regulations. Quite frankly, the journalist who asked the original question should be at the top of your list if a leak does occur in the future.

Finally, if all else fails, you can stay on message and keep repeating that defensive message, regardless of the question asked. You could respond with: "The effluent leaving this facility is carefully monitored and never exceeds strict environmental regulations."

This is where staying on message belongs, as the last choice of a number of defensive strategies. It should never be used as a tactic to "get the word out," nor should it be used as a way to tell someone—a reporter or anyone else, for that matter—what's really important during an exchange.

Key Takeaways

1. To strategically prepare to deal with reporters, it's important to know which medium you are addressing. The best way to divide media is along the lines of communication traditions we've had for thousands of years: literacy and orality. Literacy is the written word; orality is the spoken word. Once you divide journalists along those lines, you can better understand how to prepare for interviews and meet their need to manage information.
2. The skill of answering questions is the most important skill to develop if you hope to protect yourself and strategically manage exchanges with journalists to win-win outcomes. Within that, you must learn to stop talking when you answer questions. If you are unable to pause, answer, and stop, you are a ticking time bomb. It is only a matter of time before you are misquoted or quoted out of context.
3. Strategic communication is about outcomes, not inputs. To be strategic, you must focus on specifically identifiable audiences and find ways to positively influence the attitudes, opinions and behaviors of those audiences. Constantly repeating a key message, regardless of how clever or appropriate it may be, is not strategic.
4. Finally, to protect yourself and your organization, there are a number of defensive strategies you can apply. The value of clear, succinct answers cannot be overstated as a defensive strategy (and as a foundation on which effective communication can be constructed), but if you are unable to use this approach, the defensive strategies we've discussed here, whether used alone or in combination, should help you extricate yourself from virtually any difficult situation—provided, of course, that you have not crossed that fine line between spin and sin.

Glossary

Accuracy: Facts included in the stories are true, or as true as they could be at the time the journalist filed the story.

Broadcast media: Media outlets that use the spoken word (regardless of whether accompanied by visual images) to convey information relevant to the audiences they serve.

Deception: The process of communicating messages meant to mislead receivers of communication believe what the senders do not.

Issues: Unresolved problems that have the potential of escalating into a dispute.

Lie: Any intentionally deceptive message which is stated

Literacy: The human communication tradition of the written word, which encompasses print media.

Live interview: An interview in which the audience hears questions and answers with minimal editing or no editing at all, regardless of whether it's played live to air or has been sitting on a website for 10-plus years.

Media: Print and broadcast outlets that keep audiences informed—quickly, accurately, and to the best of their ability—on matters that significantly affect those audiences.

Orality: The human communication tradition of the spoken word, which encompasses broadcast media.

Polarization: The process of driving two sides further and further apart during a dispute.

Print media: Media outlets that use the written word to convey information relevant to the audiences they serve.

Sound bite: Small verbal quotes from a spokesperson, usually less than 12 seconds in length, that are inserted into a broadcast story.

Spin: Linking together facts in a way that attempts to portray an individual or organization in the best possible light.

References

Bergman, Eric. *At Ease with the Media.* San Francisco: International Association of Business Communicators (IABC), 2006a.

Bergman, Eric. *Media Training with Excellence: A Balanced Approach.* San Francisco: International Association of Business Communicators (IABC), 2006b.

Bok, Sissela. *LYING: Moral Choice in Public and Private Life.* New York: Vintage Books, 1999.

Grunig, James, editor. *Excellence in Public Relations and Communication Management.* Mahwah, NJ: Lawrence Erlbaum Associates, 1992.

Mearsheimer, John. "Lying in International Politics." Paper presented at the American Political Association conference, Chicago, Il, September 2004.

CHAPTER FOURTEEN

When People outside the Organization Need Information: Strategically Communicating with External Stakeholders

J. David Johnson and Anna Goodman Hoover

The Legacy of Silence: The Paducah Gaseous Diffusion Plant Case Study

Stakeholder relations at the Paducah Gaseous Diffusion Plant (PGDP) in western Kentucky exemplify what can happen when an organization attempts to replace former policies rooted in secrecy with increased informational openness. As of summer 2012, the PGDP is the only operating uranium enrichment facility in the United States. For almost 60 years, the plant has produced fuel—initially for military reactors and nuclear weapons and, later, for commercial reactors. The plant was owned and operated by the United States Department of Energy (DOE) until 1992, when its operations were leased to the United States Enrichment Corporation. However, DOE retains management of the site's cleanup, infrastructure, hazardous wastes, and environmental restoration.

In 1988, samplings of private drinking wells on properties adjacent to the plant revealed traces of both the radioactive isotope technetium-99 and the industrial degreaser trichloroethylene. Subsequent testing also found contaminants in nearby creeks. As a result, the U.S. Environmental Protection Agency added the plant to its National Priorities List of Superfund sites in 1993. DOE assumed responsibility for cleaning up the site and for supplying safe, potable water to residents whose properties had been contaminated.

As Slovic, Flynn, and Layman (1991) have discussed, only in recent years has DOE revealed numerous instances of past waste mishandling at many nuclear facilities. The PGDP is one such facility. For decades, internal concerns were raised about worker radiation exposures and environmental impacts at the plant; however, DOE was not forthcoming

---

to its stakeholders about these concerns. As evidence of mismanagement continued to mount, DOE Secretary Bill Richardson issued a formal apology to employees in 1999 for the agency's concealment of information about exposures and potential impacts (Bruce and Becker 2007).

Successful organizations must maintain good relationships with a variety of external stakeholders. Successful managers, therefore, must evaluate the needs of clients, shareholders, regulatory agencies, the media, and other constituencies frequently, weighing whether, when, and how to meet these needs. Often, stakeholder demands center around the exchange of information and, more specifically, around access to accurate, timely, and relevant reports about the organization itself.

What happens when an organization with a history of providing minimal information to information-hungry stakeholders, such as PGDP, attempts to adapt its policies for increased disclosure? This already challenging process is further complicated in the PGDP case, and in many other quasi-governmental/private partnerships (e.g., Freddie Mac), with blurring organizational boundaries and confusion as to who are stakeholders, actors, regulators, and often, among private investors, guarantors of last resort. Frequently, the organization's transition toward a more responsive model is not a smooth one.

When stakeholders try to make sense of an organization's actions within a broader context, they must rely upon past experiences to assess what is possible within a given circumstance. Having neither direct nor immediate knowledge of internal organizational workings, individuals use what they know of an organization's past actions to assess the motivations for and appropriateness of current organizational actions. This sense-making process helps individuals determine the seriousness of a situation, choose how to react to the situation, and interpret the situation as it changes. Thus, yesterday's organizational actions directly bear upon today's stakeholder decisions, including whether to rely upon information provided by the organization itself or to seek additional information elsewhere, possibly from inaccurate and/or unfriendly sources. If the organization's past actions have indicated an unwillingness to provide credible, timely information, returning the relationship to a positive state can be a long, arduous task.

As this volume details, organizations interact with their external environments in a number of ways. In this chapter, we will focus on how key external stakeholders, especially government officials and investors, obtain information they need from organizations.

Stakeholder Relationships

Reflecting classic approaches to organizations, before modern system theories emphasized the open boundaries of organizations, management tended to focus exclusively on internal operations. The legacy of this tradition has been a lack of transparency and the general lack of accessibility to internal organizational information. In today's technology-driven world, in-depth organizational information can be provided with great ease across multiple channels; however, external stakeholder wishes may conflict directly with an organization's willingness to supply such information. In terms of data sharing, yesterday's inward organizational gaze has been supplanted, to some extent, by today's concerns that sharing certain information could threaten the intellectual property rights of organizations, suggest insider trading issues, create security threats, and/or result in legal liabilities. Such concerns greatly inhibit truly participative relations with key stakeholders.

As organization-stakeholder relations have become more dynamic and complex, managers and scholars alike have had to rethink the classic paradigm. Today, stakeholder satisfaction is widely accepted as a key to organizational success. The last 30 years have seen the formation of new types of organizational coalitions to develop innovative products and services, while modern logistics models focus on ever-closer relationships between organizations and their suppliers. These shifts have been reflected in the dramatic growth of outsourcing and the use of private contractors who often are quasi-employees. Recent controversies at Federal Express and elsewhere illustrate some of the challenges associated with such changes. As in the Paducah case, these quasi-governmental organizations often increase the complexity of stakeholder information seeking.

Organizations are beginning to realize the benefits of closer stakeholder relationships in a number of other areas. New ideas and applications have been both proposed and developed by customers themselves. Work forces have been expanded with volunteers, including citizen scientists who help leverage scant resources by conducting such activities as environmental sampling for state agencies and other nonprofit organizations.

> In the face of budget cuts, the Michigan Department of Natural Resources has activated its publics to help maintain hiking trails, track wildlife, and so on. Departments of Transportation across the country have established adopt-a-highway programs that illustrate the willingness of individuals and organizations to work together toward mutual goals.

The citizen movement provides another strong example of the shift in stakeholder involvement, with individuals attempting to influence policy and practice at a number of levels. Citizen journalists, including online bloggers and community radio practitioners, present their work to increasingly large audiences, while citizen scientists who do not agree with organizational and/or governmental assertions often conduct their own testing and analyses, reaching and publicizing independent conclusions. Such individual efforts have expanded into the public relations arena, as well, with individuals using the Internet, and especially social media, to promote their own efforts and causes, sometimes leading to the creation and expansion of viral marketing campaigns. Reciprocity norms in the sharing of information are essential to modern stakeholder relations (Tangpong, Li, and Johns 2010).

In the face of such fluid boundaries, the maintenance of stakeholder relationships remains a key issue for organizational management. Stakeholder concerns cut across public-private and corporate-nonprofit sectors, with the mediating role of information transfer from organization to stakeholder at the crux of the relationship. Therefore, managers must choose whether, when, and how to meet the information demands of key stakeholders.

Stakeholder Identity Orientations

The first step toward making such important decisions is to answer two very important questions: (1) who is perceived as a legitimate stakeholder, and (2) to what extent should legitimate stakeholder information needs be proactively addressed? These questions are intimately bound to an organization's adoption of one of three identity orientations: individualistic, relational, or collectivistic (Basu and Palazzo 2008).

In individualistic organizations, decision making is guided by self-interest (Basu and Palazzo 2008). Managers take a pragmatic approach to identifying legitimate primary stakeholders, whose needs are addressed chiefly when there is a direct threat to the organization or when some other organizational interest is served. The relative number of acknowledged stakeholders for individualistic organizations tends to be somewhat smaller than those of other identity orientations, while the organization's willingness to provide information is somewhat reduced. Thus, both the target audience and the amount of information provided likely will be smaller for individualistic organizations.

In contrast, organizations that adopt relational identity orientations emphasize the establishment and maintenance of stakeholder partnerships (Basu and Palazzo 2008). Such an approach to stakeholder management indicates a somewhat broader view of the relationship between organizations and their stakeholders, implicitly recognizing their symbiotic nature. Relational organizations, therefore, are more likely to perceive a larger number of stakeholders as legitimate and have an increased willingness to provide information to those individuals and groups.

Finally, organizations with collectivistic identity orientations speak in "universal" terms, envisioning themselves as part of a broader network of interested parties (Basu and Palazzo 2008). These organizations incorporate pro-social goals into their agendas and see themselves as one of many stakeholders involved in larger processes. These commitments drive collectivistic organizations to provide information widely to broader publics.

Each of the three identity orientations points to different perceptions of stakeholder legitimacy and varying organizational willingness to provide information. This is not to say, however, that any single orientation is uniformly preferable to any other in the dissemination of information to stakeholders. For example, an individualistic organization that supplies limited information to stakeholders who have little desire for such information as design decisions may have less need to adapt its strategy than a collectivistic organization freely sharing vast amounts of product specifications with stakeholders who have little or no need for the information.

> One example of an information technology that did not fulfill its initial promise is the adoption and implementation of electronic health records. Despite considerable national policy interest, physicians and hospitals have proven to be slow adopters of the technology (Johnson 2009b). Seeing an opportunity several years ago, Google unveiled a personal health record that individuals could develop on their own. Although considerable effort, publicity, and partnerships with a variety of vendors converged around the product, Google recently abandoned the effort because of lack of public interest.

As interrelationships among organizations and individuals become increasingly complex, so too must organizations develop more complex ways of building and maintaining goodwill in those relationships. Organizations must be ever more attuned to their environment, especially when concerns arise about the potentially disruptive impact of some innovations on their operations and stakeholder relationships. Managers therefore face a daunting task in today's rapidly expanding, ever-changing information environment: providing the necessary amount of information to meet stakeholder needs. Since stakeholders must come to intelligent judgments about an organization and its operations based on the welter of facts, forecasts, gossip, and intuition that makes up their information environment, the general thrust of modern organizations is to be more responsive and adaptive to external stakeholders.

Moreover, Emery, and Trist (1965) and Lawrence and Lorsch (1967) note that as an organization's involvement with its environment grows, its internal structures become more complex, leading to front-back designs, facilitated by information technology (Galbraith 1995). Traditionally, organizations have taken a "field of dreams" approach—that is, "If we build it, they will come." Unfortunately, such endeavors rarely work well anywhere other than a big screen cornfield, as assumed stakeholder interest in information technology applications often does not materialize.

The recognition that stakeholder interest in specific business endeavors cannot be taken for granted represents just one of many forces driving increased organizational efforts to share information with external audiences. Pressure from government entities, sometimes spurred by various legal actions, including e-discovery, as well as legal requirements for open meeting and open records, and other statutory requirements have steered many organizations toward more proactive approaches to information provision.

Coorientation/Matching

It is important for organizations to effectively match their stakeholders' needs in the amount and types of information that they make available. One way to navigate complex organization-stakeholder relationships and the related impacts on information flow is to implement a coorientation approach. Originating in psychology to illustrate the relationship between psychological balance and mutual benefit (Heider 1946), coorientation models have been adopted by public relations professionals as tools for understanding relationships between organizations and their stakeholders (Broom 1977; Grunig and Hunt 1984). Since the model can be adapted to the specific challenges of organization-stakeholder information matching, organizations can identify their own placement within the four conditions of mismatch and match, thus better positioning themselves to adapt information strategies and improve stakeholder satisfaction.

Adversarialism, such as the initial history of the Paducah case, describes a coorientation condition in which stakeholder information needs are high, but organizational willingness to provide information is low. This condition arises when the organization determines that its internal need to keep information private outweighs its stakeholders' desire for more information. The Paducah facility supported an industry that was born during wartime, with the earliest applications of the technology appearing as weaponry and military reactors; thus, a high level of secrecy was perceived as vital to national security. Other, somewhat less extreme, reasons that managers sometimes give for withholding information from stakeholders include fear of external sanctions, potential legal actions, or loss of proprietary data. When a lack of willingness to disclose information is perceived, stakeholders can become suspicious of organizational motives for "concealing" the information. When the organization is seen as an adversary rather than an ally, stakeholder satisfaction drops, increasing the chances of potential stakeholder abandonment and, ultimately, loss of organizational legitimacy.

Inundation describes the opposite condition, in which an organization provides vast amounts of information to stakeholders who have little desire for it. Inundation resembles adversarialism in exemplifying a motivation-driven approach to corporate social responsibility, with the organization placing its own wishes ahead of its stakeholders' needs. In the case of inundation, the organization has determined that its intrinsic desire for openness outweighs the external influence of low stakeholder needs. The excess of undesired information can lead stakeholders to "tune out," ignoring potentially important messages from the organization as the signal gets lost amidst noise.

The third coorientation state, apathy, describes a condition in which both stakeholder information needs and organizational willingness to provide information are low. From the organization's perspective, this match can result either from an internal organizational focus that ignores potential stakeholder information needs or from the belief that stakeholder information needs actually are low. While apathy can indicate a level of mutual contentment, organizations must be vigilant in performing stakeholder needs assessments. If stakeholder needs increase with no subsequent organizational response, the relationship could transition easily into adversarialism.

The fourth condition, satisfaction, arises when the organization has a strong willingness to meet stakeholders' high levels of information need. Organizations relying upon performance-driven approaches rooted in expectancy matching or stakeholder-driven approaches that examine the needs of external stakeholders have greater probability of achieving satisfaction. However, even the satisfaction condition holds potential challenges, as organizations must conduct frequent stakeholder needs assessments. If stakeholder needs decrease without an ensuing organizational response, the relationship could devolve into the inundation condition.

Those Who Seek: Needs of External Stakeholders

For this coorientation approach to work, managers must determine exactly who the organization's stakeholders are, thus helping identify what types of information are needed as stakeholder interests and information needs are closely coupled. In general, stakeholders support organizational functioning, whether by providing labor, financial support, a potential market, positive exposure, or some other function. Stakeholder typologies distinguish between primary stakeholders, whose role is essential to organizational survival, and secondary stakeholders, who are not essential to survival but whose actions, nevertheless, can affect the organization (Clarkson 1995).

While relations with internal stakeholders, such as employees, are covered in volume one of this set, this chapter's primary focus is stakeholders who are external to the organization. Among these key stakeholders are policymakers and government agencies who create and enforce laws that affect operations. In addition, organizations depend upon the investors who finance operations, as well as small-business and corporate partners who assist in jointly leveraging resources to meet common goals. Each of these stakeholder categories requires specific kinds of information at specific points in the life cycle of the organization—requirements that managers must determine when and how to meet.

How They Seek

"Efficiency requires members of the audience to be treated amorphously and to bend to the institution. Effectiveness requires that individuals be helped on their own terms" (Dervin 1980, 85).

Stakeholders who require information about an organization have a variety of options for gathering this information, many of which are provided directly by the organization itself. Frequently, the most immediately accessible source is the Internet. Organizational websites often go beyond superficial boilerplate overviews to include investor relations sections, complete with annual reports, investor news, and earnings reports. Many of these items, created by the organization itself, also are provided regularly to investors via surface and/or e-mail, especially for publicly held companies. Further, various regulatory agencies require the organization to create and submit detailed reports of operational matters ranging from financial activities to potential environmental impacts.

One challenge for organizations, however, is insuring that stakeholders use the informational materials that they provide. As noted previously in this chapter, the traditional internally focused management model has lent itself to an approach to information sharing that falls within the adversarialism section of the coorientation model; that is, organizations have provided little information to external stakeholders, leading to concerns about how forthcoming they really are and what "spin" they might be applying. Because individuals base their assumptions about present conditions on past experiences, such historical issues can lead to distrust of materials produced by organizations. Therefore, to create a holistic, unbiased picture of organizational operations, stakeholders often seek information about the organization from other sources, then integrate and analyze all of the collected information before making decisions.

Traditionally, managers have approached stakeholder communication via a one-way, top-down flow of communication. They have relied on mass media campaigns to reach large numbers of people efficiently. These authoritative dicta and the lack of interactivity possible through the preferred communication channels were meant to discourage or preempt, rather than stimulate, information seeking. Many approaches and assumptions of traditional media research often were implicit in this approach. Somewhat akin to mass media's historical bullet theory, stakeholders were thought to be a relatively passive, defenseless audience whose input was sought solely through surveys or focus groups to determine the best way of changing their minds and their subsequent behaviors.

> Bullet theory reflected early beliefs that messages from the mass media could be "shot" into a relatively defenseless and passive audience who could be easily influenced.

More contemporary approaches to stakeholder relations are likely to stress a dialogic view of external communication, with both parties initiating and attending to messages in turn. These views incorporate a much more specific role for information seeking, which in traditional views was almost totally ignored. Managers' most important role in these more modern perspectives is as stimulus or cue to action, identifying stakeholder concerns and helping define the agenda of the most important issues that stakeholders face. Thus, a critical role of managers is that of managing attention.

This approach suggests that a precursor to improved dialogue would be to increase the stakeholder's knowledge base by providing alternative information sources. Indeed, one objective of information campaigns should be to sensitize individuals to other sources of communication. For example, stakeholders can increase their information seeking through the use of apps that provide corporate intranet data to mobile devices, thereby increasing the access of outsiders to what has traditionally been internal information. Today's external stakeholders have access to package tracking, reservation data, and other information that were previously the sole domain of those within the organization. Acquainting individuals with sources that are relevant and useful for their immediate purposes is a critical first step to developing better stakeholder information-seeking habits.

Tactics

In some ways, stakeholders are like organizational newcomers, in that they often have to uncover for themselves, using various tactics, what an organization is really like. Thus, discussions of external stakeholder information seeking can be informed by recent research lines related to information seeking by organizational newcomers, especially during organizational entry or job changing (Ashford, Blatt, and VandeWalle 2003). Of particular interest have been the tactics that these individuals use to uncover information about task, cultural, and other expectations that an organization might have (Miller and Jablin 1991). A newcomer to an organization often is confronted with a vast array of information that s/he must make sense of to determine appropriate behaviors. Active information seeking on the part of newcomers and stakeholders often is necessary because organizations frequently withhold information, whether inadvertently or purposively.

The vast array of information that newcomers or stakeholders are exposed to, along with the gaps in provided information, can result in high levels of stakeholder uncertainty. As this uncertainty engenders uncomfortable feelings, stakeholders are driven to seek information that would reduce it. In doing so, they may be doubly vexed because inexperienced information seekers may not know what tactics are appropriate or useful. As a result, their information seeking also may be more thoughtful, with newcomers and stakeholders consciously weighing the efficacies of various strategies they might employ.

The most obvious strategy, and seemingly the most efficient, is to ask *overt questions* on the topic of interest. A new investor, therefore, may ask what the expected return is. This strategy is more likely to be used when individuals feel comfortable with a situation—when they want a direct, immediate, and authoritative reply. Individuals may feel uncomfortable asking direct questions if they perceive others will view them as constantly pestering for information or if the question reveals more about their own inexperience and/or ignorance of the topic than they want others to know. Questioning also involves selecting a target for the question, which in itself may be a difficult choice. For example, would it be wiser to approach the investor relations officer or to ask a relative or friend who works for the firm? Similarly, there is the risk that a question, such as "Are we tanking?" could result in a negative answer that both parties would like to avoid.

Indirect questions often are employed in cases where someone is uncomfortable. Such questions usually take the form of a simple declarative sentence or observation that is meant to solicit information, often disguised within an apparently casual conversation. For example, a statement like, "You seem to be incredibly busy—your business must really be thriving," could be a somewhat discrete attempt to validate organizational success.

Another, more dangerous, strategy that individuals might pursue is *testing limits*. For example, an individual who really wants to find out how an organization operates could engage in drop-in visits.

A less direct strategy is that of *observing*. In such cases, stakeholders can watch the actual behaviors of a target organization, weighing those actions against the organization's words. There are limits, however, to what a stakeholder can directly observe.

Beyond these well-established and documented information-seeking strategies relied upon by newcomers, such strategies as skimming, berry-picking, chaining, and monitoring key sources for developments also might pertain to the external stakeholder's information-seeking challenge (Johnson 2009a). Perhaps the most interesting of these options is browsing, because of its random, nonrational surface appearance.

> Blau (1955) classically found workers establishing occasions for information seeking by hanging out with others; merely being present at informal events. Thus, geographic proximity in places such as Silicon Valley can help stakeholders get a feel for the "buzz."

Browsing essentially involves scanning the contents of a resource base and is used as an early strategy in a search process or when someone is scanning his/her environment. A key element of browsing is preparedness to be surprised and to follow-up (Chang and Rice 1993). Browsing in social contexts often takes the form of informal networking. Casual group conversations, including gossip, may take on elements of browsing, with more intensive follow-ups on specific topics that interest the information seeker. Browsing is facilitated by accessibility, flexibility, and interactivity, which also can provide an occasion for the use of such other strategies as indirect questions.

While walking around, an information seeker might pause to "shoot the breeze" with others. This conversation will be of limited informational value if the stakeholder allows the other conversants to do all the talking. Instead, the information seeker must be prepared to ask neutral questions and to listen with care to responses.

> No one can go to the direct source of information regularly; there is not sufficient time. Instead, a stakeholder can use many of Burt's suggestions (1992) related to structural holes, developing a wide range of strategically located, nonredundant sources to provide the widest-possible view of the organization. In doing this, stakeholders also should develop sources of information external to the organization, such as the media, who can offer a more independent view of organizational operations. At the same time stakeholders are developing this breadth of ties, they should insure that there are sufficient redundant ties to provide alternative sources of information on critical issues.

The final newcomer strategy is to use a *third-party* intermediary within the organization to gather information. Thus, rather than approaching the chief financial officer, who would serve as a primary source, a stakeholder might ask questions of his/her administrative assistant, who can serve as a secondary source of information. This strategy is employed most often when a primary source is unavailable or when the seeker feels uncomfortable approaching him/her directly. The downside to this strategy is that the secondary source must be trustworthy and a true surrogate for the primary one. It helps to have key informants for particular domains of information. Traditionally, these individuals have been described as gatekeepers because of their role in filtering information, often in a condensed, understandable fashion.

Recognizing the effort and sophistication needed to satisfy their information needs, individuals often rely on intermediaries to conduct their searches for them. The increasing use of secondary information disseminators, or brokers, is really a variant on classic notions of opinion leadership (Katz and Lazarsfeld 1955). Opinion leadership suggests that ideas flow from the media to opinion leaders to less-active segments of the population. Opinion leaders not only serve a relay function, but they also provide social support information to individuals, reinforce messages by their social influence over them, and validate the authoritativeness of the information. Thus, opinion leaders both disseminate ideas and, because of the interpersonal nature of their ties, provide additional pressure to conform as well. However, these highly intelligent seekers also may create unexpected problems since they may create different paths and approaches to dealing with problems an organization may be having.

The emergence of the Internet as an omnibus source of information appears to have changed the nature of opinion leadership; both more authoritative sources, such as Bloomberg news feeds for financial information, and more interpersonal sources, such as advocacy groups supporting specific policies and practices, are readily accessible online. The risk, however, is that individuals can quickly become overloaded or confused in an undirected environment. In essence, while the goal may be the provision of great amounts of information to reduce uncertainty or to help bridge a knowledge gap, the actual effect can be increased uncertainty and, ultimately, a decreased sense of efficacy, inhibiting the desire to conduct future searches. A stakeholder literacy approach, then, would help people gain the skills to access, judge the credibility of, and effectively utilize a wide range of organizational information from multiple sources.

Increasingly, formal groups are becoming opinion leaders and information seekers for individuals. A big advantage of investor groups is their access to informal contacts. These contacts can provide critical information before it is available from more traditional sources. In addition, such groups can prepare someone psychologically for a more active and directed search for information. More and more, these formal groups, acting as crowd-sourced investors, support the everyday information needs of stakeholders.

The last half-century has seen the emergence of advocacy groups that support the needs of their individual members; such groups also may seek to change policies and practices, as well as societal reactions to their members, attempting to insure that sufficient resources are devoted to the needs of their groups. At times, these groups have agendas that do not necessarily coincide with an individual's need for information that might contrast with or directly oppose the advocacy group's goals. While the entrepreneurial broker is an individual's agent, advocacy groups need members to advance the group agenda. For example, while a mining company might downplay or omit environmental impact information in its corporate communications, an environmental organization advocating against certain types of mining might downplay or omit the company's economic impact information from its communications. Information literate stakeholders would be able to collect, assess, synthesize, and weigh these disparate types of information to support decision making related to the organization.

An example of the delicate balancing act that advocacy groups need to perform to keep their credibility with both the organizations they seek to influence and the stakeholders they represent can be found in American Association of Retired Persons' role in policy debates on cutting the budget deficit. Recently, to keep their credibility with government officials, AARP suggested that the organization might be receptive to some changes in Medicare and Social Security, much to the consternation of many whom they represent.

Given the amount and variety of information available on the Internet, some individuals have expressed concern that lay people may bypass organizational intermediaries in existing power structures. The notion of the citizen scientist, for example, has gained increased attention. Most compelling, however, has been how this informed-citizen movement is driving research. The Army of Women, a patient group that advocates for improvements in breast cancer research, exemplifies this trend by generating funds for clinical studies, enhancing participation in trials (particularly challenging in rare diseases), and garnering support for more trials.

Promoting Information Seeking

Johnson (1996, 1997) has summarized the basic approach to information seeking by individuals, with Case (2007) making very similar arguments in a more recent review. First, people seek out information that is the most accessible. Second, mere information access is of little utility without the proper information-seeking skills and training for successful retrieval. Third, people follow habitual patterns in their information seeking. Fourth, face-to-face interpersonal communication is *the* preferred mode of communication for information seeking. Therefore, the quality of an individual's interpersonal networks has important implications for information seeking; people want to consult others, such as opinion leaders, who have digested and evaluated an array of information (Johnson 2009a). Fifth, different types of persons use different sources of information; this point is reinforced by norms and standards of care that vary across professions (e.g., engineers vs. lawyers). Sixth and finally, individuals have cognitive limits on the amount of information that they can process, especially in short-term memory.

Managers in the current environment must effectively facilitate the flow of information to insure support for an appropriate information infrastructure that recognizes how stakeholders typically acquire information. Many organizations have realized that promoting information technologies advances strategic advantages, especially in enhancing quality, maintaining market share, and developing innovations. Indeed, it has become commonplace for almost all hospitals and managed care providers to have active information programs for their clients. Obviously, a key role for managers lies in facilitating and encouraging stakeholder attempts to seek and find information. This represents a significant shift in management priorities, as well as a major change in the way stakeholders are viewed.

Organizations increasingly attempt to shape the richness of their stakeholders' information fields. For example, some organizations provide access to corporate intranets, allowing customers to track purchases. This strategy removes barriers to the acquisition of information. Simple scanning of information on the web also can increase the knowledge base of individuals, making it possible for external stakeholders both to communicate more effectively with managers and to make more informed decisions about appropriate solutions to challenges. Creating richer information fields through such practices as "self-serving" in retrieving information from databases, for example, makes for a more informed stakeholder who is likely to consume less managerial time "being brought up to speed" on basic information.

In essence, an information architecture serves three data-related functions: storing, transporting, and transforming (Cash et al. 1994). Increasingly, the blending and integration of these functions is creating exciting opportunities for satisfying information needs. The benefits and possibilities are captured under the heading of informatics.

Databases may be thought of as those information repositories that are the key elements of an organization's memory. Essentially, databases provide a means for storing, organizing, and retrieving information. Electronic storage enhances the possibilities of linking various databases to create increasingly sophisticated searches. Shared databases are at the center of developing information systems, since they provide a common core of information. Traditionally, data storage has meant physical storage of information in filing systems; however, the exponentially growing volume of information has rendered paper-based systems increasingly unwieldy (Johnson 2009a). Modern conceptions of storage have broadened this function considerably to include verification and quality control of information entering a storage system. Once information has been stored, security systems, which bear directly on information-seeking possibilities, become very important. For example, who should have access to personal information, and how is such access granted? Security issues also involve developing and implementing means to insure that no one can tamper or change information residing in a database.

Data transport is the acquisition and exchange of information. The previously mundane world of data transmission has become the stuff of headline news, with innovative apps by Google, Apple, and other companies providing easier access to information that receives prime placement across major press outlets. Networks, like the Internet, usually combine enhanced telecommunication capabilities with (frequently database driven) software that allows linkage and exchange of information between users. The Internet's ability to provide easy access, both in terms of low cost and reduced barriers, and the user-friendliness of search software and associated applications have been exciting developments for information seekers. Telecommunication systems, such as fiber optic cables and satellite systems, provide the hardware that links individuals and provides enhanced access to systems, largely through the availability of various handheld devices. Telecommunication systems maintain communication channels (e.g., e-mail) through which information can be accessed and reported. Specifically, these systems enhance the information seeking of stakeholders by creating new channels for sending and receiving information, helping them filter this information, reducing their dependence on others, leveraging their time to concentrate on the most important tasks, and enhancing their ability for dealing with complexity.

Communication technologies, such as bulletin boards and discussion lists, permit sending messages to a communication space characterized by potential similarities of messages and communicators, rather than to specific individuals. Such developments enhance participation and access by allowing individuals who share similar interests to identify each other and communicate within the same electronic space.

These technologies represent a transition to more truly interactive, dialogic systems involving social media and Web 2.0. While Web 1.0, or the read-only Web, operated much as a traditional library that promoted more efficient searches and passive reading of available materials (Strecher 2008), Web 2.0 has increased interactivity tremendously. Users can create and share information via text, graphics, and video through a variety of social media applications (Sarasohn-Kahn 2008). These collaboratives promote greater knowledge transfer, concerted action, and greater voice when approaching policymakers for funding, regulation, and other objectives.

While the Internet remains the primary source of Web 2.0 applications for most individuals, some have suggested that a better label would be Interactive Communication, which would encompass personal digital assistants, mobile phones, computer tailored print materials interactive voice response, computer-driven kiosks, DVDs, and so on (Strecher

2008). Four types of interactivity are particularly relevant: user navigation, collaborative filters, human-to-human interaction, and expert systems (Strecher 2008). User navigation is somewhat analogous to searching
for information in a library. Collaborative filtering involves sophisticated
software written for identifying user behavior and linking individuals who
have similar preferences; this type of application is found on Amazon.
com, where recommendations are provided based on the purchases of others who have chosen similar products. Human-to-human interaction mediated by the web can take the form of information brokers or investor
services that include an instant messaging service, combining the best features of the Internet with traditional financial advisors.

The efforts of advocacy groups now can be more easily pooled as advances in information technology, social networking, and other information tools produce more informed consumers who can share information
with each other and whose collective knowledge may even exceed that
of some professionals. Such collectives can result in knowledge transfer,
greater voice, concerted action, and formal collaborations. These activities
are somewhat similar to the citizen scientists' movement in the hard sciences in which large numbers of participants observe, measure, and assess
phenomena with the assistance of the Internet and modern computing.
Accelerating these trends are a host of technology and decision-support
related advances, including enhanced access to authoritative web-based
information resources, personal decision aids, and social networking
capabilities.

The Internet has spawned many flexible information search and retrieval services that provide substantial benefits. Expert search engines,
such as those found in tailoring applications, try to accommodate the different learning and search styles of users, adapting approaches to specific
individuals. Messages might be screened, sorted, and prioritized based on
several categories: the urgency in which a response is needed, cognitive
domains (e.g., key words), social dimensions (e.g., more attention given to
friends, those higher in the hierarchy), future communication events (e.g.,
the agenda for an upcoming meeting), and so forth. Many corporate sites
now develop user profiles that keep abreast of self-defined areas of interest as relevant material is added to a database through such tools as RSS
feeds and Twitter. Such approaches combine both push, with controlled
messages delivered to mass audiences, and pull, with messages sought out
by audience members because of their inherent interests wherever they
might be. Twitter, for example, provides a perfect platform for announcing
new product developments, profit statements, and so on. Various IT tools
also are being developed for tracking and identifying different stakeholders and their interests (Chung, Chen, and Reid 2009).

Social networking services are primarily technology and software facilitators for people to form relationships with each other. Facebook, for example, describes itself as "a *social utility* that *connects you* with the people around you" (http://www.facebook.com/). Typically, social networks define a universe of users through directories. They also can define the types of relationships users would like to have with others. Users often are seen as members of particular communities, and in some applications, social networks facilitate the development of communities of practice around particular interests and activities, such as Yahoo! groups and such real-time interactive games as Scrabble and Farmville. Recent research in instructional communication has shown that such computer-based interactivity can increase the engagement levels of message recipients (Emmons et al. 2004).

The content features of these websites, especially in terms of facilitating the flow of complex information in such diverse forms as textual, graphic, visual, and so on, can greatly facilitate the flow of information. The social tagging of websites by various users on del.icio.us, for example, provides one method of sharing communally identified websites. Different technologies and platforms associated with the sites enhance the possibilities for interacting: babble, chat, blasts, blogging, discussion boards, e-mail, loops, pokes, likes, requests, reviews, shouts, tagging, and Track Back Ping are just a few of the ever-increasing number of ways to communicate online. These features have been associated with the development of Web 2.0, which encourages the development of collective intelligence through the democratic participation of users (Boulos and Wheeler 2007).

The integration of data storage and transport with sophisticated software offers unique opportunities for solutions that transcend the limits of individual information processing. Such applications are especially helpful for novices, but they also are a boon for experienced professionals who need to make decisions under pressure. To use a familiar example, a car's dashboard contains a number of instruments that help the driver use a complex system that interacts with its outside environment through an array of sensors. Some of the visual displays indicate that appropriate action needs to be taken quickly (e.g., a significant decline in oil pressure, or a rise in coolant temperature), others give feedback on current performance (e.g., miles per hour), while still others provide longer-term information (e.g., maintenance is required, oil life is diminishing). More modern vehicle dashboards also have inferential capabilities (e.g., projected range, miles per gallon, traffic avoidance) to provide more detail on particular areas of concern to drivers. To be useful, a careful balance must be struck between providing too much information, which may distract the driver from the task at hand, and too little. Careful thought must be given to what indicators really are critical to system performance. Extending the metaphor, an investor's personal web page could serve as a sort of dashboard, with a visual cue indicating that things had gone into the red zone, thus signaling the need for an immediate response, whether buying, selling, or following-up for additional information.

One method of fully engaging information seekers with computer technologies is to introduce interactivity, which Street and Rimal (1997) describe as computer technologies that allow stakeholders to access, control, and respond to relevant information. Information system designers thus may wish to encourage a state in which individuals feel that they are in the "groove," that is, that they are jamming with the information environment around them (Eisenberg 1990). People want to maximize their cognitive load, as well as their enjoyment (Marchionini 1992), and they do not like tasks or information systems that add to their frustration. Instead, they prefer systems that are intrinsically gratifying and that have an intuitive, game-like feel (Paisley 1993).

For example, people do not like two-step information systems that cite sources of information that they must later seek out. The concept of flow, which captures playfulness and exploratory experience, can encourage people to use new and unfamiliar information technologies. Flow theory, most associated with the work of Csikszentmihalyi, suggests that involvement in a flow state is self-motivating because it is pleasurable and encourages repetition (Trevino and Webster 1992). Thus, search engines that provide direct answers or hyperlinks work better than citing sources that someone needs to look up separately.

Traditional approaches have pushed targeting messages to particular audience segments. Audience segmentation breaks down the mass audience into groups that are as homogeneous within, and as different from, each other group as possible. Considerable evidence points to the importance of effective audience segmentation for the design and implementation of successful campaigns. With improved identification of audience knowledge and beliefs comes an increased ability to create messages that appeal to a specific group of stakeholders. Understanding the beliefs of message recipients is necessary at all levels, from crafting an effective message to its delivery by a salient source through an appropriate channel (Atkin 2001). Lack of specificity in audience targeting not only runs the risk of decreased message effectiveness but also may increase the potential for unintended effects, even promoting the opposite of the intended behavior through boomerang effects.

Organizations need to recognize the fundamentally different nature of various segments of their audience and develop different strategies to reach them. In segmenting stakeholders, organizations need to focus on the importance of different groups (e.g., who most needs to change?) and on their receptivity (e.g., who is most likely to be influenced) (Atkin 1992). This type of approach essentially seeks to understand the stakeholder so well that it sells itself by the mere provision of information. Classical segmentation has been done by demographic characteristics, taking a targeting approach.

In contrast to targeting that focuses on groups of individuals who share similar characteristics, tailoring focuses on individuals who have unique clusters of attributes. The utilization of tailored messages, which have been shown to be more effective than generic messages (Neuhauser and Kreps 2003), within new media interventions provides a fascinating avenue for exploration. There is evidence across a number of domains that tailoring is superior to nontailoring of messages for campaigns. This, in part, is based on the classic formulation that impact equals efficacy times reach, with tailoring argued to have both high efficacy and high reach (Noar, Banac, and Harris 2007). In broad form, tailoring involves the use of computer algorithms to match personalized messages designed to impact behaviors. Tailoring provides a means of generating interactive computer interventions to disseminate very specific messages to individual combinations of socioeconomic, ethnic, gender, interest, and other groups while maintaining the logistical and cost advantages typically provided by mass media outlets.

A tailoring approach focuses on the unique attributes of individuals and mimics some of the classic characteristics of interpersonal channels (Kukafka 2005; Noar, Pierce, and Black 2010). These systems use *personalization* by gathering specific information during assessment (e.g., name, age, and so forth); *feedback* by involving expert systems recommendations for the individual; and *adaptation* by involving the development of content packages tailored specifically to the person's information needs (Lustria et al. 2009). Message tailoring goes hand-in-hand with segmentation and has seen considerable advances over the last couple of decades, especially with the advent of new media and technologies that facilitate its application. At the same time that tremendous growth has occurred in terms of consumer tools for acquiring information, a concomitant increase has occurred in marketing and advertising these tools (Tomes 2010). The applications have demonstrated greater influence than classic mass media one-size-fits-all approaches. In part, this has been accomplished by the greater relevance of messages delivered to specific audiences (Strecher 2008).

In the Internet age, erroneous, incomplete, or biased information that is promoted and sustained in the blogosphere can pose a significant threat to an organization's relationships with its stakeholders and, ultimately, to its operations. Investors face growing problems with where to obtain objective information, since professional analysts often self-censor information. Conversely, factual and news-oriented blogs can serve as a valid means of disseminating comprehensive organizational information to stakeholders. More and more, traditional mailing lists for organizational press releases are being expanded to include bloggers and other citizen journalists.

Outcomes

> "Brains have difficulty processing all the relevant information—there is too much, it may not fit with expectations and previous patterns, and some of it may simply be too threatening to accept" (Mintzberg 1975, 17).

In the modern age, individuals are faced with three fundamental information-seeking problems: (1) they have more choices than ever before; (2) they have more sources of information regarding these choices; and (3) they increasingly receive information targeted at influencing their behavior rather than simply communicating facts (Marchionini 1992). Thus, stakeholders must constantly struggle with the question of where to invest their time and what to investigate, confronting the question of how much is enough for particular purposes.

Information pollution has become an increasing concern of even the popular press because the wealth of information stored on Internet resources creates some difficulty in determining the reliability of that information. Even when the sources are reliable, such as government agencies, information can be presented as "data dumps," with poor website navigability and a lack of user friendliness. Such situations limit stakeholders' ability to access and retrieve relevant data, potentially frustrating them and discouraging future information-seeking attempts. A related strategy that may be very effective for inhibiting information seeking is to drown people with information and then interpret it for them. There also is reason to be concerned about the commercial or self-serving motivations of many information providers. One unresolved area is who is liable for erroneous information on a database: the host of a website, the author of a message, or the person providing the information they have gleaned from the website to another? These trends suggest a need to revisit simplicity. There also is a need to think carefully about what information should be excluded from an individual's information processing.

All of the forgoing findings relate to the "costs" of information seeking compared to the value or benefit of the information sought, particularly as that information relates to decision making (March 1994). While more and more information can be produced and provided more efficiently, there is a concomitant increase in the costs of consuming (e.g., interpreting, analyzing) this information. The costs of information acquisition are many and include the psychological, the temporal, and the material. Many stakeholders appear to assume that having easily obtained information, no matter how incomplete or dubious, is preferable to expending additional effort to gather complete and valid information.

Costs have been articulated in various "laws" of information-seeking behavior. The classic law of "least effort" has been evoked to articulate why channels are chosen first that involve the least exertion. Mooers's law suggests an information source or system will be less desirable if the specific information it contains is deemed more painful or troublesome than the absence of that information (Johnson 2009a). In short, the costs of overcoming ignorance at times outweigh the gains. (And what is amazing is how low the costs are that establish absolute barriers to information seeking.) It is even possible, at least for particular topics, to be sated—that is, to have acquired enough information. Thus, there may be as many, if not more, reasons for not seeking as for seeking information.

All of this points to the benefits of organizations adopting easy-to-use push technologies that guide stakeholders, as well as using multiple channels to reach stakeholders. Following the traditional top-down approach to stakeholder communication, organizational websites provide one point of stakeholder exposure to information; however, unlike traditional media channels, such websites have dialogic capabilities. Organizations can use their official online presence to gather information from stakeholders, ranging from basic demographic data to concerns and priorities elicited through online surveys. Organizations also can implement social networking approaches to supplement these efforts, not only to provide information but also to build relationships with stakeholders, creating another arena in which the "temperature" of stakeholder information needs can be taken. Further, organizations can expand the recipients of official communications, such as press releases and annual reports, to include more nontraditional targets, including citizen journalists, respected and relevant blogs, and citizen science groups.

Conclusions

As made explicit earlier in this chapter, it is important that the information provided by organizations meets the perceived needs of stakeholders to the extent possible. Corporate monitoring of Twitter, advocacy groups, and sophisticated tracking of stakeholders and their requirements on the web is key for achieving appropriate coorientation (Chung et al. 2009). By providing the right amount of information to the right stakeholders, organizations can contribute to a state of shared satisfaction in the information exchange.

Returning to the case study detailed earlier, in compliance with federal laws and community right-to-know provisions, DOE has attempted in recent years to redress legacy trust issues with its stakeholders in a number of ways. Following the site's addition to the Superfund National Priorities List, DOE established the PGDP Citizens Advisory Board, or CAB, to assist the community in understanding technical information about the site. Both DOE and the CAB have conducted extensive public meetings about a number of historical and current matters, including property contamination around the facility and options for future waste disposal after the plant is decommissioned. In addition, DOE created an Environmental Information Center in Paducah, featuring access to administrative records, reports, and other information about the facility. Many site-specific reports also are available through the information center's website (http://www.pppo.energy.gov/pad_eic.html).

Despite such efforts, the tensions created by decades of adversarialism remain. As recently as 2006, one representative of a local stakeholder group wrote a letter to the then chair of the House of Representatives Subcommittee on Energy and Water Development, decrying DOE's "shroud of secrecy (KRCEE 2007)." Even more recently, researchers in Paducah who asked local stakeholders to identify credible PGDP information sources were told by numerous individuals that DOE is no longer a trustworthy source of information for many in that community (KRCEE 2011).

It seems clear from the PGDP case study that DOE's previous unwillingness to share relevant information with stakeholders who needed it still has negative ramifications long after the organization has attempted to alter its information sharing policies. Perhaps, to borrow a cliché, the best defense against such a contentious situation is a good offense—that is, an organization should adopt an information-matching approach to avoid adversarialism from the outset, providing the best information it has in the quantities desired by its stakeholders. Otherwise, countless resources and extensive time could be required to repair stakeholder relationships, if, in fact, those relationships can be repaired at all.

When a mismatch occurs between available organizational information and stakeholder needs, the resulting states of adversarialism or inundation can reduce stakeholder satisfaction and potentially harm the organization's operations. Even when information supply and demand are matched, as in the low-low apathy state, there is the potential for relationship devolution if either stakeholder needs or organizational willingness to supply information changes without a complementary shift from the other party. Thus, it is key that managers continually scan their organizations' stakeholders to determine the desired level of information sought, along with making internal determinations about what information can be safely shared. In doing so, organizations can support the establishment of information architectures that meet stakeholder information needs while also satisfying organizational strategic goals. Often this is a very delicate balancing act for organizations.

Key Takeaways

1. Managers in our new information environment must effectively facilitate the flow of information by insuring support for an appropriate information infrastructure that recognizes how stakeholders typically acquire information. They must understand where stakeholders are by applying a coorientation framework, bringing them up to speed, and having them self-serve, while tailoring information as much as possible.
2. Stakeholder information, and the means of providing it, is a strategic asset that should be systematically incorporated into managerial planning. This resource-based strategy can provide organizations with unique advantages (Tangpong et al. 2010).
3. Managers need to lobby federal and state governments to develop and maintain critical information infrastructures, such as publicly available databases. Corporations can substantially exploit existing government databases and have a vested interest in helping to maintain them.
4. Organizations must be ever vigilant against threat-rigidity relations with their environment (Staw, Sandelands, and Dutton 1981). The tendency to circle the horses and withdraw behind walls is illustrated by early information-disclosure decisions in Paducah. Such approaches play directly into the creation of adversarial relations with stakeholders, leading to external concerns about an organization's perceived secrecy and trustworthiness. In the absence of timely and relevant information from the organization, stakeholders are likely to attempt to fill that vacuum with information from other sources that may directly oppose the organization's goals.

Glossary

Brokers: Third parties who stand between parties in transactions, providing services that would normally be unavailable to them.

Coorientation: A type of model developed in psychology and public relations that predicts the nature of harmony or conflict relationships based upon matching the motivations and actions of the parties.

Information architecture: An information architecture serves three data-related functions: storing, transporting, and transforming.

Information seeking: Purposive acquisition of information from selected information carriers.

Information-seeking tactics: Approaches that individuals use to uncover information about task, cultural, and other concerns.

Opinion leadership: The social process where ideas flow from the media through opinion leaders to less active segments of the population.

Stakeholders (external): Individuals or groups who are either impacted by or who can impact an organization's operations.

Strategic communication: Purposive attempts to achieve identified outcomes that are important for an organization's performance.

References

Ashford, Susan J., Ruth Blatt, and Don VandeWalle. "Reflections on the Looking Glass: A Review of Research on Feedback Seeking Behavior in Organizations." *Journal of Management* 29 (2003): 773–99.

Atkin, Charles K. "Designing Persuasive Health Messages." In *Effective Dissemination of Clinical and Health Information,* edited by Lee Sechrest, Thomas E. Backer, Everett M. Rogers, Timothy F Campbell and Mary L. Grady, 99–107. Rockville, MD: Agency for Health Care Policy and Research, 1992.

Atkin, Charles K. "Theory and Principles of Media Health Campaigns." In *Public Communication Campaigns,* edited by Ronald E. Rice and Charles K. Atkin, 49–68. London: Sage, 2001.

Basu, Kunal, and Guido Palazzo. "Corporate Social Responsibility: A Process Model of Sensemaking." *Academy of Management Review* 33, no. 1 (2008): 122–36.

Blau, Peter M. *The Dynamics of Bureaucracy: A Study of Interpersonal Relations in Two Government Agencies.* Chicago: University of Chicago Press, 1955.

Boulos, Maged N. Kamel, and Steve Wheeler. "The Emerging Web 2.0 Social Software: An Enabling Suite of Sociable Technologies in Health and Health Care Education." *Health Information and Library Journals* 24 (2007): 2–23.

Broom, Glen M. "Coorientational Measurement of Public Issues." *Public Relations Review* 3 (1977): 110–18.

Bruce, Alan S., and Paul J. Becker. "State-Corporate Crime and the Paducah Gaseous Diffusion Plant." *Western Criminology Review* 8, no. 2 (2007): 29–43.

Burt, Ronald S. *Structural Holes: The Social Structure of Competition.* Cambridge, MA: Harvard University Press, 1992.

Case, Donald O. *Looking for Information.* 2nd ed. New York: Academic Press, 2007.

Cash Jr., James I., Roger G. Eccles, Nitin Nohria, and Richard L. Nolan. *Building the Information Age Organization: Structure, Control, and Information Technologies.* Boston: Irwin, 1994.

Chang, Shan-ju, and Ronald E. Rice. "Browsing: A Multidimensional Framework." In *Annual Review of Information Science and Technology,* edited by Martha E. Williams, 231–76. Medford, NJ: Learned Information, 1993.

Chung, Wingyan, Hsinchun Chen, and Edna Reid. "Business Stakeholder Analyzer: An Experiment of Classifying Stakeholders on the Web." *Journal of the American Society for Information Science and Technology* 60, no. 1 (2009): 59–74.

Clarkson, Max B. E. "A Stakeholder Framework for Analyzing and Evaluating Corporate Social Performance." *Academy of Management Review* 20, no. 1 (1995): 92–117.

Dervin, Brenda. "Communication Gaps and Inequities: Moving toward a Reconceptualization." In *Progress in Communication Sciences,* edited by Brenda Dervin and Melvin J. Voight, 74–112. Norwood, NJ: ABLEX, 1980.

Eisenberg, Eric M. "Jamming: Transcendence through Organizing." *Communication Research* 17 (1990): 139–64.

Emery, Fred, and Eric Trist. "The Causal Texture of Organizational Environment." *Human Relations* 18 (1965): 21–32.

Emmons, Karen M., Mei Wong, Elaine Puleo, Neil Weinstein, Robert Fletcher, and Graham Colditz. "Tailored Computer-Based Cancer Risk Communication: Correcting Colorectal Cancer Risk Perception." *Journal of Health Communication* 9 (2004): 127–41.

Galbraith, Jay R. *Designing Organizations: An Executive Briefing on Strategy, Structure, and Process.* San Francisco: Jossey-Bass, 1995.

Grunig, James E., and Todd T. Hunt. *Managing Public Relations.* New York: International Thomas Publishing, 1984.

Heider, Fritz. "Attitudes and Cognitive Organization." *Journal of Psychology* 21 (1946): 107–12.

Johnson, J. David. *Cancer-Related Information Seeking.* Cresskill, NJ: Hampton Press, 1997.

Johnson, J. David. *Information Seeking: An Organizational Dilemma.* Westport, CT: Quorom Books, 1996.

Johnson, J. David. *Managing Knowledge Networks.* Cambridge, UK: Cambridge University Press, 2009a.

Johnson, J. David. "Profiling the Likelihood of Success of Electronic Medical Records." In *The Culture of Efficiency: Technology in Everyday Life,* edited by S. Kleinman, 121–41. New York: Peter Lang, 2009b.

Katz, Elihu, and Paul F. Lazarsfeld. *Personal Influence: The Part Played by People in the Flow of Mass Communications.* New York: The Free Press, 1955.

KRCEE. *Community Visions for the Paducah Site.* Lexington: Kentucky Research Consortium for Energy and the Environment, 2011.

KRCEE. *Property Acquisition Study for Areas near the Paducah Site.* Lexington: Kentucky Research Consortium for Energy and the Environment, 2007.

Kukafka, Rita "Tailored Health Communication." In *Consumer Health Informatics: Informing Consumers in Improving Healthcare,* edited by Deborah Lewis, Gunther Eysenbach, Rita Kukafka, P. Zoe Stavri and Holly B. Jimison, 22–33. New York: Springer, 2005.

Lawrence, Paul R., and Jay W. Lorsch. *Organization and Environment: Managing Differentiation and Integration.* Boston, MA: Harvard Business School, 1967.

Lustria, Mia L. A., Juliann Cortese, Seth M. Noar, and Robert L. Glueckauf. "Computer-Tailored Health Interventions Delivered over the Web: Review and Analysis of Key Components." *Patient Education and Counseling* 74 (2009): 156–73.

March, James G. *A Primer on Decision Making: How Decisions Happen.* New York: Free Press, 1994.

Marchionini, Gary. "Interfaces for End User Information Seeking." *Journal of the American Society for Information Science* 43 (1992): 156–63.

Miller, Vernon D., and Fredric M. Jablin. "Information Seeking During Organizational Entry: Influences, Tactics, and a Model of the Process." *Academy of Management Review* 16 (1991): 92–120.

Mintzberg, Henry. *Impediments to the Use of Management Information.* New York: National Association of Accountants, 1975.

Neuhauser, Linda, and Gary L. Kreps. "Rethinking Communication in the E-Health Era." *Journal of Health Psychology* 8, no. 1 (2003): 7–23.

Noar, Seth M., Christina N. Banac, and Melissa S. Harris. "Does Tailoring Matter? Meta-Analytic Review of Tailored Print Health Behavior Change Interventions." *Psychological Bulletin* 133, no. 4 (2007): 673–93.

Noar, Seth M., Larson B. Pierce, and Hulda G. Black. "Can Computer-Mediated Interventions Change Theoretical Mediators of Safer Sex? A Meta-Analysis." *Human Communication Research* 36 (2010): 261–97.

Paisley, William. "Knowledge Utilization: The Role of New Communication Technologies." *Journal of the American Society for Information Science* 44 (1993): 222–34.

Sarasohn-Kahn, Jane. *The Wisdom of Patients: Health Care Meets Online Social Media.* Oakland, CA: California Healthcare Foundation, 2008.

Staw, Barry M., Lance E. Sandelands, and Jane E. Dutton. "Threat-Rigidity Effects in Organizational Behavior: A Multilevel Analysis." *Administrative Science Quarterly* 26 (1981): 501–24.

Slovic, Paul, James H. Flynn, and Mark Layman. "Perceived Risk, Trust, and the Politics of Nuclear Waste." *Science* 254, no. 5038 (1991): 1603–37.

Strecher, Victor J. "Interactive Health Communications for Cancer Prevention and Control." In *Handbook of Cancer Control and Behavioral Science: A Resource for Researchers, Practitioners, and Policymakers,* edited by Suzanne M. Miller, Deborah J. Bowen, Robert T. Croyle and Julia. H. Rowland, 547–58. Washington D.C.: American Psychological Association, 2008.

Street, Richard L., and Rajiv N. Rimal. "Health Promotion and Interactive Technology: A Conceptual Foundation." In *Health Promotion and Interactive Technology: Theoretical Applications and Future Directions,* edited by Richard L. Street, William R. Gold, and Timothy R. Manning, 1–18. Mahwah, NJ: Lawrence Erlbaum Associates, 1997.

Tangpong, Chanchai, Jin Li, and Tony R. Johns. "Stakeholder Prescription and Managerial Decisions: An Investigation of the Universality of Stakeholder Prescription." *Journal of Managerial Issues* XXII, no. 3 (2010): 345–67.

Tomes, Nancy J. "The 'Information Rx'." In *Medical Professionalism in the New Information Age,* edited by David J. Rothman and David Blumenthal, 40–65. New Brunswick, NJ: Rutgers University Press, 2010.

Trevino, Linda K., and Jane Webster. "Flow in Computer Mediated Communication: Electronic Mail and Voice Mail Evaluation and Impacts." *Communication Research* 19 (1992): 539–73.

CHAPTER FIFTEEN

Stopping the Island Mentality: Harnessing Communication during an Age of Globalization

Mary M. Meares

The Daimler-Chrysler Merger and a Clash of Cultures

In 1998, Daimler (German manufacturer of Mercedes-Benz cars) and the U.S.-based Chrysler merged to form DaimlerChrysler (Vlasic and Stertz 2000). At that time, Chrysler was the most profitable automotive company in the world, producing vans, light trucks, SUVs, and large sedans, with 23 percent of the U.S. market in sales. It was known for its risk taking and creative problem solving after coming close to bankruptcy several times. Chrysler aimed to increase sales in Europe and protect itself from potential future challenges by aligning with Daimler. Daimler produced luxury sedans, valued for their quality and exacting engineering. However, their production was much more expensive than other luxury car makers and they hoped the merger would help them to lower costs and increase sales in North America.

Mergers can be difficult between any two companies; however, this was labeled a "merger of equals" (Grässlin 2000, 155) by one co-CEO of the merged company. Financial analysts hailed the potential of the new corporation. Initially, German and American senior executives of the new merged corporation met face-to-face in Spain to get to know each other and discuss future plans (Vlasic and Stertz 2000). While there was some concern expressed about the importance of speed in decision making versus working in committees, the executives got to know each other over food and drinks, developing a good sense of rapport. However, soon differences in style and expectations began to be apparent. The American co-CEO gave an emotional closing speech to the gathered executives, talking about his plans to step down after a few years; the Germans found this confusing and couldn't understand why he would make an announcement like this so far in advance of his plans—they thought he must be planning to resign right away and were confused when he didn't.

Differences in work style became apparent after that initial meeting. The German executives worked long hours, smoking and drinking while in the office working, activities that were banned at the U.S. sites. American workers talked of working smarter, not harder. Decisions were made differently, with the Germans having subordinates do extensive research and preparing position papers, then working up the chain of command to the top; once a decision was made it was seen as fixed. The Americans executives, on the other hand, made decisions more quickly after consultation with engineers or other specialists, taking initiative, often without approval from the upper echelons. These types of differences led to negative judgments on both sides. Employees became verbally critical of those from the other country, measuring competence by the perspective of their own culture. Concerns about differences in style between the two co-CEOs became prominent. Why was it so difficult for the Germans and Americans to work together? What should the CEOs have done to prevent or repair these rifts? Is it possible for companies with employees from different countries to merge effectively?

Place a call for customer service from the United States and your call may be routed to a call center in India or Ireland. Attend a professional baseball or basketball game and it is likely that members of the teams come from different countries and speak different languages; memorabilia you purchase may have been manufactured in countries you know little about. Buy a computer or other electronic item, and chances are good that it will have components manufactured in many different countries. Journalist Thomas Friedman (2005) provided an example of globalization in the business world when he described asking a Dell Computer manager about the origin of his laptop. The manager answered that it was designed by engineers in Texas and Taiwan working together; the microprocessor was made by Intel by workers in one of their factories in the Philippines, Costa Rica, Malaysia, or China; and the memory was produced in a factory in Korea, Germany, Taiwan, or Japan. Along with the addition of other components manufactured in various other places (often in foreign-owned factories), the computer was assembled in Taiwan. When components of a product are manufactured in different locations, culture plays a part when employees are coordinating production schedules, goals, assembly, and marketing of final products. Being able to work effectively across cultures is important in all of these situations.

Globalization refers to the increasing interconnectedness of economic systems and organizations worldwide as seen in trade agreements and multinational/international corporations. Globalization results in increasing contact and need to work effectively with people from cultural backgrounds different from one's own.

Globalization is increasingly a reality for organizations of all types. Large organizations conduct business in various locations and have employees from diverse cultural backgrounds. Governmental and nongovernmental organizations (NGOs) may have employees and volunteers working globally. For some, contact with culturally different others comes in the form of international moves. For others, with improvements in technology at competitive prices, contact with employees from other countries comes in the form of membership on global virtual teams. Cynthia Stohl (2001) described various types of organizations (see Table 15.1), based on their level of globalization, both in terms of operation and identification. Some organizations operate on a global level; however, their employees still have expectations and make judgments based on the cultures they have experienced.

One of the greatest challenges facing global organizations, although often under recognized, is the impact of the various cultures of their members on organizational functions and interaction. While some aspects of cultural differences (e.g., linguistic differences) may be obvious, less

Table 15.1   Types of Organizations

Organization Type	Description
Domestic	Organizations based in one country, reflecting the dominant culture; no recognition of different cultural ways of working
Multicultural	Organizations based in one country, but reflecting differences in cultural groups within that country
Multinational	Organizations based in one country, but doing business in other countries; recognition of cultural differences in work practices and customers, but inherently reflecting the interests of one nationality
International	Organizations based in multiple, culturally distinct countries; reflecting the interests of diverse national orientations
Global	Organizations that identify as being beyond the domain of a specific nation, organizational affiliation seen as more important than national loyalty.

Source: Adapted from Cynthia Stohl (2001, 329–30).

obvious are the differences in worldview and expectations that can have a profound impact on how individuals communicate in daily interactions and decision making. The ability to understand and explain these differences and how they can be overcome is vital in operating successfully in the global context.

> Culture is a historically based system of meaning among a group of people. Our culture (or cultures) tells us what to pay attention to and as we communicate with others from our culture, shared values and worldview are developed. Culture can be based on nationality, ethnicity, region, religion, gender, socioeconomic status, or other group identities; however, when we focus on globalization, national identity is usually the most salient.

Cultural Differences in Values and Worldviews

When we look at different countries or cultures, it is helpful to have criteria by which to compare them. One useful concept is that of cultural values. Cultural values are the guiding principles that reflect how a group of people collectively tend to judge the world and their experiences. Cultural values reflect how people believe the world should be. For example, while the United States is a very diverse country, we generally value individual achievement, financial success, and youth. Our cultural values contribute to the individual's and group's worldview, or how they see the world as actually being. Our view of reality is shaped by our cultural experience.

> Cultural values are the deeply held beliefs held by a group that reflect what is important to them and how they believe people should behave and how the world should be.

A number of researchers have developed cultural values dimensions on which we can compare general tendencies of different cultures. There are limitations to this approach and concerns have been raised about the tendency to stereotype based on country-level descriptions, the reality that we all belong to multiple cultural groups, and cultures change over time (albeit slowly). However, these dimensions give us ways to make cross-cultural comparisons and, thus, understand where cultural differences may cause difficulty.

One set of cultural value dimensions was developed by Geert Hofstede (2005, 2001), while he worked as a researcher for IBM and observed differences in IBM employees from different countries. Hofstede conducted surveys, first of IBM employees, then of others in the corporate world, including hundreds of thousands of participants. In spite of a strong corporate culture at IBM, differences in cultural values and expectations were evident in several key areas. Based upon his work, he proposed, measured, and graphed countries based on five cultural orientations: power distance, individualism/collectivism, uncertainty avoidance, long-term orientation, and masculinity. I describe each of these in the following text.

Power Distance

Power distance (Hofstede 2005) measures how much people with less power accept and expect differences in status and access to power. While power differences exist in every culture, some more egalitarian cultures have less difference in status and power than others. Individuals from high power distance countries may expect to defer to those with more power and may look for ways to support hierarchies, whereas those from more egalitarian countries may challenge status differences directly. This can lead to embarrassment to those who expect to be deferred to. Status and power differences are demonstrated by manner of address (first or family name) and the use of titles. In the workplace, high power distance cultures are more likely to be characterized by centralized decision making, multi-layered hierarchy, formal rules, authoritative leaders, and the expectation that subordinates will follow their supervisors' instructions. Low power distance cultures value decentralized decision-making structures, flat organizational structures, fewer supervisors and rules, and a consultative or democratic leadership style.

> Power distance is the difference in status and access to power in a culture between people at the low end of the hierarchy and those at higher levels. In the United States our ideal is to have very low power distance, but in reality we enact differences in status and power on a daily basis in our homes, schools, and the workplace.

Hofstede (2005) found that Malaysia, Guatemala, Panama, and the Philippines had high differences in power, which was accepted as normal and natural for those at lower levels of the hierarchy. In contrast, Australia, Israel, and Denmark had the least difference in status and access to power (the lowest power distance). The United States is relatively low in power difference expectations.

Individualism and Collectivism

Individualism is the degree to which members of a culture make decisions based on the individual assessment of options versus deferring to the wishes of others or the welfare of the group. People who are more collectivistic will make choices based on the group identity or defer to those with more status in the group to decide for them (often elders or supervisors). They tend to value belonging and interdependence. Those from more individualistic cultures tend to be more competitive and focus on their own goals, valuing privacy and independence.

> While we all interact with others, the cultural value of individualism refers to the degree to which we make decisions based on what we think is best—not what others do. This does not mean that we do not solicit input from others, but that we trust ourselves to make decisions. Collectivists put their trust in the collective, rather than the individual. From a collectivist perspective, individualism can be seen as selfish.

Hofstede's (2005) findings show the United States, Australia, Great Britain, and Canada as the most individualistic countries, along with other countries in Europe. Countries in Central America (Guatemala and Panama), South America (Ecuador, Venezuela, and Colombia), and Asia (Indonesia and Pakistan) were the least individualistic. Hofstede also found a tendency for low power distance countries to be more individualistic, while a higher power distance was related to collectivism. While individualism is a variable measured at the cultural level, we can also look at individuals and whether they are typical of their culture. While surveys show that U.S. Americans are very individualistic, some individuals are quite interdependent and collectivistic.

Uncertainty Avoidance

While much in life is uncertain, uncertainty avoidance (Hofstede 2005) is the measure of a culture's need for certainty and the tendency to avoid ambiguity and uncertainty. Cultures high in uncertainty avoidance put an emphasis on rules, regulations, and laws to govern behavior, minimizing the potential for unpredictability. They also tend to be those who respect older people and view difference as dangerous. In work settings, loyalty is valued and but innovation may be constrained by the desire for predictability. Cultures with a low need for uncertainty avoidance are more accepting of difference and tolerant of expression of different viewpoints. They tend to respect youth and change, and have fewer rules than high uncertainty avoidance cultures. In the workplace, countries with low uncertainty avoidance emphasize creative solutions to problems and employees may not be as loyal to a specific employer.

As with all dimensions, there are variations in levels of openness to difference and novelty among individuals. However, Hofstede (2005) found that Greece, Portugal, Guatemala, and Uruguay had the highest levels of uncertainty avoidance. Singapore, Jamaica, Denmark, and Sweden had the lowest levels of uncertainty avoidance. The United States was also moderately low in uncertainty avoidance.

Masculinity/Femininity

According to Hofstede (2005), masculine cultures are those which differentiate between gender expectations, with men expected to be assertive and women more gentle and caring. Masculine cultures encourage competition among men, a focus on a challenging and stressful workplace, respect for the strong, and males are expected to focus on task, not relationships. In contrast, feminine cultures have little differentiation between men's and women's expectations and roles. They emphasize relationships, cooperation, a balanced life, and compassion for the weak. There is an expectation from this perspective in group decision making, security in employment, performance-based promotion, and an emphasis on emotional maturity and stability.

Japan, Austria, Venezuela, Italy, and Switzerland are ranked highest in masculinity (Hofstede 2001). In contrast, Sweden, Norway, the Netherlands, and Denmark are the least masculine countries. The United States ranks moderately high on masculinity, implying differences in gender expectations, in spite of a legal commitment to equal opportunity based on gender.

Long-Term Orientation

Long-term orientation, a dimension Hofstede (2001) added to his original list of cultural values, was influenced by study of Confucianism and Asian cultures. The original four dimensions reflected a western bias in thinking; this dimension, which can apply to any culture (not just Confucian ones) expands understanding of differences between Asian and non-Asian countries. Long-term orientation focuses on "persistence and thrift" (Hofstede 2001, 351), whereas short-term orientation focuses on respect for traditional ways and individual consistency. Countries with a long-term orientation focus on the future, view relationships as bound by status and hierarchy, have a sense of shame, and focus on saving. In the workplace, there is a focus on adapting tradition to changing situations, building a firm foundation and strong market share, and investing in the future. Short-term orientation countries focus on getting quick results, reciprocation in relationships (where status in unimportant), having leisure time, and respect for tradition. In the workplace, they focus on immediate profitability, spending capital, and maintaining traditions.

While the data on this variable is not as extensive, China, Hong Kong, Taiwan, and Japan have the highest long-term orientation (Hofstede 2001). Pakistan, Nigeria, the Philippines, and Canada have the lowest long-term orientation scores, reflecting a short-term orientation. The United States scores relatively low on long-term orientation as well.

Other Cultural Value Dimensions

While Hofstede's (2005) work is well known, many other researchers have studied other cultural value dimensions. One example with implications for organizations is relationship to time. Florence Kluckholn and Fred Strodtbeck (1961) described past, present, and future orientations. While related to long-term orientation, these orientations focused more specifically on time. In the workplace, organizations from cultures that emphasize a future orientation are likely to be goal oriented, with specific deadlines for achieving objectives. Present-oriented organizations are likely to focus less on goals and achievement, instead encouraging members or employees to reflect on their current experience. Organizations in past-oriented culture focus on traditions and past icons to guide current practice.

Cultures may have more of a past, present, or future orientation, depending on where members of the culture place their focus—on future goals, enjoying the present, or maintaining traditions with respect for the past.

Edward T. Hall (1976) addressed time with the concepts of monochronic and polychronic time orientations. Monochronic cultures are those in which one thing is done at a time and activities are sequenced in a linear fashion, as in a schedule of appointments. Polychronic cultures are those in which multiple things are done simultaneously, multitasking without reducing time to a commodity and parceling it out linearly. Western organizations tend to prefer a monochronic approach; a polychronic approach may be seen as inefficient.

> Monochronic cultures are those in which time is treated in a linear fashion, following a schedule, with one activity following another. Cultures that are more polychronic treat time as more fluid, with multiple activities happening simultaneously with less focus on scheduling discrete events.

Hall (1976) also described two different ways of communicating: high context and low context. High-context cultures put most of the message in the contextual clues, rather than directly in the words. This is common in more homogeneous cultures. Low-context cultures, in contrast, put most of the message in the words that are spoken or written. The United States and other heterogeneous cultures tend to be more low context—when people do not share the same background, it is less likely they will understand clues from the context. In organizations, the level of directness and explicitness of the specific verbal message may vary, depending on the cultural backgrounds and expectations of the workers as well as their experience with the task at hand. However, when an employee does not know the context, explicit messages (seen as rude or condescending from a high-context perspective) may be needed. From a low-context cultural perspective, high-context messages may be seen as rambling and without a point, yet be clear to members from that culture because they have the clues to interpret the message.

> High-context cultures are those which put the message in the written or spoken words. Low-context cultures put much of the meaning in the context, rather than in the words, and are more indirect.

These and many other cultural value dimensions can serve as tools to unravel and understand differences in employee behaviors in contexts where employees come from different cultures and countries. However, the natural reaction to difference is to judge it based upon one's own expectations. In the next section, we examine this challenge.

Cultural Ethnocentrism and the "Island Mentality"

Our discussion so far has focused on cultural differences, but when people experience cultural difference there is a natural tendency to judge different norms and practices based on one's own experience and cultural norms. For example, the German executives judged the American DaimlerChrysler co-CEO based upon how his actions would be interpreted from a German cultural perspective. Based on this, they mistook his motivations. Many cultural gaffes are a result of analyzing situations without taking differences in culture into consideration.

Milton J. Bennett (1986) examined the phenomenon of ethnocentrism and described a developmental model of intercultural sensitivity, moving from ethnocentric to ethnorelative stages. It is developmental in the sense that as individuals have experience with other cultures and become increasingly sophisticated in their mental categories for thinking about difference, they may move from one stage to the next. The three stages of ethnocentrism are all characterized by the fact that one's own culture is the standard upon which others are judged.

> "The island mentality" is the tendency for people to believe in the superiority of a specific culture or country (usually their own), judging others with different norms, values, and expectations to be inferior. This is also known as "ethnocentrism." This may be due to lack of contact with other cultures, fears and defensiveness about the other, or a belief that all other cultures are inferior versions of one's own.

The first stage of ethnocentrism is denial, where an individual may have either never had contact with culturally different others, or may have been in a situation where the contact had no impact on him or her (Bennett 1986). An individual at this stage may intellectually know that there are people who are "foreigners" or different in some way, but there are no categories for thinking about difference other than to label them different. As an individual gains more knowledge and experience of another culture or cultures, he or she may progress to the next stage, defense.

In Bennett's (1986) defense stage, the individual has more cognitive complexity to think about cultural differences, but they are viewed in terms of what is wrong with the other culture as it is not like one's own and must then be inherently inferior. This attitude may be more or less aggressive and potentially dangerous. Individuals may have a "siege mentality," perceiving their own values, livelihood, or well-being to be threatened by those who are culturally different. Concerns about foreign-born residents or minorities taking jobs away from members of the dominant group are prime examples of the defense stage. Negative stereotypes abound at this stage and can affect an employee's ability to work with those from other backgrounds. Organizations characterized by the defense stage are likely to be perceived as arrogant or overbearing to employees, customers, or clients from other cultures (Bennett and Bennett 2004). At this stage, organizations may present a hostile environment to anyone from nonmajority backgrounds and may avoid recruiting employees from minority groups because of concerns about their "fit" with the other employees. However, for individuals, if constructive relationships can be built at this stage, it can encourage movement to the next stage, minimization.

Bennett's (1986) third stage of ethnocentrism is minimization. At this stage, individuals may be interested in superficial cultural differences in dress, food, and customs, but still believe that members of the other culture are inherently the same as their own. This still creates a judgment based on a fixed idea of right and wrong, and as a result is still ethnocentric. While cultural differences at this stage are treated more pleasantly and hospitality is extended to those from other backgrounds, there is still stereotyping and prejudice at play when "the other" does not act the way they "should." Members of organizations that are characterized by minimization may perceive themselves as being more culturally sensitive than they are, and thus appear condescending or hypocritical (Bennett and Bennett 2004).

The later three stages of Bennett's (1986) model are ethnorelative, or not characterized by judging cultural others based on one's own culture. Acceptance is the first ethnorelative stage, where while an individual may not like or agree with all cultural differences, nonetheless she or he recognizes that there are inherent cultural differences in norms, values, and worldview that are equally valid. This can be a challenging transformation as individuals ideally learn to negotiate their ability to act while not imposing their own view on others. Organizations at this stage grapple with issues of cultural diversity as well, bringing members into discussion about how to balance individual cultural values with collective needs.

Adaptation (Bennett 1986) follows acceptance and is necessary, when, based on more intense and direct experience, one must learn to cognitively shift one's frame of reference to another cultural perspective. This shifting perspective extends beyond empathy to include adapting to feelings and behaviors from a host culture, acting appropriately, and being able to shift from one culture to the other. This adaptation involves a deep level of knowledge as well as competence in enacting that knowledge, but can lead individuals to question their own identity and authenticity. Adaptation is likely to happen for individuals when they have the opportunity to work outside their own culture, to work extensively with people from another culture, or are part of a minority culture. Organizations characterized by adaptation take an active role in providing training to their employees so that they can learn cognitive and behavioral skills appropriate for their role (Bennett and Bennett 2004). The organizational climate is respectful of domestic and international diversity, and diverse perspectives are seen as a valuable resource for the organization. Global organizations that are able to work at the adaptation stage are positioned to assist their employees in navigating these issues in order to accomplish organizational goals.

Bennett's (1986) final stage of intercultural sensitivity is integration. Integration is most likely to be seen in individuals who are bicultural or multicultural; they are able to integrate different cultural frameworks into their own individual identity, but may become "cultural marginals" (Bennett 1993, 109) losing some of their sense of connection to their original culture. This can be a constructive position as those in integration often serve as cultural teachers or guides for others, but also leads to a certain level of detachment. Organizations that are characterized by integration include discussion of cultural context in daily discourse and are fully multicultural (Bennett and Bennett 2004).

Global organizations, by their very nature, put individuals in contexts where they are interacting with coworkers and customers from different cultural backgrounds. Sensitivity to intercultural differences in communicating is vital and there are many things organizations can do to encourage this. While not every employee needs to be at the most advanced stages, an employee who is ethnocentric can seriously damage an organization's reputation and functioning.

Intercultural Training

There are two ways for an organization to have a culturally sophisticated workforce: hire workers who are interculturally competent and sensitive or help employees to develop an intercultural mindset and skills to utilize it. Oftentimes, as in the Daimler-Chrysler merger, employees do not need sophisticated skills until a change in the business context necessitates a change in their work responsibilities to involve working with those from another culture. However, in some countries and contexts, diversity of the domestic population (as in the United States) means that cultural diversity will always be present.

Historically, intercultural training is a relatively new field, developed in the latter half of the 20th century as globalization increased. Much of our understanding of culture grew from the failure of government and corporate employees to successfully complete their missions, resulting in the recognition that culture should be studied for its practical knowledge, not just by academic anthropologists (Pusch 2004). Edward T. Hall was a pioneer in this area, working at the Foreign Service Institute for the U.S. State Department. In this role, he developed training materials with his colleagues and tested methods of training. Later, student exchange programs and the U.S. Peace Corps extended his work to examine the best ways to prepare students and volunteers to live, study, and work effectively for extended periods of time outside of their own cultural context. In the corporate context, early intercultural training took the form of predeparture briefings for executives and their families moving for overseas assignments. As globalism has increased in the last few decades, more and more corporations have recognized the need to have intercultural consultants provide advice, training of employees, and coaching for executives on cultural issues as they relate to teamwork, virtual work, crises, and supervising those from different cultures. Knowledge of the level of intercultural sensitivity of the trainees and the organization can help trainers to utilize methods that are appropriate for decreasing ethnocentrism.

Intercultural training programs may have a variety of goals. Many aim to raise awareness and knowledge of cultural differences, providing information on culture and cultivating empathy in order to provide the potential for constructive communication. However, some training programs work to develop skills (including communication skills), a much more challenging task, involving more time and energy. Training can be culture general or cultural specific (Fowler and Blohm 2004). Culture-general training provides knowledge of constructs, such as cultural values, that can be used with any culture. In contrast, culture-specific training targets a specific culture, helping the trainees to learn about that culture. Training may also be context general or context specific. One common specific context is orientation. Often corporations contract with relocation companies to provide predeparture training or orientation upon arrival in a new country. At the start of a new project involving employees from different countries, an intercultural trainer may be hired to work on general expectations of team members, provide tools to talk about culture, and negotiate cultural differences in expectations in order to establish a constructive foundation for future work. DaimlerChrysler might have benefited from this type of training at the start of their merger process. In addition, some organizations provide general intercultural training in order to encourage employees to be aware of the impact of culture on their work and how their cultural assumptions affect others. Training can provide tools for talking about cultural differences and encourage participants to expand their understanding of culture and culture's impact on communication. In a global organization, this knowledge helps employees to do their work in a way that supports the organization's goals.

Conclusion

The case of the DaimlerChrysler merger illustrates the challenges in merging not just corporate cultures, but also national differences in cultural expectation related to leadership, decision making, and workplace norms. While not every company from the same culture is the same, we can see general tendencies based upon the employees' cultural values and worldview. While both of these countries are similar in their future and short-term orientation and level of masculinity, the German norms, exemplified by Daimler-Benz employees, are characterized by high uncertainty avoidance, more emphasis on hierarchy, somewhat more collectivism, and a preference for bureaucracy. The U.S. norms, demonstrated by the Americans at Chrysler, are characterized by lower uncertainty avoidance, low power distance, high individualism, and a bias toward decisive managerial action. Members of both nationalities, however, demonstrated an island mentality, judging others based on their own cultural expectations.

In the end, the DaimlerChrysler merger failed. After nine years and a tremendous financial loss, DaimlerChrysler sold the Chrysler group to a financial management organization. However, current Chrysler officials maintain optimism about the potential for international mergers. At the time of this writing, Chrysler was in the process of merging with the Italian car company, Fiat (Walsh 2011). According to Chrysler executives, this merger has more potential for success this time as their Italian-born CEO, Sergio Marchionne, leads the integration efforts with his experience in global contexts.

Global organizations and international mergers can be successful in spite of cultural differences, but successful organizations are those that recognize differences in norms, values, and worldviews, and provide employees with training on cultural differences and how to talk about them. While ethnocentrism is a natural reaction to difference, intercultural training can help employees to overcome the tendency to judge others and stop the "island mentality" from destroying productivity and resulting in loss to individuals and organizations.

Key Takeaways

1. Culture influences how we see the world, what we think is important, and how we perceive the actions of others, including in the workplace.

2. Understanding cultural differences can help us to understand the conflicts that occur in global situations with employees from different cultural backgrounds.
3. Cultural value dimensions such as power distance, individualism/collectivism, long-term orientation, masculinity/femininity, past/present/future orientation, monochronic/polychronic, and low/high context are tools for analyzing, describing, and understanding cultural differences.
4. While ethnocentrism is a natural stage (or set of stages), individuals and organizations benefit from moving beyond the island mentality.
5. Intercultural training can help individuals and organizations develop intercultural sensitivity and become more productive.

Glossary

Collectivism: The cultural tendency of members of a group to make choices based on the group identity or defer to those with more status in the group to decide for them (often elders or supervisors).

Cultural values: The deeply held beliefs held by a group that reflect what is important to them and how they believe people should behave and how the world should be.

Ethnocentrism: The tendency to judge others based on one's own culture, judging others to be inferior.

Ethnorelativism: The ability to not judge others based upon one's on culture.

Feminine cultures: Cultures that have little differentiation between expectations of men and women based on gender roles.

High-context cultures: Cultures in which most of the message is expressed in the verbal (spoken or written) words.

Individualism: The degree to which members of a culture make decisions based on the individual makes decisions based on the individual assessment of options versus deferring to the wishes of others or the group.

"Island mentality": The tendency for people to believe in the superiority of a specific culture or country (usually their own), judging others with different norms, values, and expectations to be inferior.

Long-term orientation: The cultural value from Confucianism that focuses on working persistently toward long-term outcomes.

Low-context cultures: Cultures in which much of the message is expressed through the context of the interaction, rather than through the verbal message.

Masculine cultures: Cultures that differentiate individuals based on gender expectations, workplace culture is competitive, and men are expected to be assertive.

Monochronic cultures: Cultures with a tendency to treat time in a linear fashion, following a schedule, with one activity following another.

Polychronic: Cultures that treat time as more fluid, with multiple activities happening simultaneously with less focus on scheduling discrete events.

Power distance: A measure of how much people with less power accept and expect differences in status and access to power.

Short-term orientation: The cultural value from Confucianism, which focuses on getting quick results, building relationships, and maintaining traditions.

Uncertainty avoidance: The measure of a culture's need for certainty, and to avoid ambiguity and uncertainty.

Worldview: How cultural groups perceive the world to be.

References

Bennett, Janet M. "Cultural Marginality: Identity Issues in Intercultural Training." In *Education for the Intercultural Experience,* edited by R. Michael Paige. 2nd ed., 109–35. Yarmouth, ME: Intercultural Press, 1993.

Bennett, Milton J. "A Developmental Approach to Training for Intercultural Sensitivity." *International Journal of Intercultural Relations* 10 (1986): 179–96.

Bennett, Milton J., and Janet M. Bennett. "Developing Intercultural Sensitivity: An Integrative Approach to Global and Domestic Diversity." In *the Handbook of Intercultural Training,* edited by Dan Landis, Janet M. Bennett, and Milton J. Bennett, 147–65. Thousand Oaks, CA: Sage, 2004.

Fowler, Sandra M., and Judith M. Blohm. "An Analysis of Methods for Intercultural Training." In *the Handbook of Intercultural Training,* edited by Dan Landis, Janet M. Bennett, and Milton J. Bennett, 37–84. Thousand Oaks, CA: Sage, 2004.

Friedman, Thomas L. *The World is Flat: A Brief History of the Twenty-First Century.* New York: Farrar, Straus, & Giroux, 2005.

Grässlin, Jürgen. *Jürgen Schrempp and the Making of an Auto Dynasty.* New York: McGraw-Hill, 2000.

Hall, Edward T. *Beyond Culture.* Garden City, NY: Doubleday, 1976.

Hofstede, Geert. *Cultures and Organizations: Software of the Mind.* 2nd ed. New York: McGraw-Hill, 2005.

Hofstede, Geert. *Culture's Consequences: Comparing Values, Behaviors, Institutions, and Organizations across Nations.* 2nd ed. Thousand Oaks, CA: Sage, 2001.

Kluckhohn, Florence, and Fred L. Strodtbeck. *Variations in Value Orientations.* Westport, CT: Greenwood, 1961.

Pusch, Margaret D. "Intercultural Training in Historical Perspective." In *The Handbook of Intercultural Training,* edited by Dan Landis, Janet M. Bennett, and Milton J. Bennett, 13–36. Thousand Oaks, CA: Sage, 2004.

Stohl, Cynthia. "Globalizing Organizational Communication." In *The New Handbook of Organizational Communication: Advances in Theory, Research, and Methods*, edited by Fredric M. Jablin and Linda L. Putnam, 323–75. Thousand Oaks, CA: Sage, 2001.

Vlasic, Bill, and Bradley A. Stertz. *Taken for a Ride: How Daimler-Benz Drove Off with Chrysler.* New York: Harper CollinsWilliam Morrow, 2000.

Walsh, Tom. "Chrysler Exec: This Fiat Merger Will Succeed where Daimler's Didn't." *Detroit Free Press,* August 2, 2011.

About the Editor and Contributors

The Editor

Jason S. Wrench (Ed.D., West Virginia University, 2002) is an associate professor and chair of the Communication and Media Department at the State University of New York at New Paltz. Dr. Wrench specializes in workplace learning and performance, or the intersection of instructional communication and organizational communication. His varied research interests include computer-mediated communication, empirical research methods, humor, risk/crisis communication, and supervisor-subordinate interactions. He regularly consults with individuals and organizations on organizational communication and as a professional speech coach for senior executives. Dr. Wrench has published eight previous books (*Intercultural Communication: Power in Context; Communication, Affect, and Learning in the Classroom; Principles of Public Speaking; Human Communication in Everyday Life: Explanations and Applications; Quantitative Research Methods for Communication: A Hands-On Approach; The Directory of Communication-Related Mental Measures; Stand up, Speak Out: The Practice and Ethics of Public Speaking;* and *Casing Organizational Communication*). Furthermore, he has published over 30 research articles that have appeared in various journals such as *Communication Quarterly, Communication Research Reports, Education, Human Communication, Journal of Communication and Religion, Journal of Criminal Justice Education, Journal of Homosexuality, Journal of Intercultural Communication, Southern Communication Journal, The Source: A Journal of Education,* and *The NACADA Journal* (National Association of Campus Advising).

The Contributors

LaKesha N. Anderson (Ph.D., George Mason University, 2010) is an assistant professor in the Department of Communication at Indiana State

University. Her research focuses primarily on health and risk management and has been featured in publications as well as at many competitive conferences.

Eric Bergman has been a communications consultant for more than 30 years. He has worked in virtually every facet of organizational communication—from government public affairs to corporate advertising. For the past 20 years, his business has focused on providing media spokesperson training to professional, corporate, not-for-profit, and government organizations in Canada, the United States, Europe, and the Caribbean. He holds a bachelor of arts in communication studies, is an accredited business communicator (ABC), and an accredited public relations practitioner (APR). In 2002, he was named a master communicator by the International Association of Business Communicators (IABC), which is the highest distinction that can be bestowed on an IABC member in Canada. In October 2006, his train-the-trainer guide for media training, *Media Training with Excellence: A Balanced Approach,* was published by IABC. The book has help move the entire industry away from the outdated paradigm of constantly repeating messages, to one in which spokespeople strive to achieve sustainable winwin outcomes during exchanges with journalists.

Shannon M. Brogan (Ph.D., Ohio University, 2003) is an associate professor of speech communication at Kentucky State University. She has published in *Human Communication, Communication Research Reports,* and the *Journal of Family Communication.* Dr. Brogan has also written organizational case studies in *Casing Organizational Communication: Applying Theory and Research to the Modern Organization.* Her research topics include family, work, and balance, consumer education, and standardized testing.

Tina A. Coffelt (Ph.D., University of Missouri) is an assistant professor in the English Department at Iowa State University. She has published in the *Journal of Family Communication, Women's Studies in Communication,* and the *Northwest Journal of Communication.*

Erin E. Gilles (Ph.D., University of Kentucky, 2009) is an assistant professor of mass communications and journalism at Kentucky State University. Her dissertation research focused on health communication in online bulletin boards and direct-to-customer pharmaceutical advertising. She has also published organizational case studies in *Casing Organizational Communication: Applying Theory and Research to the Modern Organization.*

Jackson Hataway (Ph.D., University of Alabama) is an associate consultant with Strategic Arts & Sciences, a strategic planning and organizational development consulting firm located in Portland, Oregon.

Anna Goodman Hoover (M.A., University of Kentucky, 2008) is deputy director of the National Coordinating Center for the Public Health Practice-Based Research Networks, where she helps organize cross-cutting and multinetwork research studies designed to evaluate and compare public health strategies implemented across diverse settings. She also serves as communications liaison for the University of Kentucky Superfund Research Program Research Translation Core, where she works with stakeholder groups to improve mutual understandings of environmental health issues, supporting the advancement of research outcomes into practice at community, provider, and policy levels. As research project coordinator for the Kentucky Research Consortium for Energy and the Environment's Paducah Gaseous Diffusion Plant Stakeholder Future State Vision study from 2008–2011, she worked with affected communities to produce a publicly approved future use for a National Priority List Superfund site. Her research focuses on incorporating participatory communication methods into public engagement processes to improve environmental health outcomes in communities. With more than two decades in the communication field, she has extensive professional experience in media, marketing, and public relations.

Tony Jaques is director of Issue Outcomes, an Australian consultancy specializing in issue and crisis management, and was formerly Asia-Pacific issue manager for a multinational American company. He is also a senior research associate at RMIT University in Melbourne, where he was awarded a Ph.D. and teaches in the masters program. He has been widely published in the field of issue and crisis management in journals including *Journal of Communication Management, Journal of Public Affairs, Asia Pacific Public Relations Journal, Public Relations Quarterly, Journal of Business Strategy, Public Relations Review, Corporate Communication, Journal of Public Relations, Disaster Prevention and Management, Organizational Development Journal, Public Communication Review,* and *International Journal of Strategic Communication.* Dr. Jaques is author of the book *Don't Just Stand There—The Do-it Plan for Effective Issue Management* and from 2002 to 2008 was a director of the Issue Management Council in Leesburg, Virginia.

J. David Johnson (Ph.D., Michigan State University, 1978) was dean of the College of Communications and Information Studies at the University of Kentucky for over a decade. He has also held academic positions at the University of Wisconsin–Milwaukee, Arizona State University, the State University of New York at Buffalo, and Michigan State University, and was a media research analyst for the U.S. Information Agency. He has published five books: *Cancer-Related Information Seeking, Information Seeking: An Organizational Dilemma, Organizational Communication Structure, Managing Knowledge Networks,* and *Innovation and Knowledge Management: The Cancer Information Service Research Consortium.* He has been recognized as among the most prolific publishers of refereed journal articles in the history of the communication discipline. He has received grants from the National Cancer Institute, Michigan Department of Public Health, Michigan Department of Transportation, and National Association of Broadcasters. He has worked extensively in an advisory capacity for various state and federal agencies in the field of health, most recently he was selected to serve on the Communication Expert Panel for the Centers for Disease Control Office of Smoking and Health, Health Communications Branch.

Doreen M. S. Jowi (Ph.D., Ohio University, 2005) is an assistant professor in the Department of Communication Studies and Managing Director of Global and Multicultural Education at Bloomsburg University of Pennsylvania. Dr. Jowi has published in the forthcoming book: *Casing Organizational Communication: Applying Theory and Research to the Modern Organization, Journal of Computer Mediated Communication, Human Communication,* and coauthored a book chapter in *Fundamentals of Public Speaking.* In addition, Dr. Jowi has coauthored a book titled: *The Directory of Communication Related Mental Measures.*

Mary L. Kahl (Ph.D., Indiana University, 1994) is a professor and chair of the Department of Communication at Indiana State University in Terra Haute, IN 47809. She is a distinguished teaching fellow and on the Committee of Scholars for the Eastern Communication Association, where she is also a former president of the organization. Her research interests include political discourses (including political campaign debates, inaugural addresses, political apologia, and other epideictic discourses of the contemporary presidency) and gender and communication (including the discourses of contemporary female politicians, gendered communication in the university, and the gendered dimensions of public memory. She has published in numerous proceedings and academic journals including *Qualitative Research Reports* and *Communication Quarterly.* She is coauthor on an advanced public speaking book along with Michael J. Hostetler called *Advanced Public Speaking: A Leader's Guide to Communication* (published by Allyn and Bacon).

Mary M. Meares (Ph.D., New Mexico) is an assistant professor and graduate program director for the M.A. in communication studies at the University of Alabama. Her research on cultural diversity in the workplace has been published in the *Journal of Applied Communication Research, The Journal of Intergroup Relations, Communication Research Reports, The Keio Communication Review, The Northwest Journal of Communication, The Texas Linguistic Forum,* and *Communication Reports.* She also has numerous published book chapters and case studies on cultural diversity in organizations.

Sherwyn Morreale is an associate professor and director of Graduate Studies in Communication at the University of Colorado at Colorado Springs. Dr. Morreale's main research and teaching interests include organizational communication, communication theory, business and professional communication, instructional communication, public speaking, and the assessment of communication competence. She is the lead author of three communication textbooks and has authored numerous articles and chapters for collected volumes and special monographs in the communication discipline. From 1997 to 2006, Dr. Morreale served as associate director of the National Communication Association, the oldest and largest association of professors in the communication discipline in the world.

Timothy L. Sellnow (Ph.D., Wayne State University) is a professor of communication and associate dean for graduate studies in the College of Communications and Information Studies at the University of Kentucky, United States. His work on crisis, risk and communication has appeared in the *Handbook of Crisis and Risk Communication, International Encyclopedia of Communication, Communication Yearbook, The Handbook of Public Relations, Handbook of Applied Communication Research, Public Relations Review, Communication Studies, Journal of Business Ethics, Journal of Business Communication, Argumentation and Advocacy, Critical Studies in Media Communication,* and the *Journal of Applied Communication Research.* Sellnow is also the co-author of four books on crisis and risk communication and past editor of the *Journal of Applied Communication Research.*

Pamela Shockley-Zalabak is chancellor and a professor of communication at the University of Colorado at Colorado Springs. The author of eight books and over 100 articles and productions on organizational communication, Dr. Shockley-Zalabak's research interests include organizational trust and cultures as they relate to overall organizational effectiveness. Prior to assuming her chancellor responsibilities, Dr. Shockley-Zalabak was vice chancellor for student success and the founding chair of the UCCS communication department. Dr. Shockley-Zalabak also is president of CommuniCon, Inc., a consulting organization working with clients in the United States, Europe, and Asia and is the producer of award-winning television documentaries aired nationally and in major U.S. markets.

Don W. Stacks (Ph.D., University of Florida), is professor of public relations program in the School of Communication and director of the public relations graduate program at the University of Miami, Coral Gables, FL. Stacks has written more than 150 scholarly articles and papers. Stacks has authored eight books on communication topics, including the award-winning *Primer of Public Relations Research*. He has won the National Communication Association's PRIDE award and was named the Measurement Standard's "measurement tool" for 2003. He has coauthored *Nonverbal Communication: Studies and Applications* with Mark Hickson and Nina-Jo More through five editions. He is the series coeditor for *Business Expert Press* on public relations topics written for the professional and editor of the *Journal of the Association for Communication Administration*.

Shari R. Veil (Ph.D., North Dakota State University) is an assistant professor of communication and the director of the risk sciences division in the College of Communications and Information Studies at the University of Kentucky, United States. Her research has been published in the *Handbook of Crisis Communication, Handbook of Communication and Corporate Reputation, Journal of Applied Communication Research, Journal of Contingencies and Crisis Management, Journal of Business Ethics, International Journal of Technology and Human Interaction, Journal of Communication Management, Management Communication Quarterly, Journal of Business Communication, International Journal of Strategic Communication, Communication Studies,* and *Public Relations Review,* among others.

Daniel L. Walsch (Ph.D., George Mason University, 2011) serves as the press secretary for George Mason University as well as a part-time professor for the Department of Communication. An expert in the field of public relations and crisis management, his work has been featured in both regional and national press outlets, as well as at several academic conferences.

Morgan Wickline is a graduate student in the College of Communications and Information Studies at the University of Kentucky, United States. Her research on instructional communication and risk and crisis communication has been funded by the Department of Homeland Security's National Center for Food Protection and Defense and presented at national and international communication conferences. Wickline has several manuscripts currently in review.

Kristin Roeschenthaler Wolfe is currently a Ph.D. candidate at Duquesne University studying the rhetoric and philosophy of communication. Previously, she spent 13 years working in advertising, public relations, and Internet usability and project management.

Catherine Karl Wright (Ph.D., Regent University, 2005) is a term assistant professor of communication with 17 years of university teaching, student advising, and research experience. Her course load includes: public speaking, interpersonal communication, business and professional communication, small-group communication, mass media and society, interpersonal communication in the workplace, website development and promotion, convention planning, and study-abroad courses. Her teaching technique emphasizes presentation skills, writing skills, and the integration of technology into coursework and assignments as well as other projects based on theoretical foundations of communication. Her research interests include computer-mediated communication (CMC), diffusion of innovation, and small-group communication and online learning communities (OLC). Her presentations at conferences have included cross-disciplinary research in communication, education, and business, exploring theoretical perspectives. Dr. Wright has previously published in the *Southwestern Mass Communication Journal.*

Index